1993
Science Year

The World Book Annual Science Supplement

A Review of Science and Technology
During the 1992 School Year

World Book, Inc.

a Scott Fetzer company
Chicago London Sydney Toronto

The Year's Major Science Stories

From an international summit on the environment to the discovery of new evidence supporting the big bang theory of the formation of the universe, it was an eventful year for science and technology. On these two pages are the stories that *Science Year* editors picked as the most memorable, exciting, or important of the year, along with details about where you will find information about them in the book.   *The Editors*

Earth summit ▶
Amid mounting concerns about the environment, leaders from more than 100 nations met in Brazil in June 1992 to discuss how humanity is changing Earth's environment. In the Science Studies section, see GLOBAL CHANGE. In the Science News Update Section, see ENVIRONMENT.

▲
Satellite rescue
Three astronauts captured a satellite using only their gloved hands during the first flight of the U.S. space shuttle Endeavour in May 1992. In the Science News Update section, see SPACE TECHNOLOGY.

Earthquake aftermath
Several earthquakes jolted California in spring and summer 1992. In the Science News Update section, see GEOLOGY.
▼

Portions of the material contained in this volume are excerpted from the 1992 edition of *The World Book Encyclopedia*.

© 1992 World Book, Inc.
525 W. Monroe
Chicago, IL 60661.

ISBN: 0-7166-1193-7
ISSN: 0080-7621
Library of Congress Catalog Number: 65-21776
Printed in the United States of America

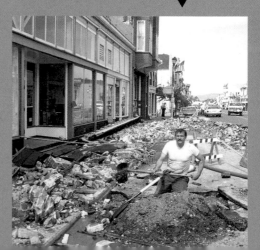

Condors released

Two California condors were released into the wild in January 1992, less than a decade after a captive-breeding program rescued the bird species from extinction. In the Science News Update section, see ZOOLOGY (CLOSE-UP).

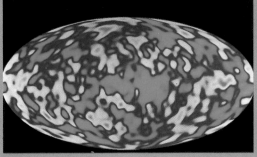

Evidence of the big bang

An examination of background radiation from throughout the universe provided evidence in April 1992 to support the big bang theory of the formation of the universe. In the Science News Update section, see ASTRONOMY, UNIVERSE; PHYSICS (CLOSE-UP).

Ancient mummy

The well-preserved body of a man who died up to 5,300 years ago was discovered in an Italian glacier in September 1991. In the Science News Update section, see ARCHAEOLOGY, OLD WORLD.

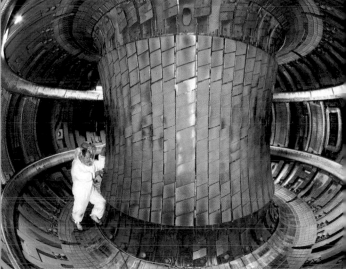

Fusion advance

A scientific team in England took a major step toward the controlled release of energy from nuclear fusion—the reaction that powers the sun—in November 1991. In the Science News Update section, see ENERGY; PHYSICS.

Volcanic eruption

Beginning in December 1991, an eruption of Mount Etna threatened populated areas in Sicily. In the Science News Update section, see GEOLOGY.

Contents

Page 17

Page 44

Science News Update

Thirty-five articles, arranged alphabetically, report on the year's major developments in all areas of science and technology, from "Agriculture" and "Archaeology" to "Space Technology" and "Zoology." In addition, seven Close-Up articles focus on especially noteworthy developments:

Science You Can Use

Five articles present various aspects of science and technology as they apply to the consumer.

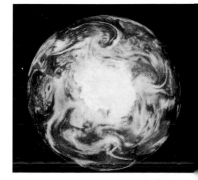

World Book Supplement

Four new or revised articles from the 1992 edition of *The World Book Encyclopedia:* "Earthquake," "Plate tectonics," "Nutrition," and "Reproduction, Human."

Index

A cumulative index of topics covered in the 1993, 1992, and 1991 editions of *Science Year*.

Cross-Reference Tabs

A tear-out page of cross-reference tabs for insertion in *The World Book Encyclopedia* appears before page 1.

Staff

Editorial Advisory Board

Contributors

Adelman, George, M.A., M.S.
Editor,
Encyclopedia of Neuroscience.
[*Neuroscience*]

Amato, Ivan, M.A.
Staff Writer,
Science Magazine.
[*Materials Science*]

Asker, James R., B.A.
Space Technology Editor,
Aviation Week & Space Technology
Magazine.
[Space Technology]

Bedford, Barbara L., Ph.D.
Assistant Professor,
Department of Natural Resources,
and Director,
Ecosystems Research Center,
Cornell University.
[Special Report, *Wetlands: Mired in
Controversy*]

Bower, Bruce, M.A.
Behavioral Sciences Editor,
Science News Magazine.
[*Psychology*]

Brett, Carlton E., Ph.D.
Professor,
Department of Geological Sciences,
University of Rochester.
[*Fossil Studies*]

Cain, Steve, B.S.
News Coordinator,
Purdue University School of
Agriculture.
[*Agriculture*]

Cantril, Albert H., Ph.D.
Consultant in Public Opinion
Research.
[Science You Can Use: *Making
Sense of Opinion Polls*]

Chiras, Daniel D., B.A., Ph.D.
Adjunct Professor of Environmental
Policy and Management,
University of Denver.
[*Environment*]

Dwyer, Johanna T., D.Sc., R.D.
Professor of Medicine and
Community Health,
Tufts University School of Medicine.
[*Nutrition*]

Fagan, Brian M., Ph.D.
Professor of Anthropology,
University of California, Santa
Barbara.
[Special Report, *Who Were the
Neanderthals?*]

Falconer, Allan, Ph.D.
Professor,
Department of Geography and Earth
Resources,
Utah State University.
[Special Report, *The Sahara's Bleak
"Shore"*]

Ferrell, Keith
Editor,
OMNI Magazine.
[*Computer Hardware; Computer
Software*]

Francis, F. J., Ph.D.
Professor Emeritus,
Department of Food Science,
University of Massachusetts at
Amherst.
[*Nutrition* (Close-Up)]

Goldhaber, Paul, B.S., D.D.S.
Professor of Periodontology,
Harvard School of Dental Medicine.
[*Dentistry*]

Goodman, Richard A., M.D., M.P.H.
Adjunct Professor,
Division of Epidemiology,
Emory University.
[*Public Health*]

Graff, Gordon, Ph.D.
Technical Editor,
McGraw-Hill Incorporated,
and Free-Lance Science Writer.
[*Chemistry; Chemistry* (Close-Up);
Science You Can Use: *The Chemistry
of Cleaning Clothes*]

Grossman, Lawrence, Ph.D.
Professor of Geochemistry,
Department of the Geophysical
Sciences and Enrico Fermi Institute,
University of Chicago.
[Special Report, *Stones from Space*]

Hart, Benjamin L., Ph.D.
Professor of Physiology and Behavior,
School of Veterinary Medicine,
University of California, Davis.
[Special Report, *Science Stalks the
Domestic Cat*]

Hay, William W., Ph.D.
Professor of Geology,
University of Colorado, Boulder.
[*Geology*]

Haymer, David S., Ph.D.
Assistant Professor,
Department of Genetics,
University of Hawaii.
[*Genetics*]

Hester, Thomas R., Ph.D.
Professor of Anthropology
and Director,
Texas Archeological Research
Laboratory,
University of Texas, Austin.
[*Archaeology, New World*]

Hofman, Helenmarie, Ph.D.
Associate Professor of Science
Education,
Gettysburg College,
and Executive Director,
Student Space Foundation.
[Special Report, *Not for Science
Students Only*]

Hyslop, John, Ph.D.
Archaeologist,
American Museum of Natural History.
[Special Report, *The Rise of Andean
Civilization*]

Jones, William Goodrich, A.M.L.S.
Assistant University Librarian,
University of Illinois at Chicago.
[*Books of Science*]

King, Elliot, M.S., M.A., Ph.D.
Editor,
Scientific Computing Magazine.
[*Electronics*]

King, Lauriston R., Ph.D.
Deputy Director,
Office of University Research,
Texas A&M University.
[*Oceanography*]

Klein, Richard G., Ph.D.
Professor of Anthropology,
University of Chicago.
[*Anthropology*]

Kniffen, Donald A., Ph.D.
Professor of Physics,
Hampden-Sydney College.
[Special Report, *Observing the
Gamma-Ray Sky*]

Kowal, Deborah, M.A.
Adjunct Professor,
Division of International Health,
Emory University.
[*Public Health*]

Lechtenberg, Victor L., Ph.D.
Executive Associate Dean of
Agriculture,
Purdue University.
[*Agriculture*]

Limburg, Peter R., B.A., M.A.
Free-Lance Science Writer.
[Science You Can Use: *Weather
Terms—Cloudy or Clear?*]

Lunine, Jonathan I., Ph.D.
Associate Professor of Planetary
Sciences,
University of Arizona.
[*Astronomy, Solar System;
Astronomy* (Close-Up)]

March, Robert H., Ph.D.
Professor of Physics and Integrated
Liberal Studies,
University of Wisconsin.
[*Physics; Physics* (Close-Up)]

Marschall, Laurence A., Ph.D.
Professor,
Department of Physics,
Gettysburg College.
[*Astronomy, Universe*]

Merz, Beverly, B.A.
Free-Lance Writer.
[*Medical Research; Drugs* (Close-Up)]

Meyer, B. Robert, M.D.
Chief, Division of Clinical
Pharmacology,
North Shore University Hospital.
[*Drugs*]

Morrill, John H., B.A.
Business Manager,
American Council for an Energy
Efficient Economy.
[Science You Can Use: *EnergyGuide
Labels: Help for the Appliance
Shopper*]

Pennisi, Elizabeth J., M.S.
Chemistry/Materials Science Editor,
Science News Magazine.
[Special Report, *Getting the Fat (and
Sugar) Out; Zoology*]

Petit, Charles, B.A.
Science Writer,
San Francisco Chronicle.
[Special Report, *Seeking the
Ultimate Cold*]

Pyne, Nanette M., Ph.D.
Director of Development,
Seattle Art Museum.
[*Archaeology, Old World*]

Salisbury, Frank B., Ph.D.
Professor of Plant Physiology,
Utah State University.
[*Botany*]

Schroeder, Don, B.S., B.A.
Technical Editor,
Car and Driver Magazine.
[Science You Can Use: *Airbags: Split-
Second Protection*]

Sforza, Pasquale M., Ph.D.
Chairman,
Department of Aerospace
Engineering,
Polytechnic University.
[Special Report, *Clearing the Air with
Cleaner Cars*]

Snow, John T., Ph.D.
Professor of Atmospheric Science,
Purdue University.
[*Meteorology; Meteorology* (Close-
Up)]

Snow, Theodore P., Ph.D.
Professor of Astrophysics,
University of Colorado, Boulder.
[*Astronomy, Milky Way*]

Tamarin, Robert H., Ph.D.
Professor and Chairman of Biology,
Boston University.
[Special Report, *The Evolution of
Genetic Medicine; Ecology*]

Thom, Derrick J., Ph.D.
Professor and Head,
Department of Geography and Earth
Resources,
Utah State University.
[Special Report, *The Sahara's Bleak
"Shore"*]

Tobin, Thomas R., Ph.D.
Assistant Professor,
ARL Division of Neurobiology,
University of Arizona.
[*Zoology*]

Visich, Marian, Jr., Ph.D.
Associate Dean of Engineering,
State University of New York.
[*Energy*]

Walter, Eugene J., Jr., B.A.
Free-Lance Writer.
[*Zoology* (Close-Up)]

Wenke, Robert J., Ph.D.
Professor,
Department of Anthropology,
University of Washington.
[*Archaeology, Old World*]

Woodwell, George M., Ph.D.
President and Director,
Woods Hole Research Center.
[Science Studies: *Global Change*]

9

Special Reports

Thirteen articles give in-depth treatment to significant and timely subjects in science and technology.

Page 21   Page 112

Page 124   Page 182

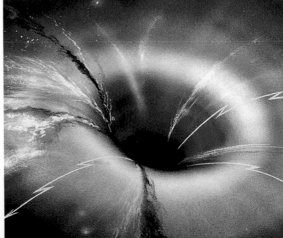

As citizens debate wetlands policy,
scientists are learning more about how
these ecosystems purify water, control
flooding, and support plants and animals.

Wetlands: Mired in Controversy

BY BARBARA L. BEDFORD

Rarely are changes to a United States government technical manual
even noticed by the public. But between August 1991 and January
1992, more than 80,000 letters poured into one of the U.S. government agencies that handles wetlands policies. The letters commented,
sometimes heatedly, on proposed changes in a government manual
used to identify and determine the boundaries of the nation's wetlands. Some letters praised the changes. Others argued they would en-
danger many of the nation's remaining wetlands.

Government policy regarding wetlands has become the focus of a
major controversy, involving land developers, farmers, environmental
groups, government administrators, scientists, and private citizens.
Some view wetlands as refuges for endangered species, spawning
grounds for commercially important fish and shellfish, and purifiers of
the nation's water supply. Others argue that the government has gone
too far in its efforts to protect wetlands.

The government has not always been in the business of protecting
wetlands. Until the 1960's, government policies encouraged—and
even helped pay for—turning wetlands to other uses. Draining and filling these water-soaked lands provided fields and pastures for farmers
and gave cities room to grow. People generally viewed wetlands in their
natural state as useless or, worse than useless, as breeding grounds for
disease-carrying mosquitoes. Since the 1780's, more than half the wet-

lands in the United States have been destroyed, according to the U.S. Fish and Wildlife Service, the agency responsible for mapping them.

The first efforts to purchase and protect wetlands came in the early 1900's from hunters who recognized these "unusable" lands as vital habitats for ducks, geese, and many fur-bearing animals. Spurred by rising public concern for the environment, states began passing laws in the 1960's to save wetlands from further destruction. In 1972, Congress placed restrictions on dumping materials into wetlands to fill them. The trend had turned toward wetland protection. In 1992, at least six bills related to wetlands were scheduled to come before the U.S. Congress, including some that would reverse the trend and reduce government protection.

Today, U.S. government policies draw criticism both from landowners and from those who seek to protect wetlands. About 75 per cent of U.S. wetlands are privately owned, and property owners claim that the burden of protecting wetlands falls to them, while the benefits go to the public. Before filling a wetland, a landowner must apply for a permit—a time-consuming process that can be costly and confusing. And sometimes permits are denied. On the other hand, people concerned with wetland protection point out that government policies exempt most wetland conversions from regulation and have failed to halt wetland losses.

Pressure from various groups, including farmers and real estate developers, led the Administration of President George Bush to call for revisions in the way the government identified wetlands. These revisions drew the storm of letters.

Which lands are wetlands?

To understand the current controversy, it's important to look at how scientists define and classify wetlands and to find out what scientists know about the role that wetlands play in the environment. Scientists as well as government regulators acknowledge that defining a wetland can be tricky, in part because of the enormous diversity of wetlands. Wetlands range in size from shallow basins that could fit in a backyard to Florida's Everglades, a marsh that covers an area larger than the state of Delaware. Among the more familiar wetland images are majestic swamps of cypress trees draped in moss; flat, open marshes fringed by cattails and dotted with ducks; and soft, spongy bogs carpeted with moss. There are many other kinds of wetlands, but despite their great variety, wetlands do share certain features.

All wetlands are just that: wet lands. Neither open water nor dry land, these areas form transitional zones between truly *aquatic* (water) systems, such as rivers or lakes, and truly *terrestrial* (land) systems, such as forests or grasslands. Because wetlands occur in landscapes that gradually shift from wet to dry, it can be difficult to determine just where a wetland starts or stops.

Wetlands typically develop in landscapes where water can accumulate: in shallow coastal bays and inland basins; along the shores of lakes

The author:
Barbara L. Bedford is assistant professor of natural resources and director of the Ecosystems Research Center at Cornell University.

and the flood plains of rivers; and on broad, flat expanses of land with poor drainage. Wetlands also can occur on gently sloping land, where water seeps from the ground or wells up in springs. Wetlands even turn up on high ground and on hilly slopes in Newfoundland, Scandinavia, and other places with heavy rainfall and little evaporation.

Water levels in most wetlands fluctuate from season to season, from year to year, and over longer climate cycles. These fluctuations also can make it difficult to identify wetlands. At least some of the time, however, a wetland lies covered—or soaked—with water. Even though a wetland may not always contain water, the source and amount of its water still determines the type of soil it has and the plants that grow in it. These soils and plants remain as evidence of the water's recurring presence.

When soil becomes flooded or water-saturated, bacteria in the soil rapidly use up the available oxygen, and the floodwaters prevent the air from reaching the soil and replenishing that oxygen. The soil becomes *anoxic* (lacking in oxygen) as a result. Wetland soils are unique because they lack oxygen at least part of the year, in most years.

Baldcypress trees grow in a southern swamp. Knobby growths called *knees* on the trees' roots protrude above the water and absorb oxygen.

To survive in wetlands, plants—all of which need oxygen—must have special means of getting oxygen to their roots. Cypress trees, for example, have knobby "knees" on their roots that break through the water's surface and absorb oxygen. Many wetland plants have hollow air spaces in their stems, which carry oxygen from the leaves above water to the roots below. (It's possible to cut off a bulrush, a plant that rings some wetlands, and use it as an underwater breathing tube.) Such adaptations enable the plants to live in wetlands, where typical dry land plants would die.

These three features—the recurrent presence of water, soils lacking in oxygen, and plants adapted to the unusual conditions—distinguish wetlands from all other ecosystems. By *ecosystem*, scientists mean the nonliving features of an environment, along with the plants, animals, and microbes that live in it, and the interactions that occur among everything in that environment.

The great diversity of wetlands

Wetlands scientists point out that there is no one correct way of classifying wetland ecosystems. Botanists, fascinated by the great diversity of plants that grow in wetlands, have developed dozens of classification schemes based on vegetation. Soil scientists distinguish wetlands by their type of soil and by how rapidly water drains from that soil. The U.S. Fish and Wildlife Service developed a wetland classification system based primarily on the wetland's importance to waterfowl.

Wetlands can be broadly classified as bogs, marshes, and swamps. Although these broad categories only hint at the great diversity of wetlands, they nonetheless convey key features that differentiate wetlands:

A multitude of wetlands

There are many kinds of wetlands, and ecologists say there is no one correct way of classifying them. Wetlands may be classified by their plant life, the type of soil beneath them, or the source and chemistry of their water. The broadest categories of wetlands, based mainly on plant life, are swamps, marshes, and bogs.

Some commonly used terms to describe wetlands

- **Bogs** are wetlands in which dead remains of plants accumulate as peat. Bogs receive water only from the atmosphere.

- **Fens**, like bogs, are peat-forming wetlands, but they receive some water from the ground and the surface.

- **Marshes** are nonforested wetlands dominated by soft-stemmed plants. Marshes may be freshwater or saltwater and occur inland or along coasts.

- **Mire** is a European term for a peat-forming wetland, such as a bog or fen.

- **Moor**, like mire, is a European term for a peat-forming wetland.

- **Muskegs** are vast expanses of peat-forming wetlands.

- **Peatlands** are peat-forming wetlands, including bogs and fens.

- **Playas** are marshes in small basins on the high plains of Texas and New Mexico.

- **Prairie potholes** are marshes in shallow basins on the prairies of the Midwestern United States and Canada.

- **Sloughs** are areas of slowly moving or still water in the flood plains of rivers and lakes.

- **Swamps** are forested wetlands, dominated by shrubs or trees.

- **Wet meadows** and **wet prairies** are nonforested wetlands dominated by grasses and sedges. They usually remain water-saturated only part of the year.

Volo Bog in northern Illinois fills a hollow created by a glacier thousands of years ago.

Marshes fed by the tides extend along the coast of Louisiana.

White cedar trees grow in a swamp in Massachusetts.

A prairie pothole in South Dakota may dry out by the end of summer or during a drought.

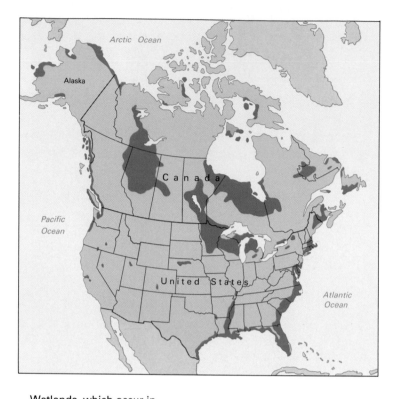

Wetlands, which occur in all climates and regions, cover about 5 per cent of the U.S. land area and about 13 per cent of Canada's. Nearly one-fourth of the world's remaining wetlands are found in Canada. Dark green areas on the map indicate regions in the United States and Canada where wetlands are prevalent.

their plant life, the chemical composition of their water, and their underlying soil.

■ *Bogs* are most commonly found at high latitudes with cool, moist climates, such as Ireland, Scotland, Scandinavia, and large parts of Canada. Bogs receive water only from rain, snow, and other forms of precipitation, which usually contain few *nutrients* (chemicals plants use as food).

Bog plants must develop special mechanisms for capturing or conserving nutrients in an environment described by one bog ecologist as a "wet desert." Some bog plants take nutrients from insects. The sundew plant, for example, has sticky fluid on its leaves that traps insects. The tubular leaves of the pitcher plant collect rain water in which insects drown. Thick carpets of moss that form on the surface of a bog are also adapted to the nutrient-poor conditions. This moss, known as Sphagnum moss, holds water in special cells in its leaves and extracts nutrients from the water through chemical reactions.

Dead plant matter breaks down very slowly in the wet, acidic, and oxygenless conditions of a bog. Partly decayed moss and other plant matter accumulate as a dense mat called peat. Peat, which makes a bog feel spongy underfoot, can be dried and used for fuel.

■ *Marshes* lie scattered throughout the world. Some marshes occur along seacoasts, fed by salt water, fresh water, or both. But most marshes lie inland and obtain fresh water from rivers, lakes, or the ground. Marshes have nonacidic water that can be very rich in nutrients, depending on the soils or rocks it travels across or through. Ground water that moves through limestone, for example, usually carries large amounts of the nutrients calcium and magnesium, components of limestone that dissolve in water. Rivers carry heavy loads of sediments if they travel across unplanted land or other easily eroded surfaces. These sediments usually contain nutrients.

Many marshes occur on mineral soils, which form from rocks that have broken apart. Whether a soil is mineral or *organic*—composed chiefly of the remains of dead plant matter, like the peat beneath a bog—determines the availability of nutrients and the soil's ability to hold water. In general, plants obtain nutrients more readily from a mineral soil, and a mineral soil holds less water than an organic soil.

Marshes lack trees and are dominated instead by grasslike, soft-

The regulatory quagmire

United States government priorities have slowly shifted from destroying wetlands to protecting them. The change was prompted by growing public concern for the environment and by scientific studies that raise questions about how continued wetland losses may threaten water quality, flood control, and commercial fisheries.

In 1972, Congress enacted the first and only nationwide wetlands regulatory program in amendments to the Clean Water Act. Section 404 of that act required landowners to obtain permits from the Corps of Engineers, a branch of the Army, to discharge such materials as dirt, sand, and gravel into U.S. waters. A court decision later broadened the definition of waters to include wetlands, and Congress in 1977 officially authorized regulatory control over wetlands under Section 404.

The Section 404 program has had a limited effect. It exempts discharges related to agriculture, forestry, and ranching from regulation and requires a permit to fill a wetland but not to drain or otherwise alter one. Each year, the Corps of Engineers approves about 10,000 permit applications and denies about 500 under the Section 404 program, according to a 1991 report to Congress. But not everyone applies for a permit, though a person who fills a wetland without a permit can be required to restore it. The Corps received reports of over 18,000 unauthorized discharges of earth materials into wetlands from 1988 through 1990.

The 1985 Food Security Act changed federal farm policies affecting wetlands. Under what has become known as the Swampbuster provision, farmers lose eligibility for certain federal benefits, including subsidies and crop insurance, by planting crops on wetlands drained after Dec. 23, 1985. In 1990, Congress strengthened the Swampbuster provision. Under the new regulations, farmers lose eligibility for benefits if they drain a wetland for cropland, even if they don't plant it.

Other government programs attempt to protect wetlands by purchase; by tax incentives to landowners who retain wetlands; and by making payments to farmers who restore farmed wetlands. Significant losses of wetlands continued, however, through the 1980's.

For this reason, the Environmental Protection Agency (EPA) in 1987 asked the Conservation Foundation, a nonprofit research organization, to convene a National Wetlands Policy Forum to recommend ways of improving wetland policy. Forum members included government officials, environmental and business leaders, farmers, and scholars. Their report summarized existing problems, noting that public and private programs to protect and manage wetlands addressed only limited aspects of the problem and had been adopted haphazardly and incoherently. This led to duplication and uncertainty, the report added, at times imposing burdensome costs on wetland owners. It further noted that many natural values of wetlands benefit the public more than the individual who owns the wetland.

The forum recommended the establishment of a national policy with a short-term goal of achieving "no overall net loss of the nation's remaining wetlands" and, over the long term, "to restore and create wetlands, where feasible." It explained that not every wetland should become untouchable, but that overall wetland losses should not exceed wetland gains. It also noted that the government must share with individual landowners the costs of restoring and creating wetlands.

Controversy over national wetland policies intensified after President George Bush took office in 1989. Implementation of the Swampbuster provision and strengthened enforcement of Section 404, combined with the confusion and delays these programs sometimes create, have angered some farmers and land developers. Those concerned with wetland protection are disappointed that the Administration has not implemented a no-net-loss policy, a policy Bush endorsed in his 1988 election campaign.

A major part of the controversy concerns what is and is not wetland. In 1989, the federal agencies directly involved in wetland management—the EPA, Corps of Engineers, Soil Conservation Service, and Fish and Wildlife Service—adopted a single manual for identifying wetlands. The manual marked an important step toward coordinating federal policy and eliminating confusion. The four agencies recognized the need to test the manual in the field and then revise it.

Revisions were underway during 1991 when the Bush Administration proposed changes. Under its proposal, wetland plants and soils could no longer be used alone to identify an area as a wetland, as they could under the 1989 manual. Instead, the area had to have standing water or saturated soil at the time of inspection, as well as wetland plants and soil. Supporters of the Bush proposal claim that the manual protected every mud hole. But critics maintain the proposed changes are scientifically flawed and would exclude large areas of readily recognized wetlands.   [B. L. B.]

The importance of wetlands

Wetlands perform a number of important ecological functions. They support a variety of plants and provide food, shelter, and breeding grounds for many species of animals. Wetlands improve water quality by removing pollutants, and they reduce flooding by storing floodwaters. Not every wetland performs all functions.

Wetlands provide habitat for at least a third of all the threatened or endangered species in the United States, such as the showy lady's slipper, *above*.

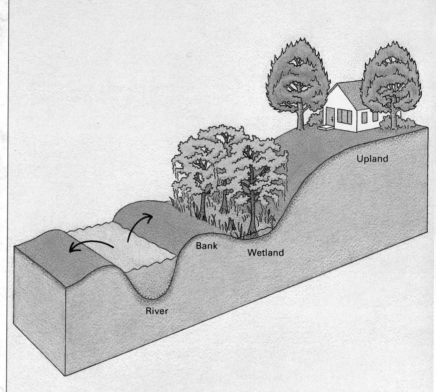

Storing floodwaters

Many wetlands lie between high, dry land and the waters of rivers or lakes. When these bodies of water overflow their banks, wetlands act as storage basins, reducing flooding downstream. The floodwaters slowly leave the wetland as water levels in the river or lake return to normal.

Wetlands provide breeding grounds for many kinds of animals, including American alligators, *right*.

Most North American ducks and geese nest in wetlands. Wetlands also serve as vital stopovers for waterfowl during migrations between northern nesting sites and southern wintering sites.

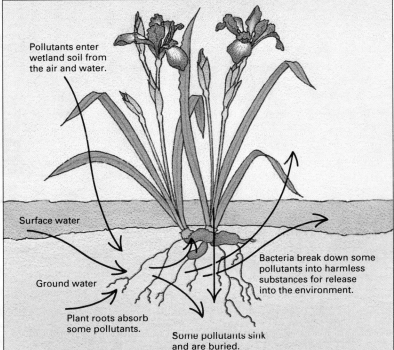

Pollutants enter wetland soil from the air and water.

Surface water

Ground water

Bacteria break down some pollutants into harmless substances for release into the environment.

Plant roots absorb some pollutants.

Some pollutants sink and are buried.

Wetlands provide food and cover for fur-bearing animals and serve as nurseries for fish and shellfish.

Purifying water

Environmental pollutants, such as nitrates and phosphates, can enter wetlands from ground water, surface water, and the air. The roots of wetland plants take up some of these pollutants. Others become bound to soil or buried in dead plant matter. Bacteria that thrive in wetland soils break down most of the nitrates, which then return to the environment as harmless nitrogen gas.

stemmed plants, termed *emergent vegetation*. These plants sink roots into submerged wetland soil, but their shoots emerge above the water to take carbon dioxide from the air for *photosynthesis*—the process of converting carbon dioxide, sunlight, and nutrients into food energy. Cattails are the best-known emergent vegetation. Other types include sedges, bulrushes, reeds, and hundreds of colorful, flowering plants.

■ *Swamps,* like marshes, occur in all regions and receive water from all sources. But unlike marshes, swamps are dominated by trees and shrubs. Many swamps develop in areas regularly flooded by flowing water, especially the flood plains of major rivers. This gives them dry periods between floods as well, enabling trees and shrubs to take root. Swamps generally have mineral soils and typically are rich in nutrients.

The term *swamp* encompasses a variety of forested wetlands. Cypress and gum trees commonly grow in swamps in the Southeastern United States. Red maples and white cedars are common in Northern swamps. Mangrove trees, which can endure salt as well as flooding, grow in swamps along the coast of Florida.

Understanding flooding patterns

Today, scientists also look at flooding patterns to understand how bogs, marshes, and swamps function and why the various types of wetlands differ. Some scientists believe that most differences among wetlands stem from how often, how long, and how deeply water saturates the soil—something they call *hydroperiod*. The water in coastal wetlands, for example, rises and falls with the tides. Wetlands fed by rivers usually flood seasonally, when heavy rains or melting snow causes rivers or streams to overflow. The larger a river's drainage basin is, the deeper and more persistent the flooding is likely to be. Wetlands fed primarily by ground water tend to have fairly constant water levels, while wetlands fed largely by precipitation may have water levels that vary greatly from season to season and year to year. Some plants tolerate a narrow range of water levels, but others require alternating periods of dry soil and periods of deep water.

The variety of wetlands helps explain the number of valuable functions they perform. Wetlands support many kinds of plants and animals, improve water quality, reduce flood damage, and replenish ground water supplies. They also are places of great natural beauty. Not every wetland provides all these services, but wetlands as a whole do.

Great egrets hunt for food in the shallow water of a wetland. The birds were threatened with extinction in the early 1900's, after their long white plumes became prized decorations on ladies' hats.

Wildlife in wetlands

Most wetlands teem with life. A spring canoe ride through a Midwestern marsh, for example, might reveal damselflies and dragonflies, whirligig beetles, painted turtles and leopard frogs, beavers and muskrats, green herons and dozens of other marsh birds, shorebirds, ducks,

America's lost wetlands

As the United States has grown, the draining and filling of wetlands has provided needed farmland and room for cities to expand. Experts calculate that by the 1980's the United States had lost more than half the wetlands it had in the 1780's.

Wetlands near populated areas deteriorate when people use them as dumping grounds, *top*. Cropland encroaches on potholes, which once dotted much of the northern prairie, *left*.

and geese. Because nutrients tend to accumulate in wetlands along with water, abundant food is available for plants. The plant remains provide a feast for small animals, which in turn are fed upon by larger animals.

Not all animals that depend on wetlands spend their entire life there. Wetlands serve as nurseries for many marine fish and shellfish. Small, fur-bearing mammals forage for food in wetlands. Many songbirds following migration routes stop temporarily in wetlands. Ducks and geese use wetlands for nesting and for stopovers during migration between summer habitats in the north and wintering sites in the south.

Wetlands also serve as havens for the shrinking number of plant and animal species on Earth. Of the plants the U.S. government lists as endangered, 28 per cent depend on wetlands, according to William A. Niering, a botanist at Connecticut College in New London. And nearly half the nation's endangered animals depend on wetlands, according to the World Wildlife Federation. These figures become even more impressive when we realize that wetlands cover only about 5 per cent of the continental United States.

Eastern painted turtles sun themselves on a log in an Illinois wetland.

Water management, naturally

Less well known than their biological richness is the critical role wetlands play in the larger environment. When rivers and streams overflow their banks, wetlands reduce flood damage downstream by storing the overflow until the flood recedes. Wetland plants slow the movement of floodwaters, robbing them of much of their force.

A study in the 1970's by Wisconsin scientists monitored the levels of floodwaters in *watersheds* (river drainage basins) with and without wetlands. The floodwaters peaked at levels 60 per cent lower in watersheds with 15 per cent of their area in wetlands than in watersheds with no wetlands. In Massachusetts, government engineers decided in the early 1970's that they could control flooding near Boston far more economically by saving wetlands along the Charles River than by building dams.

Some wetlands also help maintain ground water supplies. The water is purified as it trickles through the soil. The town of Amherst, Mass., for example, gets most of its water from an underground supply refilled by a large swamp. The Everglades helps replenish the underground water supply for southern Florida. That supply is threatened, however, by the diversion of water for irrigation and flood control.

Water generally is cleaner when leaving a wetland than when entering one. Some wetlands intercept waters contaminated by sewage and by fertilizers from cropland before the polluted waters reach lakes and rivers. Phosphorus, an ingredient in most fertilizers, binds to dirt particles that sink in wetland sediments. Wetland plants also take up phosphorus in their roots. If the dead plants later become buried in wetland soils, the phosphorus locked in them goes into long-term storage.

Nitrates, compounds of nitrogen and oxygen, also enter wetlands in water that drains from farmland. Bacteria that live in anoxic wetland soils convert the nitrates to harmless nitrogen gas, which then escapes into the atmosphere. This conversion of nitrates occurs at higher rates in wetlands than in any other ecosystem.

Other studies have shown that wetlands can remove metals that drain from mining sites and pollute water. Such metals as iron, aluminum, and copper, for example, bind to carbon in wetland soils and become buried in wetland sediments. Studies also have shown that chemical reactions that occur in wetlands can neutralize the acidity of pollutants that fall as acid rain.

Many wetlands clear water of the sediments that erode from farmlands or stream channels. Wetlands have this ability because they commonly form in basins or backwaters where the flow of water slows, allowing sediments to drop out and settle. Plants that grow in wetlands also slow the water.

Scientists have long known how wetlands cleanse water, but only in the 1970's and 1980's did scientific studies begin to measure the varying rates at which such processes occur. These studies also demonstrated that wetlands' ability to cleanse water does have limits and that a wetland can be destroyed when more pollutants get dumped into it than it can handle.

The idea that wetlands might help stabilize the world's climate began to draw increasing attention in the 1980's. Scientists believe that rising levels of carbon dioxide in the atmosphere may cause *global warming*—a process in which carbon dioxide and other heat-trapping gases lead to higher than normal temperatures around the world. Burning *fossil fuels* (coal, oil, and natural gas) releases carbon dioxide, as does the process of decay. Plants, in contrast, remove carbon dioxide from the air during photosynthesis. Wetlands, moreover, act as "carbon sinks" because large amounts of dead plant and animal matter, which is rich in carbon, stay trapped in the water-logged soils. Wetlands thus prevent the organic matter from decaying and releasing carbon dioxide gas into the atmosphere.

Lost wetlands

Every hour since the 1780's, what are now the continental 48 states have lost more than 24 hectares (60 acres) of wetland, according to government figures. California has lost the largest percentage of its wetlands—91 per cent—and Florida the greatest area—3.8 million hectares (9 million acres). By the mid-

Restoring wetlands

Efforts to replace lost wetlands include a project by scientists at Oregon State University in Corvallis to restore a salt marsh along Oregon's Salmon River.

The project's site was a pasture created from a salt marsh by building dikes to hold back the river's water in the 1960's.

In 1978, after the dikes were removed, salt water flowed in and killed the pasture plants.

Sedge, a grasslike wetland plant, dominated the restored salt marsh in 1988, 10 years after the restoration project began.

1980's, Illinois, Indiana, Iowa, and Ohio had each drained from 85 to 90 per cent of their wetlands to create cropland and pasture. Wetlands were lost to cities as well as farms. In the 1800's, America depended on rivers, canals, and other waterways to transport goods and people. And cities grew up where land met open water—just where wetlands were likely to be. Major American cities built in part on drained or filled wetlands include Boston, Chicago, New Orleans, and Washington, D.C.

The latest government inventory, conducted in the mid-1980's, revealed that about 41.7 million hectares (103 million acres) of wetlands remained in the United States. Inland freshwater wetlands made up 95 per cent of that total; and coastal wetlands, the remainder.

Agriculture still claims more wetlands than any other human activity. As farmers pump water from the ground for irrigation, dig drainage ditches, and divert water in rivers and streams to control flooding, wetlands lose needed water. Forested wetlands have been hit hardest in recent years, especially in the Southeastern United States.

Lost acreage, however, does not tell the whole story. Some types of wetlands—such as Nebraska's seasonally flooded flatlands—have nearly disappeared. Only remnants are left of others, including the wet prairies of the Midwest and the marshes of California's Central Valley.

Few wetlands have escaped changes in the quality and quantity of their water. Toxic pollutants, for example, commonly turn up in the sediments of wetlands along the Great Lakes. Moreover, few large tracts of undisturbed wetlands remain in the United States. Roads, railways, and utility line corridors have chopped up wetlands near cities and along major transportation routes. Canals to reach oil wells have fragmented wetlands along the Gulf of Mexico.

Replacing lost wetlands

As wetlands are destroyed, a few new ones are created. Interest in restoring and creating wetlands has grown since the early 1980's, in part to comply with government regulations but primarily to gain specific benefits.

Florida, for example, in the 1980's began restoring marshes along the flood plains of the Kissimmee River, both to improve the quality of the river's water and to provide habitat for wading birds and other wildlife. The town of Arcata, Calif., restored and extended a marsh to cleanse sewage wastewater before it entered the Pacific Ocean. The marsh has attracted more than 200 species of birds. And the North American Waterfowl Management Plan, an agreement signed by the U.S. and Canadian governments in 1986, calls for restoring farmed prairie wetlands in an attempt to increase waterfowl populations.

Scientists are carefully monitoring these projects. But no one has monitored, even for a short time, most of the thousands of other wetlands created in the United States. Thus, scientists don't know what plants and animals inhabit these new wetlands, what functions they perform, or even if they will last. Two leading wetlands experts—Joy Zedler of San Diego State University and Milton Weller of Texas A&M

University in College Station—point out that although some evidence indicates such wetlands can look like natural ones, there is little data available to demonstrate that they function like natural ones.

Wetland scientists know that it is possible to construct wetlands for a specific purpose, such as floodwater storage or habitat for waterfowl. But they are still trying to learn if it is possible to create entire wetland ecosystems that can serve many functions and sustain themselves. Some wetland-creation projects require systems of pumps and dikes to raise and lower water levels in an effort to mimic nature. Building, maintaining, and monitoring such systems is expensive—too expensive for most restoration projects.

Another unanswered question concerns our ability to restore wetlands so that they maintain biological diversity. Most of the recently created or restored wetlands have been salt marshes along the Atlantic coast or shallow ponds fringed with cattails or other emergent vegetation. No one has tried to create a bog, and little effort has gone into restoring forested wetlands and other threatened wetlands.

Attitudes toward wetlands have changed greatly since the mid-1900's as the value of these resources has become better understood. More and more people now question the wisdom of draining and filling wetlands. But the question remains whether we are wise enough to find ways of preserving our existing wetlands that are fair both to the people who own them and to the society that benefits from them.

For further reading:

Niering, William A. *Wetlands.* Knopf, 1985.
Niering, William A., and Littlehales, Bates. *Wetlands of North America.* Thomasson-Grant, 1991.
Wetlands: A Global Perspective. Ed. by M. E. Moser and C. A. Finlayson. Facts on File, 1991.

Questions for thought and discussion

Suppose it is your job to decide whether to issue permits allowing people to drain or fill wetlands. One day, you receive an application for a permit to fill a large marsh a few miles from a major city. The marsh is a stopover for migrating ducks and geese. You visit the site and are struck by the marsh's quiet beauty—and its closeness to a suburban development of expensive homes. While you are there, you meet with the landowners, an elderly couple. They explain that medical expenses require them to sell their land as quickly as possible. But, they tell you, the presence of the huge wetland has made the property almost impossible to get rid of. They beg you to grant them the permit.

Questions: What information would you gather before making your decision? Can you think of a solution that would address both the environmental issues and the couple's concern?

Meteorite collisions with Earth may have helped shape the history of life on this planet. The rocks themselves hold clues to the formation of the solar system billions of years ago.

Stones from Space

BY LAWRENCE GROSSMAN

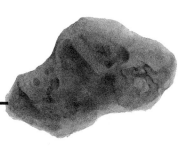

The asteroid was 795,000 kilometers (494,000 miles) from Earth when astronomers at the Spacewatch Telescope at Kitt Peak Observatory in Arizona spotted it moving across the night sky on Jan. 18, 1991. By measuring the brightness of the rocky object, the astronomers determined that the asteroid was fairly small—only about 5 to 10 meters (16 to 33 feet) in diameter. Twelve hours later, the asteroid, in orbit around the sun, made its closest approach to Earth. Traveling at about 20 kilometers (12 miles) per second, the asteroid passed 170,000 kilometers (106,000 miles) away—less than half the distance between Earth and the moon.

Although this asteroid never collided with Earth, other pieces of matter from space slam into Earth's atmosphere all the time. Most of these particles are no bigger than a pea. Others, however, have been large enough to create huge impact craters.

These visitors from space interest scientists for a number of reasons. Their impacts helped shape the early Earth and, scientists have recently learned, may have had a major effect on the history of life on this planet. Some of these rocks from space are the only intact survivors from the birth of the solar system. And, as I and other researchers have found, they hold precious chemical clues to processes that occurred 4.6 billion years ago, just before the sun and planets formed from a swirling disk-shaped cloud of gas and dust known as the *solar nebula*. Moreover, scientists in the late 1980's and early 1990's found that some

of these space rocks contain star dust, mineral grains that formed
around stars tens of millions of years older than our own sun. This star
dust is the only direct evidence we have of the processes that fuel the
nuclear fires that burn within stars, of the stars' chemical makeup, and
of the raw material dying stars contributed to the solar nebula.

The author:

Lawrence Grossman is a professor of geochemistry in the Department of the Geophysical Sciences and at the Enrico Fermi Institute at the University of Chicago.

Where meteorites come from

Most of the solid objects that enter Earth's atmosphere are pieces of
asteroids, small planets no larger than 1,000 kilometers (620 miles) in
diameter. Asteroids should not be confused with *comets,* balls of ice and
dust that shed dust particles and gas molecules and that form bright
halos and long tails when their orbits take them close to the sun. Most
asteroids orbit the sun in a region between the orbits of Mars and
Jupiter—known as the asteroid belt—that contains millions of pieces
of rock left over from the formation of the solar system.

In the crowded asteroid belt, there are occasional collisions between
asteroids, causing them to break into smaller pieces. Scientists usually
call pieces with a diameter of about 1 kilometer (0.6 mile) or less a meteoroid. Some of the asteroids and meteoroids kicked out of the asteroid belt during collisions go into a new orbit that crosses Earth's orbit.
Eventually—perhaps not for millions of years—Earth and the asteroid
or meteoroid will meet at the crossroads of their orbits, and the two
will collide.

When an asteroid or meteoroid plummets through Earth's atmosphere, friction causes its outer surface to heat up and glow. If the object is so small that it is completely *vaporized* (changed to gas) during its
descent, it is called a meteor. Meteors cause streaks in the sky called
shooting stars when they occur at random and meteor showers when
relatively large numbers of them appear on the same date each year.

Meteorites are objects large enough to survive the intense heat of
their passage through the atmosphere and reach the ground. Some
meteorites strike Earth with such force that they explode and create
huge depressions called impact craters. At first, scientists were slow to
accept that such depressions were, in fact, created by impacts. But today we know that the impact of even a relatively small object from
space can create a huge crater on Earth's surface. Meteoroids and asteroids travel through space at speeds of about 25 kilometers (16
miles) per second. Friction with the atmosphere does not even slow objects weighing more than 1,000 metric tons (1,100 short tons). And at
these speeds, even meteoroids with small diameters have such large
amounts of *kinetic* energy (energy of motion) that they may create
large craters.

Meteor Crater in Arizona, for example, is about 1,265 meters (4,150
feet) wide and 174 meters (571 feet) deep. Scientists believe it was created 50,000 years ago by the impact of a meteorite that was only 60 meters (200 feet) in diameter but that landed with an explosive force
1,000 times greater than that of the atomic bomb dropped on Hiroshima, Japan, in 1945.

By analyzing the rock at and near craters and by laboratory experiments, geologists have been able to determine what happens when a meteorite crashes into Earth. In a typical impact, almost all of a meteorite's kinetic energy is released as a shock wave that transmits heat and pressure into the surface rocks at the point of impact. The shock wave compresses the surface rocks, squeezing some downward and lofting others outward at speeds of several kilometers per second. Some of the surface rock is vaporized and some melted in place. Some rock is crushed and the pieces are almost instantaneously cemented together again, forming breccia, a type of rock containing angular fragments.

As the shock wave travels outward from the point of impact, it lifts, overturns, and folds the surface rock, forming a bowl-shaped crater with a raised rim all the way around it. The impact of a large meteorite also may result in the formation of a peak in the center of a crater, created by rock compressing and then rebounding. Meteorite impacts can also form numerous concentric rims around the crater.

Identifying impact craters is easiest when a crater's bowl-shaped basin, raised rims, or central peak are preserved. Unfortunately, most impact craters on Earth's land surface are so old that they are difficult if not impossible to recognize. Over thousands of years, erosion, the advance and retreat of glaciers, and other geologic processes have worn away the craters' raised rims and central peaks. Some have been filled in with and even buried by sediments. Even the presence of breccia is not proof that a circular structure is, in fact, an impact crater, because other geologic events, such as landslides and volcanoes, can produce breccia.

The most conclusive evidence that a circular depression is an impact crater is the presence of shocked rocks. Such rocks may contain *shatter cones* (rocks fractured in conical patterns). Or they may have distinctive patterns of microscopic cracks in certain minerals, which indicate that they were suddenly subjected to high temperatures and pressures. Geologists can also identify impact craters by the chemical composition of the rocks. Meteorites leave chemical calling cards—high concentrations of nickel, platinum, and iridium, elements generally found in low concentrations in Earth rocks.

Meteorites shaped the history of Earth

One major reason for studying impact craters is to learn more about the history of our planet. An intriguing recent development in the study of meteorite impacts, for example, has been the discovery of evidence suggesting a link between at least one impact and a period of *mass extinction,* a biological crisis of major proportions that occurs when a large number of species become extinct over a short time period. Some scientists believe that a large meteorite impact may have been responsible for a mass extinction that occurred about 65 million years ago at the end of the Cretaceous Period and the beginning of the Tertiary Period. Scientists had long known from the study of fossils that many species became extinct at that time. These species included

Rocks from space

More than the nine planets orbit the sun. Smaller chunks of rock also inhabit our solar system. These rocks are called *asteroids* or *meteoroids*, depending on their size.

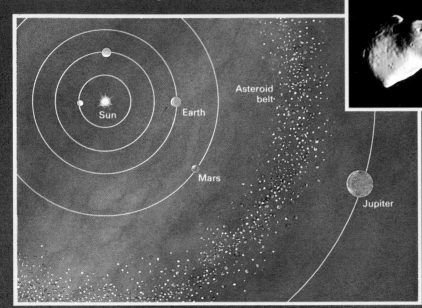

The asteroid belt

Most asteroids and meteoroids orbit the sun in a region called the asteroid belt between the orbits of Mars and Jupiter, *above*. An *asteroid* (inset) is a small planet at least 1 kilometer (0.6 mile) in diameter.

Out from the asteroid belt

In the asteroid belt, asteroids occasionally collide and break into fragments. Fragments with a diameter smaller than 1 kilometer are called *meteoroids*. The collision may knock the fragments out of their orbit and set them on a new path that eventually crosses Earth's orbit.

Stones from the sky

Eventually, Earth and these space rocks meet at the crossroads of their orbits, and the rocks streak into Earth's atmosphere. A rock so small that it is *vaporized* (changed to gas) during its fiery descent is known as a *meteor*. These glowing objects, popularly called *shooting stars*, cause meteor showers when they appear in large numbers, *below*.

Crash landing

Some of these space rocks are large enough to survive their passage through Earth's atmosphere. These are called *meteorites*, and when larger ones slam into the ground, *right*, they create big craters.

Signs of an ancient catastrophe

Meteor Crater in Arizona, which is about 1,265 meters (4,150 feet) wide and 174 meters (571 feet) deep, was created by the impact of a meteorite only about 60 meters (200 feet) in diameter. Scientists estimate that the meteorite landed with a force 1,000 times greater than that of the atomic bomb dropped on Hiroshima, Japan, in 1945. Such craters are the most obvious evidence of meteorite collisions with Earth.

Another type of evidence of an impact is the presence of crystals of minerals such as quartz with a pattern of microscopic cracks, *top*, and breccia, crushed and re-formed rock containing angular fragments, *above*.

all marine and flying reptiles, the last of the dinosaurs, and almost all species of small marine organisms called plankton. Some groups, however, such as land plants, snakes, and mammals, were hardly affected.

In 1980, a team of scientists led by physicist Luis Alvarez of the University of California at Berkeley reported finding high concentrations of iridium in a layer of clay in northern Italy. The layer dated from the end of the Cretaceous Period and the beginning of the Tertiary Period, which scientists refer to as the K-T boundary. Since iridium is not abundant in Earth rocks, the scientists proposed that it had been deposited during a meteorite impact. The discovery of high iridium concentrations in sediments at the K-T boundary in Denmark and New Zealand indicated that the process responsible occurred throughout the world. Today, scientists generally agree that Earth was indeed struck by a meteorite about 65 million years ago.

They believe that the meteorite was probably about 10 kilometers (6 miles) in diameter. A meteorite of that size hitting Earth would have released energy 5 billion times greater than that of the Hiroshima bomb and produced a crater with a diameter of about 200 kilometers (120 miles).

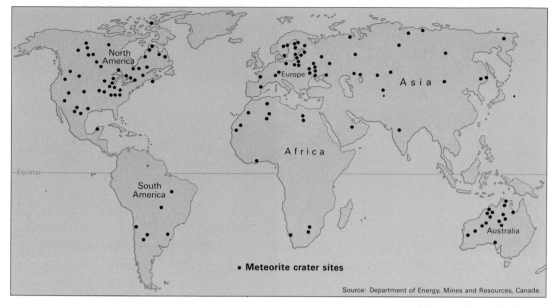

Meteorite crater sites

Source: Department of Energy, Mines and Resources, Canada.

Advocates of the theory that a meteorite caused the Cretaceous extinction contend that such an impact would have ejected so much dust into the upper atmosphere that the entire Earth would have been shrouded in darkness and cold for at least several months. The lack of sunlight would have shut off photosynthesis during this period, killing off all marine plants and, ultimately, nearly all marine animal species. Land plants would have died also, but they could have regenerated a few years later from seeds and spores. Dinosaurs, which required large amounts of food, would have starved or frozen. But smaller mammals probably survived by eating decaying vegetation and insects.

Some scientists, however, argue that other effects of the impact may have been as significant as the loss of sunlight. For example, the heat generated by the meteorite impact may have ignited massive wildfires that burned up vegetation and created huge clouds of soot. The vaporization of rock by the impact may have produced chemicals that poisoned the atmosphere.

The location of the crater left by the Cretaceous impact remains a question. Many possible sites have been proposed, but none has won universal scientific acceptance. In 1990, geologists Alan R. Hildebrand and William V. Boynton of the University of Arizona in Tucson suggested that the meteorite may have landed on the Yucatán Peninsula of Mexico. Although evidence of an impact has been found at the site, some scientists believe that the crater was formed earlier than 65 million years ago.

Studying impact craters has also provided scientists with clues to the frequency with which Earth has been struck by meteorites in the past. Although the rate of bombardment has fallen dramatically since the planet's formation about 4.6 billion years ago, large meteorites still enter the atmosphere from time to time. How great is the danger from meteorite impacts? Only those asteroids and meteoroids in Earth-cross-

Scientists have firmly identified only about 130 impact craters, most of them in areas accessible to geologists. Many other meteorites have landed in the ocean. Other impact craters are not easily identifiable because they have been filled in or buried by sediments or their rims have been destroyed by erosion or other geologic processes.

Some scientists believe that a meteorite impact about 65 million years ago was responsible for the extinction of numerous species, including the last of the dinosaurs. They believe that the impact threw up a huge cloud of dust that prevented sunlight from reaching Earth, dramatically cooling Earth's climate.

ing orbits have a chance of colliding with Earth. Until recently, scientists relied solely on cameras attached to telescopes to search the sky for these objects. But these devices can perceive only those meteoroids with a diameter greater than 1 kilometer (0.6 mile). In 1990, however, scientists at the Spacewatch Telescope at Kitt Peak began searching the sky with more sensitive electronic detectors capable of seeing objects as small as 10 meters (33 feet) across.

Early reports from the Spacewatch project indicate that there are many more relatively small objects in Earth-crossing orbits than scientists had believed. In fact, the Spacewatch scientists have calculated that objects 50 meters (160 feet) wide collide with Earth about once every century. Such a collision rate is surprisingly high and has sparked serious scientific discussion about how we could protect ourselves from such an impact. Unfortunately, locating and determining the orbits of large numbers of near-Earth objects would be a massive task. Blowing them up in space would probably not help, because many of the fragments—including larger ones—would still hit Earth. Some experts suggest that detonating a nuclear warhead or other explosive device near the object could cause meteoroids or asteroids to veer away from the Earth.

Analyzing meteorites

While some scientists investigate impact craters to learn more about the history of our planet, other scientists study meteorites themselves. Scientists have been analyzing meteorites since the early 1800's, when people began to accept the idea that meteor trails in the sky were made by stones entering the atmosphere from space. Today, scientists classify meteorites according to the relative amounts of rock and metal they contain. *Iron meteorites* consist almost entirely of a metallic iron-nickel alloy, something rarely found naturally on Earth. *Stony-iron meteorites* consist of about half silicates—the chief minerals in soil and rock on Earth—and half metallic iron-nickel. *Stony meteorites* are made mostly of silicates but also have significant amounts of metallic iron-nickel.

Stony meteorites are further classified as achondrites or chondrites. Achondrites were formed by volcanic action. Most of them come from asteroids, but a few are pieces of the moon, and some are believed to be from Mars—in both cases thrown into space by a meteorite impact.

Chondrites are the rarest and most scientifically valuable type of meteorite. They contain tiny spheres of crystals and glass called chondrules that have never been found on Earth. Scientists believe that chondrites are probably the only objects that have survived almost unchanged since the solar system formed. All other objects in the solar system were altered by heating processes such as those that accompanied the formation of the planets. Studies have revealed that the material in this class of meteorites probably formed before any other type. This discovery in the mid-1950's helped scientists determine that 4.6 billion years is the age of the solar system.

Analyses of chondrites have provided clues to the puzzle of why different planets in the solar system have different chemical compositions. All the planets formed from the same solar nebula, a swirling cloud of gas and dust. So we might expect that the planets would have the same composition. But they don't. The inner planets—Mercury, Venus, Earth, and Mars—are made of rocky material. The outer planets—Jupiter, Saturn, Uranus, Neptune, and Pluto—consist chiefly of gases. Some process must have been responsible for the separation of the elements as the hot nebula began to cool and matter began to clump together to form the planets.

In the late 1960's, I and a number of other scientists began exploring the theory that differing temperatures of *condensation* (the process by which a gas changes to a solid) could account for the differences. In other words, we thought that some elements in the solar nebula must have condensed and formed mineral grains while temperatures were still so high that other elements remained in a gaseous state. These first grains became the building materials for some of the larger bodies called protoplanets that collided, broke up, and recombined to form the planets and asteroids. Grains that condensed later became the building blocks for other protoplanets. I had calculated, for example, that as the solar nebula began to cool, aluminum, calcium, and titanium would have been among the first elements to form mineral grains. But we had no way to simulate the condensation of the solar nebula in the laboratory.

We thought that *carbonaceous* (carbon-containing) chondrites, the oldest objects in the solar system, might hold some evidence that would confirm our theories. However, this type of meteorite was very hard to come by. Carbonaceous chondrites are still very rare today. Twenty years ago, researchers could get only small samples—pieces about the size of a fingernail—from museums.

Then, in February 1969, the Allende meteorite, a carbonaceous chondrite weighing nearly 2 tons, landed in Mexico. This enabled scientists to remove and study large slices of this kind of meteorite. We found that the Allende meteorite contained irregularly shaped particles. When scientists analyzed these particles, they found that they consist of aluminum, calcium, and titanium, in just the mineralogical forms predicted by my calculations. This finding indicated that elements had indeed condensed from the solar nebula at different temperatures and so verified the theory of condensation, accounting for the different compositions of the planets.

Meteorites aid the study of stars

In the late 1980's and early 1990's, scientists discovered star dust in carbonaceous chondrites—a finding that has revolutionized research into the nature of stars. Before this discovery, scientists wishing to study stars could do so only indirectly and at great distances. For example, they could use instruments called spectrographs to measure the patterns of light emitted by stars. These patterns, which vary according to the mix of elements in a star, can be used to determine a star's chemical composition and the temperature on its surface. Scientists could also use powerful atom-smashers, more accurately called particle accelerators, to study the properties of *isotopes* created in stars. (Isotopes are varieties of an element. The different isotopes of an element have the same number of subatomic particles called protons but different numbers of neutrons in their *nuclei* [cores].)

Scientists used their findings to develop theories that would enable them to predict which isotopes would be found in what proportions in various types of stars. They also theorized about how nuclear reactions within stars had produced the elements and isotopes in the proportions found in the solar system. Before we could confirm these theo-

Fascinating facts about meteorites

The single largest meteorite ever found is the Hoba Meteorite, discovered in 1920 in the south-west African country of Namibia. It weighs an estimated 60 metric tons (66 short tons).

The largest known impact crater is the Sudbury Crater in Ontario, Canada. It is about 200 kilometers (120 miles) in diameter. Scientists believe it was created 1.85 billion years ago by a meteorite with an estimated diameter of 10 kilometers (6 miles).

The only person in the United States known to have been struck by a meteorite was Mrs. Hewlett Hodges of Sylacauga, Ala. She was resting on a sofa in 1954, when a meteorite weighing about 4.5 kilograms (10 pounds) crashed through the roof, bounced off a radio, and bruised her thigh, according to news reports at the time.

Although meteorites land all over the world, Antarctica is one of the best places to find them. One reason is that Antarctic ice sheets hold a large store of meteorites that have landed over time and have become buried in the ice. The meteorites are carried along as the ice sheets move toward the sea. Sometimes, the ice sheets are pushed up against mountains that block their path. The upward moving ice is then eroded by wind, and the meteorites are exposed. Meteorites landing in Antarctica are also less likely than meteorites falling elsewhere to have been damaged by such geologic processes as weathering or to have been contaminated by human beings or other organisms.

The English word *meteor* comes from a Greek word meaning "thing in the air."

Meteors fall through the atmosphere around the clock. But their trails cannot be seen during the day because the sky is too bright.

Impact craters created by meteorite crashes have been found on Mercury, Venus, and Mars and on the moons of Jupiter, Saturn, Uranus, and Neptune.

The most astonishing encounter between Earth and a meteorite in the 1900's may have been the explosion of the Tunguska Comet in Siberia on June 30, 1908. The object, which had an estimated diameter of 100 meters (330 feet), exploded in the atmosphere. The explosion scorched and leveled trees over hundreds of square kilometers. The shock wave from the explosion traveled around the world.

Scientists believe that about 27 metric tons (30 short tons) of meteoritic dust falls on Earth every day.

Meteorites are seldom spherical. Most have an irregular shape.

Meteor showers, also called *meteor swarms*, occur when Earth moves through a trail of small rocks and dust particles. The cloud of particles is usually the orbiting debris from a burned-out comet.

One of the most spectacular meteor showers of the 1900's was the Leonid meteor shower in 1966. The Leonid shower occurs each year in mid-November. It usually produces a weak display, though the shower is noted for its blue and green meteor trails. But about every 33 or 34 years, the Leonid shower stages a spectacular show. In 1966, the latest of these displays, tens of thousands of shooting stars filled the sky for several hours. Astronomers believe that the Leonid meteor shower in 1998 or 1999 may be as dazzling.

Scientists began accepting the idea that meteorites are extraterrestrial objects in 1803 after several thousand meteorites fell in one night near the French town of L'Aigle. French scientists who hurried to the site confirmed that the stones were not Earth rocks.

Although the temperature of the external surface of meteorites can exceed 2,000 °C (3,600 °F) as they travel through Earth's upper atmosphere, they are cool by the time they land.

From ancient stars to us

Scientists have discovered that chondrites, the oldest type of meteorite, contain star dust, tiny mineral grains that formed around distant stars billions of years ago. These grains provide evidence about the materials and processes that formed the chemical elements from which our solar system is built.

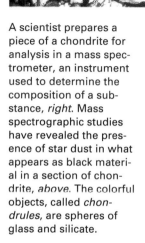

A scientist prepares a piece of a chondrite for analysis in a mass spectrometer, an instrument used to determine the composition of a substance, *right*. Mass spectrographic studies have revealed the presence of star dust in what appears as black material in a section of chondrite, *above*. The colorful objects, called *chondrules*, are spheres of glass and silicate.

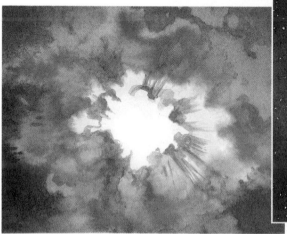

Scientists theorize that the star dust's trek to Earth began when an exploding star, or *supernova,* ejected gas and dust grains into space.

Gas and dust grains from numerous exploding stars accumulated in space, forming an interstellar cloud. The cloud broke into pieces called *nebulae.*

ries, however, we had to know the composition of the matter in the solar system. We gained this knowledge by analyzing the elements and isotopes in meteorites, rocks on Earth, and, later, moon rocks. But the problem with this approach was that these rocks represent a composite of the different elements and isotopes from all the ancient stars that contributed material to the solar nebula.

The center of every star is a nuclear "furnace," where the nuclei of atoms of lighter elements and isotopes fuse to form heavier ones. The isotopes produced by a particular star depend on the chemical material from which the star formed and on the nuclear fusion reactions taking place within the star. As a result, each star has a distinctive "signature," a particular mix of elements and their isotopes.

The outermost regions of some stars also contain "star dust," mineral grains that formed because the gases there were cool enough to condense. The ratios of isotopes of a given element in these mineral grains match those of the gases from which they formed.

Over time, stars lose gas and dust in several ways. But most star dust comes from *supernovae*, the violent explosions of massive stars that have run out of nuclear fuel. The gas and dust ejected from numerous exploding, dying stars accumulate in interstellar space, forming enormous, cold clouds. Eventually, gravity pulls the molecules in a cloud together, and the cloud collapses, heats up, and breaks into fragments. Scientists believe that our solar nebula formed from such a fragment.

The center of the solar nebula would have been so hot that all the dust grains there were completely vaporized. As individual dust grains

As our solar nebula began to swirl and grow hot, most of the original dust grains were vaporized. The remaining grains mixed with new grains created as the gas cooled, forming rocks that became building blocks for planets.

Some rocks with original dust grains were not incorporated into large planets and survived in the small, cold asteroids. Pieces of these asteroids later landed on Earth as meteorites, carrying with them the dust from ancient stars.

disappeared, so too did the record of the unique isotopic signatures of the stars around which they formed. As a result, the gas in the inner solar nebula became a well stirred, isotopically uniform mixture. The gas in this part of the nebula eventually cooled and condensed into new mineral grains whose isotopes were identical to those of the gas.

When scientists analyzed an entire chondrite using a technique called mass spectrometry, they found that the overall mixture of isotopes in the meteorite was similar to that in Earth rocks. However, there were slight differences in the isotopic ratios of *noble gases*, particularly xenon. (Noble gases do not react readily with other elements and so may remain essentially unchanged for long periods.) When scientists heated pieces of a chondrite, they found that the ratios of xenon isotopes released at certain temperatures were very different from those of Earth rocks. Some scientists suggested that the minerals in the chondrites in which the xenon was locked might be older than the solar system. They might even be the unchanged dust of dead stars. If any grains of star dust existed, however, they were present in extraordinarily small amounts. In order to find them, scientists would have to find a way to separate them from the material that makes up the bulk of the meteorite.

Finding star dust in the stones

In the early 1970's, a team of scientists at the University of Chicago headed by chemist Edward Anders began working on this problem. Between 1987 and 1991, they announced that they had found three types of star dust in a sample of carbonaceous chondrite—diamonds, graphite, and silicon carbide.

Using several strong acids and other chemicals, the scientists had dissolved more and more of the chondrite until only about one-fifth of 1 per cent of the sample remained. Then they added ammonia to the sample. When they did, some of the very finest particles clumped together. These particles turned out to be diamonds. The diamond grains were extremely small, only about 50 atoms across. The scientists then determined that other solid particles in the sample were grains of graphite. These grains were about 600 times larger than the diamond grains. Finally, when the scientists added two more acids to the remaining sample of the chondrite, they found grains of silicon carbide about 30 times larger than the diamond grains.

When Anders and his colleagues heated the three types of star dust, a variety of isotopes of xenon and of neon were released. The relative proportions of the isotopes of each of these gases were so enormously different from those found in the solar system that the scientists had no doubt that the grains were star dust.

Anders and his colleagues theorized that some xenon isotopes found in the diamond grains were formed when matter in the core of a star was exposed to a sudden, massive burst of subatomic particles called neutrons. The other xenon isotopes were created when matter from deep in a star was blasted through a thick outer layer of hydrogen. Both processes are believed to occur in supernovae. The scientists suggested that the diamond crystals had probably condensed in the cool outer atmosphere of the star before it exploded. The force of the explosion implanted the freshly created xenon isotopes into the tiny diamond crystals.

The scientists also theorized that the distinctive proportions of xenon and neon isotopes found in the silicon carbide and graphite crystals formed in a *red giant star,* a star that has exhausted its hydrogen fuel and has begun to expand and turn reddish in color. They suggested that blobs of cooler material in the surface layers of a red giant sank, forcing upward hotter material that had formed in the interior. This hotter material, which contained the neon and xenon isotopes, became trapped in grains of silicon carbide and graphite as they condensed from the outer atmosphere.

Why had this star dust survived? Theories answering that question bear on conditions that existed in the solar nebula. For example, scientists theorize that the grains may not have been vaporized and mixed in the solar nebula because they happened to be in the outer part of the cloud, where temperatures were cooler than in the center. Or perhaps the entire nebula cooled relatively quickly, before the grains could evaporate completely, like hot tea cooling before all the ice cubes dropped into it melt.

However this happened, the scientists also suggested the grains were incorporated into protoplanets that never became part of a planet. Because they were not subjected to the heat that accompanied the formation of the planets, they remained cold and unaltered for the entire history of the solar system. As a result, the isotopic signatures of their parent stars were preserved.

Studies of interstellar grains have thus yielded the first direct information on the isotopic composition of the stars that contributed matter to our solar system. These data have allowed astrophysicists to refine their theories about the nuclear reactions that take place within stars. Scientists also have been able to use the grains as clues to the physical conditions, such as temperature, density, and circulation patterns, inside the stars that produced them.

It could be that a meteorite may ultimately influence our fate. Meanwhile, however, studies of these stones from space continue to reveal fascinating new insights into our beginnings.

For further reading:

Grieve, Richard A. F. "Impact Cratering on Earth." *Scientific American,* April 1990, pp. 66-73.

Raup, David M. *Extinction: Bad Genes or Bad Luck?* Norton and Company, 1991.

Dodd, R. S. *Thunderstones and Shooting Stars: The Meaning of Meteorites.* Harvard University Press, 1986.

Archaeologists excavating ancient ruins in and near the Andes Mountains of South America are finding evidence of complex societies that flourished as early as 4,500 years ago.

The Rise of Andean Civilization

BY JOHN HYSLOP AND DAVID DREIER

Lustrous gold, the wealth of a dead civilization, gleamed in display cases in late 1990 as the Museum of the Nation in Lima, Peru, showcased treasures from an ancient Indian religious ceremonial center. At a remote site called Kuntur Wasi, high in the Andes Mountains of northern Peru, a team of Japanese archaeologists had found the treasures in richly appointed tombs dating from about 700 to 500 B.C. Who were the obviously high-ranking persons who had been buried there so long ago? The best guess is that they were priest-rulers, but they might also have been wealthy merchants or artisans. Whatever part these individuals once played in the ancient society's ruling class, they were now dust, their bodies reduced to fragmenting skeletons. But many of the artifacts that had rested with them through the centuries were unmarred. The archaeologists found ceramic bottles and figurines, and bodily adornments fashioned from beads, seashells, and stones. And they found gold: golden spools that were worn in the ears, golden *pectorals* (breast ornaments), and two crowns of finely worked gold.

The Kuntur Wasi burials are among the earliest-known tombs of rulers in the Americas. But the Kuntur Wasi society, which was probably closely related to one known as Chavín (*chah VEEN*), was far from being in the first wave of Andean cultures. Since the 1970's, excavations in Peru have uncovered architectural remnants of several other highly organized societies that existed long before the time of Christ. In fact, many ruins of temples and other monumental structures that have emerged recently from the dry Andean earth are among the oldest in the world—some as ancient as the pyramids of Egypt. These discoveries have revolutionized our view of when and how complex societies developed in the Americas. And they have led scientists to rethink the very nature of civilization itself.

A new view of early Andean cultures

In the early 1900's, archaeologists thought that civilized societies in the Americas first emerged in Mexico and Central America about 2,000 years ago. According to that view, the influence of these cultures, particularly that of the Maya, then spread to South America and gave rise to several Indian civilizations in the Andes. The Andean societies culminated with the Inca, who were subdued by the Spanish conqueror Francisco Pizarro in the 1530's.

In the 1940's, a Peruvian archaeologist named Julio C. Tello challenged this view of South America as an inheritor, rather than originator, of civilization. It was Tello who discovered the Chavín culture. Working at a site in central Peru called Chavín de Huántar, Tello in the late 1930's and early 1940's found artifacts and the remains of buildings from a previously unknown people. He named the society Chavín after the name of the site.

Tello argued that Chavín, which flourished from about 800 to 200 B.C., was the first Andean civilization. He also believed that it emerged independently from the cultures of Mexico and Central America. Tello reasoned that because the Andes were so isolated from Central Amer-

The authors:
John Hyslop is an archaeologist at the American Museum of Natural History in New York City. David Dreier is a senior editor of *Science Year.*

ica, early Andean societies most likely evolved free of outside influences. Moreover, the artistic style of Chavín bore little resemblance to that of any early civilization in Mexico or Central America.

Today, many archaeologists think Tello was at least half right. They agree that Andean civilization did indeed arise independently. In fact, the Andes region was apparently one of only a few places in the world, including Egypt, India, Mesopotamia, and China, where complex societies emerged in the 2,000 to 3,000 years before the time of Christ.

But was Chavín the first civilization in the Andes? That is a trickier question. Archaeological work in Peru from the 1970's through the 1990's has shown that complex societies existed in the Andes long before the emergence of Chavín. If these earlier, nameless societies were true civilizations, then the ancient societies of the Old World of Asia and the Middle East did not "beat" the New World of the Americas in developing civilized societies.

What is civilization?

The uncertainty stems from the fact that archaeologists cannot agree on what precisely marks a true civilization. They generally concur that all societies through history have had several characteristics in common. Every such society has had a dependable food source based on agriculture and, in most cases, the breeding of animals, which made it possible to accumulate surpluses and support a large population. A sizable portion of the people in the society were not involved in food production and worked full-time at other occupations—for example, as soldiers or artisans. Political power was concentrated in the hands of a small elite class. And, finally, the society erected monumental buildings and carried out other projects requiring a large labor force.

When all these criteria were first met in South America is still being debated. The overriding question, however, is whether all indeed *must* be met for a society to be considered truly civilized. Archaeologists have already had to make some adjustments in their concept of civilization. Writing, for example, had long been considered a hallmark of civilized people, but we now know that advanced societies can function without a system of writing, and no Andean society ever invented writing. Likewise, wheeled vehicles, used widely by the ancient civilizations of Asia and the Middle East, were unknown in the Andes—or anywhere else in the Americas.

Civilization, then, is a rather slippery concept. But, whether truly civilized or not, the early cultures of the Andes were remarkable in their own right, not least of all because they got a late start compared with societies elsewhere.

Settling South America

South America was the last continent of the world to be populated by human beings. Near the end of the last Ice Age, which lasted from about 2 million to 10,000 years ago, people migrated from Asia to

Glossary

Early Horizon: An era, from about 800 B.C. to 200 B.C, that may represent the dawn of true civilization in the Andes.

Huaca: An earthen mound formed from the eroded remains of ancient buildings.

Initial Period: An epoch in Andean history, lasting from about 2000 B.C. to 800 B.C., during which people established many large settlements along the coast and in the mountains and constructed many massive buildings.

Late Preceramic Period: The era, beginning in about 2500 B.C. and lasting 500 years, marked by the establishment of the first Andean settlements with large public buildings.

Midden: An ancient refuse heap, which archaeologists search for evidence of how people in long-ago societies lived from day to day.

What makes a civilization?

Archaeologists trying to determine when civilized societies arose in the Andes or elsewhere look for evidence of a culture with a complex social system that included the following characteristics:

A dependable food source, such as agriculture, enabling the society to accumulate surpluses and support a large population.

A class of people freed from tasks relating to food production and therefore able to work full-time at other occupations.

The concentration of power in the hands of an elite group.

The construction of monumental buildings and the achievement of other endeavors requiring mass labor.

North America over a land bridge that existed during much of that time between Siberia and Alaska. Archaeologists have been unable to determine with certainty when the first migrations took place, but evidence suggests that it was before 13,000 B.C. At any rate, the newcomers had apparently occupied considerable parts of North America by about 12,000 B.C.

The Indians who made the New World their home continued to wander, but why they did so and what routes they took are unknown. These earliest Americans were hunting and gathering people, equipped with spears and stone tools. It is most likely that they moved frequently in search of the game and plants that made up their diet. Slowly, over the centuries, Indian populations spread across North America and into Central and South America, reaching the Andes by about 11,000 B.C.

The archaeological evidence shows that by about 9000 B.C., human beings had inhabited most of South America. Some archaeologists, however, argue on the basis of other findings that the migrations through the New World were fairly rapid and that the populating of South America was concluded earlier, by about 11,000 B.C. But that theory has not been accepted by many experts.

Giving up the nomadic life

Regardless of which date is correct, it is clear that the South American Indians spent several thousand more years leading a nomadic hunting-and-gathering existence. Then, finally, they settled into villages and adopted a new way of life—one that led to the rise of civilization.

The people who settled in the Andes region of western South America began to domesticate plants and animals about 6000 B.C. Domestication is a genetic change in a species, attained through generations of cultivation or breeding, that makes it more useful and productive for human use. By 5000 B.C., the Andean peoples had domesticated a few animals—notably llamas and Andean camels—and a great variety of plants, including cotton, squashes, beans, chili peppers, and many types of potatoes.

At about the same time, a number of groups established settlements west of the Andes along the coast of the Pacific Ocean. Abundant food was there for the taking. Although the Peruvian coastal plain

From Asia to the Andes

Migrating hunting-and-gathering people from Asia came to the New World across a land bridge linking Siberia and Alaska prior to about 13,000 B.C. From Alaska, the newcomers migrated through North America and down through Central and South America, reaching the Andes by about 11,000 B.C. (inset map). In later periods, the people of the Andes established many settlements along the coast of what is now Peru and in the Andean highlands (large map).

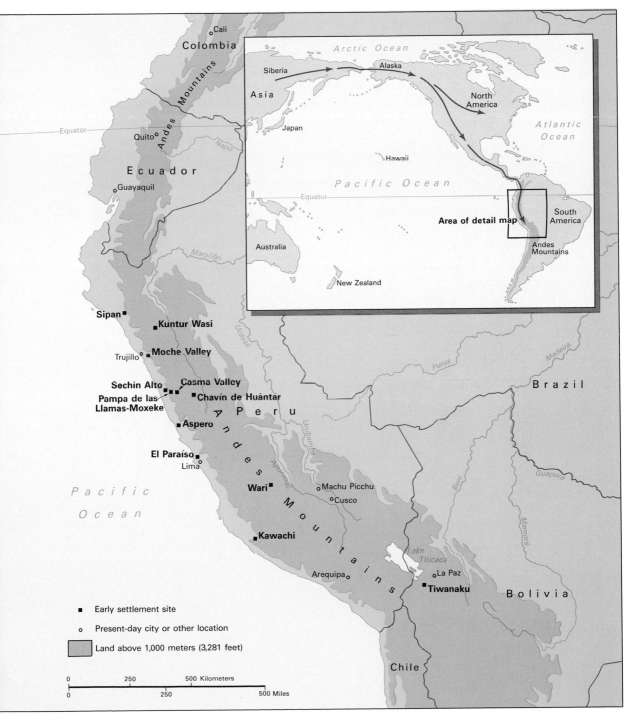

gets very little rainfall and is one of the world's driest deserts, the Pacific waters abound with anchovies and other fishes. Excavations of coastal *middens* (garbage heaps) since the 1970's show that these villagers ate a diet rich in seafood—not only fish, which they trapped in large nets woven from plant fibers, but also the clams and mussels that littered the shore and could be gathered by the basketful.

Because the coastal region had such a dependable and plentiful supply of food, it is not surprising that some of the first major population centers in Peru developed there. In about 2500 B.C., the same time that the Egyptians were completing the great pyramids at Giza, the ancient Peruvians began establishing dozens of seaside towns with large public buildings. Unlike the simple villages of earlier centuries, these newer settlements were centers of religious and political activity. Construction began at these sites before the people had learned how to make ceramic pottery, so archaeologists refer to the era as the Late Preceramic Period. Two notable towns from the Late Preceramic Period are at excavation sites named Aspero (*as PAR oh*) and El Paraíso (*el puh rye EE zo*).

Aspero is on the sea about 160 kilometers (100 miles) north of Lima. The site, which covers at least 12 hectares (30 acres), includes plazas, terraces, the foundations of houses, and about a dozen large

Timeline of Andean cultures
While civilizations rose, flourished, and declined in other parts of the world, one culture also succeeded another in the Andes until the A.D. 1500's.

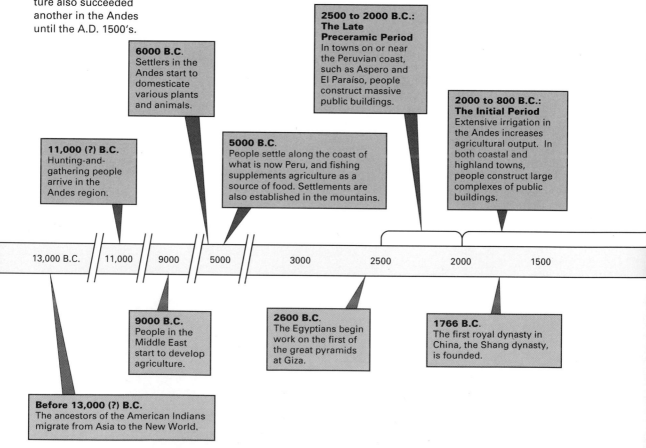

11,000 (?) B.C.
Hunting-and-gathering people arrive in the Andes region.

6000 B.C.
Settlers in the Andes start to domesticate various plants and animals.

5000 B.C.
People settle along the coast of what is now Peru, and fishing supplements agriculture as a source of food. Settlements are also established in the mountains.

2500 to 2000 B.C.: The Late Preceramic Period
In towns on or near the Peruvian coast, such as Aspero and El Paraíso, people construct massive public buildings.

2000 to 800 B.C.: The Initial Period
Extensive irrigation in the Andes increases agricultural output. In both coastal and highland towns, people construct large complexes of public buildings.

13,000 B.C. 11,000 9000 5000 3000 2500 2000 1500

Before 13,000 (?) B.C.
The ancestors of the American Indians migrate from Asia to the New World.

9000 B.C.
People in the Middle East start to develop agriculture.

2600 B.C.
The Egyptians begin work on the first of the great pyramids at Giza.

1766 B.C.
The first royal dynasty in China, the Shang dynasty, is founded.

mounds. These and other such mounds are known as *huacas* (*WAH kuz*). Huaca is an Inca word that has come to mean an ancient building or place, and archaeologists apply the term to any mound formed from the ruins of an ancient structure. In most cases, after 3,000 to 4,000 years of erosion, these mounds bear almost no resemblance to the buildings they once were.

The huacas at Aspero, the largest of which is 10 meters (33 feet) high, are the remains of some of Peru's first monumental buildings. These were large temples built as platforms with sloping sides, each platform topped with an enclosure consisting of several interconnecting rooms. The buildings were constructed of packed rubble enclosed by walls of stone and mud-mortar, and it is clear that they were periodically enlarged. Archaeologists excavating the site have deduced this from complicated patterns of rebuilt chambers and floors within the mounds. Every once in a while, it seems, the people of Aspero filled in the rooms atop a temple with rubble, creating a higher platform on which they erected a new enclosure.

The somewhat haphazard way these structures were built suggests that the society lacked a center of authority to oversee construction according to a master plan. Some archaeologists speculate that the resi-

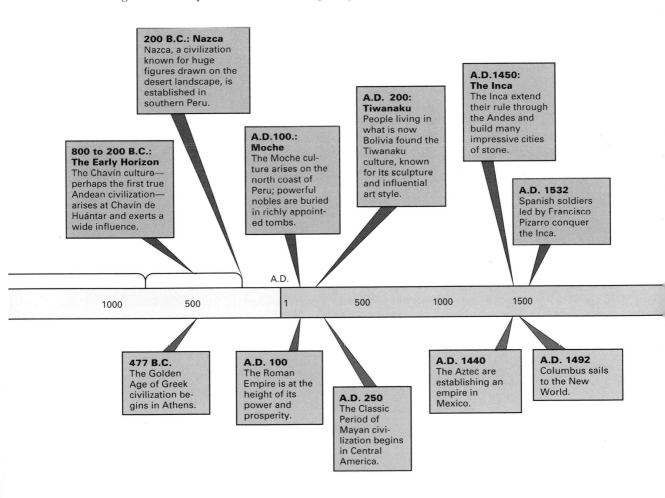

200 B.C.: Nazca
Nazca, a civilization known for huge figures drawn on the desert landscape, is established in southern Peru.

A.D. 200: Tiwanaku
People living in what is now Bolivia found the Tiwanaku culture, known for its sculpture and influential art style.

A.D.1450: The Inca
The Inca extend their rule through the Andes and build many impressive cities of stone.

800 to 200 B.C.: The Early Horizon
The Chavín culture—perhaps the first true Andean civilization—arises at Chavín de Huántar and exerts a wide influence.

A.D.100.: Moche
The Moche culture arises on the north coast of Peru; powerful nobles are buried in richly appointed tombs.

A.D. 1532
Spanish soldiers led by Francisco Pizarro conquer the Inca.

A.D.

1000   500   1   500   1000   1500

477 B.C.
The Golden Age of Greek civilization begins in Athens.

A.D. 100
The Roman Empire is at the height of its power and prosperity.

A.D. 250
The Classic Period of Mayan civilization begins in Central America.

A.D. 1440
The Aztec are establishing an empire in Mexico.

A.D. 1492
Columbus sails to the New World.

Early coastal settlements

Clay figurines, *right,* are among artifacts found at Aspero, a Peruvian coastal site from the Late Preceramic Period, which lasted from about 2500 to 2000 B.C. Another major site from that era is El Paraíso, where archaeologists have excavated the ruins of a large public building, *below,* perhaps a temple. Bags made from plant fibers, *bottom,* were probably used by workers at El Paraíso to carry rocks and debris used in constructing such buildings.

The people of Aspero catch fish in nets and gather clams and mussels on the shore. Like the people of other coastal settlements of the Late Preceramic Period, the inhabitants of Aspero were assured of an abundant supply of food from the Pacific Ocean. During this period, workers in Aspero constructed some of the first monumental buildings erected in the Andes—large temple platforms with sloping sides, background.

dents of Aspero and other coastal settlements may have enlarged their temples whenever they agreed among themselves to do so, though the times they chose may have had some ceremonial significance. This theory would also account for the apparent absence of royal tombs at this and other Preceramic sites. But other archaeologists argue that the construction of monumental buildings is unlikely if no one is in control. So if there were no actual rulers at Aspero, perhaps there were at least councils of elders or some other figures of authority who decided when it was time for everyone to get to work on the temples.

The largest of the Late Preceramic sites is El Paraíso, located 2 kilometers (1.2 miles) inland on the Chillon River just north of the modern city of Lima. El Paraíso covers 58 hectares (143 acres) and includes six low temple mounds. One of those mounds is the biggest in area that has been found at any Late Preceramic settlement. Although the original temple was not very high—perhaps as tall as a three-story building—it measured 50 by 250 meters (164 by 820 feet) at its base. According to one estimate, 90,000 metric tons (100,000 short tons) of stone went into the construction of El Paraíso's major structures. Like those at Aspero, they were built in stages over a long period of time.

Although the best-known Late Preceramic settlements with large public buildings were constructed along the coast, some groups of people established fairly sizable towns in the mountains. Those communities relied mostly on farming the fertile soil of the highland valleys. So, contrary to the theory of some archaeologists that the bounty of the sea was crucial to the rise of early Andean civilization, a number of settlements seemed to get along quite well without it.

The ruins of some buildings at the mountain sites contain chambers with central pits blackened from fire. Here, evidently, the people gathered to honor their gods with burnt offerings. But what sorts of gods the people of either the highland or coastal settlements worshiped, or what they offered up to those deities, is unknown.

In both the coastal and mountain communities of Late Preceramic times, people began making textiles from dyed cotton yarn. Archaeologists have discovered the remnants of cotton fabrics with complicated designs depicting cats, condors, and other animals. One design, a double-headed snake, continued to appear in Andean art for another 4,000 years.

A new era dawns in the Andes

Starting around 2000 B.C., Andean civilization underwent dramatic change. In the next 1,200 years, the people of the Andes laid the final foundations for the advanced civilizations that would come after them, so archaeologists call this era the Initial Period or Lower Formative Period. Although some coastal settlements continued to thrive during this epoch, the people relied less on fishing and more on agriculture, constructing extensive irrigation systems that turned large tracts of the desert plain into farmland. Agriculture also flourished in the highlands, supporting ever larger populations there. Ceramic pottery made

its first appearance in the Andes during the Initial Period. The Andean people acquired the know-how for pottery making from the Indians of northern South America or from the Amazon regions to the east of the Andes.

The Initial Period was marked especially by an increase in the number and size of sites with monumental buildings. A characteristic style of the period was a U-shaped arrangement consisting of a large temple platform or pyramid, with several adjacent structures forming a courtyard. Several dozen of these U-shaped complexes have been found at sites on the northern coast. Some of the buildings at these sites contain remnants of their original adobe wall sculptures and colored murals. In some cases, architectural elements are fierce or gruesome. At one location, a series of large and angry adobe heads 2 meters (6.5 feet) high glower with bared teeth. At another site, representations of detached body parts are carved into the stones of a retaining wall surrounding a templelike building. Archaeologists theorize that religious leaders may have intended such images to frighten people into obedience in the absence of a strong government.

Archaeologists have discovered some of the most striking Initial Period architecture at two sites in the Casma Valley, near the coast in north-central Peru. One of these sites, which contains what is probably the most remarkable collection of pre-Chavín ruins so far excavated, is Pampa de las Llamas Moxeke (*PAHM pa day lahs LAH mas mo HECK ay*). This site encompasses about 200 hectares (500 acres) and is dominated by two large mounds. Each of the mounds covers an area larger than a football field. One mound, the remains of an enormous pyramid, is the height of a 10-story building. The other mound, designated Huaca A, is rectangular and about three stories high. Archaeologists think Huaca A was once a huge warehouse where the people of Pampa de las Llamas-Moxeke stored surplus food and other goods. The walls

Workers clear rubble from the remains of a large structure that archaeologists think was used as a warehouse for storing surplus food and other goods. The building is part of a large site near the coast in north-central Peru called Pampa de las Llamas-Moxeke, which was a major settlement of the Initial Period, an era lasting from about 2000 to 800 B.C.

Farmers bring their surplus produce to the huge warehouse at Pampa de las Llamas-Moxeke. The building, bigger than a football field, has been left open to the sky because so little rain falls in the area. A large pyramid situated about 1.2 kilometers (0.75 mile) from the warehouse, background, towers to the height of a modern 10-story building. Between the two structures is a huge public plaza. The town also encompassed many other structures, right, which may have included houses and workshops. These buildings, apparently also without roofs, were made of stones set in mud mortar. The warehouse and pyramid, in contrast, were constructed of adobe.

flanking the narrow main entrance, where guards may once have stood to control access to the building, are carved with huge images of scowling catlike beasts. Both the pyramid and the warehouse were constructed of packed earth faced with adobe.

The remainder of Pampa de las Llamas-Moxeke consists of many small mounds, a number of plazas of varying size, and the foundations of several hundred small stone structures, many of which may have been houses. The stone walls of these buildings were cemented with mud mortar.

Another remarkable Casma Valley site is Sechin Alto (*SECH een ALL toe*), which also covers about 200 hectares. The focal point of the site is a mound measuring 250 by 300 meters (820 by 980 feet) at its base and rising to a height of about 44 meters (144 feet)—equivalent to a 12-story building. This huge mound was once an enormous stepped pyramid, the largest Initial Period pyramid that has so far been discovered at any site in the Andes. Other remains include four large plazas, three with circular sunken courts. The size and number of buildings at Sechin Alto indicate that at the height of its prosperity, about 1500 B.C., the city may have been the most populous human settlement in the Americas.

Mysteries of the monumental structures

Our knowledge of the Initial Period, like that of the Late Preceramic Period, is sketchy. Archaeologists are still trying to determine the purpose of many large buildings of the Initial Period. The monumental structures erected with so much expenditure of time, labor, and materials must have been a focus of public life, but it is still unclear what political and administrative functions most of the buildings served or what rituals or other activities were performed in them.

Archaeologists have engaged in a lively debate about the organization of Initial Period societies. Although no one has argued that those societies were part of a unified nation under a central political authority, most scholars think Initial Period communities may have been more structured than those of the Late Preceramic era. Some experts have suggested that settlements such as Sechin Alto were the capitals of small regional states, while others have proposed that they were more like the even smaller city-states of ancient Greece. But excavations of Initial Period population centers, like those at Late Preceramic sites, have turned up no royal tombs or evidence of projects requiring forced labor. So even if governments of some sort did exist during the Initial Period, they evidently had little power to command people to do their bidding.

But could the architecture of the Initial Period, which was so much more massive than anything the Andes had seen before, have been constructed without force? The answer, while by no means certain, seems to be yes. The work may have been directed by religious leaders who used persuasion—or perhaps fear of the gods—to motivate peo-

Artifacts of the first true Andean civilization?
A ceramic vessel, *left,* depicts the principal god of Chavín, which archaeologists think may have been the first true civilization in the Andes. A head combining human and catlike features, *above,* adorns a temple wall at Chavín de Huántar, a site high in the mountains of central Peru that was once a leading center of the Chavín society.

ple. Moreover, the buildings, like those in Late Preceramic settlements, took shape over a period of centuries, so the burden placed on any one generation during the Initial Period was probably not particularly oppressive.

The unifying influence of Chavín

Around 800 B.C., the culture of the Initial Period began giving way to the next phase of Andean society, which was apparently the dawn of full-fledged civilization in the Andes. This era, which lasted until approximately 200 B.C., was marked by the rise of the Chavín culture. By about 500 B.C., Chavín had spread its influence and art style across most of central and northern Peru, and so the era is known as the Early Horizon. The term *horizon* is used for several periods in Andean history when wide areas were culturally and politically united.

The place that was once the center of Chavín society, Chavín de Huántar, covers about 40 hectares (100 acres). The site, at an altitude of 3,180 meters (10,400 feet) in the mountains, contains impressive stone platforms, plazas, and sculptures. Some of these structures show that the people of Chavín, in developing their own artistic and architectural style, borrowed heavily from earlier cultures. One great platform, for instance, was built in the familiar U shape.

Nonetheless, the Chavín society was clearly a departure from those that had come before. Evidence from homes and especially from burials reveals sharp class differences among the population. For example, in a few tombs of this era, luxury goods made by highly skilled artisans, including gold jewelry and fine textiles, appear for the first time. Only members of a rich and powerful elite could have obtained such items.

The sculptures at Chavín de Huántar feature complex designs that included human and animal forms, which evidently had religious importance. Archaeologists have found the same figures copied on metal objects, textiles, and pottery that they have unearthed at coastal and highland Early Horizon sites. This evidence shows how widespread the Chavín culture became in Peru.

That culture must have been a forceful one to influence so large a region, but archaeologists are divided on what sort of culture it was. Many argue that it was primarily religious, spreading a faith that appealed to large numbers of people. Other authorities, however, say that Chavín's influence more likely resulted from a complex trading system or a series of military conquests.

Chavín's impact is undoubted, but was Chavín indeed the first true civilization of the Andes? The answer remains as elusive as the definition of civilization itself. Chavín clearly had many of the characteristics we usually attribute to civilized societies, and it tied together diverse peoples who earlier had experienced only limited contact with one another. On the other hand, Chavín may not have established an interregional state, which to some scholars' minds would exclude it from the ranks of true civilizations. It is also possible that Chavín was a true civilization, but not the first—further archaeological research may show that one or more of the Andean cultures that preceded Chavín deserves to be called civilized.

The cultural legacy of Chavín lives on

Whatever was the actual status of Chavín, its day in the sun came to an end about 200 B.C., and Chavín de Huántar sank into decay. But the influence of Chavín continued, and aspects of the Chavín culture were adopted in the dozens of Andean societies that flourished in the centuries that followed. Several of those societies founded large unified states and thus were civilizations in every sense of the word.

As Chavín was dying, a culture called Nazca (*NAHZ kuh*) developed on Peru's south coast. Nazca's main ceremonial center was Kawachi, an imposing assemblage of platforms and enclosures. Much remains to be learned about the Nazca people, who are best known for scraping hundreds of gigantic figures in the desert soil. From the air, the huge markings can be made out as geometric designs and depictions of plants and animals, together with hundreds of straight lines. There has been much wild speculation about the purpose of the figures, but experts agree that they were probably used for some sort of ritual. Research in the 1980's established that most of the lines drawn among the figures were used as pathways for ceremonial processions. The Nazca culture died out about A.D. 600.

On the north coast of Peru, a people known as the Moche (*MO chay*) in about A.D 100 built a strong centralized state that flourished for some 600 years. At their administrative center in the Moche Valley, this society erected one of the largest structures ever built in the Americas, a pyramid 40 meters (130 feet) high and 300 meters (980 feet) on a side. Since 1988, archaeologists working at a Moche site called Sipán (*see PAHN*) have excavated the tombs of several gold-bedecked individuals—the richest burials ever found in the New World. From such evidence, there can be no question that Moche society was divided between the few who had wealth and power and the many who did not.

Another important Andean culture arose about A.D. 200 on the high plateau of Bolivia. It is called Tiwanaku (*tee wah NAH ku*), after the name of its capital, a city built at the astonishing elevation of 3,850 meters (12,600 feet). The people of Tiwanaku were llama herders and experts in high-altitude agriculture. The artistic motifs of Tiwanaku, which included figures of animals with eyes divided vertically into black and white halves, were adopted by another society, called Wari, which lived to the north. After A.D. 500, this art style spread over a wide region of the Andes stretching from what is now northern Peru to northern Chile. The Tiwanaku and Wari cultures collapsed sometime after A.D. 800.

And finally, the Inca

The joining of Andean cultures was achieved on a greater scale hundreds of years later by the Inca. From the mid-1400's to the early 1500's, the Inca conquered an expanse of territory stretching from northern Ecuador to central Chile, a distance of about 4,000 kilometers (2,500 miles). Great builders, the Inca bound their far-flung empire together with more than 23,000 kilometers (14,300 miles) of roads, and they constructed great cities of stone: their capital, Cusco (*COOS ko*), in southern Peru; the magnificent city of Machu Picchu (*MAH choo PEEK choo*); and many others.

The Inca empire was the largest state ever founded in the New World before the time of Columbus. It was also the last, the final flowering of Native American civilization.

After their downfall, the Inca tried to explain their culture to the Spanish conquerors. Largely ignorant of the Andean peoples who had preceded them, the Inca claimed to have invented their civilization from nothing. But the truth was far more complex than the myths they created for themselves. The Inca were in fact heirs to a cultural legacy at least 4,000 years old, a heritage that is now being rediscovered. Having left no written record, the early Andean societies may always be something of a mystery. Archaeologists must reconstruct their story from the arid, crumbling remains they left behind. But at last that story, however incomplete, is being told.

For further reading:

Burger, Richard L. "Long Before the Inca." *Natural History,* February 1989.
Moseley, Michael. *The Incas and Their Ancestors.* Thames and Hudson, 1992.

To meet increasingly strict pollution-control regulations, scientists and engineers are continuing decades of refinements in the design of automobile engines and fuels.

Clearing the Air with Cleaner Cars

BY PASQUALE M. SFORZA

Designers of the cars of the future knew in 1991 that they would begin taking some dramatic turns. In November 1990, United States President George Bush had signed into law the Clean Air Act Amendments, which challenged automakers to concentrate harder than ever on styling cars that offered not only mechanical muscle and slick bodies but also engine systems that dirtied the air far less than did cars already on the road. Bush described the law as "the most significant air pollution legislation in our nation's history."

The legislation targets all sources of air pollution. It requires that by 1994 many new cars—and by 1996 all new cars—be designed to produce significantly fewer *emissions,* the by-products and pollutants they release into the air. The vehicles must also be able to meet these new emissions standards for 10 years or 100,000 miles, twice as long as required before.

The automotive industry has been modifying car engines, exhaust systems, and controls since the 1950's, when experts first realized that automobiles contributed to air pollution and smog. The newest laws will require the most extensive changes in engine designs to date. They also challenge the oil industry to develop fuels that will be less polluting as we drive into the year 2000.

In order to create cleaner-operating cars and better fuels, scientists and engineers study every detail of the workings of the internal-combustion gasoline engine. This engine design, which was first created in

Glossary

Carbon monoxide: A poisonous gas created when fuel is burned without adequate oxygen.

Combustion: A chemical reaction in which fuel and air are ignited to produce heat.

Combustion chamber: A small area in which fuel is burned. In automobiles, this area lies at the top of each cylinder.

Gasoline engine: An engine that burns gasoline to produce hot gases, which expand and push on movable parts, setting them in motion.

Hydrocarbons: Compounds composed of hydrogen and carbon that are the basic ingredients of gasoline.

Nitrogen oxides: Compounds, made of nitrogen and oxygen, given off during combustion in a gasoline engine and considered highly polluting.

Photochemical smog: The result of a chemical reaction between unburned hydrocarbons and nitrogen oxides in the presence of sunlight. This smog contains *ozone,* a gas that can irritate the eyes and cause respiratory problems in people.

The author:
Pasquale M. Sforza is chairman of the Department of Aerospace Engineering at Polytechnic University in New York City.

Germany in the late 1800's, has propelled American automobiles since they first pulled onto the road nearly 100 years ago. It is a clever device for using fuel to produce heat, which in turn produces mechanical work to move the car.

Combustion, the process of burning fuel in the presence of oxygen, breaks the chemical bonds of the fuel, releasing energy in the form of heat. To achieve combustion, air is drawn into the engine and mixed with a fine spray of fuel—usually gasoline—in a *combustion chamber,* a closed region at the top of a cylinder. One wall of the chamber is the head of a *piston,* a metal rod that moves up and down inside the cylinder. The piston moves up to compress the mixture of fuel and air. Then a small spark from a spark plug ignites the mixture. An explosion follows in which the gasoline is burned, producing hot, expanding gases that force down the piston. The piston is attached to a crankshaft, which the piston's movements turn. This motion is the primary movement that makes the car go. So a car engine can be thought of as an energy transformer, converting chemical energy to *thermal* (heat) energy to mechanical energy, all in one neat package.

Combusted gas exerts enormous force on the typical piston—equivalent to having the defensive line of a professional football team stand on the piston head. The attractive feature of gasoline engines is that such great power is produced in a fairly small space.

Compactness of this sort is due to the nature of gasoline, which packs more energy per pound than does dynamite. Although gasoline is a convenient, powerful fuel, it can pollute the air. Some gasoline pollutes the atmosphere simply because the fuel evaporates at the gas-station pump or through small leaks in the car's fuel tank or fuel line connections. Gasoline combustion also pollutes.

How combustion leads to pollution

Most efforts at creating cleaner cars focus on limiting emissions formed as by-products of gasoline combustion. These emissions come out of the car's exhaust system and are among the major factors contributing to air pollution in urban areas. Scientists trying to solve these pollution problems study what happens to the fuel when it is burned and what can influence the outcome of the combustion process.

Gasoline is made through the refining of crude oil or petroleum. Like all petroleum products, the gasoline used in automobiles is composed of *hydrocarbons,* molecules consisting primarily of atoms of hydrogen and carbon. Most gasoline is not pure, however. Other elements, such as nitrogen, oxygen, and sulfur, may be present in the mixture as impurities.

If a mixture of gasoline and air were free of impurities, then, in theory, it could be burned completely. For example, if pure gasoline, composed solely of carbon and hydrogen atoms, were burned in pure air, consisting only of molecules made of two atoms of oxygen and two of nitrogen, then some oxygen atoms would attach to the gasoline's hydrogen atoms to form water (H_2O) and some would attach to the gaso-

Cleaning up hazardous automobile emissions

Automobiles produce several types of pollutants, most notably unburned *hydrocarbons* (compounds of hydrogen and carbon), carbon monoxide gas, and *nitrogen oxides* (compounds of nitrogen and oxygen), *below*. Since the United States first established minimal standards for auto pollution control in the late 1960's, U.S. cars have become increasingly cleaner. Standards for future models call for even greater emission control, *below right*.

Automobile emissions and their harmful effects

Hydrocarbons

Some types of unburned hydrocarbons can cause lung inflammation and other respiratory problems when breathed in. Hydrocarbons also combine with nitrogen oxides in the atmosphere to give rise to ozone, a component of photochemical smog, which can irritate the eyes and cause breathing difficulties.

Carbon monoxide

Carbon monoxide is a poisonous gas that can reduce the supply of oxygen to the body's organs and tissues. This can damage the heart and blood vessels, and, in some cases, cause death.

Nitrogen oxides

Nitrogen oxides in the atmosphere mix with moisture to create acid rain, which damages plants and wildlife. The compounds can also cause lung inflammation in human beings.

Reducing emissions in passenger cars

Hydrocarbons

Before 1968	Unrestricted emissions
1975	Reduced by 32%
1990	Reduced by 81%
2010	To be reduced by 97%

Carbon monoxide

Before 1968	Unrestricted emissions
1975	Reduced by 21%
1990	Reduced by 75%
2010	To be reduced by 94%

Nitrogen oxides

Before 1968	Unrestricted emissions
1975	Increased by 7%
1990	Reduced by 58%
2010	To be reduced by 91%

Figures are based on average, per-vehicle emissions from all makes and models on the road during the given year.

Source: U.S. Environmental Protection Agency, Motor Vehicle Emission Laboratory.

line's carbon atoms to form carbon dioxide (CO_2). No free oxygen would remain, the nitrogen would be unaffected, and no other harmful by-products would be created. (Carbon dioxide, which is linked to *global warming*, the projected rise in Earth's average temperature, is an unavoidable by-product of the combustion of gasoline or other types of fossil fuels.)

However, other factors, such as the ratio of fuel to air, affect combustion. For complete combustion to occur, about 6 per cent of the weight of the fuel-air mixture must be in the fuel. If the fuel makes up a larger percentage, the mixture is said to be "rich." If it composes a smaller percentage, the mixture is "lean." A minimum and maximum percentage of fuel to air must exist for combustion to occur at all.

Internal combustion and how it causes pollution

An automobile's internal combustion engine has cylinders in which *combustion,* the burning of fuel and air, occurs. The force exerted by combustion, followed by the release of exhaust gases, cause the piston in each cylinder to move up and down. This mechanical work is transferred to a crankshaft and ultimately turns the car's wheels. Incomplete combustion and imperfect fuel and air mixtures can create harmful compounds that may pollute the atmosphere.

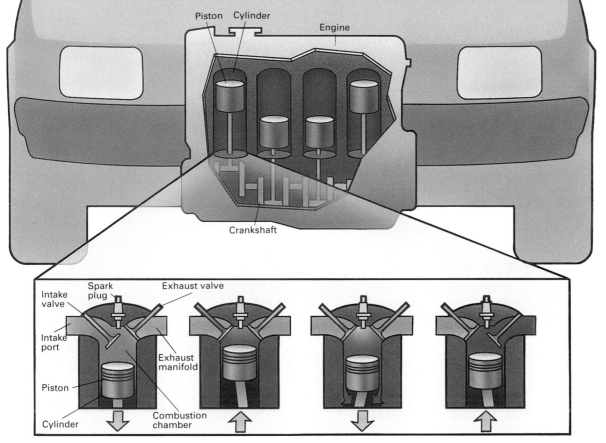

In a four-stroke gasoline engine, fuel and air are mixed together and travel through an intake port to each cylinder. An intake valve then opens to allow the fuel-air mixture to flow into the cylinder's combustion chamber. If too much air is mixed with gasoline, combustion can cause the formation of nitrogen oxides.

As the intake valve closes, the piston within the cylinder moves up to compress the fuel-air mixture. If the mixture is ignited prematurely—that is, before it is fully compressed—incomplete combustion will result, producing nitrogen oxides.

A spark from a spark plug ignites the fuel-air mixture, turning it into hot, swelling gases. This explosion exerts tremendous force on the piston, pushing it down. Some gases may push past the piston and escape the engine as pollutants.

The exhaust valve opens and the piston moves back up the cylinder to push the gases out into the exhaust manifold. These gases contain some pollutants, such as carbon monoxide, nitrogen oxides, and soot.

When too much air is in the mixture, excess oxygen atoms from the air can link up with the nitrogen to produce nitrogen oxides, compounds that contain varying numbers of oxygen atoms. Nitrogen oxides can harm both the environment and human beings. If inhaled, nitrogen dioxide can cause inflammation of the lungs. Continued exposure may lead to long-term lung disease and increased risk for infections of the respiratory system. Nitrogen oxides can also mix with moisture in the atmosphere to form nitric acids that fall to Earth as precipitation, commonly referred to as *acid rain*, which can damage plants and wildlife.

If the fuel-air mixture contains too little air, the result is incomplete combustion. Not all the gasoline's carbon and hydrogen atoms can hook up with oxygen atoms to form water or carbon dioxide. When a carbon atom hooks up with only one atom of oxygen, a molecule of carbon monoxide (CO) is formed. Carbon monoxide is a poisonous gas that can deprive the human body of oxygen. High CO concentrations are known to damage the heart and blood vessels, particularly in people with heart disease.

Unburned carbon, or soot, appears as smoke or as black deposits on buildings and other surfaces and is another result of incomplete gasoline combustion. Soot particles inhaled from the air may cause lung inflammation and breathing problems. And unburned hydrocarbons, some of which are thought to cause cancer, constitute another dangerous emission from automobiles.

Hydrocarbons and nitrogen oxides in the air can react in the presence of sunlight to produce photochemical smog. Smog contains *ozone* (molecules composed of three oxygen atoms), high levels of nitrogen dioxide, and a wide variety of hydrocarbon molecules that have partially combined with oxygen. Although ozone in the upper atmosphere helps shield the Earth from the sun's ultraviolet rays, ozone in the lower atmosphere causes eye, nose, and throat irritation, as well as impaired breathing and coughing. These effects are most severe in the very young and the very old.

Other factors that lead to pollution

Obviously, combustion of even the purest gasoline and purest air can easily give rise to pollutants if the fuel and air are not in perfect proportion. The fuel and air must not only be properly balanced, they must also be thoroughly mixed. If they are not, some parts of the combustion chamber may contain lean mixtures and others rich, even though the total amount of fuel and air is perfect.

In addition, the walls of the combustion chamber may further foster incomplete combustion of a perfect fuel-air mixture. A tiny burr or soot deposit protruding from the combustion chamber wall is likely to become hotter than other areas of the chamber and could cause the fuel-air mixture to ignite before it should. This can produce nitrogen oxides. By the same token, cool areas in the chamber can enhance the formation of carbon monoxide.

The fuel itself contains impurities that can create harmful compounds when burned. Even the air drawn into the engine contains impurities. And it is unlikely that either gasoline or air will ever be perfectly pure. In fact, to enhance automobile performance, gasoline contains additives, which may promote pollution. Lead, for example, was once added to gasoline to help prevent preignition of the fuel-air mixture. Later, lead was generally banned as a pollutant that posed serious health hazards.

Probing the combustion process

To control the production of pollutants, scientists must first understand what is occurring in the combustion chamber and related areas before, during, and after combustion. Scientists at research centers such as Sandia National Laboratories in Livermore, Calif., and Southwest Research Institute in San Antonio try to measure such factors as the flame speed and temperature during combustion and the quantities of fuel and oxygen present. Obtaining such data presents a great challenge because the combustion process takes place in a small chamber, under hostile conditions of extreme pressure and temperature, during time frames that are measured in thousandths of a second.

Two major technological advances aid scientists studying automotive engine combustion: the laser and the computer. Both came into widespread use in the mid-1970's and now are the mainstays of combustion research.

The *laser,* a device that emits an intense beam of light, allows scientists to "probe" into the very heart of the combustion process without inserting any instruments that might react with the hot gases. The laser light is pulsed in flashes that last only millionths of a second or less. In effect, this technique allows scientists to observe the chain of chemical reactions as if they were a slow-motion film.

To see the combustion process, scientists developed combustion chambers with windows made of quartz or sapphire. They also used transparent pistons. Researchers at the General Motors Research Laboratory in Warren, Mich., even developed a totally transparent cylinder to allow them to view every angle of the combustion process.

Typically, researchers shine a laser through one of the clear areas of the combustion chamber. Through another window, they capture the laser's light and analyze how it passes through the gases. This enables the researchers to determine the temperature of the expanding gases, the speed at which they are traveling, and the types of molecules and number of particles present at each stage of the combustion process.

A computer scans and processes this data rapidly. Computer graphics also can be used to reconstruct the various stages of the combustion process from the data the laser analysis provides. Cray Research Incorporated in Eagan, Minn., has developed a computer model that can simulate the flow and mixing of the fuel and air, the valve and piston movements, and the resulting emissions. In addition, chemists can compute the rates of the individual chemical reactions that make up each step of the combustion process. Powerful supercomputers aid these studies.

Such tools have enabled scientists to understand combustion in greater detail and helped them to develop engines that run better yet pollute less. Research advances have ranged from changing the size and construction of cars, to chemically changing the composition of emissions, to redesigning both the fuel and the engine.

Engineering lighter cars

Because a lighter car uses less fuel—and one way to reduce carbon dioxide and other emissions is to reduce the amount of fuel burned— auto engineers have created lighter, smaller cars. A 1975 federal law initiated the trend toward smaller cars. It required automakers to increase average fuel efficiency from 6 kilometers per liter (14 miles per gallon) to 11.7 kilometers per liter (27.5 miles per gallon) by 1985.

In response to this law, engineers put automobile engine parts on a diet of high-strength, low-weight materials, such as aluminum alloys. Many composite materials, such as fiberglass, graphite epoxy, and kevlar aramid, have found their way into engine components and accessories as well.

Although lighter cars reduced fuel consumption and, therefore, the total amount of emissions, they did not change the types of emissions leaving the car. Consequently, engineers have devised a number of ways to prevent many of the emissions from entering the atmosphere.

A cylinder made of heat-resistant sapphire provides a clear view of the type of combustion that occurs in a four-stroke engine. Light from lasers beamed through the cylinder illuminates tiny particles seeded into the burning gases. By viewing the motion of these glowing particles, researchers can determine such variables as combustion speed, temperature, and density. They then can adjust the fuel mixture and spark timing to alter these variables and promote more complete combustion.

Devices that capture emissions

Because the piston must move up and down in the cylinder, there is a slight space between the piston and the cylinder wall. Although piston rings encircle the piston and fill the space between the piston and the cylinder wall, some combustion by-products "blow by" the piston rings and enter the crankcase of the engine. Until the 1960's, cars were equipped with only a tube that allowed these gases to escape out of the crankcase and into the atmosphere. Then engineers introduced the positive crankcase ventilation system (PCV). In a PCV system, a hose and valve direct the vapors in the crankcase back into the engine's *intake manifold* (a pipe that carries fuel and air to the cylinder) where they are returned to the combustion chamber to be recycled. This keeps all the combustion gases in the exhaust system, where the heat produced by combustion can consume some of the pollutants.

Since 1973, autos have had a similar system for returning some gases emitted through the exhaust valve—the main path taken by combustion by-products—back to the intake manifold to be reburned. This system, exhaust gas recirculation, reduces nitrogen oxide emissions.

Researchers have also studied the possibility of using the exhaust manifold as an "afterburner" to combust the exhaust gases before they enter the atmosphere. The manifold would have to be larger and its temperature maintained well above 500 °C (932 °F) to achieve combustion. But cars have been getting smaller, leaving little room for a large, hot "afterburner."

Farther down the exhaust pipe there is one final opportunity for capturing pollutants before they enter the outside air. In 1975, to meet emissions standards mandated by the Clean Air Act, automakers began to equip their vehicles with a *catalytic converter,* a device containing pellets or a honeycomb type of structure coated with a blend of such metals as palladium, rhodium, and platinum. When exhaust gases pass through these metals, unburned hydrocarbons, carbon monoxide, and nitrogen oxides undergo a chemical reaction that changes them into less harmful compounds, such as carbon dioxide and water vapor. Although catalytic converters significantly reduce pollutants, they lose their effectiveness over time.

Fine-tuning the fuel-air mixture

Researchers have also tried to reduce emissions by improving the mixture of fuel and air. By controlling more precisely the amount of fuel and air in the combustion chamber, they have increased the likelihood that the mixture will burn more completely and leave fewer polluting residues.

The technology to produce such tailor-made mixtures was made possible by the development of inexpensive, powerful *microprocessors* (tiny electronic components on silicon "chips") located in a central computer system under the car's dashboard. Combined with *sensors* (devices that react to such variables as temperature, motion, and oxygen levels), microprocessors can determine how much fuel is needed for the amount of air being drawn in. Because drivers operate cars under numerous weather and road conditions—and demand that their vehicle start, stop, speed up, and slow down at the drop of a foot—all the monitoring and decision-making needed to achieve proper fuel-air mixtures must be done accurately and rapidly, in some cases many times per second. This difficult task is made to order for computers, which were introduced into automobiles in the 1980's and are now standard operating equipment on almost all new cars.

The air-mass flow sensor measures the amount of air entering the engine and alerts the computer, which is also receiving other information about the engine from other sensors and microprocessors. The computer calculates how much fuel is required and sends a command to the fuel injection system, which sprays the correct amount of fuel into the air flowing through the intake ports of the cylinders. The computer also tells the fuel injection system precisely when to release the fuel so that the fuel and air will be properly mixed as they enter the chamber.

Other sensors determine if the fuel-air mixture ignites too quickly, before the piston rod is in the correct position to be forced down by the combusted gases. The sensors then alert the computer to alter the timing of the fuel-air injection to correct this situation.

The design of the combustion chamber itself can also help control the fuel-air mixture. For example, the *stratified* (layered) charge combustion chamber, pioneered by Texaco Incorporated in the 1960's and developed by several automakers since then, is designed so that the fuel-air mixture is richest near the spark plug and then becomes leaner farther away. The richer mixture is always easier to ignite, so combustion is assured and less fuel is needed overall.

After combustion occurs, an exhaust valve opens to allow the gases produced by combustion to escape from the cylinder through an exhaust port and into the exhaust manifold, which leads to the exhaust pipe that carries the gases away from the engine. Researchers today are developing ways to control both the intake and exhaust valves more precisely to foster more complete combustion.

Rethinking engine designs and materials

In addition to improving the various components of the engine and exhaust system, engineers have worked on changing the overall design of the engine. Almost all automobile engines operate on a four-stroke cycle, in which each cycle—fuel-air intake, compression, firing, and exhaust—requires one up or down stroke of the piston. The first two functions and the last two functions may be combined so that only two strokes are required.

Two-stroke engines are simpler in design and smaller and lighter than four-stroke engines. Thus, they produce more power per pound. But because the two-stroke engine has traditionally burned more fuel and created more emissions than the four-stroke, automakers have

Engineering a cleaner car

The need to reduce automobile pollution has challenged engineers to redesign the car's engine and exhaust system and to explore the use of alternative fuels.

Positive crankcase ventilation (PCV)

To capture gases that escape around the piston during combustion, the PCV system was introduced in the 1960's. Gases that have blown by the piston into the engine's crankcase are routed through a tube back to the intake manifold to be reburned. The PCV valve controls the amount of gases recirculated to the intake manifold.

Electronic fuel injection

A fuel injector sprays gasoline into the air flowing through the engine's intake port. Sensors tell a computer how much air is flowing by. The computer controls the timing and quantity of the fuel so that the fuel and air will be mixed thoroughly and burn more cleanly when they enter the combustion chamber. Fuel injection was introduced into cars in the 1980's.

New materials for hotter engines

High temperatures in cylinders help ensure more complete burning of fuel. A ceramic (nonmetallic) coating on the walls of an engine's cylinders can withstand temperatures up to 1,300 °C (2,370 °F). Researchers in the 1990's were developing ceramics that could be used to line the combustion chamber and to replace metals in other engine components. They also were developing plastic components that are lighter, less apt to corrode, and cheaper than metals.

Muffler

Exhaust pipe

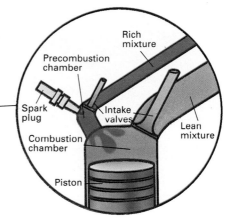

Rich mixture

Precombustion chamber

Spark plug

Intake valves

Lean mixture

Combustion chamber

Piston

Stratified-charge engines for better burning
A burning fuel-air mixture rich in gasoline streams from a precombustion chamber into the main combustion area. There it ignites another fuel-air mixture lean in gasoline that is delivered by a separate intake port. Because the rich mixture is easy to ignite, and the burning consumes less and less gasoline as it spreads through the combustion chamber, this design, developed in the 1980's, fosters combustion and reduces fuel consumption.

Emissions

Pellets

Catalytic converter to clean exhaust
Installed along the exhaust pipe, the catalytic converter contains thousands of tiny beads or a ceramic honeycomb coated with such metals as platinum and palladium. As exhaust gases pass through the device, hydrocarbons, carbon monoxide, and, in some cases, nitrogen oxides undergo a chemical reaction that converts them to less harmful compounds. Converters, first used in 1975, are now installed on all new cars sold in the United States.

added to it some of the emission-reducing features of the four-stroke.

Manufacturers are also experimenting with the gas turbine engine, which is widely used in airplanes. Like a traditional gasoline engine, this engine combusts a fuel-air mixture. The advantages of gas turbines include the potential for operating at low emission levels, a simple design, reduced fuel consumption, and minimal maintenance.

Finally, the high performance levels sought for advanced engines requires engineers to develop materials that not only will remain strong under high temperatures in corrosive environments but also will be inexpensive to purchase and mold. Ceramics may meet these goals. For example, a ceramic coating applied to engine components that get very hot will act as a thermal barrier, reducing the amount of wasted heat and minimizing the engine's cooling needs. Plastics reinforced with graphite fiber, which have been used in the hot engines of racing cars, also are likely to find their way into passenger automobile engines. Such high-temperature materials could help reduce emissions by keeping heat in the cylinder, where it can do the job of pushing down the pistons.

Powering cars of the future

While some researchers concentrate on the car and improving its systems and materials, others focus on the fuel that feeds the car. On at least one occasion, car improvements and fuel refinements went hand in hand. When catalytic converters were developed, the petroleum industry had to make gasoline lead-free. Leaded gasoline produces emissions containing lead, which coats the metals in the converter, rendering them ineffective. Because lead has been linked to cancer and can cause nervous-system damage in children, lead-free gasoline was an important development against automobile pollution.

Researchers continue to search for ways to make better gasoline. Refining crude oil to produce gasoline involves heating the oil and drawing off various types of hydrocarbons as they evaporate. Some hydrocarbons, such as butane, are lightweight molecules that evaporate easily. Others, such as benzene, are heavier, have a tendency to form deposits and particulates, and may be cancer-causing.

Petroleum companies can create gasolines that pollute less by using more hydrocarbons from the middle of the weight spectrum—those that are neither very light nor very heavy. Refiners can also break down or "crack" some of the heavier hydrocarbons to yield lighter compounds. Some gasoline additives, such as methyl tertiary butyl ether—commonly known as MTBE—include oxygen atoms in their structure. This helps promote more complete fuel combustion.

Researchers are also investigating fuels other than gasoline. Methanol (an alcohol made from ingredients derived from such sources as natural gas, wood, coal, sewage, or garbage) emits smaller quantities of pollutants normally associated with gasoline combustion. But it has less potential energy than does gasoline, and it is more difficult to ignite. Methanol also can *corrode* (eat away) many of the metals, sealants, and

The Impact, a car from the General Motors Corporation, flashes a sleek exterior but no gasoline engine. The Impact runs on electricity from a battery and, like other electric vehicles, emits no pollutants. Automakers throughout the world in 1991 introduced a variety of electric cars that will come to market by 1998, when at least 2 per cent of cars sold in California must be emission-free. Although electric vehicles are much cleaner than gasoline-powered models, they run for only about 100 miles before the battery needs recharging.

resins used in automobiles. Finally, methanol produces formaldehyde, a toxic compound that can irritate the eyes, nose, and throat, and which is thought to cause cancer. On the positive side, methanol burns more completely than does gasoline, and when mixed with 15 per cent gasoline to form a fuel called M-85, it achieves satisfactory starting performance. A "flexible fuel" engine can run on either gasoline or methanol or a combination of both. Special sensors determine the type of fuel in use and relay this information to the central computer system.

Natural gas is another abundant fuel that experts consider an alternative to gasoline. It is composed mainly of methane gas and is cheaper and much cleaner than gasoline. This fuel's major drawback is that, unlike gasoline and methanol, it is not available as a liquid at normal air temperatures and pressures. Natural gas must be carried in a pressurized tank, or, as a liquid, in an insulated tank—unfamiliar additions to a car's design that consumers may reject. Refueling with natural gas could take up to several hours.

Some scientists are interested in hydrogen as the fuel of the future. Hydrogen burns much more cleanly than do other fuels and is easy to produce. But complex technical problems must be solved before it can be widely used in cars.

Electric vehicles are quiet and virtually emission-free. However, the batteries from which they draw energy usually contain toxic chemicals, which become pollutants when the batteries are disposed of. Today's electric cars cannot go as far or as fast as gasoline-driven vehicles because the battery does not offer the same amount of energy as does gasoline combustion. Furthermore, the battery must be recharged regularly, and the energy to do this comes from power plants that are also a source of pollution. Nevertheless, electric vehicles are the likely choice for meeting zero-emission laws that have been established in some areas, such as California.

The ongoing search for ways to make cars cleaner poses a demanding challenge to engineers, as well as chemists, materials scientists, and technicians. The widespread research reflects our newly heightened concerns for the environment along with our old desire to maintain the freedom of movement that the automobile has brought to the developed world.

For further reading:

Stockel, Martin W., and Stockel, M. T. *Auto Mechanics Fundamentals.* The Goodheart-Willcox Co., Inc. 1990.
Seiffert, Ulrich, and Walzer, Peter. *The Future for Automotive Technology.* Frances Pinter Ltd., 1984.

Research on the domestic cat spotlights the animal's unusual physical characteristics—and the conflict between cats' natural behaviors and the human world.

Science Stalks the Domestic Cat

BY BENJAMIN L. HART

Have you ever wondered why falling cats always seem to land on their feet? Or why cats are compelled to hunt birds and rodents no matter how well the pets are fed? Like cat owners, many scientists are intrigued by the cat's behavior and physical features. Ecologists say that the sheer number of cats kept as pets—about 67 million in the United States alone—means that the animals have a significant influence on the ecology of urban areas. And studies of the domestic cat's physical makeup and behavior not only add to our knowledge of all members of the cat family, but also provide practical benefits for millions of pet owners.

Much of the current scientific interest in cats stems from their changing relationship with human beings. For years, most cats in the United States lived in wild or semiwild states in cities, on farms, or in the countryside. They reproduced and flourished because people brought them food or because stored food attracted rodents, which the cats preyed upon. Today, although there are still many *feral* (wild) cats, millions of others have achieved the status of family members and live in a human-dominated environment. And, after long being neglected as subjects for scientific inquiry, the cat has caught the interest of biologists.

Domestic cats belong to the *Felidae* family of the animal kingdom, which also includes such large cats as the lion, tiger, cheetah, and leopard. The wild ancestor of the domestic cat is *Felis libica*, commonly called the African wild cat. This species still exists in Africa, but because it is most active at night, it is rarely seen and therefore difficult to study. Scientists have learned, however, that the African wild cat lives a solitary life on a well-marked territory. Male and female adults interact very little other than during mating. Later, females interact with their own kittens.

The cat is the most recently domesticated mammal. Domestication in its broadest sense refers to a process in which an animal species becomes tame and unafraid of people. But for biologists, domestication also means that a species has been genetically altered to produce traits desirable to people. In contrast to dogs, cattle, and other domestic animals, the domestic cat is the least altered anatomically and behaviorally from its wild ancestor. This is partly because people have lacked a reason to breed specific traits in cats as they have with cows, for example, to produce more milk.

Fascinating feline physiology

Like their wild ancestor, domestic cats are physically adapted for hunting small prey. Although their vision is not especially keen, they see well in dim light and readily perceive motion. Their padded feet and flexible muscles allow them to silently stalk prey or give chase by running about 48 kilometers (30 miles) per hour.

Researchers studying the cat still have much to learn about the animal and its relatives. A wide range of felines, for example, exhibit unusually playful or sexual behavior when they smell the catnip plant. No other animal responds to the plant in this way. Although research has shown that the catnip response occurs in about 50 per cent of all cats and appears to be an inherited trait, exactly how the odor affects the cat brain is still unknown.

Biologists have been a little more successful in understanding how cats purr. In February 1991, physiologists Dawn Frazer and David A. Rice of Tulane University in New Orleans, La., and G. Peters of the Alexander Koenig Museum in Germany reported that purring consists of low frequency sound produced by vibrations of the cat's *larynx* (voice box) during inhaling and exhaling. These researchers recorded the sounds through instruments that they placed on various parts of the cat's body. They found that the sounds were not linked to the sounds of the cat's breathing pattern, which is why purring is continuous. Purring may in fact occur simultaneously with other vocalizations.

Scientists do not know the purpose of purring, however, especially as it might have served the cat's wild ancestor. Purring appears to be a

The author:
Benjamin L. Hart is professor of physiology and behavior at the School of Veterinary Medicine, University of California, Davis.

sign of contentment, yet even cats that are ill and in discomfort may purr. Cat owners recognize that purring occurs when cats are around people, but the presence of people is not essential for purring. Cats may purr during mating—and kittens, while nursing. But cats of any age do not purr while they are sleeping.

How cats survive falls

Perhaps more intriguing than purring is the cat's ability to survive falls. The research of veterinarians Wayne Whitney and Cheryl Mehlhaff at the Animal Medical Center in New York City shed light on this ability in 1987. The cat's habit of falling out of open windows provided the researchers with an opportunity to study 115 cats that had fallen from high-rise apartments in New York City. The average fall was 5.5 stories. Of the 115 cats studied, 90 per cent survived, including one cat that fell 32 stories onto a sidewalk and suffered only a mild chest injury and a chipped tooth. Interestingly, cats that fell from 9 or more stories suffered fewer injuries than those falling from lower heights. Among cats that fell from 9 to 32 stories, only 5 per cent suffered fatal injuries, but 10 per cent of those that fell from 7 or fewer stories died.

How do cats manage to take falling so easily? For one thing, in comparison to human beings, a cat is much smaller and lighter. Also, a cat has more body surface area in proportion to its weight than a human being has. This increase in surface area results in greater air resistance, which slows the fall. The important thing, however, is that a falling cat apparently positions itself to form a sort of parachute. Less than one second after it starts to fall, a cat quickly rights itself in midair with all four legs pointing downward. The cat's inner ears act like an internal gyroscope, telling the cat which direction it is falling. With the legs pointed downward, the cat then spreads its legs so that its body forms a sort of parachute that increases air resistance. With its limbs flexed, the cat also cushions the force of impact by landing on all four legs. The force of the impact is distributed through the muscles and joints.

Whitney and Mehlhaff believe that the parachute effect comes into play mainly above four stories, at the point where the cat has reached its greatest rate of descent. Of the 115 cats the researchers studied,

Domestic cats have been the most popular pet in the United States since the mid-1980's. Research on the animal's health and behavior yields practical benefits for millions of pet owners.

The cat family

The domestic cat and the large wild cats belong to the same family of animals, *Felidae, right*. The tiger is the largest cat, with males averaging about 190 kilograms (420 pounds). Most domestic cats weigh only from 3 to 7 kilograms (6 to 15 pounds). But all members of the cat family have long, muscular bodies and short, strong jaws with 30 sharp teeth for grasping and shredding prey. The domestic cat is most closely related to *Felis libica, below,* its wild ancestor. *Felis libica* still exists in Africa, but the solitary animal is rarely seen.

Tiger

Cheetah

Leopard

Jaguar

Lion

Mountain lion

Lynx

Ocelot

Domestic cat

only 1 of 13 cats that fell nine or more stories sustained a bone fracture, whereas most of the cats that fell from lower stories suffered some type of broken bone.

Researching feline disease

Cats may be able to escape injuries from falls, but many suffer from serious diseases, such as feline leukemia; infectious *peritonitis,* an inflammation of the membrane that lines the walls of the abdomen; and *panleukopenia* (cat distemper). Since the mid-1980's, veterinary researchers have made great strides in understanding two other major diseases: a type of heart disease called dilated cardiomyopathy and a type of AIDS that strikes only cats.

For years, dilated cardiomyopathy was recognized as a significant cause of death of pet cats in the United States. This disease is characterized by enlargement and weakening of the heart to the point where it is incapable of pumping blood. Until 1987, the cause of the disease was unknown, and veterinarians could offer no cure. In 1987, veterinarians Paul Pion and Mark Kittleson and their colleagues at the University of California, Davis, School of Veterinary Medicine reported that cats suffering from dilated cardiomyopathy had a deficiency of an amino acid called taurine. (Amino acids are the building blocks of protein.) Giving the cats taurine supplements reversed the disease and led to a full recovery.

Before the California study, cat specialists had thought that taurine deficiencies occurred only in cats fed commercial dog food or home-cooked food that was nutritionally unbalanced. But the California veterinarians discovered that cats fed exclusively with some types of commercial cat food could develop the heart disease. Since the 1987 study, manufacturers of the cat foods have added more taurine to their products, and there has been a dramatic decrease in the number of cases of the disease.

Another important discovery was the recognition of feline AIDS in 1988 by veterinarian Neils Pedersen and his colleagues at the University of California, Davis. The disease is caused by a virus called the *feline immunodeficiency virus* (FIV). FIV is usually transmitted during a fight through the saliva of an infected cat that bites another cat, puncturing the skin. Because cat fights generally occur outdoors, feline AIDS is found mainly in cats that are allowed to roam freely or in multiple-cat households that adopt wild or homeless cats. In many areas of the United States where there is a large population of freely roaming cats, about 5 per cent of the feline population is infected. Since the disease was first diagnosed in 1988, veterinarians have found feline AIDS in cats throughout the United States, Canada, South Africa, Australia, New Zealand, and Japan.

The virus and the disease pattern are similar to that of human AIDS, but cats do not get the human virus, and people are not susceptible to the cat virus. Veterinarians had observed the symptoms of FIV infection for many years, but investigators did not recognize the disorder as

A cat's ears move independently of one another. By aiming the cup of an ear toward a sound, the cat can improve its perception of the noise.

What makes a cat, a cat?

From its whiskers to its tail, the domestic cat has many special physical features.

A sense organ in the cat's mouth helps detect scents.

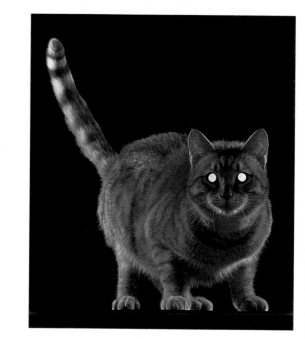

A cat's eyes glow when light strikes them at night because of a special layer of cells at the back of its eyes called the *tapetum lucidum*. This structure reflects light and thus helps the cat see in dim light, but not in total darkness.

The cat's whiskers, which grow on the chin, at the sides of the face, and above the eyes, are attached to nerves in the skin. As the whiskers brush against objects, the nerves relay the sense of touch to the brain.

Spongy footpads on the bottom of each paw make movement virtually noiseless. A cat's forepaw has five toes, including a thumblike toe called a *dewclaw*. A cat's hindpaw has four toes. Hooklike claws extend from each toe when the cat climbs or grasps an object and retract under the skin when not needed.

A cat appears to glide when it walks because it moves the front and rear legs on one side of its body at the same time, an unusual trait for most four-legged animals. Special construction of its hip joint helps the cat leap with ease.

The cat can run with grace and speed because most of its muscles are long and thin. The domestic cat can reach a running speed of about 48 kilometers (30 miles) per hour.

A stop–action photographic technique reveals how a cat rights itself in midair less than one second after it starts to fall. When falling long distances, a cat positions its body to form a sort of parachute that slows its descent, helping to prevent serious injury.

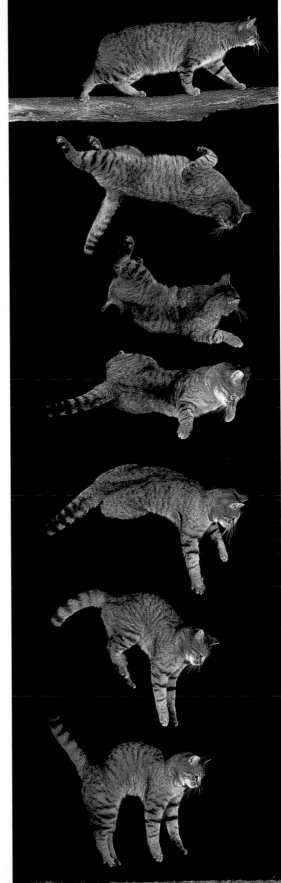

a type of AIDS until the symptoms of human AIDS were recognized as a disease.

Like human AIDS, feline AIDS attacks the body's disease-fighting immune system. The feline disorder has two stages. The first stage begins when a cat is infected through a bite. About four weeks after the initial infection, the cat becomes ill with a fever but usually recovers. The second stage begins about two to four years after infection and is marked by the appearance of infections in the mouth and respiratory system and on the skin. These infections are called *opportunistic* because they afflict only cats whose immune systems are too weak to fight off the infection-causing microbes. Death from these AIDS-related infections is inevitable.

According to veterinarians, cat owners can best protect their cats from FIV infection by not allowing the cats to run free. If a cat is kept indoors even with an infected animal, the likelihood of transmission is small because indoor cats rarely bite each other.

Focusing on cat behavior

Another major focus of research is cat behavior. Many people think of cat behavior merely as grooming, scratching, and sleeping. However, just because cats are not often seen performing tricks does not mean that cats do not easily learn. Animal behaviorists say the intelligence or learning ability of cats is no greater or less than that of dogs. But comparing different species is difficult, because tests of their learning abilities must take into account differences in the animals' sensory and motor capabilities and in their inherited behavioral predispositions. For example, cats being tested for learning ability will not respond to the reward of petting as consistently as dogs will.

Nevertheless, as early as the 1920's, researchers found that cats can learn complex tasks, especially if the reward is food. And in highly structured tests of learning ability, cats often outperformed dogs in the ability to master conceptual problems. In the 1950's, animal behaviorist J. M. Warren at Pennsylvania State University at University Park described the cat's ability to master "oddity learning" in which the animal is shown three objects and is rewarded for selecting the one that is most unlike the other two. In the test, cats learned to paw a square block rather than two round blocks presented at the same time, because food was hidden beneath the square block. In similar tests, the cat chose the different object when presented with one round block and two squares.

Such tests require the ability to understand concepts, in this case, that of similarity and dissimilarity. Researchers have found that some cats do as well with this type of conceptual learning as monkeys. And, aside from monkeys and other primates, cats are among the most adept at learning by observing the successes and failures of other animals attempting to complete tasks to obtain a reward.

Frequent grooming is another natural behavior of the cat. The feline tongue's prickly surface acts as a brush to remove loose hairs, para-

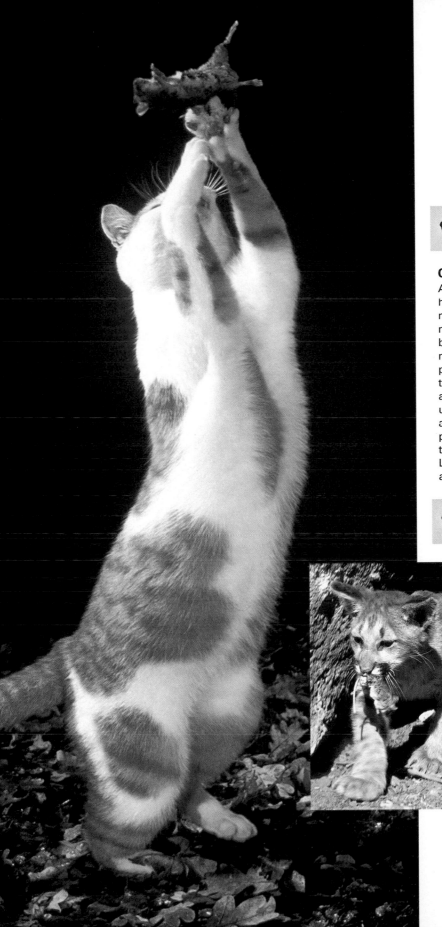

Catching prey

All cats are instinctive hunters. A young mountain lion, *below,* must hunt to survive, but even well-fed domestic cats will catch prey. A domestic cat tosses a mouse in the air, *left,* to release pent-up predatory energy and not necessarily for pleasure, according to the work of Paul Leyhausen, a German animal behaviorist.

Marking territory

A domestic cat scratches a carpet-covered post, *right,* for the same reason that a mountain lion scratches a log, *below.* Both are making visible markers of their territory. Scratching also rubs secretions from the cat's paws onto the marker. The secretions have a distinctive odor that signals the animal's presence to other cats.

Grooming

A lioness's prickly tongue removes loose hairs, parasites, and other foreign material in her cub's coat, *above*. A domestic cat, *left,* exhibits similar grooming behavior, which helps account for the cat's reputation for cleanliness.

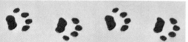

Playful fighting

When young domestic cats, *right,* or tigers, *below,* play with each other, they mimic the behavior of fighting an enemy. The defensive cat on its back or side uses its hind claws to rake the soft underside of the opponent, and with front claws extended, it reaches to grasp the head. Experts say that this social play may increase intelligence and rarely results in injury.

sites, and other foreign material from the coat. The saliva a cat transfers from its mouth to its coat contains proteins that may play a role in conditioning the hair. Unfortunately, the saliva also contains a protein that causes an allergic reaction in some people. Allergists have recently learned that most of the nearly 10 per cent of people in the United States who are allergic to cats are sensitive to this protein in cat saliva. When these people are exposed to loose cat hairs in a room, they may come in contact with the protein and suffer an allergic reaction, such as sneezing, runny nose, or difficult breathing.

Collisions between feline and human worlds

In some ways, the cat's natural behavior matches the life style of many families. The home is empty for much of the day, and that suits the cat because it has the genetic makeup and behavioral instincts to be a loner. But living with a pet cat may also bring us into confrontation with some behaviors that are normal for the wild cat, but which can be quite undesirable in our homes. For example, scratching one or two tree trunks outdoors is perfectly normal behavior for a wild cat. One function of scratching is to remove the worn outer layer of the claw, exposing a new claw underneath. This behavior also enables cats in the wild to mark their territories. A cat will scratch one or more trees or other prominent areas, and in the process of scratching, rub secretions from its feet onto the tree trunk. This gives the scratched area a distinct odor that other cats in the territory recognize. To maintain its territorial marker, the cat repeatedly scratches and freshens the visual and chemical marks.

Pet cats have the same instinctual response to mark a territory. Just as an outdoor cat chooses a prominent tree, an indoor cat chooses a prominent object, such as a couch or chair. The domestic cat also freshens its marker by repeatedly scratching it. But, a domestic cat that scratches furniture or drapes can prove costly to the cat's owner.

Pet owners are often disappointed that their cats do not read the label designating a carpet-covered post as a scratching post and that they continue to scratch a couch or chair. Training a cat to stop scratching furniture may mean removing or covering the mutilated furniture and replacing it with an alternative object, such as a scratching post, in the same prominent place. Cats like to take long vertical strokes when scratching, so they prefer posts covered with a material that has vertically oriented threads. Cats also will use redwood or pine posts, if the posts are roughed up first with a wire brush. Because cats like to stay with a territorial marker once they have started scratching it, owners find that once a cat starts scratching a post, they can move the post to a less prominent place.

Urine spraying is another normal territorial behavior of cats in the wild that can become a major frustration for domestic cat owners. In the wild, this behavior familiarizes the cat with its territory and home range. The urine odor probably makes it feel self assured and comfortable and signals its presence to other cats in surrounding areas.

Veterinary behaviorist Leslie Cooper of the University of California, Davis, and I found in 1984 that 5 per cent of female domestic cats and 10 per cent of neutered male domestic cats become problem sprayers. The cat sniffs a target area a foot or so above the floor, and then turns and directs a stream of urine toward the target. Males and females spray using basically the same posture, but the behavior is most common in males. Neutering male cats markedly reduces the occurrence of this behavior, but even the neutered males and females may ruin household furniture or stereo speakers by their spraying behavior.

Frequently, a pet cat begins spraying after the introduction of a new adult cat or kitten into the household. A cat owner may have mistakenly believed that a cat needed company and brought home another cat, only to find that the resident pet is not at all thrilled with the newcomer. In this situation, the original cat begins to spray because it is anxious or otherwise threatened by the invasion of its territory.

Until 1991, the most common veterinary treatment to stop a cat from spraying was to administer a drug that mimics the female hormone progesterone. This treatment proved effective in controlling spraying behavior in about 50 per cent of neutered male cats but was much less effective in female cats. In 1991, Amy Marder, a veterinary behaviorist in Boston, introduced the notion of treating spraying cats with the human tranquilizer diazepam, also known as Valium. In a clinical study reported in March 1992, Cooper and I found that diazepam controlled spraying in 55 per cent of male and female cats.

Diazepam has side effects in cats, however, just as it does in people. The drug often causes excessive drowsiness and a temporary lack of coordination. Diazepam also produces physiological and behavioral dependency. In 1992, I—working with Robert Eckstein and Karen Powell at the University of California, Davis, and Nicholas Dodman of Tufts University in Medford, Mass.— found that the tranquilizer buspirone, another drug gaining some popularity for the treatment of anxiety in people, is at least as effective as diazepam in controlling spraying behavior without producing the side effects of diazepam.

The need for drug treatments shows that as we remove cats from their natural environment, the expression of their normal behaviors may conflict with our human-oriented environment. Veterinary behaviorists may have to use ingenuity, and sometimes borrow from the area of human drug therapy, to help felines adjust to our environment.

Backyard predators

We will also need ingenuity to solve problems stemming from the cat's natural hunting behavior. Much of what we understand about the predatory behavior of cats is the work of Paul Leyhausen, a German animal behaviorist, who spent the 1950's through the 1970's studying domestic cats and related felines.

Leyhausen believed that rodents are a cat's natural prey. Being naturally solitary creatures, *Felis libica* could successfully hunt rats and mice alone, whereas to hunt larger prey, two or more predators had to cooperate. Usually, the cat waits in front of a rodent's burrow until the rodent strays from its shelter. Then the cat stalks after it, slinking along a trail or ditch and pausing to wait for the opportune moment to pounce on the prey. Actually, the odds generally favor the prey. From his observations, Leyhausen estimated that a cat makes about three attempts before it catches one mouse.

Most cat owners have seen cats play with mice before killing them. The cat tosses the mouse in the air, bats it, rolls it over, clasps it, and kicks at it using its hind claws. The reasons cats play with their prey is not clear. Leyhausen favored the explanation that this play represents the release of pent-up energy associated with predatory behavior and is not necessarily done for pleasure.

A disturbing picture of feline backyard predatory behavior emerged in a 1989 study by biologist Peter Churcher of Bedford School in Bedfordshire, England, and ecologist John Lawton of the University of London. These investigators recorded the number and kind of prey brought home by 77 normal pet cats living in a village in Bedfordshire. They found that in a year's time almost 1,100 prey were claimed by the cats. About 64 per cent of the kill were small mammals, and 36 per cent were birds, including song thrushes, blackbirds, and robins. When they used these figures to calculate the impact of the entire population of 5 million house cats throughout Great Britain, they estimated the pet cats kill at least 20 million birds a year.

The larger number of cats in the United States probably prey on rodents and birds in much greater numbers. In fact, ecologists say that the British study no doubt underestimated the number of birds cats kill, because house cats bring home only about half their victims. In January 1992, California scientists said that cats have all but eliminated the wild bird population in San Francisco's Golden Gate Park.

Making sure that a pet cat is well fed may combat this carnage. But the hunting will probably continue because of the cat's strong predatory instincts. Still, in 1980, the work of animal behaviorist Tim Caro of the University of California, Davis, showed that many cats require experience with a particular type of prey in order to hunt it successfully. Cats exposed to mice as kittens gain efficiency killing rodents, but their success does not carry over very well to killing birds. Thus, one way of improving the odds of having a pet cat that will not hunt birds may be to adopt a kitten that has never been exposed to that prey.

The cats' increasing presence in human society suggests a growing interest in this most recently domesticated mammal. Many scientists share this interest and are pursuing research into just what it means to be a cat in a human world.

For further reading:

Corey, Paul. *Do Cats Think*. Book Sales, 1990.
Eckstein, Warren. *How to Get Your Cat to Do What You Want*. Random House, 1990.

The chairperson of the National Commission on AIDS talks about how the United States is responding to the challenge of the epidemic.

A Presidential Adviser on AIDS

AN INTERVIEW WITH JUNE E. OSBORN
CONDUCTED BY JINGER HOOP

Science Year: You've had a distinguished career as a pediatrician, medical researcher, academic dean, and now chairperson of the National Commission on AIDS. Obviously, dealing with the AIDS epidemic takes a great deal of your time and attention today. But do you remember when you first heard of cases of the disease we now call AIDS?

Osborn: I remember the day the first report came out—June 5, 1981. Even then, I was probably as close to being professionally involved in that area as anybody. I had done research on viruses, and I had been a government adviser on sexually transmitted diseases. So I was instantly aware of that first report, which described cases of a rare type of pneumonia in five young men in Los Angeles.

SY: At first, the disease seemed to be confined to homosexual men who had many sex partners and who lived in certain cities. When did you begin to suspect that AIDS might become a full-scale epidemic?

Osborn: Immediately. I don't think that any of us knew what "full-scale" would eventually mean. But it was quite obvious from the very beginning that this was a sexually transmitted disease, and we already were having a massive epidemic of sexually transmitted diseases. So I knew that whatever AIDS was, it had a pretty fertile field to grow in.

SY: Since that time, you've been working to try to halt the epidemic. From your perspective, what's the outlook for the future?

Osborn: In the United States, we have at least a million people infected with HIV, the virus that causes AIDS. So we're about to have an awful lot of people get sick and die. About 100,000 people died of AIDS in the United States in the first 10 years of the epidemic. Another 200,000 will die in only 2 more years.

SY: In a November 1991 meeting with U.S. President George Bush, you warned him that "a bad decade is coming," a statement that made headlines in newspapers across the United States.

The author:
Jinger Hoop is the associate editor of *Science Year*.

"**W**e've got to take care of the people who are about to develop AIDS, but we're not prepared to. . . . A lot of people who have never received medical care are dying of AIDS on the streets, in homeless shelters, and in emergency rooms."

Osborn: Yes. We've got to take care of the people who are about to develop AIDS, but we're not prepared to. Right now it's a national disaster. A lot of people who have never received medical care are dying of AIDS on the streets, in homeless shelters, and in emergency rooms.

SY: Yet we've made great strides in understanding AIDS. By the mid-1980's, only a few years after the first cases of the disease were reported, scientists had discovered that HIV infects white blood cells and is spread through the exchange of bodily fluids. What's been the biggest obstacle to curbing the epidemic in the United States?

Osborn: Public attitudes: denial that the epidemic is happening, fear of homosexuals, and a really quite hateful tendency to care more about some people in our society than others. AIDS first appeared among homosexuals, and gay men still make up the largest number of infected people in the United States. It used to be said rather cynically early in the epidemic that if AIDS mainly struck bankers' sons instead of gay men, just imagine how the nation would respond. I think it's our business to recognize that AIDS is a risk to all our sons and daughters.

SY: Do you think the solution lies in increased government funding for AIDS research?

Osborn: Of all the areas of AIDS funding, research is the closest to adequate, probably because it's the easiest and least painful kind of AIDS funding for Congress to support. Congressional leadership has been tremendously important to get us to where we are, but in terms of funding efforts for prevention and care, we are very far behind.

SY: What sort of prevention programs would you like to see?

Osborn: Every type of effort to help people avoid high-risk behavior. Research shows that in order to change behavior in a sustained way, we need to use multiple media and multiple repetitions of the message. So we need AIDS education in schools. We need sex education in the

June E. Osborn

When the first cases of AIDS were reported in 1981, June E. Osborn was ideally suited to become a key player in the fight against the disease. A physician with expertise in the study of viruses, Osborn had been a scientific adviser to the United States government and was comfortable dealing with policymakers and the press. Today, more than a decade after the disease emerged, she has become a persuasive advocate of forceful and compassionate steps to combat the epidemic.

Born in Endicott, N.Y., on May 28, 1937, Osborn was the younger of two daughters in a family devoted to education and science. Until 1950, her father was a professor of psychiatry and her mother was a professor of childhood education at the University of Buffalo. When June was a teen-ager, the family moved to Madison, Wis., where her father became director of the state's mental hygiene department and professor of psychiatry at the University of Wisconsin and her mother began a second career as a psychiatric social worker.

Osborn and her sister followed in their mother's footsteps by pursuing challenging careers at a time when few women were encouraged to do so. While her sister studied for advanced degrees in economics, Osborn attended Oberlin College in Ohio, studying chemistry as an undergraduate. But she decided she was better suited to a career in medicine—not as a physician in private practice, but as a professor and medical researcher.

Osborn began medical school at Case Western Reserve University in Cleveland in 1957. There, she studied under physician-scientists she considered marvelous role models, including Frederick C. Robbins, who in 1954 had shared the Nobel Prize in physiology or medicine for his research on the virus that causes polio. Osborn decided to follow Robbins' example and become trained in both pediatrics and *virology* (the study of viruses and viral diseases).

After graduating from medical school, she spent three years as an intern and resident in pediatrics at Harvard hospitals in Boston. In 1964, she began two years of research on viruses at Johns Hopkins Hospital in Baltimore and at the University of Pittsburgh School of Medicine in Pennsylvania. In 1966, she moved back to Madison to join the faculty of the University of Wisconsin medical school with appointments in microbiology and pediatrics.

Then, in the early 1970's, the Administration of President Richard M. Nixon began opening doors for women as scientific advisers to government agencies. Osborn's background made her a sought-after scientific authority. She served as an adviser on vaccines for the U.S. Food and Drug Administration, the National Institutes of Health (NIH), and the Centers for Disease Control.

Government officials requested Osborn's help in dealing with the AIDS epidemic in 1983. At the time, the first AIDS cases were being reported among people who had received transfusions of blood or blood products. In January 1984, the NIH asked Osborn to chair a special committee to help create policies for dealing with HIV and the nation's blood supply. She helped draw up guidelines for testing donated blood that protected the privacy of blood donors while making the U.S. blood supply much safer.

With the scope of the AIDS epidemic growing, Osborn became more and more involved in the fight against it. A divorced mother of three who refers to parenthood as "the process of growing your own best friends," she took pains to make sure her children understood the importance of her work and why it preoccupied her time. In 1988, she became a member of the World Health Organization's Global Commission on AIDS. One year later, the members of the National Commission on AIDS selected her as their chairperson. The commission, an independent agency, was created by Congress to advise the President and Congress on the AIDS epidemic and national policy.

Today, Osborn juggles many responsibilities. She is dean of the University of Michigan School of Public Health in Ann Arbor, a post she has held since 1984. At the same time, she chairs the National Commission on AIDS and works with its executive director and 20 staff members in Washington, D.C. She tries to average one day a week in Washington and otherwise relies on the telephone and fax machine to help her handle both jobs. Her schedule is too irregular to allow her to teach her own university courses, but she lectures in other professors' courses and relishes her position as dean because it gives her the opportunity to guide and direct the careers of young faculty members and students. She counsels young people to "grow their ambitions big enough" to realize their talents.

And Osborn sees herself as a teacher whenever she talks to the public about AIDS. In doing so, she has developed a reputation for being direct—often pointedly frank—in assessing how American society has responded to this new challenge and what is yet to be done.   [J. H.]

schools so that kids understand the AIDS education. We need an approach using television, radio, and print media. We must tell people what constitutes risky behavior and what ways there are to avoid it. We need community-based efforts so that people who speak different languages—either literally or figuratively—can still hear the message about AIDS.

SY: In 1988, the U.S. Department of Health and Human Services mailed AIDS information pamphlets to every household in the United States, in what was called the nation's most ambitious health-education attempt. What effect do you think that had?

Osborn: Those pamphlets were written in educated English and educated Spanish. America is the most diverse society in the world, and many of our people can't read, so the brochures were not anywhere near enough. To understand how uncommitted our approach is, think of what a company does when they want to sell a new brand of toothpaste. They'll invest $90 million to get an extra 5 per cent share of the market. We haven't made a comparable investment to combat this epidemic, and yet we're talking about our kids' lives.

SY: You're the mother of three children, all in their early 20's. Other parents may be interested to learn how and when you told your children about AIDS.

Osborn: I've had a unique opportunity with my children because they've been with me throughout this epidemic. They've traveled around the world with me to conferences and heard me give speeches on the subject.

In general, though, parents need to be both informed and available. Young people should be told that AIDS is a very important life-threatening infection that can be avoided with good judgment about sexual behavior and about the use of intravenous drugs. Unprotected sex with many partners greatly increases the risk of getting AIDS, as does the sharing of needles among intravenous drug users. If parents are well and comfortably informed, and if they can communicate the importance of this in terms their child can understand, I think they're doing a good job.

SY: Do you think most parents are well informed enough to educate their children on this issue?

Osborn: Right now there is a kind of disjointed communication about AIDS in many families. The kids may learn something at school that's actually quite good, but the parents are underinformed or misinformed and may find that they don't like the message. That suggests that the parents just don't understand how important it is. I would like to have workplaces as well as schools become centers for AIDS education. If parents get good AIDS information at work, and if the kids come home from school well informed, then the information meshes and the message is reinforced.

SY: Is it unrealistic to assume that all children and teen-agers feel comfortable discussing these issues with their parents?

> "Think of what a company does when they want to sell a new brand of toothpaste. They'll invest $90 million to get an extra 5 per cent share of the market. We haven't made a comparable investment to combat this epidemic, and yet we're talking about our kids' lives."

"Young people should be told that AIDS is a very important life-threatening infection that can be avoided with good judgment about sexual behavior and about the use of intravenous drugs."

Osborn: At least in some families, some questions are easier for kids to ask elsewhere. And so we need to have a lot of sources of information about AIDS available in this society.

SY: You've said in the past that telling young people that sexual abstinence is the only way to avoid AIDS would be as unsuccessful as the "Just Say No" antidrug campaign. What did you mean?

Osborn: I certainly much prefer abstinence for teen-agers. But with a lethal disease out there, we cannot restrict ourselves to that message. The word *just* is the problem in the "Just Say No" messages. *Just* implies that saying "no" is easy. Those people who think that it's easy forgot what it was like to be an adolescent. Saying "no" can be the hardest thing in the world.

AIDS is spreading rapidly among the poor, but it's extremely hard to promote abstinence for adolescents who are so poor that they feel they have no future. For them, the likelihood of being shot within the next 2 years is much greater than their perceived likelihood of getting sick from AIDS within the next 10 years.

SY: You mentioned earlier that sharing drug-injection equipment is a major way HIV is spread. Curbing addiction entirely would be the ideal solution to this problem, but it appears particularly difficult. Do you support attempts to distribute free needles to drug addicts in an effort to stop the spread of AIDS?

Osborn: "Free needles" is quite an evil phrase because it sounds like we're out there trying to give people needles for the fun of it. In point of fact, what we're trying to do is keep the lack of drug-addiction treatment from being an automatic death sentence.

The National Commission on AIDS's first recommendation is that people who want to escape addiction should be able to receive treatment when they decide to get treated—so-called "treatment on demand." That's the cornerstone of any rational policy for the epidemic among injecting drug users. But treatment on demand is not available in any major city in this country right now. A poor person who wants to stop being addicted cannot get into treatment in less than four weeks or, in many cities, several months. When treatment on demand is not available—and even when it is for people who cannot bring themselves to be treated for other reasons—there must be a way to interrupt the spread of this virus.

SY: So, in your view, this involves somehow stopping the sharing of contaminated needles?

Osborn: Yes. The one way HIV can flare out of control unpredictably is through sharing needles—because this is one of the most efficient ways to spread this virus. Even the most risky forms of sex do not always result in HIV infection. But sharing injection apparatus between infected and uninfected people results in HIV infection a much greater percentage of the time. That's how we ended up with a massive East Coast epidemic in only a few years. More than 50 per cent of injecting drug users are now infected. In Edinburgh, Scotland, the percentage of HIV infection among injecting drug users went from almost 0 per cent to 50 per cent during an 18-month period. A similar increase happened in Bangkok, Thailand, between January 1988 and July 1989.

We're sitting on the edge of a volcano in most big U.S. cities, where right now the percentage of infected injecting drug users is around 10 per cent. At any time we could suddenly have a massive increase in the number of infected people, all of whom are sexually active and can infect their partners. If we ignore and neglect the drug side of this epidemic, it will flare like a brush fire.

SY: Many of these suggestions for combating the epidemic are quite controversial.

Osborn: People should look at it this way: Every time this epidemic expands its range, it gets to be more threatening to everyone. I've often referred to what I call "double-digit seroprevalence," which means the point when you've got 10 per cent, 20 per cent, or more of your population infected. If that happens, you no longer can even think about protecting yourself by knowing your sex partner. If you have one or two sex partners before choosing a relationship, the odds of getting infected would be very high.

> "The one way HIV can flare out of control unpredictably is through sharing needles. . . . If we ignore and neglect the drug side of this epidemic, it will flare like a brush fire."

So if we blow this next decade the way we blew the 1980's, then we're into a very different problem. Then we won't be able to use the one weapon we've got against this virus—which is knowledgeable avoidance.

SY: You've mentioned the AIDS epidemic in nations other than the United States. Has your participation in the World Health Organization's Global Commission on AIDS convinced you that some countries are handling the epidemics within their borders better than the United States?

Osborn: The nations of what we used to call Western Europe are doing a much better job. They recognized that everyone was at risk right away and started pushing for condom use. All the things Americans are now beginning to talk about just a little bit, they've been doing for years. If you get off an airplane at London's Heathrow Airport, the first thing you see is a picture of a condom with a little sign that says "Life Insurance: 15 pence."

In the United States, we still don't have condom advertising on the major TV networks, and we're forbidden to do the most rudimentary

> " **I** think [Magic Johnson's announcement that he was HIV-infected] helped instantly. It let people know that everyone is at risk. . . . We're now at a different level of public understanding about AIDS and likely to remain so."

government surveys of sexual behavior. It is very difficult to explain to Europeans what's happening in this country, because they see us with a vastly worse problem and not even doing the simplest things about it. Europeans think we're out of our minds, and I sort of do, too.

SY: What about AIDS prevention in nations other than Western Europe?

Osborn: In general, there's a lot to be learned by looking at prevention efforts around the world. In almost every country, there has been the initial effort to say "Oh, well, AIDS is not going to happen to us, or only to the bad people in our country, whom we don't care about." That's a very dangerous stance to take with a virus that takes 10 years to express itself and is spread by sexual intercourse—a behavior that most adults and many teen-agers engage in. The People's Republic of China took the stance that they didn't have HIV, but since about 1990 they've admitted that they do. They have AIDS associated with a big intravenous drug problem in South China. Now, Thailand has a disastrous situation as well, and there's reason to worry that India has a similar epidemic, perhaps one that's even worse.

SY: It's often said that the character of the AIDS epidemic in the United States is different from that of some other countries. For example, AIDS seems to be spread more commonly by heterosexual contact in Africa than in the United States. Is this kind of distinction useful?

Osborn: Not really. About 75 per cent of the world's epidemic is heterosexually spread. Why Americans have spent so much time trying to pretend that everyone isn't at risk, I will never understand. We are the same species. And we've had instances of heterosexual spread in the United States from the very beginning.

And I think that Americans sometimes don't appreciate the fact that the United States is the epicenter of this disaster. The AIDS epidemic began here, and we have the largest number of cases of any nation in the world. In some parts of Africa, the epidemic started a little later, but it spread more quickly, chiefly because they don't have the resources to screen the blood supply and because their attempts to communicate public-health messages were poor. AIDS simply is harder to control in places that don't have resources.

SY: Many people were surprised when basketball star Earvin (Magic) Johnson, who apparently had not engaged in homosexual intercourse or intravenous drug use, reported that he had become HIV infected.

Osborn: They wouldn't have been so surprised if they'd been listening to what's been said since the beginning of the AIDS epidemic. Sex is universally risky in the sense that people must be thoughtful about sexual partners. Abstinence is the only safe decision in the absolute sense, but safer sex can be achieved by minimizing the number of sexual partners and using condoms. After all the safer-sex messages that we've been giving for years, I don't know why so many people haven't been listening.

SY: Do you think Magic Johnson's announcement helped people start listening?

Osborn: I think it helped instantly. It let people know that everyone is at risk. No doubt there are some people still trying to explain it away, but I don't think that's the most common reaction. We're now at a different level of public understanding about AIDS and likely to remain so. For one thing, it's not going to be possible to pretend that this isn't happening because we're about to have hundreds of thousands of Americans become ill and die. If so many people hadn't been grieving in secret, everybody already would know somebody they cared about who had been lost to AIDS or who is dying.

SY: It's become almost a cliché to speak of AIDS as a modern plague. Are we dealing with something on the scale of the bubonic plague?

Osborn: The only plague that's worth equating AIDS with is syphilis, another potentially fatal sexually transmitted disease. The other epidemics do not share the kinds of characteristics that make a meaning-

> "About 75 per cent of the world's epidemic is heterosexually spread. Why Americans have spent so much time trying to pretend that everyone isn't at risk, I will never understand."

ful comparison. We've had epidemics of influenza and measles, but these diseases are transmitted through contact that doesn't involve intimacy. Bubonic plague was dependent on rats and crowding. AIDS is not spread in these ways.

SY: Can we learn some lessons about controlling AIDS based on how public-health officials handled syphilis?

Osborn: We should be pretty humble about this, because we haven't done well with syphilis, either. One of the statements that irks me the most is that public-health workers should go back to "tried-and-true" methods for dealing with sexually transmitted diseases. Well, we failed when the approach was a very heavy-handed policy of tracing the sexual contacts of the people we knew had the disease. And now, despite having a cure for syphilis, we have a fresh syphilis epidemic on our hands. Fifty thousand new cases were reported in the United States in 1990.

> "People are very frightened about hugging HIV-infected people, shaking their hands, caring for them, being compassionate. They shouldn't be!"

SY: What other misconceptions need to be corrected?

Osborn: People often say that they know about AIDS. And, if you question them about how HIV is spread, a lot of them will get it right. But if you ask how the virus is *not* spread, most people are much less sure. In point of fact you can't spread it any way other than by the exchange of bodily fluids. This virus just isn't transmitted by other routes. That's important, because people are very frightened about hugging HIV-infected people, shaking their hands, caring for them, being compassionate. They shouldn't be!

SY: We often hear reports of people with AIDS being subjected to a great deal of discrimination.

Osborn: The things that are happening to HIV-infected people are beyond description. People burn crosses on their lawns. I have a friend who is not HIV infected, but his wife and kids were. My friend had to bury his first child himself because the undertaker was afraid to touch someone who'd died of AIDS.

SY: Some experts say that proposals to require HIV testing of health-care workers are rooted in this type of fear.

Osborn: That's a good example. No one has ever suggested that an HIV-infected health-care worker posed any threat to any patient except under very rare circumstances in certain surgical procedures. This is as close to zero risk as you can get. And yet government agencies in various states have started reacting to the knowledge that a health-care worker is infected in the most awful sorts of ways, chasing them out of their practices, keeping them from using their training and talent.

The public has insisted on the right to panic at an enormous cost to the society as well as to those people. I hope there comes a day when we turn around and look at that behavior in complete embarrassment. I hope we'll be ashamed that there was a time when we were willing to indulge ourselves in unsubstantiated fear to the extent of running people out of their jobs, careers, and lives. It's appalling that this nation, which says we value each individual, should be behaving that way.

SY: Do you agree with those experts who say that mandatory AIDS testing is always inappropriate?

Osborn: Other than testing donated blood, there is no excuse for unknowing mandatory testing of anyone. I object strongly to the phrase "routine AIDS testing." There's nothing routine about an HIV test, and it isn't like other so-called screening tests done routinely. If you get disturbing results on a blood cholesterol test, you change your diet. If you get a positive result on an HIV test, you're more likely to commit suicide than if you'd just been told you had full-blown AIDS or even cancer. A positive HIV result is one of the most potent motivations for suicide that has ever been measured. The concept of using HIV tests routinely without the knowledge of the patient, without counseling the patient, is inexcusable.

If you rely strictly on screening tests in this epidemic, you've missed the whole point. Counseling with or without testing is very useful. Testing without counseling may be worse than useless because you can give false reassurance to people who test negative but are still engaging in risky behavior.

SY: Are these issues part of a larger problem—which is that the public isn't sufficiently educated about science and scientific methods to be able to appreciate the significance of scientific research?

Osborn: There is really a lot that most people don't know how to approach—for example, issues of relative risk. A scientific study may find that a new high-blood-pressure drug has a certain risk of complications. Or that a better way of making electric power lines leaves open a small question about the health risk of the electromagnetic fields. These scenarios are likely to get a panic reaction out of people because people focus mainly on the risk. It's very hard for them to keep the benefits and costs—as well as the risks—of a new technology in mind as they're making personal decisions.

In my field of infectious disease, for instance, people insist on worrying when they get cold feet that they're going to get a cold. But research has shown us that's not how you get a cold! You get a cold from infection with a virus.

People are absolutely closed-minded to the results of research that discredits similar old wives' tales. Scientists know a lot of things now, and if we had the public with us, we could make much better use of this knowledge. And people really don't have to understand the rigor of science as long as they recognize that scientists have a tightly controlled way of asking questions that yields data like nothing in history has ever done.

> "Scientists know a lot of things now, and if we had the public with us, we could make much better use of this knowledge."

SY: Is miscommunication between scientists and the public the root of this problem?

Osborn: One of the things that confuses the public the most and that scientists are really quite poor about explaining is that the essence of the scientific method is to try to disprove something that the scientist thinks is correct. If you can't find evidence that disproves the theory, that strengthens its likelihood of being a useful idea.

So scientists are trained to say, "There is no evidence that cold feet cause colds," for example, rather than saying "Cold feet do not cause colds." Unfortunately, this way of phrasing things can make people who are not used to science think the scientist isn't really sure that cold feet don't cause colds. This is one of the most regular sources of conflict between scientists and the public, oftentimes with the media caught between. Therein lies an enormous amount of our problem in taking full advantage of the progress that science has made.

SY: Given these difficulties, how do you see your role as a scientist in Washington, D.C., trying to advise policymakers?

Osborn: A scientist almost by definition has a very intense, narrow focus. This allows you to look at a problem or a question in a careful and controlled way and come up with new insight or information. A scientist who tries to address issues of public policy must have some way of making the transition from the narrowly focused fact-finding that makes good science to the understanding of broader social issues that makes good policy. If you can't make that transition, then you become either useless or a nuisance as a scientific adviser.

A good example right now is in the development of AIDS vaccines. Scientists who never look up from a laboratory bench to see what else is going on may announce that they have an exciting new development in the fight against AIDS because they've had one good vaccine experiment. The experiment in fact may be exciting, but there will still be several years' worth of testing before a vaccine can be used. And there are ethical issues involved in choosing whom you test the vaccine on, especially when there may be 11 competing vaccines and not enough people to test more than 5. Then there's the whole problem of making the vaccine available both in the United States and around the world. If the scientists are not at least aware of these issues, they can badly distort public policy for a little while when they discuss their experiment. They may also distort people's attitudes about AIDS prevention because people who think a vaccine is right around the corner may stop listening to messages about changing risky behavior.

An adviser who can be honest in both the scientific context and the broader social context can be enormously useful. That turns out to be an extremely powerful and unusual approach to things in Washington, D.C., and is one of the reasons that I have fared relatively well there. I try very hard, if I do nothing else, to stay completely up to date on scientific research. Then I can bring to bear whatever information is available, or be quite honest about it if I'm dealing from a lack of information. People have come to realize that I will say "I don't know" if I don't know.

SY: What accomplishments are you proudest of? Have you had many victories in the fight against AIDS?

Osborn: There have been a lot of victories for the National Commission on AIDS, but they're hard to talk about. For instance, I said to myself on New Year's Eve 1990 that 1991 was going to be a terrible year. I feared that we were going to be overtaken by the stampede for mandatory testing of health-care workers, a complete nonissue that threatens the careers of many wonderful and well-trained people and serves no public-health interest. I told myself that, if really badly done, this could cost us 10 years' worth of progress in keeping us from mandatory testing. I remember muttering that 1991 will be the year we lose this battle. But we did not lose it. And, not only have we not lost, I think we will win.

So, what I feel proudest of are things that didn't happen that otherwise might have. I have a little rule that I have taught all of my friends on Capitol Hill. I tell them that if we really believe this prevention stuff, we have to learn to celebrate things that don't happen.

BY BRIAN M. FAGAN

Who Were the Neanderthals?

For more than 150 years, scientists have debated whether these "other" human beings were direct ancestors of modern people or a side branch on the family tree.

A gray sky settled over the deep river valley on a winter day 75,000 years ago. Chill winds rippled the weathered hides covering the mouth of a limestone cave near the frozen Vézère River in what is now southwestern France. Thin trails of white smoke rose from hearths inside. In front of the cave, a short, powerfully built Neanderthal woman dressed in a fur loincloth squatted over a reindeer skin fastened to the ground with pegs. Slowly, she scraped the pelt with a crescent-shaped stone scraper. A baby slept in a skin slung over her shoulder. Nearby, two fur-clad Neanderthal men sat by a fire, skillfully shaping pieces of flint. From each rounded stone, the men chipped four or five triangular, sharp-edged spearpoints. Later, the men would bind the lethal points to long wooden staves and set out to hunt.

The Neanderthals were expert Ice Age hunters and gatherers. In small bands such as this, they occupied a vast area that encompassed Europe, the Middle East, and western Asia from about 120,000 years to about 32,000 years ago. The Neanderthals were among the last survivors of an ancient world that had its beginnings in tropical Africa with the origin of the first human beings more than 2.5 million years ago. Their simple technology and way of life were legacies from this remote time. But their rituals and burial customs set them apart from earlier human beings and placed them at the threshold of the modern world.

The Neanderthals pose a fascinating problem for modern scientists because they were so similar to and yet so different from us. As a result, we are not sure how to apply our knowledge of modern human beings and other primates to the Neanderthals.

Shifting opinions and perplexing questions

Scientific opinion about these ancient people has changed dramatically since the first discovery of Neanderthal fossils more than 150 years ago. Probably because most Neanderthals were stocky with thick bones and heavily muscled bodies, they were long depicted as slow-witted, brutish cave dwellers who were given to clubbing not only prey but also one another. In fact, anthropologists have discovered since the 1950's that the Neanderthals were nimble, skilled people who made tools and weapons and had a relatively complex way of life, even though their intellectual abilities were almost certainly more limited than our own.

The author:
Brian M. Fagan is a professor of anthropology at the University of California, Santa Barbara, and the author of many books on anthropology and archaeology.

The most perplexing questions about the Neanderthals have focused on their fate—and fueled one of the greatest ongoing debates in anthropology. By about 32,000 years ago, the last of the Neanderthals had vanished. In their place were early modern human beings—people who looked like us—who created cave paintings, engaged in long-distance trade, and produced more efficient weapons. Were the Neanderthals the direct ancestors of these modern human beings? Or did the Neanderthals die out without leaving a genetic legacy? Although several findings in the late 1980's and early 1990's suggest that the Neanderthals were a side branch on the human family tree, unanswered questions continue to fuel the debate. The importance of this inquiry extends beyond the Neanderthals. It bears on attempts to determine who we are and where we came from.

Seeking answers in the fossils

The first recognized Neanderthal fossils—a skull and limb bones—were discovered in the Neander Valley in northwest Germany in 1856. The skull, with its thick walls, large and bony brow, and bulging sides, raised a storm of controversy. At first, some scientists refused to believe that the bones were ancient. British biologist Thomas Huxley, however, was among those who recognized that the skull was prehistoric and, in a brilliant essay published in 1863, convincingly argued that the skull had belonged to an extinct form of human being.

The portrait of the Neanderthals as shambling savages originated in part from an analysis of a nearly complete Neanderthal skeleton found in 1908 at La Chapelle-aux-Saints, a cave in southwestern France. After studying the skeleton, a French anthropologist named Marcellin Boule proclaimed that the La Chapelle man had been slow-witted and short and had lumbered along in a stooped position with his head thrust forward. According to Boule, the Neanderthals were neither direct human ancestors nor even members of the species *Homo sapiens*, to which all modern human beings belong.

Since Boule's day, growing evidence of the similarities between the Neanderthals and modern human beings has convinced many anthropologists that the Neanderthals should be considered *Homo sapiens*. But they say that the differences are significant enough to classify the Neanderthals as a human subspecies—*Homo sapiens neanderthalis*. Modern human beings are grouped in another subspecies—*Homo sapiens sapiens*. Other scientists, however, maintain that the Neanderthals

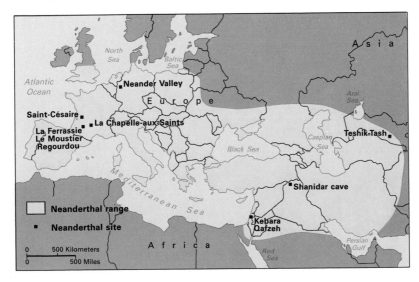

Where they lived
The Neanderthals lived throughout Europe and in western Asia from as early as 120,000 years ago to as late as 32,000 years ago. Archaeologists have found Neanderthal bones as well as tools, weapons, and other artifacts at many sites.

What Neanderthals looked like

Although Neanderthals and modern human beings are classified as members of the same species, Neanderthals were much stockier and more muscular than modern human beings are. Many scientists believe the Neanderthals' physical features, some of which helped them conserve energy, evolved as a means of survival in their Ice Age environment.

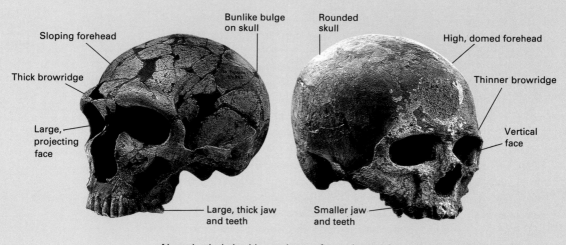

Sloping forehead

Bunlike bulge on skull

Rounded skull

High, domed forehead

Thick browridge

Thinner browridge

Large, projecting face

Vertical face

Large, thick jaw and teeth

Smaller jaw and teeth

Neanderthals had large, heavy faces that projected outward and massive jaws and teeth. Their browridge was thick and protruding. The top of their skull was slightly flat and the back had a bunlike bulge. In contrast, modern human beings have a high, domed forehead and smaller jaws and teeth. The browridge barely protrudes from a vertical face. The skull is rounded.

Neanderthals had broad shoulders, massive upper arms, short forearms and lower legs, and powerful knees. Neanderthal men had an average height of about 168 centimeters (66 inches). Neanderthal women stood about 152 centimeters (60 inches) tall.

Early modern human beings were lightly built. The men stood about 183 centimeters (72 inches) tall, while women averaged about 168 centimeters. Early modern human beings were not as strong as Neanderthals were, nor could they run as fast.

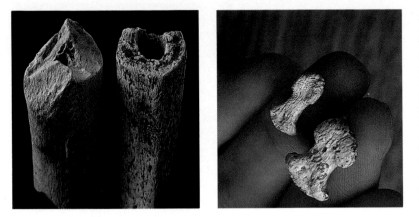

A Neanderthal thigh-bone, *far left*, was much thicker than that of even a modern weight lifter. Scientists believe Neanderthals' heavy bones supported huge muscles. A Neanderthal fingertip bone, *left*, is at least twice the size of a fingertip bone from a modern human being. Neanderthal fingers could exert massive force when gripping.

should be classified as a distinct species called *Homo neanderthalis*.

Anthropologists do agree that Neanderthals descended from *Homo erectus*, the first prehistoric human species to spread out of Africa. The oldest undisputed Neanderthal fossils, which have been found in Europe, are believed to be about 120,000 years old. By 90,000 years ago, the Neanderthals were also living in the Middle East and western Asia.

A vast intellectual and physical chasm separated the Neanderthals and early modern human beings. Although the Neanderthals survived as a group for nearly 100,000 years, their intellectual abilities were probably far inferior to those of the first modern human beings. Researchers say "probably" because no Neanderthal brains have survived. But the artifacts the Neanderthals left—or failed to leave—behind support this position. For example, their tools changed little over time, which suggests a lack of inventiveness. In addition, they made only limited use of their natural resources. Unlike early modern human beings, the Neanderthals apparently never used bone as a raw material for tools and weapons.

Neanderthal anatomy

The Neanderthals also looked different from early modern human beings. The Neanderthals had long and broad skulls, with sloping foreheads, thick, strongly arched brows, large noses, and faces that projected outward. These features contrasted sharply with the high, domed foreheads, rounded skulls, thinner noses, and vertical faces of modern human beings. Neanderthal jaws and teeth were much bigger and stronger than those of modern human beings.

The Neanderthals were stocky, with thick arm and leg bones and huge muscles. They had broad shoulders and brawny upper arms, and their thumbs could exert massive force when gripping. Fossil studies have also revealed that Neanderthals stood and walked upright without slouching. Boule, who had based his theories of Neanderthal anatomy on only the La Chapelle fossil, had not realized that this individual had suffered from severe arthritis, which had caused him to stoop. Studies

A Neanderthal hunt

Neanderthals were expert hunters who killed game of all sizes with sharp-edged stone spearpoints, *right*, tied to wooden sticks. Neanderthal hunters cautiously stalked their prey for long periods before attacking at close quarters, *below*. After wounding the animal, the hunters waited for it to weaken before delivering the final blows. The Neanderthals then butchered the carcass and dried the meat for future use.

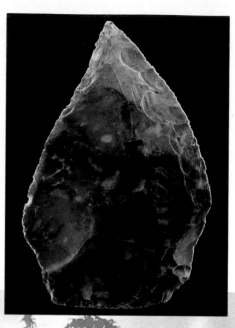

of Neanderthal fossils have also revealed that these prehistoric people were agile and capable of running fast.

Although some Neanderthals lived in temperate areas—in southern Europe, the Middle East, and western Asia—they are often thought of as Ice Age people. The physical features scientists consider as "classic" Neanderthal appear most pronounced in the Neanderthals who lived in Europe toward the end of the most recent Ice Age, which lasted from about 70,000 to about 10,000 years ago. Experts believe that the anatomy of the Neanderthals was an adaptation to the climate of nine-month winters and weeks of subzero temperatures. For example, the Neanderthals, like the Inuit, Lapps, and other modern inhabitants of cold areas, had short forearms and shins. Such features help preserve heat typically lost in the limbs when the human body is exposed to cold. The Neanderthals, who had only simple tools and weapons and lived in small, isolated groups, may have needed such powerful bodies in order to survive and reproduce under harsh conditions. In contrast, early modern human beings relied on technology to protect them from the elements. For example, modern human dwellings were better designed, and modern human clothing was warmer.

Questions about whether the Neanderthals could speak—and if so, how—have intrigued scientists for years. Unfortunately, the vocal tract consists of soft tissue that, unlike bone, is rarely preserved in fossils. As a result, scientists such as anatomist Jeffrey T. Laitman of the Mount Sinai School of Medicine in New York City, have had to rely on evidence of the speech center in casts of Neanderthal brains and on reconstructions of the Neanderthal *voice box* (larynx and pharynx). These reconstructions are based on studies of the voice boxes of modern human beings and ancient human ancestors. The evidence suggests that Neanderthals were capable of speech.

However, it does not indicate that the Neanderthals spoke as clearly as we do. Laitman, for example, believes they may not have been able to articulate certain vowel sounds, such as *a, i,* and *u,* as well as we can because their voice box may have been located higher in the throat. As a result, the sound-producing area in their throat was not as large as ours is. Nor do these studies provide any evidence that the Neanderthals had a well-developed language. The Neanderthals' ability to communicate was probably more primitive than our own.

A hunter-gatherer life style

Hard evidence of the way in which the Neanderthals lived is also scanty. Judging from studies of modern hunters and gatherers, some anthropologists speculate that Neanderthals probably lived in small groups made up of a few closely related families. Like some modern hunter-gatherers, Neanderthal bands may have come together in the spring and autumn to hunt and to engage in other communal activities. For example, at these gatherings, people may have arranged marriages and traded fine-grained rock for toolmaking. But archaeological evidence of such gatherings is lacking.

The Neanderthals made and used a variety of stone tools, including scrapers, saw-edged flakes for woodworking and shredding skin and meat, and small axes. Although they may also have made tools out of wood, none of these has survived.

The variety of fossilized fruits, vegetables, and seeds found at Neanderthal sites suggest that these people were opportunists, who took advantage of the profusion of plant foods that grew during the short summers of the Ice Age. But the Neanderthals were, above all, expert hunters in contrast to their more primitive predecessors, who relied heavily on scavenging from the kills of animal predators. The animal bones that the Neanderthals left behind indicate that they hunted every type of Ice Age animal, including arctic foxes, birds, the elephant-like mammoth—the largest Ice Age animal—and even the fierce, now-extinct cave bear. Many of the bones found at Neanderthal sites are those of animals in their prime, rather than old or young animals that would be easier to catch.

The Neanderthals' favorite prey, however, appears to have been reindeer. Ice Age Europe was a paradise for these migratory animals, who traveled over long distances between summer and winter pastures. In summer, they grazed on the open tundra in what is now central Europe. Then in autumn, they moved into the sheltered valleys of southwestern France, southern Germany, and other areas. Perhaps, as the reindeer migrated in spring and autumn, the Neanderthals ambushed them in narrow passes and at shallow river crossings. Here, groups of men and women could have stampeded large numbers of animals and killed them easily. They may have butchered the carcasses and dried the meat for use in the winter months.

Unlike their predecessors, who hunted with spears made of stone or fire-hardened wood, the Neanderthals used a more efficient weapon of their own invention—the stone-tipped spear. The key element in this innovation was the Neanderthals' ability to manufacture large numbers of relatively standard-sized, sharp-edged stone flakes. They did this by carefully shaping lumps of flint and other fine-grained rock into triangular and oval-shaped pieces. Then they would skillfully remove as many as half a dozen flakes from the piece, each of which could be used as a scraper or spearpoint with only minimal additional trimming. The deadly points may have been lashed onto long wooden staves. But because the Neanderthals used neither bows and arrows nor throwing sticks, their success in a hunt would have depended in large measure on their ability to get close to their prey without being detected.

On a Neanderthal hunt

A typical Neanderthal hunt would have been a lengthy enterprise, because stalking and approaching animals at close range takes much longer than does the attack and kill. We can imagine such a scene in southwestern France: Sleek bison graze peacefully on the lush summer grass, their tails lashing at circling mosquitoes. Nearby, the fast-running Vézère River murmurs as the late-afternoon sun paints the pine

A Neanderthal burial

Neanderthals were the first human beings known to have buried their dead, which suggests they believed in an afterlife. At Shanidar cave in Iraq, archaeologists found the remains of a 30-year-old Neanderthal man, *below,* who died 50,000 years ago. The body had been placed in a shallow grave in the cave floor, then covered with dirt and rocks, *bottom.*

trees in somber colors. In our re-creation, three Neanderthal hunters crouch behind a clump of low bushes, watching their prey. As a bison suddenly raises its head to listen, the men freeze. When the bison resumes grazing, the hunters relax. As the hours pass, the men move imperceptibly forward, slowly encircling a young bull at the edge of the small herd. By sunset, they are only a few feet away from their quarry.

Then, one of the men gives an inconspicuous nod. Quickly, he and the other two rise to their feet and jump alongside the bison. One man aims a sharp-tipped spear between the bison's shoulders. The other two men jump on the beast's back to slow it down. As the wounded bison stampedes, tossing its large horns, one man is thrown to the ground, a great gash in his side. The others jump clear and then watch the weakened animal in its death throes. As darkness falls, the animal finally collapses and the hunters deliver the death blow. Within minutes, blazing pine torches illuminate the kill as men, women, and children efficiently cut away the hide and dismember the bison before wild animal predators can move in.

Concern for the living and the dead

Neanderthal life was short and often brutal. Few adults lived beyond age 40. Many Neanderthal fossils show evidence of injury, such as broken bones, or of disease, such as malnutrition or arthritis. Yet such evidence also seems to testify to the Neanderthals' concern for one another. Many Neanderthals survived their injuries and illnesses, indicating that others had cared for them. One of the most interesting examples of this is the fossilized skeleton of a man found at the Shanidar cave in what is now northern Iraq. Despite having been born with a withered right arm, which almost certainly would have prevented him from hunting, the man had lived for about 30 years.

Although the Neanderthals apparently followed the same way of life for tens of thousands of years, they were responsible for some social innovations. They were the first known prehistoric people to bury their dead. The La Chapelle man, for example, had been laid in a shallow grave, surrounded by stone tools. In a nearby rock shelter named Le Moustier, archaeologists in 1909 found the skeleton of a Neanderthal boy who was about age 15 when he died. He had been buried with his head pillowed on one forearm. Also in the grave were burnt wild ox bones and a well-made stone ax.

Between 1909 and 1972, archaeologists found at least six Neanderthal graves—four of children and two of adults—at La Ferrassie, a cave near the Vézère River. Fifteen other empty graves lay nearby and may once have contained either skeletons or goods buried with the dead. A Neanderthal grave found at Teshik-Tash, a cave in Uzbekistan in central Asia, marks the eastern boundary of the Neanderthal homeland. There, in the late 1930's, archaeologists found the skeleton of a boy buried about 50,000 years ago. Six pairs of mountain goat horns lay around his head.

This concern for the dead was a major development in human prehistory. For hundreds of thousands of years, human beings simply abandoned their dead. Broken skulls and limb bones have provided evidence of such abandonments. In contrast, the Neanderthals buried their dead in shallow pits, sometimes with offerings such as mountain goat horns, as if they believed in an afterlife.

At Regourdou in southwestern France, for example, archaeologists in the late 1950's and early 1960's found a rectangular pit lined with stone and divided by a wall of stone slabs. One side of the pit held the skeleton of a young man, believed to have died approximately 80,000 years ago. In the other half of the pit, archaeologists found the carefully arranged bones of a cave bear along with the remains of more than 20 other cave bears.

Of course, we have no means of knowing what rituals might have been played out at Regourdou or the roles rituals might have played in Neanderthal life. Perhaps they served the same purpose as rituals traditionally have—to invoke supernatural protection during a harsh

Direct ancestor or dead end?

Nearly all scientists agree that Neanderthals evolved from *Homo erectus*, the earliest human species to spread out of Africa. But they continue to debate whether Neanderthals were direct ancestors of modern *Homo sapiens*—the species to which all living human beings belong—or were an evolutionary dead end. This debate has resulted in the development of two main theories to explain the Neanderthals' fate.

One theory states that Neanderthals were direct human ancestors, one of several forms of primitive *Homo sapiens* to evolve from *Homo erectus*. Modern *Homo sapiens* developed as a result of interbreeding between Neanderthals and other forms of primitive *Homo sapiens*.

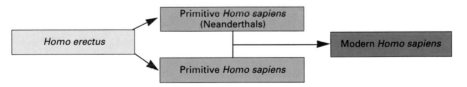

The other theory proposes that Neanderthals left no modern descendants. They were one of several forms of primitive *Homo sapiens* to develop from *Homo erectus*. But modern *Homo sapiens* evolved from another type of primitive *Homo sapiens* in Africa. Modern *Homo sapiens* then spread throughout the world, replacing Neanderthals and all other forms of primitive *Homo sapiens*.

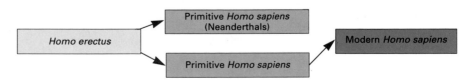

life that could end suddenly and violently, to explain the unknown, to transmit information from generation to generation, or to establish or reinforce connections between bands or family members.

What happened to the Neanderthals?

The most perplexing question about the Neanderthals, however, concerns their fate. By about 32,000 years ago, all the Neanderthals had vanished. Were they the ancestors of the modern human beings who replaced them? Or were they evolutionary dead ends?

One group of scientists, including C. Loring Brace and Milford H. Wolpoff of the University of Michigan in Ann Arbor, argue that the Neanderthals were among the direct ancestors of early modern human beings. They contend that groups of *Homo erectus* in Europe, the Middle East, and Asia slowly and independently evolved into several versions of primitive *Homo sapiens*. The Neanderthals represented one of these versions. Cross-breeding between Neanderthals and the other groups of primitive *Homo sapiens* resulted in the evolution of early modern human beings.

An opposing and more widely accepted viewpoint is that proposed by such experts as Christopher Stringer of the British Museum in London and physical anthropologist Erik Trinkaus of the University of New Mexico in Albuquerque. They contend that the Neanderthals were a specialized offshoot from the main evolutionary line to modern human beings. They point to significant physical differences between the Neanderthals and early modern human beings as evidence that the Neanderthals contributed little or nothing to the physical characteristics of modern people.

This theory was based, in part, on studies into the origins of modern human beings using mitochondrial DNA (deoxyribonucleic acid). DNA is the molecule of which genes are made. Most DNA is found in the cell nucleus and represents a combination of genetic material from both parents. Mitochondria, which are found outside the nuclei of cells of many plants and all animals, serve as the "engines" of the cells, converting food and water into energy. Mitochondrial DNA, however, passes from one generation to the next only through females and so is unaltered by genetic mixing.

In 1987, a team of scientists led by biochemist Allan C. Wilson of the University of California at Berkeley reported that their studies of the mitochondrial DNA of living women from many parts of the world indicated that modern human beings were descended from a woman who lived in Africa 200,000 years ago. From Africa, they said, modern human beings had spread throughout the world, replacing existing primitive human populations, including the Neanderthals. In early 1992, two groups of researchers independently attacked the statistical methods used in the 1987 study. They speculated that other groups of prehistoric people elsewhere in the world may be among the direct ancestors of modern human beings. However, in 1991, scientists led by molecular biologist Linda Vigilant of Pennsylvania State University in

University Park had conducted new molecular studies using more advanced techniques and mitochondrial DNA from 120 Africans from six parts of Africa. Their findings supported the African-origins theory.

In general, the archaeological evidence seems to support the dead-end theory. The oldest sites containing fossils of early modern human beings and their artifacts in Western Europe date from about 40,000 years ago. The latest known Neanderthal remains—found in 1979 at Saint-Césaire in France—are about 36,000 years old. If these dates are correct, then Neanderthals and early modern human beings coexisted in Europe for at least several thousand years. If that is so, it is unlikely that early modern human beings descended from the Neanderthals.

Early modern human beings may have occupied certain areas in the Middle East before the Neanderthals did. In 1988, French researchers reported that early modern human fossils found at the cave site of Qafzeh in Israel in the 1930's were about 92,000 years old, about twice as old as previously believed. To make this estimate, the researchers dated pieces of burnt flint from the site using *thermoluminescence*, a process in which objects that have been heated long ago are reheated and the amount of light they emit is measured. The longer the interval since the object was first heated, the more light the object emits.

Using the same technique, the French researchers also examined burnt flints from Kebara, a nearby cave where Neanderthal fossils had been found in 1931. They reported that these fossils were only about 60,000 years old. Such evidence suggests that early modern human beings actually arrived in the Middle East before the Neanderthals.

The Neanderthals, with their simple technology and inferior intellectual powers, were no match for early modern human beings. It seems unlikely that early modern people killed off the Neanderthals, but they may have pushed the Neanderthals from the best hunting grounds or simply outhunted them. In the end, the more primitive Neanderthals were unable to compete with modern human beings, and the last Neanderthals became extinct about 32,000 years ago.

Perhaps one of the most poignant findings about the Neanderthals was made at Saint-Césaire. There, buried among the Neanderthal fossils, were primitive versions of the type of tools associated with early modern human beings. If the Neanderthals had begun to adopt the more advanced technology of their modern cousins, they apparently did so too late.

For further reading:

Fagan, Brian. *The Journey from Eden*. Thames Hudson, 1990.
Fischman, Joshua. "Hard Evidence." *Discover*, February 1992, pp. 44-51.
Shreeve, James. "The Deepening Conundrum of Neanderthal Man." *Smithsonian*, December 1991, pp. 114-127.
Thorne, Alan G., and Wolpoff, Milford H. "The Multiregional Evolution of Humans." *Scientific American*, April 1992, pp. 76-83.
Wilson, Allan C., and Cann, Rebecca L. "The Recent African Genesis of Humans." *Scientific American*, April 1992, pp. 68-73.

BY DERRICK J. THOM AND ALLAN FALCONER

The Sahara's Bleak "Shore"

Scientists once thought that the Sahara was expanding south into an area called the Sahel. But new research finds that the desert ebbs and flows into this land of drought and famine.

Glossary

Desertification: A process in which a region becomes arid or a desert.

Erg: A desert area of sand dunes.

Oasis: A fertile, vegetated area in a desert where underground water is close enough to the surface for wells or springs to exist.

Reg: A plain of stones and pebbles in the central Sahara, deposited by ancient rivers as they flowed from mountains.

Sahara: The world's largest desert, stretching more than 5,630 kilometers (3,500 miles) across northern Africa.

Sahel: A region south of the Sahara extending from the Atlantic Ocean almost to the Red Sea.

Wadi: A dry valley or riverbed that carries water only during rare rainstorms.

The authors:
Derrick J. Thom is professor of geography and head of the Department of Geography and Earth Resources at Utah State University in Logan. Allan Falconer is professor of geography at the same university.

Along a sandy track on the eastern frontier of Niger is the village of Bouri, a small farming community in this west African republic. The villagers belong to an ethnic group called the Kanuri. For centuries, the Kanuri have cultivated millet on the surrounding dunes and grown corn, wheat, sorghum, melons, and some vegetables on irrigated lands adjacent to Lake Chad. They have raised cattle, fished the waters of the lake, and shared their environment with a group of nomadic herders, who migrate through the area with their animals.

Stories of "big rains" and "great floods" are common in Bouri folklore. Some people can even remember when the shore of Lake Chad came up to the edge of the village. But in 1992, Lake Chad was more than 50 kilometers (30 miles) away and no longer a large shallow lake but two smaller lakes. And since 1968, there have been no big rains. In fact, rainfall in this region has been below average, causing periodic crop failures that have led to food shortages and, at times, even famine and death.

The villagers live in a region called the *Sahel* (an Arabic word meaning *coast* or *shore*), which borders the great Sahara to the north. Like the waves of an ocean, the sands of the Sahara ebb and flow along the Sahel's shore. Because of an ongoing drought, parts of the Sahel are undergoing *desertification* (processes by which a region becomes arid or a desert). The sands of the Sahara have crept southward, pushing back previous boundaries of the Sahel and covering areas where people once grew crops or raised cattle. As a result of this, thousands of people have starved to death. Hunger in some places has become a way of life and is driving many people away from their villages. In some places, sand dunes have buried entire villages.

The current dry spell in the Sahel has scientists from all around the world studying the Sahara-Sahel border and asking important questions: Is the region's climate changing permanently, thus allowing the sands of the Sahara to relentlessly encroach into the Sahel? Or is this dry spell just part of a natural long-term fluctuation in rainfall that will end someday, causing the Sahara's sands to retreat?

The immense and arid Sahara

Stretching northward from the Sahel, the Sahara, the world's largest desert, reaches almost to the Mediterranean Sea. From the Atlantic Ocean on the west to the Red Sea on the east, the Sahara extends more than 5,630 kilometers (3,500 miles), covers an area of about 9 million square kilometers (3.5 million square miles), and includes parts of 10 countries. To place the Sahara in perspective, it is almost the size of the 48 midcontinental states of the United States. But, in contrast to the United States population of 253 million, the Sahara's population is only about 2 million to 3 million, less than one person per square mile. And most people live in scattered oases, where underground water comes to the surface to form springs or is close enough to the surface to be reached by digging.

Although seas of sand dunes, called *ergs*, are features of the Sahara

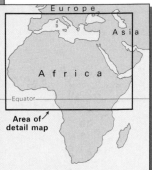

The Sahara and the Sahel

The Sahel is south of the Sahara, a vast desert in Africa. The Sahel extends through parts of Senegal, Mauritania, Mali, Burkina Faso, Niger, Nigeria, Chad, Sudan, Ethiopia, Kenya, and Somalia.

landscape, they represent less than 15 per cent of the total area and form only an outer ring of the desert. More than half the total area of the Sahara, inside the ring of ergs, are stone-covered plains called *regs*. Plateaus and wind-eroded rocks protrude from these bleak but gently undulating tracts of stones and pebbles. Finally, at the center of the Sahara, amid the regs, are outcrops of volcanic mountains.

Scientists do not agree on a single definition of a desert, though most say a desert is a region that can support little plant life because of insufficient moisture and dry soil. Areas near the North and South poles, for example, are considered deserts because they are so cold that the moisture is frozen and cannot stimulate plant growth. The Sahara is classified as a desert because of its low rainfall, less than 25 centimeters (10 inches) each year. Low rainfall limits plant growth, and, consequently, vegetation consists of scanty tufts of short grass and scattered patches of scrub bushes and dwarf trees. In an oasis, however, there is enough water to support date palm trees.

In addition to low rainfall, deserts may have considerable differences between day and night temperatures. Temperatures in the Sahara can rise to more than 50 °C (122 °F) during a day in July, yet drop to 20 °C (68 °F) at night because the clear, cloudless skies allow the land's absorbed heat to quickly escape into the atmosphere.

The semiarid Sahel

The Sahel is an area of semiarid *steppe* (vast plain) with short, grass-type vegetation, low-growing trees, and thornbushes. The Sahel region stretches southward from the Sahara to Africa's *savanna* (grassy plain)

Inhospitable lands

The sand dunes of the Sahara, *above,* make up 15 per cent of the desert. At the desert's fringes, the sand merges with scrubby plains in the irregular "coastline" called the Sahel. There, *right,* drought is common and soils are poor, though people still rely heavily on agriculture.

and extends west to east through parts of Senegal, Mauritania, Mali, Burkina Faso, Niger, Nigeria, Chad, and Sudan. Some geographers also consider the dry regions of Ethiopia, Kenya, and Somalia as belonging to the Sahel.

The Sahel is a transition zone between the arid Sahara and the well-watered savanna to the south. The Sahel is also a transition area of human activity. North of the Sahel, in the Sahara, people mainly keep herds or flocks of animals. South of the Sahel, people engage mainly in agriculture. But in the Sahel, people do both. Nomadic and seminomadic herders move their livestock into the desert during the rainy season and return to the Sahel during the dry season. Over the centuries, farmers and herders maintained a balance between the Sahel's human and livestock populations and water and land resources.

The region's green past

The land of the Sahara and the Sahel tells a dramatic story of past climate change. Geoligists have found that thousands of years ago the area was covered by grasslands, forests, and lakes. Ancient people hunted, fished, and farmed in a lush, green land. Geologic evidence shows that rivers once flowed across the now arid landscape of the Sahara and Sahel. For example, geologists have discovered that ancient rivers formed the regs. These rivers flowed from the central mountains into basins, picking up rocks along the way. The rivers deposited the larger, heavier rocks nearest the mountains and smaller, lighter gravel at the outer edges of the basins. These ancient rivers also cut ravines down through the rocks that form the central mountain ranges of the Sahara. The ancient river beds, called *wadis,* now channel water only during rare rainstorms when runoff from the surrounding area drains into them.

By studying land features, geologists also have discovered ancient natural drainage systems in the Sahara, including river courses, lakes, and deltas. This evidence has been supported by images of river channels revealed by special radar imaging equipment flown aboard the space shuttle by the U.S. National Aeronautics and Space Administration (NASA) in 1981. Geologists say that the Sahara region began to slowly dry out at the end of the last

125

Life in a world of sand

Some parts of the Sahel are under siege by the Sahara. In Mauritania, for example, the sand has drifted relentlessly over crops, pastureland, and entire villages, forcing many people to leave their homes.

Camps for refugees from drought-stricken lands press against the former boundaries of the city of Nouakchott, Mauritania's capital, *below.* Tens of thousands of people have abandoned their agrarian or pastoral way of life to crowd into shanties on the outskirts of towns and cities.

Men shovel sand away from their house after a sandstorm, *right.* Because winds blowing across the desert pick up and deposit sand and dirt in the area, sweeping sand from houses and bulldozing it from roads is a daily task.

A woman waters her tiny garden near Tiguent, a city south of Nouakchott. The fence, made of cloth and netting, was erected to keep animals from eating or trampling the plants.

Monitoring the shifting sands

Scientists examine satellite data and rainfall measurements to learn what is happening in the Sahel. So far, such measurements indicate that the Sahara's ebb and flow is closely tied to annual and seasonal rainfall.

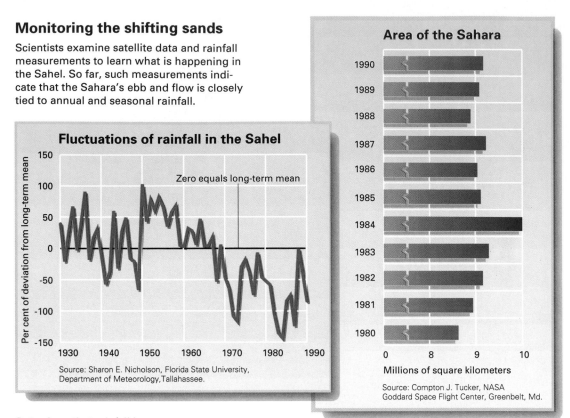

Fluctuations of rainfall in the Sahel

Zero equals long-term mean

Source: Sharon E. Nicholson, Florida State University, Department of Meteorology, Tallahassee.

Area of the Sahara

Millions of square kilometers

Source: Compton J. Tucker, NASA Goddard Space Flight Center, Greenbelt, Md.

Data show that rainfall in the Sahel is highly variable, *above,* but that since 1968 the region has experienced persistent dry conditions. A 1991 study of satellite data showed that from 1980 through 1990 the Sahara both expanded into and withdrew from the Sahel, *right.* The greatest expansion occurred in 1984. Researchers concluded that the shifts were due to annual rainfall variation.

Ice Age, about 10,000 years ago. As the ice sheets then covering northern Europe retreated farther northward, the Sahara region gradually began to expand, and by about 4000 B.C., it occupied an area similar to the present desert.

Many parts of the Sahara that are now virtually without life supported human settlement in ancient times. Thousands of rock and cave paintings, particularly in the Tassili-n-Ajjer plateau in the central Sahara, depict wild animals, hunting scenes, and people herding goats, sheep, and cattle. Archaeologists have discovered that the scenes depict life in the region from before 5000 B.C. to about 1000 B.C. To trace the climate change from wet to dry in the Sahara and the expansion of this vast desert over thousands of years, climatologists have studied the Tassili paintings and the written histories of the Egyptian dynasties (Dynasty I began at about 3100 B.C., and Dynasty XX ended at about 1070 B.C.) and the Roman Empire (27 B.C to A.D. 476).

Patterns of rainfall in the Sahel

The Sahel as a whole receives an average of 25 to 50 centimeters (10 to 20 inches) of rainfall yearly, an amount greater than in the Sahara. But the amount varies considerably from one location to another. The towns of Ouagadougou in Burkina Faso and Timbuktu in Mali illustrate the rainfall variability typical of the Sahel. Both have a dry season from November through April. In Ouagadougou, average rainfall for August is 26 centimeters (10 inches) and the annual total rainfall is 88 centimeters (35 inches). About 480 kilometers (300 miles) north in Timbuktu, the average August rainfall is only 8 centimeters (3 inches), and the total annual rainfall is only 23 centimeters (9 inches).

Scientists have found that rainfall for the region as a whole also varies considerably from year to year. Several years of above-average rainfall can follow several years of below-average precipitation. And every 25 to 35 years, drought occurs in the Sahel. A drought results when the average rainfall for an area drops far below the normal amount for a long period of time, for months or even years. Droughts of varying duration occurred in the Sahel in 1910, 1940, 1970, and 1984.

Ecological and human crisis in the Sahel

The years of below-average rainfall from 1968 until the 1990's have gained considerable attention for two reasons. The dry conditions have persisted over a longer period of time than in the past. And today, this dry spell affects many people, because the population in the Sahel has grown dramatically since the 1940's.

Before the 1940's, a lack of water had helped prevent significant increases in the numbers of people and animals in the Sahel. But beginning in the 1940's, Western aid and technology enabled people to drill hundreds of deep wells that tapped ground water far below the surface. Beneath the Sahara and Sahel, a vast amount of ground water has accumulated over thousands of years. The water in most places is at a depth of more than 2,000 meters (1.25 miles). Also, during the 1950's and early 1960's there was above-average rainfall. With abundant water available, human and livestock populations in the Sahel increased dramatically. Natural vegetation was cleared to grow more crops to feed more people, and more cattle were raised to support greater numbers of nomadic herders. In many areas, the increased water supplies helped support twice the number of people and animals that could have survived before the wells were drilled.

Then in 1968, the long dry period began. The pressing needs of the growing population resulted

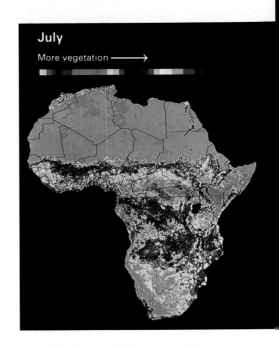

July

More vegetation ———→

A satellite image of Africa shows the Sahel (brown, white, and blue) and the Sahara (tan and orange) in July 1983, a month of the peak growing season north of the equator.

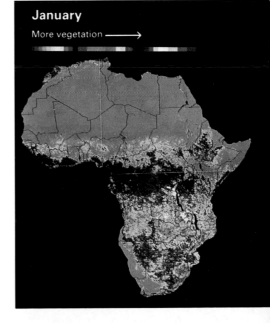

January

More vegetation ———→

Six months later, during the dry season, an image shows the Sahara "invading" the Sahel. In the desert south of the equator, the seasonal shifts, though reversed, show a similar ebb and flow.

in overcultivation of crops and overcutting of trees for fuel. The increased number of cattle caused overgrazing. Livestock herds began to congregate regularly around the wells, trampling and destroying virtually all vegetation for a radius of more than 32 kilometers (20 miles) around each well. This depletion of vegetation caused soil erosion. Topsoil was blown away during the long, dry, windy seasons, and experts say that in some places of the Sahel, damage to the land is virtually irreversible.

The situation became critical with the drought that began in 1970 and persisted until 1974. Crops failed and people starved. The people of the Sahel and Western relief agencies were unprepared for such a catastrophe. Perhaps as many as 300,000 people died, despite food relief efforts by the United States, France, Britain, the European Community, and the former Soviet Union. Livestock perished in every country of the Sahel. Estimates of animals lost ranged as high as 20 million cattle and 12 million sheep.

Between 1974 and 1983, though the dry spell persisted, average annual rainfall was sufficient once again to produce crops. Then in 1984 and 1985, drought occurred once again. It was not as devastating as in the 1970's, and Western relief was better prepared to meet this emergency—but not before thousands more people and cattle died.

Climate change or land abuse?

Beginning in the 1970's, the cause of the Sahel's persistent dryness spurred considerable speculation worldwide. Some experts suggested that permanent climatic change was occurring. A number of reports on the Sahel announced that the Sahara was advancing southward at rates of 3 to 10 kilometers (2 to 6 miles) per year. Indeed, weather data suggested that the Sahara-Sahel border, which receives 20 centimeters (8 inches) of rain, had shifted about 150 kilometers (93 miles) to the south. Such revelations seemed to support theories that the Sahara was continuing the expansion begun thousands of years ago.

Concerned over desertification in the Sahel and other parts of the world, the United Nations held a conference in 1977 in Nairobi, Kenya, to define and discuss the complex processes involved. The principal causes of desertification in Africa, the experts concluded, appeared related to land use, especially through overcultivation, overgrazing, and the cutting down of trees. The conference developed a plan of action to halt desertification by improving land-use practices. The plan called for an investment of $2.4 billion each year for 20 years. But by mid-1992, little of lasting benefit had been done. Reversing land degradation is a low priority for most African governments and is not attractive to many foreign investors, who are interested in more visible economic development programs.

Nevertheless, at least one positive outcome arose from the Nairobi conference. Scientists wanted to monitor the Sahara in more precise and detailed ways than ever before. Prior to the 1970's, scientists studying the Sahel had used a variety of methods. Climatologists had ob-

Worsening the problem

Experts say that human activities in the Sahel encourage desertlike conditions. Men, *below,* lead camels loaded with firewood into the capital of Niger. When people cut down trees faster than they can be replenished, the deforestation hastens soil erosion.

Camels nibble the leaves of a shrub that once was part of an oasis in Mauritania, *above.* Overgrazing adds to the problems created by drought because livestock trample the ground near oases and devour what is left of the plants.

served annual weather conditions, read historical accounts of floods and droughts, and analyzed general records of climatic trends. After the 1970's, scientists intensified their studies. But in many cases, researchers concentrated only on relatively small areas of the region. For example, a study by ecologist Hugh Lamprey, commissioned by the UN and published in 1988, based its conclusions on aircraft observations of sand dunes in northern Sudan. The study compared the vegetation boundary in 1958 with the boundary in 1975 and concluded that the desert in that region of Sudan had moved 97 kilometers (60 miles) southward.

But contrary evidence also emerged in the 1980's, when Swedish scientists from Lund University published the results of a detailed study conducted in northern Sudan. Using data from satellites and extensive ground investigation, they found no evidence of a current expansion of the Sahara in Sudan. Instead, the studies suggest that long-term drought and famine in the Sahel are caused by natural fluctuations of rainfall. This research stresses the Sahel environment's resiliency and ability to recover rather than its fragility.

Determining the causes of drought in the Sahel would enable international organizations, such as the United Nations, to develop better programs for aid to the region. The West has donated billions of dollars in food, equipment, and technology, but with little long-lasting benefit. The development programs have included planting and irrigating trees to stabilize sand dunes—a very expensive undertaking that has shown virtually no success in halting the encroachment of the desert sands. Partly as a result of new studies, some aid organizations have changed their focus from one of attempting to hold back the desert to one of addressing land abuse.

Tracking the Sahara's shifting border

One of the most important new studies reported in 1991, contradicting the idea that the Sahara is relentlessly moving southward, was reported by physicist Compton J. Tucker and his colleagues at the Goddard Space Flight Center in Greenbelt, Md., and at Texas Tech University in Lubbock. Tucker wanted to determine the extent of the Sahara by determining its entire southern boundary with the Sahel. These scientists pointed out that reports of constant southerly expansion into the Sahel were based on study data from only a few locations, and the studies did not take into account the droughts of the 1970's and 1980's. Given the vastness of the Sahara and Sahel and their characteristic rainfall variability, these scientists held that data from a few locations do not indicate trends for the entire region.

The scientists began by analyzing data obtained by weather satellites over Africa from 1980 through 1990. Weather satellites were designed to gather data showing the location and movement of cloud masses. However, there are many days with no cloud cover over desert regions, and consequently the satellites provided views of the ground. These images could be analyzed for indications of growing vegetation. The scientists theorized that the variation in rainfall over the Sahara and Sahel should correspond with the variation in vegetation greenness in the region. To measure the greenness of vegetation, the scientists looked at satellite images of visible light and reflected infrared rays, both of which reveal plant growth on the ground. The researchers used a ratio between visible light and reflected infrared rays to create a "vegetation index" for each month of the 11-year study.

The satellite images showed that the Sahara border actually shifted back and forth, somewhat like the ebb and flow of ocean tides. The vegetation shifted with the changes of precipitation during normal seasonal cycles in the Sahel. For example, in July—which is summer in the Northern Hemisphere—the scientists saw an area of greenness north of the equator and a reduction in the apparent size of the Sahara. By January, when it was summer in the Southern Hemisphere, the Sahel was experiencing its long dry season, and there was little plant growth. At this time, the Sahara appeared larger, and the vegetation greenness index showed that there was maximum plant growth between the equator and the southern tip of Africa.

Tucker calculated that from 1983 to 1984, the average southward movement of the border between the Sahara and the Sahel was 99 kilometers (62 miles). But from 1984 to 1985, the border moved to the north an average of 110 kilometers (68 miles). And from 1985 to 1986, it moved northward again, this time an average of 33 kilometers (21 miles). Although the Sahara's southern boundary in 1990 was an average of 130 kilometers (80 miles) south of where it was in 1980, its annual fluctuations during the study period were so great, the scientists said, that no long-term trend could be established.

Tucker's study also showed a close relationship between greenness (according to the vegetation index) and rainfall data collected from 42 locations in the Sahara. The study defined the southern boundary of the Sahara as the area with a rainfall total of 20 centimeters (8 inches) per year. By this definition, the scientists found that the Sahel fluctuated north or south within a 233-kilometer (145-mile) zone during the study years. Within that zone, it was sometimes possible to grow food and at other times it was not.

The movement of the Sahara as measured by the vegetation index or by the amount of annual rainfall was not uniform along the southern boundary of the Sahel. In many areas, the desert's boundary fluctuated greatly. But in some parts of southern Mauritania and from central Niger through western Chad, the variations in rainfall and in the location of the desert boundary were very small. These areas are of particular significance for future studies of desertification, according to the scientists, because it should be easier to detect changes to vegetation from other causes without having to deal with such a variable factor as rainfall.

Scientific evidence seems to point to a bewildering future pattern of rainfall and drought for the people of the Sahel. Climatologists say that at least 10 more years of study will be required before they can say whether the shifting boundary of the Sahara signals long-term expansion or contraction. In the short term, drought and intense human activities continue to threaten the land.

For further reading:

Porch, Douglas. *The Conquest of the Sahara.* Fromm International, 1986.
Salgado, Sebastiao. *Sahel: End of the Road.* Aperture, 1990.
Tristram, H. B. *The Great Sahara.* Darf Publications, 1985.

Chemists and food technologists are creating low-calorie substitutes for fat and sugar. But designing a tasty, safe, and practical product isn't easy.

Getting the Fat (and Sugar) Out

BY ELIZABETH J. PENNISI

The author:
Elizabeth J. Pennisi is the Chemistry/Materials Science Editor for *Science News* magazine.

An American in 1992 could eat a lunch consisting of a hamburger, baked potato with sour cream, soda pop, cake, and ice cream—and truthfully call it a low-fat, low-calorie meal. This type of meal is made possible by the sugar-free and fat-free foods and beverages that have recently made their way into grocery stores and fast-food restaurants.

In 1991, there was the introduction of a frozen dessert containing substitutes for both the fat and sugar of ice cream. Fake fats that could replace the real fat in commercially prepared cakes, puddings, sauces, cheeses, soups, and spreads also made their debut. A ground beef product with much of its fat replaced by a substance derived from oats appeared at grocers' meat counters. And the McDonald's Corporation introduced hamburger patties containing a fat replacement made from seaweed.

A 1991 survey done for the Calorie Control Council in Atlanta, Ga., showed that about 124 million—or two-thirds—of all adult Americans eat or drink low- or reduced-fat foods and drinks, and 101 million use low-calorie, sugar-free foods. Most of them choose no-calorie and low-calorie alternatives in response to changing ideas about the types of foods that should make up a healthy diet.

Excessive calories from sugar can contribute to weight problems, and sugar is also well known for its ability to promote tooth decay. Too many calories from fat have also taken their toll on the public's health. In 1988, the U.S. surgeon general issued a report linking high levels of fat intake to an increased risk for *obesity* (usually defined as weighing 20 per cent or more above a person's ideal weight). Obesity is a risk factor for high blood pressure, stroke, and diabetes. Research has also shown a relationship between high levels of fat in the diet and cancer. In addition, scientists have linked some types of fat to high blood cholesterol levels, which may lead to heart disease.

Such reports have prompted health experts and nutritionists to recommend that adults and children over age 2 not only watch their sugar intake but also limit their fat intake to a maximum of 30 per cent of their total calories. This has encouraged many people to turn to products made with fat and sugar substitutes.

Low-calorie sugar substitutes have been around for decades, but the recent trend in eating "light" has created a boom in this branch of food-technology research. Today, food chemists are seeking better substitutes by modifying existing foods, searching for new compounds in nature, and concocting entirely new substances. But the research process is complicated by our incomplete understanding of how the human body interacts with the chemicals we eat. For example, scientists do not yet know exactly why some substances taste sweet. Other questions involve the safety and usefulness of artificial fats and sweeteners.

Creating sugar substitutes

The first step in creating an artificial sweetener is to develop something that looks, tastes, and behaves like the real thing—sugar. Sugar belongs to the class of nutrients called *carbohydrates,* which also in-

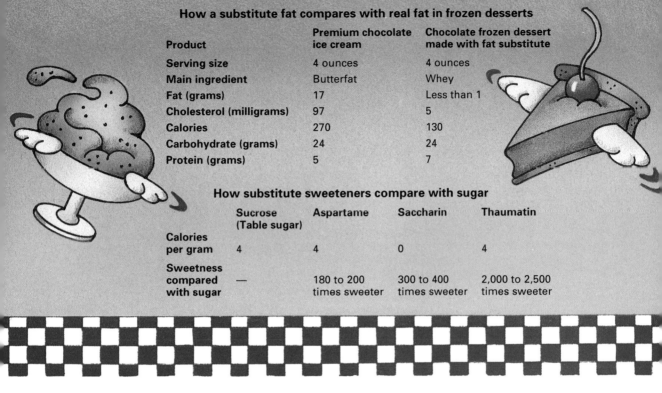

How a substitute fat compares with real fat in frozen desserts

Product	Premium chocolate ice cream	Chocolate frozen dessert made with fat substitute
Serving size	4 ounces	4 ounces
Main ingredient	Butterfat	Whey
Fat (grams)	17	Less than 1
Cholesterol (milligrams)	97	5
Calories	270	130
Carbohydrate (grams)	24	24
Protein (grams)	5	7

How substitute sweeteners compare with sugar

	Sucrose (Table sugar)	Aspartame	Saccharin	Thaumatin
Calories per gram	4	4	0	4
Sweetness compared with sugar	—	180 to 200 times sweeter	300 to 400 times sweeter	2,000 to 2,500 times sweeter

cludes starches. The most common sugar, table sugar, is called *sucrose.* In its most basic form, sucrose is a compound consisting of one molecule of *glucose,* which the body depends on for energy, and one of *fructose,* which makes fruit taste sweet. In the small intestine, molecules called *enzymes* cause a chemical reaction that breaks a sucrose molecule into its basic components of glucose and fructose. These smaller molecules are then absorbed through the intestine into the bloodstream and used by the body or, sometimes, stored as body fat. Sugar, like all carbohydrates, provides four calories per gram. (About 28 grams equal 1 ounce.)

Food scientists have a hard time tricking the mouth into tasting sugar when a sugar substitute is eaten. As many as 10,000 taste buds in the mouth and on the tongue sense sweet, as well as bitter, sour, salty, and, possibly, other flavors. As food is taken into the mouth, some food molecules make contact with tiny pores on taste buds. Scientists do not know exactly how taste-bud cells "taste" a molecule, but many think that different types of food molecules, such as sucrose, are shaped to fit different sites on taste buds called receptors. Through the nervous system, the receptors relay the message about taste to the brain.

Sugar, fat, and substitutes in the body

Substitutes for fat and sugar may have an authentic taste and texture—with few or none of the calories of the real thing. Scientists do not know exactly how the compounds affect the body, but they have developed some understanding of how substitutes for sugar, *right,* and for fat, *opposite page,* work in taste and digestion.

In the mouth, food molecules encounter some 10,000 taste buds located on the tongue, inner cheeks, roof of the mouth, and throat. Each taste bud has 60 to 100 receptors into which food molecules may fit. The receptors sense sweet, salty, sour, bitter, and other tastes.

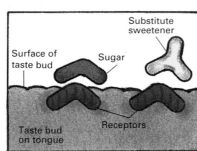

The sweet taste of *sucrose* (table sugar) molecules may be linked to their ability to fit into receptors on taste buds that convey a "sweet" message to nerves leading to the brain's taste center. Substitute sweeteners can be made of molecules that are different from sucrose, but they probably taste sweet because their shape allows them to fit into the "sweet" receptors. Some sweeteners may taste sweeter than others because they interact longer with receptors, or because they reach receptors faster and in greater numbers than other molecules.

In the digestive tract, compounds called enzymes break down specific types of food molecules such as proteins and carbohydrates. The food is then absorbed into the bloodstream and used as energy or stored. Some sweeteners are noncaloric because the body lacks a proper enzyme to break them down. These compounds pass through the digestive tract and out of the body. Other substitutes contain proteins or carbohydrates. But because they are much sweeter than sugar, they can be used in tiny amounts that contribute almost no calories.

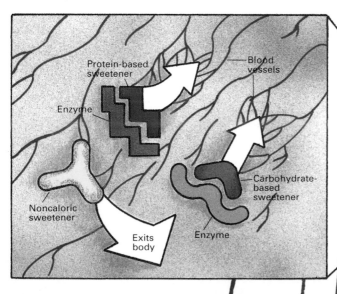

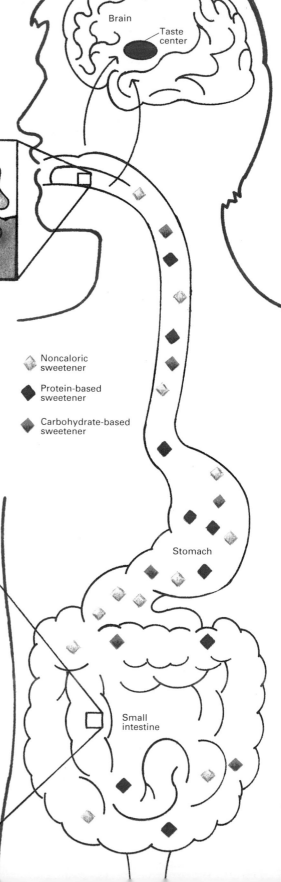

The "mouth feel" of fat is a slippery, creamy texture that substitute fats try to imitate. Substitutes made from foods such as egg whites or cornstarch may consist of microscopic particles that are soft and flexible, giving the substance the texture of fat. Some fat substitutes achieve the mouth feel of fat because they, like real fat, are composed of molecules called fatty acids.

The brain monitors the number of calories we consume. When the usual number of calories is reduced by eating substitute fats, the brain may signal the body, possibly through hunger, to eat more to replace the "missing" calories. Thus, fat substitutes alone may not help consumers lose weight or cut back on fat intake.

In the small intestine, certain enzymes break fat molecules into components that can be absorbed into the bloodstream. Other enzymes break down substitute fats made from proteins or carbohydrates—nutrients that provide fewer calories than does fat. But no enzyme exists in the body to break down some substitutes made of fatty acids. These compounds pass out of the digestive tract and contribute no calories.

Brain

♦ Artificial fat from fatty acids

♦ Protein-based fat substitute

♦ Fat

Stomach

Small intestine

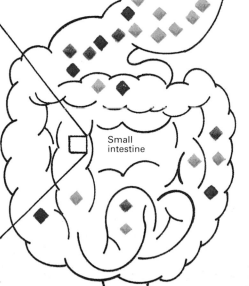

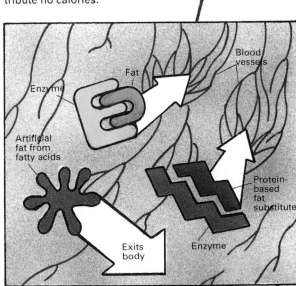

Fat

Blood vessels

Enzyme

Artificial fat from fatty acids

Protein-based fat substitute

Exits body

Enzyme

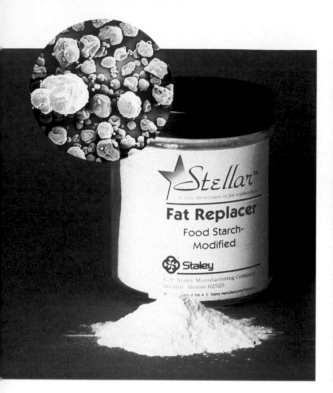

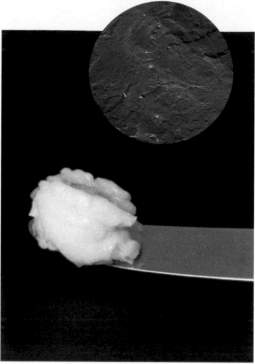

A fat substitute made from foods such as cornstarch may begin as a powder. Viewed through a microscope, the powder consists of tiny particles (inset). They are then mixed with water and subjected to extreme pressure, a process called *shearing*.

Shearing thoroughly distributes the microscopic starch particles throughout the water (inset). This process forms a substance with a smooth, creamy texture—similar to that of fat—that can replace fats used in food.

    Shape and also size may also determine the sweetness of sugar-substitute molecules. Murray Goodman, a chemist at the University of California in San Diego, found that many artificial sweetener molecules consist of two rings of atoms, which are connected by a short, bent chain of atoms. Unless the two rings in such molecules were lying in a plane (level with each other), they did not taste sweet. Several sugar substitutes look like this, Goodman said. Even though their chemical composition is different from sugar, such substitutes probably fit the taste-bud receptors that signal sweetness.

    No one knows why some substitutes taste so much sweeter than sugar. Some scientists think the molecules in the compounds may stimulate sweetness receptors longer or more intensely than sugar does.

    Researchers may create sweeteners by tinkering with the structure of chemicals found in nature to make them intensely sweet. By mixing a natural compound with other chemicals, or by subjecting it to heat, electricity, or other forms of energy, scientists can cause a chemical reaction that adds or subtracts atoms from the compound's structure. The scientists then perform taste tests to determine the sweetness of the new compound. Some experiments have yielded creations claimed to be thousands of times sweeter than sugar. The best substitutes are so much sweeter than sugar that only a tiny amount is needed for sweetness, and few or no calories are added to the diet.

Scientists can also make an entirely new substance, a synthetic one not found in nature. Synthetic compounds are considered noncaloric because the body lacks a digestive enzyme to break them down. Presumably, if they are not digested, they are not absorbed into the body and cannot provide nutrition or energy—or body fat.

For any sweeteners, additional tests investigate how the compound will behave under various conditions, such as in a hot, cold, moist, or acidic environment. A sugar substitute should remain *stable* (not break down or change) under many conditions. Tests also are conducted to demonstrate the product's safety for human consumption.

Saccharin and other sweeteners

Saccharin, the first sugar substitute to gain widespread use, was discovered by accident in 1879 by chemists at Johns Hopkins University in Baltimore. Saccharin is a white powder derived from a petroleum-based chemical. It is about 300 to 400 times sweeter than table sugar but has a bitter aftertaste. Saccharin came to market in 1900 and was widely used during the 1910's and 1940's.

The popular sugar substitute aspartame consists of compounds already found in foods. Chemist James Schlatter at G. D. Searle and Company in Skokie, Ill., discovered aspartame in 1965. The sweetener made its dietary debut in gumballs in 1981 and now sweetens more than 4,000 products. Gram for gram, aspartame—whose trade name is NutraSweet—contains as many calories as sugar, but it packs in so much more sweetness—180 times that of table sugar—that food companies do not need to add very much to get the desired flavor. Aspartame's disadvantage is that its molecules break down at high temperatures, making it difficult to use in baking.

In 1967, two German chemists discovered a new chemical that was similar to saccharin, had its atoms arranged in a ring, and was 200 times sweeter than sugar. This sweetener, Acesulfame-K, can be used in both hot and cold foods but, like saccharin, can have a bitter aftertaste. The human body cannot digest the compound, so it contributes no calories. Acesulfame-K received approval from the U.S. Food and Drug Administration (FDA) in 1988 to be used as a tabletop sweetener and in chewing gum, dry beverage mixes, puddings, and gelatin. The Hoechst Celanese Corporation in Somerville, N.J., markets this sweetener under the trade name Sunette.

Scientists have also found sweeteners by analyzing plants that people have used as flavorings or medicines. For example, thaumatin, a substance 2,000 to 2,500 times as sweet as sucrose, is derived from a west African plant whose leaves were used to wrap food before cooking. Thaumatin now flavors some chewing gum sold in the United States.

Some biochemists are trying to make substitutes from sugar itself, altering the molecules to make them intensely sweet as well as indigestible. Other researchers are hoping to market a sugar molecule that

A food technician studies a computer image of the NutraSweet molecule to understand how its size and shape may affect its sweetness. Sweet compounds tend to have similar shapes. Therefore, scientists can use computer graphics to design new types of sweetener molecules.

has the same chemical makeup as sugars used by the body, but is a mirror image of those sugars. These new sugars would look, cook, and handle just like table sugar and brown naturally when baked. But because the body lacks an enzyme to break them down as an energy source, mirror-image sugars would be noncaloric. However, further tests are needed to determine how these sugars might otherwise affect the body.

Scientists continue to modify and create substitute sweeteners because none of those discovered or produced so far tastes exactly like sugar. Furthermore, no single substitute works well under all the conditions in which sugar is used.

Developing fake fats

Many of the considerations challenging developers of sugar substitutes also confront the makers of fat substitutes. Like sugar replacements, "fake fats" mimic the real thing.

Most dietary fat is made of compounds called *triglycerides,* each of which contains three *fatty acid chains* (strings of carbon atoms with varying numbers of hydrogen atoms attached). Each of the chains is attached to a molecule of *glycerol,* a type of alcohol. As with sugars, special enzymes break fats down in the small intestine. The fatty acids are then absorbed through the intestinal lining into the bloodstream, where they are either used for energy or stored in the body. Fats are a concentrated source of energy, providing nine calories per gram.

Unlike sugar, fat by itself has little flavor. But it may enhance other flavors, perhaps by coating the mouth and distributing food molecules more effectively than can water. Most important is fat's smooth and creamy texture, which has a pleasant "mouth feel."

Fat substitutes must consist of particles that are too small for the tongue to distinguish individually, so they can be perceived as slick or creamy. Food scientists produced the first fat substitutes during the 1970's from starches that were used for thickening and stabilizing foods. These replacements consisted of carbohydrate molecules from potatoes, tapioca, corn, rice, or oats. When mixed with water, the molecules swell up, forming a thick gel. In this state, they whip and blend like fat or oil. Fine particles of the starch roll over each other like ball bearings, adding to the creaminess sensed in the mouth.

The new fat substitutes

Food technologists at A. E. Staley Manufacturing Company in Decatur, Ill., employ a different method to obtain the mouth feel of fat. In this process, acid turns cornstarch into a fine white powder, which is then mixed with water and *sheared* (subjected to extreme pressure). Shearing turns the mixture into a smooth, white cream. Because this product is mostly water—which is calorie-free—it has only one calorie per gram. It was introduced in June 1991 and called Stellar.

Food technologists at Hercules, Incorporated, in Wilmington, Del., use shearing to create a fat substitute made with *pectin,* a carbohydrate found in fruits and vegetables. Pectin is the usual gelling ingredient used in jellies. The company makes the fat substitute, called Slendid, by extracting pectin from citrus-fruit peel and turning it into a powder. Then technicians mix it with a little calcium chloride and a lot of water to form a gel. The gel is sheared to produce tiny, squishy particles that feel like fat to the mouth. Slendid, also introduced in 1991, contributes "essentially no calories" to food, according to its maker. Like Stellar, Slendid can be used in a variety of cold foods, such as commercially prepared salad dressings, margarine, sauces, frozen desserts, puddings, cakes, cookies, frosting, and soup.

United States Department of Agriculture scientists used the powder-to-gel process with a combination of oat starch and fiber. In gel form, this substitute, called Oatrim, contains about one calorie per gram and can be used in cold foods, baked goods, meat, and peanut butter.

Other fat substitutes use protein to create the mouth feel of fat. Like carbohydrates, protein provides four calories per gram. The only commercially available protein-based substitute is Simplesse, which the NutraSweet Company introduced in 1990 in Simple Pleasures, a fat-free "ice cream." A 110-gram (4-ounce) serving of Simple Pleasures contains less than 1 gram of fat, down from the 7 to 15 grams of fat in regular ice cream.

Simplesse originally was made of egg whites and a milk protein. To give these proteins the same sensory properties of fat, technologists blended, heated, and rapidly cooled them. This process, known as *microparticulation*, turns individual particles of protein into tiny spheres that easily roll over one another. However, when this product was heated, it became gritty. NutraSweet introduced a new version of Simplesse in August 1991. This product contains *whey*, another milk protein, and it can be used for cold foods or for baked goods.

Another group of fat substitutes are molecules not naturally found in the diet, though they contain fatty acids. These synthetic fats are indigestible, so they add no calories to the diet.

One synthetic fat, called olestra, has been under development for more than 20 years at the Procter & Gamble Company in Cincinnati, Ohio. Olestra may represent a breakthrough in the field of fat substitutes because it can be used for frying foods, while other substitutes, which contain water, cannot. Even though olestra is a synthetic product, it mimics fat closely because its molecules contain chains of fatty acids, just like real fat. Unlike fat, olestra has a sucrose molecule at its core instead of glycerol, and it contains six, seven, or eight fatty acids instead of three. The body's enzymes cannot break down this bulky, complex molecule, so it passes through the digestive system intact, unabsorbed and adding no calories.

Scientists at Procter & Gamble and other companies are making substitute fats whose molecules contain glycerol. But the fatty acids are longer than those that make up natural fats, so the body can only partially digest them. Thus, they add fewer calories than regular fat. One, called caprenin, is derived from rapeseed, coconut, and palm-kernel oils. Caprenin has five calories per gram instead of nine and is used by the M&M Mars Company in the Milky Way II candy bar.

Safety questions

Simply creating an artificial fat or sweetener does not mean that the ingredient will ever find its way onto our dinner tables. Most developed nations have government laws that regulate the use of additives in products sold for human consumption. In the United States, the FDA administers these laws. The U.S. regulations are complex, but, in general, modifications to food ingredients that have been in the diet for many years do not require testing or FDA approval.

Most brand-new food products do require government approval. These products include old ingredients used in completely new ways, synthetic additives, natural products that have never been used before, or natural ingredients that have not been previously combined. In these cases, the manufacturer must carry out safety tests and submit them to the FDA for approval. Some new ingredients may never receive approval. A few products may be approved only to be banned later if evidence comes to light showing that they may cause adverse effects in human beings.

Scientists usually test how much of a food additive can be consumed safely by feeding large amounts to laboratory animals and monitoring

Selected fat and sugar substitutes

Fat substitutes

Product	Composition	Characteristics	Current use in the U.S.	Potential uses	FDA status
Simplesse	Whey or egg whites and milk protein.	Digestible; 1 to 2 calories per gram; tends to break down at high temperatures.	Simple Pleasures frozen dessert.	Mayonnaise, salad dressings, yogurt, dips, sour cream, butter, margarine, cheese.	FDA affirmed its Generally Recognized as Safe (GRAS) standing in 1990.
Olestra	Sucrose poly-ester (sucrose and fatty acids derived from edible oils).	Indigestible; 0 calories per gram; withstands high temperatures and can be used for frying.	None.	Hot and cold foods, deep-fried snack foods, such as potato chips and French fries.	Waiting since 1987 for FDA approval as a new food additive.
Caprenin	Natural fatty acids.	Partially digestible; 5 calories per gram; similar to cocoa butter.	Milky Way II candy bar.	Candy and confectionery coatings.	Manufacturer's request for GRAS standing under FDA review in 1992.
Stellar	Water, mixed with a modified food starch made from corn.	Digestible; 1 calorie per gram; stable in baking but not deep frying.	Commercially prepared salad dressings, Danish pastry, hot dogs, sausages.	Pudding, gravies, soups, margarine, dairy products.	Meets GRAS standards; no limitations set for its use.
Slendid	Pectin—a type of carbohydrate derived from citrus-fruit peel—mixed with water and a gelling agent.	Digestible; 0 calories per gram; stable for baking but not deep frying.	Cookies, cheese products.	Salad dressings, meat products, soups, margarine, sauces, pudding.	Meets GRAS standards; no limitations set for its use.
Oatrim	Oat bran and flour treated with enzymes.	Digestible; 1 calorie per gram; stable for baking but not deep frying.	Healthy Choice brand ground beef product.	Frozen desserts, margarine, mayonnaise, cheese, peanut butter, baked goods.	Meets GRAS standards; no limitations set for its use.

Sugar substitutes

Product	Composition	Characteristics	Current use in the U.S.	Potential uses	FDA status
Aspartame (trade name: NutraSweet)	Combination of two plant-derived proteins.	Digestible; 4 calories per gram; loses sweetness over time and at high temperatures; cannot be used in baking.	Tabletop sweetener with the trade name Equal, soft drinks, instant cold drink mixes, cold desserts.	—	Approved in 1974, banned in 1975, and reapproved in 1981 for use as a tabletop sweetener and in certain foods and beverages.
Saccharin	Synthetic compound made from sodium.	Indigestible; 0 calories per gram; bitter or metallic aftertaste; can be used in baking.	Tabletop sweetener known as Sweet 'N Low, soft drinks, drink mixes, canned fruits, preserves, jams, salad dressings, baked goods.	—	FDA proposed banning saccharin in 1977 after it was linked to cancer in laboratory animals. Congress revoked the proposal and imposed a moratorium on the ban. President George Bush in October 1991 extended the moratorium to May 1997.
Acesulfame K	Synthetic compound made from potassium salt.	Indigestible; 0 calories per gram; stable for long periods of time and at high temperatures; may produce a bitter aftertaste.	Tabletop sweetener, beverages, food.	Baked goods.	Approved in 1988 as a packaged tabletop sweetener and for use in chewing gum, beverages, gelatin, pudding. Petitions pending for other uses.
Thaumatin	Plant-derived protein.	Digestible; 4 calories per gram; stable in heat; licoricelike aftertaste.	Chewing gum.	Flavor enhancer for meat, fish, coffee, pet food.	Meets GRAS standards for chewing gum only.

their health. The results of these tests help determine how an additive may affect people who eat a small amount per day over the course of a lifetime. Data is often also collected from studies of effects in humans.

Over the years, saccharin has fallen in and out of favor with safety experts. Products containing this sweetener bear a warning label, because studies during the 1970's linked saccharin to bladder tumors in rats fed large daily doses of the substance. The FDA in 1977 proposed banning the popular product, but public protest against the idea led the U.S. Congress to pass a law allowing its use. Scientists now believe that saccharin did not directly cause the cancer seen in the rats. Instead, the saccharin stimulated the rats' bodies to produce a protein in the urine, which, in turn, caused production of substances that led to bladder cancer, according to biologist Samuel M. Cohen at the University of Nebraska Medical Center in Omaha. Human beings do not produce these substances, he adds.

Cyclamate, a sweetener used in the United States from 1949 to 1969, was taken off the market because it also seemed to cause cancer in rats. In 1982, cyclamate's manufacturer asked the FDA to reconsider the ban and submitted results from 59 new studies showing evidence that cyclamate does not cause cancer. As of the end of 1991, the FDA had not determined that cyclamate could be reintroduced to the market.

The popular aspartame also concerned some safety experts. The FDA first approved aspartame for use in 1974, banned it the next year, then reapproved it in 1981. By 1988, however, the FDA had received about 6,000 consumer complaints regarding perceived side effects, such as headaches, mood changes, or allergic reactions, from aspartame. Yet several studies of the product undertaken by the FDA and other government health agencies did not uncover evidence that aspartame caused widespread harmful effects in people.

Fat substitutes have not elicited as much safety debate as have artificial sweeteners because many of them closely resemble foods that people eat already. Stellar and Slendid, for example, needed no special approval from the FDA. Fat substitutes also have been on the market for only a brief period of time.

But a few fat substitutes, most notably olestra, which has been awaiting FDA approval since 1987, undergo close scrutiny. Some experts are concerned, for example, that consuming large quantities of indigestible synthetic fats might cause diarrhea or interfere with the body's ability to absorb nutrients or medication.

An uncertain role in healthy eating

Even if tests show that a substitute is completely safe, it may not necessarily help people lose weight or become healthier. It is not clear whether the use of sweeteners helps people cut back on sugar, for example. Federal government reports indicate that from 1966 to 1988, Americans' annual sugar consumption increased by 15 per cent, suggesting that the growing use of sugar substitutes has not led to a decline in overall sugar consumption, at least among the population as a whole. Nevertheless, other studies have indicated that substitute sweeteners may help people reduce their intake of sugar and calories.

Scientific studies on the effects of consuming substitute fats have also shown varying results. Researchers at Johns Hopkins University reported in 1991 the results of a study in which 24 men of average weight ate breakfasts in which olestra was substituted for 20 or 36 grams of the fat the men had normally consumed. The researchers found that the participants replaced those missing calories by eating more during the rest of the day. However, the replacement calories did not come from fat, indicating that a fat substitute could help people reduce their fat intake, if not their overall caloric intake.

But fat, too, may sneak back into the diet. Scientists at the Monell Chemical Senses Center in Philadelphia reported in 1991 the results of a study in which 16 adults were fed lunch every day and asked to keep records of what they ate during the remainder of the day. The participants did not know that their lunch was adjusted to contain different amounts of fat during each week of the study. But they tended to make up for any missing fat by consuming more calories—including calories from fat—with other meals or snacks.

Some nutrition experts think a psychological component may be at work. They believe that some people consume low-calorie and low-fat foods so that they feel less guilty about later indulging in their favorite treats. But experts say that the only way people will benefit from fat and sugar substitutes is by using them as part of a balanced, low-calorie, low-fat diet—and that requires effort and discipline.

From our head to our heart to our stomach, many factors play a part in determining what goes into our mouths. As scientists sort out the body processes that determine how we taste, digest, absorb, and use food, they may not only be able to create new fat and sugar substitutes, but also understand further how their creations can be safe and effective alternatives to the flavorful foods we love.

Questions for thought and discussion

Imagine that chemists at a major university announced that they had created the perfect junk food—a compound that tasted rich and sweet and had no calories. But before the additive could be put on the market, two studies found that when laboratory rats were force-fed extremely high doses, 1 in 10 eventually developed bowel cancer. Four similar studies showed no such evidence.

While a government panel was reviewing the evidence, a prominent consumer group argued that even if the food does cause cancer in laboratory rats, it might save human lives by reducing the incidence of heart disease and obesity. They asked the government to require the substance to carry a warning label but to give consumers the option of purchasing the product.

Questions: If you served on the government panel reviewing this product, would you recommend that this food additive be made available to the public immediately? Why or why not?

The Space Science Student Involvement
Program offers contests that challenge
students talented in art and writing as
well as those interested in basic science.

Not for Science Students Only

BY HELENMARIE HOFMAN

Adam Bloom, a 9th-grade student in Silver Spring, Md., is designing
an experiment for producing structural foam aboard a space station.
Melissa Petruska, a 12th-grader in Allentown, Pa., is writing articles on
astronomy. Isaac Richter, a high school student in Long Beach, Calif.,
is drafting a design for a human settlement on Mars.

What do all these students have in common? In addition to an en-
thusiasm for space science and technology, they are all participants in
the Space Science Student Involvement Program (SSIP). SSIP is a
joint project of the National Aeronautics and Space Administration
(NASA) and the National Science Teachers Association (NSTA). It is
designed to inspire, encourage, and lend direction to students' interests in space science and technology by organizing national competitions for high school students across the United States.

Although SSIP is devoted to fostering interest in space science, it is
not aimed solely at students who are interested in the sciences. In the
belief that future space projects will require the participation of people with widely different skills and talents, SSIP also sponsors competitions for students interested in art, engineering, journalism, advertising, and marketing.

The program began in 1980, when NASA's Education Affairs Division and what is now the NSTA's Space, Science, and Technology
Division formed a partnership to design and implement SSIP. The

Tommy Ng, *opposite
page top*, the 1991 na-
tional winner of the
Space Science Student
Involvement Program
(SSIP) general illustra-
tion contest, stands be-
side his winning entry
with his teacher, Brian
Gerber.

149

first SSIP competition called for experiments designed to be carried out in space, with the winning students' experiments to be flown aboard space shuttles. By the early 1990's, more than 20 SSIP experiments had made it into space. Then in 1985, SSIP broadened its focus to include contests for junior high school students, as well as competitions in art, engineering design, journalism, computer science, and other fields.

By 1992, there were 14 competitions involving junior and senior high school students interested in art and writing as well as in science and engineering. And SSIP is adding mathematics and technology contests, which will encourage students to create designs for robots.

The SSIP competitions

There are four SSIP competitions for scientifically inclined senior high school students. In the first of these contests—an extension of the original SSIP space shuttle contest—students design experiments concerned with the long-term effects of weightlessness to be performed aboard the proposed U.S. space station. In another contest, computer buffs propose experiments to be performed on a supercomputer. A third contest requires students to create experiments that can be performed in a zero gravity facility—a "drop tower" in which the effects of zero gravity can be briefly simulated. For the fourth contest, students propose ideas for space-vehicle designs that can be tested on models in a wind tunnel, a facility capable of generating high-speed winds.

Two SSIP writing contests are of interest to young journalists in high school or junior high school. A feature article competition invites students to submit articles on space science that have been published in their school newspapers. A second journalism competition encourages students to develop their skills in advertising. For this contest, students create ads that will encourage others in their school to compete in the various SSIP contests. As in the article contest, each advertisement must appear in the student's school newspaper.

For young artists in junior and senior high school there are drawing competitions involving illustrations of Mars settlements. In one of these competitions, the student creates an overall picture of a human settlement on Mars. The illustration must show life-support systems, transportation facilities, and recreation areas, along with other essential features of a settlement designed especially for the Martian environment.

A second illustration contest asks students to use their potential drafting and engineering skills to make a detailed diagram of a Mars settlement, including information about how such systems as internal transportation and life-support work. The drawing must also show where settlers work and perform scientific experiments.

There are also two team competitions. The Moon Base Project, open only to junior high school students, requires teams to gather information about the moon and then design their own bases for human set-

(Text continued on page 159)

The author:
Helenmarie Hofman is associate professor of science education at Gettysburg College in Pennsylvania and the executive director of the Student Space Foundation in Washington, D.C.

Contests for young writers

SSIP sponsors two contests for students interested in writing news features or promotions. In one, students create advertisements for the SSIP contests that appear in their school newspapers. In the other contest, high school journalists write a news or feature article about an aspect of space or space science for their school newspaper.

Melissa Petruska, editor in chief of *The Leader*, the school newspaper at Louis E. Dieruff High School in Allentown, Pa., was the national winner in the newspaper article contest in 1991. In this excerpt from her series of articles on astronomy, Petruska, a 12th-grader, reports on the 25th anniversary of her school's planetarium, which is run by Gary Becker, a teacher at the school:

✍ . . . *Planetariums are a feature of cities; they are unnecessary in remote areas because in these regions, people have access to a clear view of the sky. "In an urban area like Allentown, the lights and pollution make the sky difficult to see," said Becker.*

He continued, "Therefore, the need arises for a place where people can observe the night-time sky minus the additives cities produce; hence a planetarium."

The main feature of the planetarium is to simulate the night-time sky. With the use of its equipment, Becker can show the motions of various celestial bodies, including the rotation and revolution of the earth, the movement of the planets, the revolution of the moon around the earth and the phase changes of the moon.

Besides this, the planetarium also compresses time. "I can show in several minutes an event which actually takes three or four months to occur," related Becker.

Through the course of the year, the planetarium welcomes approximately 8,000 students from across the Lehigh Valley area. Students in grades three, four, five and eight in the district all attend a program at the planetarium coordinated by Becker. . . .

A contest for young artists

In this contest, students create a picture of a human settlement on Mars. SSIP requires participating students to include details in their drawings about life-support systems and facilities for transportation and recreation. It also asks students to indicate how human settlers will interact with the Martian environment.

1991 Honorable Mention:
Allen Obciana
Diamond Bar High School
Diamond Bar, Calif.

Allen Obciana's vibrantly colored illustration of a Mars settlement shows a telecommunications tower; "Oxy Lab 1," a facility designed to create oxygen for the population; and a wing called "Thermal," where energy for the community is produced by tapping into a Martian volcano.

Isaac Richter's depiction of a multilevel human settlement on Mars shows one main above-ground structure covered by a large dome. This structure houses water tanks, land vehicles, and crop plants. The community's other structures are below-ground. There, a main compartment houses medical, recreation, dining, and recycling facilities. Smaller compartments house laboratories, computer rooms, and living quarters for the settlers.

1990 Honorable Mention:
Isaac Richter
Wilson High School
Long Beach, Calif.

Tomoko Anezaki's view of a future Mars settlement shows a structure about 1.6 kilometers (1 mile) in diameter. Designed to support a population of 1,000, the settlement includes a waste recycling center, communication and recreation facilities, and a large, open green where settlers can relax. The settlement's transportation facilities are located underground.

1991 Honorable Mention:
Tomoko Anezaki
Glenbrook North High
School
Northbrook, Ill.

*1991 National Junior High
School Winner:*
Bethany Flippin
North Stokes Junior High School
Danbury, N.C.

Bethany Flippin's illustration depicts a Mars settlement covered by transparent domes. An orbiting satellite provides a communications link with Earth. Plant life is abundant in Flippin's settlement, nourished by rain from condensation under the domes.

Contests for young scientists

SSIP sponsors two contests of interest to high school science students. In one, the National Aerospace Internship Contest, students propose experiments that could be performed on a supercomputer, in a wind tunnel testing facility, or in a drop tube research facility, which mimics the effects of near zero gravity. The winning students compete for one-week educational internships at a NASA research center.

Reena Barnett, a 10th-grade student at the Bronx High School of Science in New York City, was a 1991 national winner in this contest. She proposed an experiment using laboratory-created proteins called monoclonal antibodies. In the summary of her experiment, Barnett suggests that zero gravity might help monoclonal antibodies link up with drug molecules, forming a potent anticancer treatment:

> *[This] experiment will attempt to join monoclonal antibodies with a drug to form conjugates in zero gravity in the drop tube research program. It is hoped that these antibodies will join more securely at a zero gravity setting. These formed conjugates can then be injected [into] patients with cancerous tumors on earth. The conjugates will attack the tumor and destroy each layer of cells.*

In a second contest—the Space Station Proposal Contest—students propose and write experiments that could be performed on a space station. Students might devise experiments that test the effects of living or working in space. They could also propose scientific experiments that need to be performed in the unique conditions offered by space.

Christine Muth, an 11th-grade student at the North Carolina School of Science and Mathematics in Durham, was a 1991 national winner for her proposal to study the growth of plant tumors in space:

> *When crown-gall tumors were grown on carrots in the microgravity environment aboard the Cosmos 782 they were significantly less massive than those tumors grown in earth's gravity. These results seemed to contradict earlier findings that living tissue grows more rapidly in a microgravity environment. The proposed experiment attributes the Cosmos results to lack of pressure regulation aboard the [satellite] and suggests that samples be placed in pressurized containers to regulate pressure and keep it at one atmosphere. Responses will then be evaluated in terms of masses of tumors formed.*

A contest for young technical illustrators

In this contest, students design a diagram or schematic of the technical features of a human settlement on Mars. SSIP asks the students to label and identify the elements of life support, transportation, work methods, medicine, science, waste disposal, and recreation that they include in their diagrams.

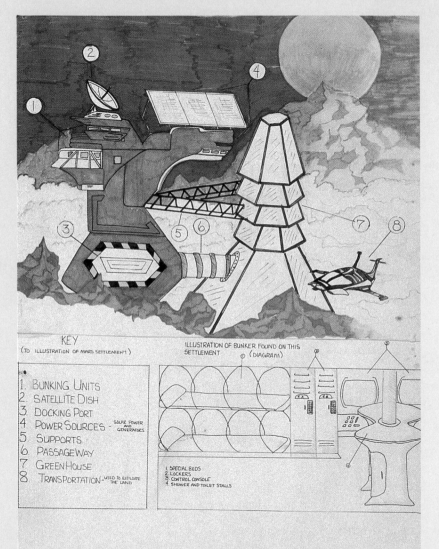

1989 National Junior High School Winner:
Joel T. Dewberry
Milwee Middle School
Longwood, Fla.

KEY
(TO ILLUSTRATION OF MARS SETTLEMENT)

1. BUNKING UNITS
2. SATELLITE DISH
3. DOCKING PORT
4. POWER SOURCES – SOLAR POWER AND GENERATORS
5. SUPPORTS
6. PASSAGEWAY
7. GREENHOUSE
8. TRANSPORTATION – USED TO EXPLORE THE LAND

ILLUSTRATION OF BUNKER FOUND ON THIS SETTLEMENT (DIAGRAM)

1. SPECIAL BEDS
2. LOCKERS
3. CONTROL CONSOLE
4. SHOWER AND TOILET STALLS

Joel T. Dewberry's diagram depicts a settlement's solar panels and backup generators, along with bunking units, a satellite dish, a flying vehicle, and its docking port. A lantern-shaped greenhouse is used to grow plants for food for the population and their livestock.

1990 Honorable Mention:
Matt Syrdal
Kellogg Middle School
Seattle, Wash.

Matt Syrdal's detailed schematic drawing includes plots where the settlers cultivate crops and a "vapor vacuum collector" that sucks water vapor from the atmosphere and converts it into liquid. Underground are living quarters and even a shopping mall with restaurants and stores. An "ice transporter module" is used to collect ice at the planet's polar caps and transport it to the settlement.

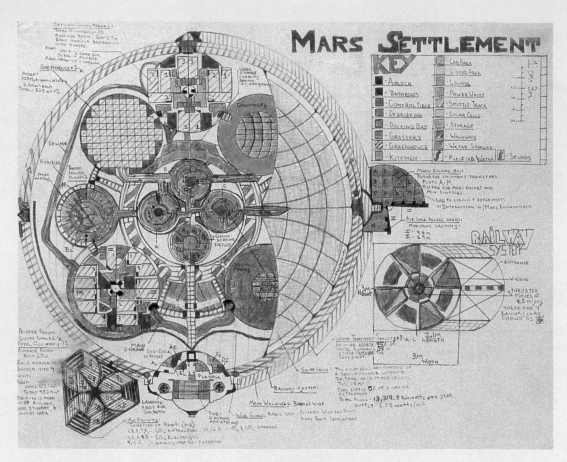

MARS SETTLEMENT

1990 National High
School Winner:
Jonathan Cohen
Comsewoque High School
Port Jefferson Station, N.Y.

Jonathan Cohen's schematic drawing of a Mars settlement includes greenhouses, three living areas, and a grassy park for recreation. A railway system links the settlement's modules, and solar cells and thermonuclear plants provide the community's power. Docking bays for shuttles from Earth are another feature of the settlement.

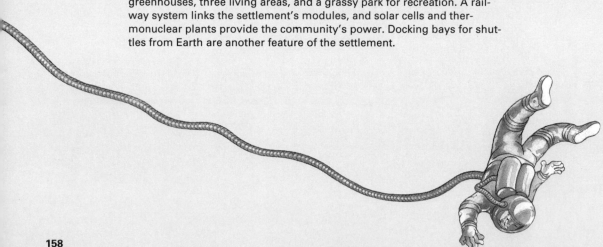

tlement there. Each team creates illustrations and a written report on how settlers on the moon will handle food supplies, transportation, safety, health, recreation, and scientific research.

Senior high school teams design Mars settlements for a contest much like the junior high moon base contest. The student teams must account for everything needed to sustain human life on Mars.

Judging and prizes

Each competition is judged by a panel of experts, including space scientists and teachers. The judges rely on several guidelines in evaluating each student's work. For example, they judge the creativity of each project and the accuracy of each student's information. In all cases, the judges demand that the project be neat, clear, and well organized, and that it give credit to published sources and to people who have helped the student.

Winners may receive an expense paid trip to a space science symposium held at a NASA center. Such trips usually include meeting astronauts and distinguished scientists. Some of the national winners in 1991 even had the privilege of meeting President George Bush in Washington, D.C., along with astronaut Charles Bolden and space-shuttle payload specialist Samuel Durrance. In recent years, the Student Space Foundation, a nonprofit organization for furthering teacher and student involvement in space science, has received donations from corporate sponsors to be given in the form of scholarships to selected national SSIP winners.

The program has encouraged many SSIP participants to continue their education and even pursue scientific careers. Meg Knowles, a 1981 regional winner from Skokie, Ill., is now a doctor with a specialty in internal medicine. "I still correspond with some of the other finalists," she says, "including John Velinger whose project subsequently flew on the space shuttle—what a vicarious thrill for me!"

"For me, this program awakened a desire to explore new frontiers of science," says Todd A. Silvestri, a regional winner in 1983 and now a chemical engineer. "I intend to make my contributions to space technology through my studies of advanced materials in the future."

The spirit of the program is perhaps best described by a tribute from Sherly L. Stuart, a regional winner in 1982-1983 and now an environmental engineer in Seattle, Wash. SSIP, she writes, "is a wonderful way to challenge high school students to use their imaginations in creating a relevant, achievable experiment. It is a great hands-on introduction to the scientific method and fundamental research. It was simply a terrific experience, and I hope it is continued for many years."

To obtain entry forms and contest rules, write:

Education Affairs Division
NASA Headquarters, Mail Code SE
400 Maryland Ave.
Washington, DC 20546

Physicists are achieving laboratory
temperatures ever closer to absolute zero—
the coldest that anything can possibly be—
in search of new properties of matter.

Seeking the
Ultimate Cold

BY CHARLES PETIT

One icy January day in Boulder, Colo., the temperature dropped to
–36 °C (–33 °F). That was awfully cold to most people there, but to a
group of scientists at the Boulder campus of the University of Colorado it was swelteringly hot. To those researchers, the coldest day ever
measured on Earth, –89.2 °C (–128.6 °F) in Antarctica in 1983, was
still sizzling. They consider even the expanses of space between the
galaxies, where the temperature is about –270 °C (–454 °F), almost
warm.

The University of Colorado researchers are among scientists pushing temperatures closer and closer to *absolute zero*. Absolute zero is not
the zero on an ordinary thermometer, like the 0 °C (32 °F) that marks
the freezing point of water. Absolute zero is the coldest temperature
anything could possibly be. The value of absolute zero is difficult to
determine, but it is very close to –273.15 °C (–459.67 °F).

In 1991, the Colorado researchers chilled atoms to the lowest temperature ever attained. Inside a special device that used laser beams to
cool the atoms by slowing them down, the temperature dropped to
about one-millionth of a degree above absolute zero.

Scientists are now trying to get things even colder. They think that
as temperatures edge ever nearer to absolute zero, matter will take on

Opposite page: Chilled
to a low temperature, a
disk takes on the proper-
ty of *superconductivity,*
loss of resistance to the
flow of an electrical current and repulsion of
other objects' magnetic
fields. The magnetic re-
pulsion allows the su-
perconductor to keep a
small magnet hovering
above it.

new properties, leading to unexpected insights into the physical laws that govern atoms and molecules. This research is being pursued in a number of countries besides the United States, including Finland, France, Germany, Great Britain, Japan, and the Netherlands.

Low-temperature studies have already led to some remarkable discoveries. Since about 1900, scientists have learned that very cold matter acts in weird ways. Many metals cooled to within a few degrees of absolute zero suddenly lose their resistance to an electrical current and become *superconductors.* Ultracold liquid helium becomes a *superfluid* that flows without friction and is able to crawl up the side of a beaker and pour itself onto the floor. Such phenomena can be explained only with the laws of *quantum mechanics,* a branch of physics dealing with the behavior of matter at the atomic and subatomic level.

Temperature measurements in the ultracold

Determining temperatures near absolute zero relies on special measurement techniques. An ordinary thermometer cannot be used for measuring ultralow temperatures, and even a thermometer using helium—which remains a liquid at the lowest temperatures—would not be accurate enough to register a difference of a millionth of a degree. Researchers thus use other sorts of instruments to measure temperatures near absolute zero. These include sensitive detectors that discern tiny changes in resistance to an electric current or differences in the speed with which the *nuclei* (cores) of atoms shift around in a magnetic field.

It is cumbersome to measure extremely low temperatures in degrees below zero Celsius or Fahrenheit, so scientists working in the realm of the supercold prefer to use the *Kelvin scale.* This temperature scale—named for the English physicist William Thomson, who received the title Lord Kelvin in 1892—starts at absolute zero. The value of each degree on the Kelvin and Celsius scales is the same. Thus, 0 °C equals 273.15 K, and 0 K equals –273.15 °C. (The degree symbol is not used in the Kelvin scale.) For simplicity, scientists often refer to degrees on the Kelvin scale as *kelvins.* For temperatures of a fraction of 1 K, they speak of *millikelvins* (thousandths of a kelvin) and *microkelvins* (millionths of a kelvin).

It was a long time before researchers had any use for such incredibly tiny temperature units. In the 1800's, when scientists first began trying to achieve extremely low temperatures, few imagined that experimenters would ever get so close to the ultimate cold.

The temperature-pressure connection

Scientific interest in low temperatures dates back some 200 years before that, to the late 1600's. Beginning at that time, several scientists, including the noted Irish chemist Robert Boyle, discovered the natural laws explaining the properties of confined gases, which pointed the way to the ultracold. These laws say that if the volume of an insulated

Glossary

Absolute zero: The lowest possible temperature.

Entropy: A measure of the randomness or disorder in matter, becoming zero at absolute zero.

Expansion cooling: Lowering the temperature of a gas by rapidly expanding its volume.

Kelvin scale: A temperature scale that has its zero point at absolute zero.

Laser cooling: Using laser beams to slow the motion of the atoms of a thin gas, thereby lowering their temperature.

Magnetic cooling: Cooling a substance by reducing the entropy of its atoms with an electromagnetic field.

Superconductivity: The loss of electrical resistance in some materials at low temperatures.

Superfluidity: The ability of very cold liquid helium to flow without friction.

The author:
Charles Petit is a science writer at the *San Francisco Chronicle.*

container is expanded, a gas within the container cools.

The reason that cooling occurs relates to the nature of heat. Heat is a form of energy—the internal energy of a substance. This energy includes the energy of motion, called *kinetic energy,* of atoms and molecules. The higher the temperature of a substance, the more kinetic energy its atoms or molecules possess—the more they race around and vibrate. Something very hot, such as boiling water, contains a great deal of energy in the form of the random motion of its molecules. It hurts to touch boiling water because the water molecules are moving so fast that they speed up the movement of molecules in the skin, causing the sensation of pain.

In the case of a gas in a sealed container, increasing the temperature causes the moving gas molecules to exert ever-higher pressure on the walls of the vessel. If the temperature of the gas is lowered, on the other hand, the kinetic energy of the gas molecules decreases, and the pressure drops.

Just as raising or lowering the temperature of a gas increases or decreases its pressure, varying the pressure affects the temperature. If you were to pull back on a piston on one side of a container of gas, thereby increasing the volume of the container and lowering the pressure, the gas would cool. In large part, that is because the molecules hitting the face of the retreating piston don't bounce back as hard as they would if the piston were standing still. As the average speed of the molecules goes down, so does their temperature. But the decrease in density of the gas created by the larger volume also plays a part in cooling the gas. At a lower density, the average distance between the gas molecules increases. As they move farther apart, the molecules must fight against atomic forces that tend to hold them close together, and in overcoming those forces, they lose kinetic energy.

First steps toward absolute zero

Using the pressure-temperature relationship of gases as a starting point, a contemporary of Boyle's, the French physicist Guillaume Amontons, attempted to determine the temperature at which a volume of gas would exert no pressure whatsoever against the sides of a container. That temperature, he reasoned, would be the lowest that could possibly be

Measuring low temperatures

Scientists working with low temperatures use the Kelvin scale, on which zero is *absolute zero,* the lowest possible temperature. A Kelvin degree has the same value as a degree in the Celsius scale. Thus, 0 K is equivalent to –273.15 °C, and 273.15 K is 0 °C—the freezing point of water.

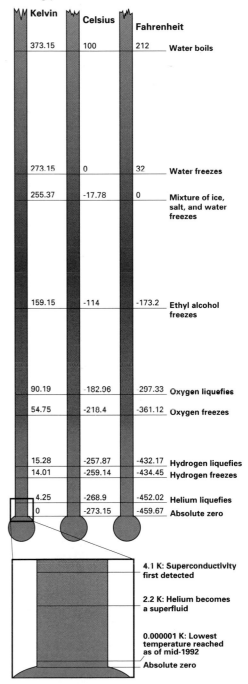

Kelvin	Celsius	Fahrenheit	
373.15	100	212	Water boils
273.15	0	32	Water freezes
255.37	-17.78	0	Mixture of ice, salt, and water freezes
159.15	-114	-173.2	Ethyl alcohol freezes
90.19	-182.96	297.33	Oxygen liquefies
54.75	-218.4	-361.12	Oxygen freezes
15.28	-257.87	-432.17	Hydrogen liquefies
14.01	-259.14	-434.45	Hydrogen freezes
4.25	-268.9	-452.02	Helium liquefies
0	-273.15	-459.67	Absolute zero

4.1 K: Superconductivity first detected

2.2 K: Helium becomes a superfluid

0.000001 K: Lowest temperature reached as of mid-1992

Absolute zero

achieved. Through a series of calculations, Amontons arrived at a temperature of −240 °C, not far from the true value of absolute zero. About 100 years later, two other French researchers, Jacques A. C. Charles and Joseph Louis Gay-Lussac, refined Amontons' formulations to arrive at the nearly exact figure of −273 °C for absolute zero.

Scientists suspected, however, that before reaching a state of zero pressure at extremely low temperatures, the gas would liquefy—turn into a liquid. In the late 1700's, the French chemist Antoine Lavoisier speculated on what would happen if Earth could somehow be dragged far from the sun. Lavoisier said the planet would get so cold that the air would rain down as a liquid.

Lavoisier was correct. The reason, scientists later discovered, is that atoms and molecules are not hard little objects that bounce off each other like ping-pong balls. They have a slight tendency to stick together due to atomic forces of attraction, and this tendency increases as they lose kinetic energy. The atoms and molecules of a gas move in a completely disorderly way, zipping about at high speed and colliding with one another. But when they get cool enough and are moving relatively slowly, atoms and molecules start to cling together, forming a liquid. In a liquid, the grip that atoms or molecules exert on one another still isn't strong enough to prevent them from sliding around, which is why liquids flow. But at a sufficiently low temperature, a liquid freezes into a solid. The atoms or molecules are now in a highly ordered state, aligned tightly into a crystal structure forming a single, rigid mass.

Lavoisier's prediction that atmospheric gases would liquefy at low temperatures was borne out by laboratory experiments in the 1800's. In 1877, still another French researcher, a mining engineer named Louis Paul Cailletet, liquefied oxygen, one of the two main gases in the atmosphere. Cailletet began by cooling oxygen gas in a strong container down to −29 °C at a pressure of about 300 times normal atmospheric pressure. He then opened a valve in the vessel to uncork the pressure. The temperature of the gas promptly fell by more than 200 °C, and droplets of liquid oxygen condensed for a few moments inside his apparatus.

The race to liquefy gases

The announcement of Cailletet's achievement excited scientists who had been trying for decades to turn atmospheric gases into liquids, and it started a race to liquefy them all. Using a somewhat more sophisticated apparatus than Cailletet had employed, scientists in Poland managed to produce cupfuls of liquid oxygen in 1883. The Polish researchers also liquefied nitrogen, the gas that makes up nearly 80 per cent of the atmosphere.

Experimentation with expansion cooling led to the development of efficient devices called *expansion refrigerators* for producing quantities of liquefied gases. In an expansion refrigerator, a piston expands a compressed gas, causing it to cool. This chilled gas is then used to cool another container of compressed gas, and this gas, in turn, is expanded

Temperature and the states of matter

All matter is made of units called atoms. A helium atom, *right,* consists of a nucleus orbited by two electrons. Atoms join together to form molecules. Water, for example, consists of two atoms of hydrogen and one atom of oxygen, *far right.* Temperature is a measurement of the energy possessed by atoms or molecules. At lower temperatures, atoms and molecules have less energy and move in an increasingly orderly way, *below.*

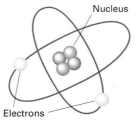

Helium atom

Nucleus

Electrons

Water molecule

Hydrogen atoms

Oxygen atom

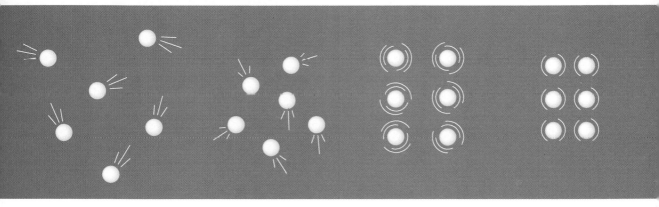

Gases consist of atoms or molecules flying about in a very disorderly way. Their energy of motion is known as *kinetic energy.* The atoms or molecules in a gas possess a large amount of kinetic energy.

Liquids form when atoms or molecules lose a certain amount of kinetic energy. They then cling together, and their motion becomes a bit more orderly. The temperature at which this occurs varies from one gas to another.

Solids form when liquids get cold enough for their atoms or molecules to line up in rigid structures. The atoms and molecules of a solid continue to move, but their movements are now very orderly.

Absolute zero would be a condition of ultimate order—atoms and molecules would be at their lowest possible energy and would move with perfect precision. But calculations show that this state can never quite be attained.

in a piston chamber. After being expanded, the gases are recompressed, and the cycle is repeated. With each cycle, heat is removed from the system, and the temperature continues to drop until the gases begin to liquefy.

By the late 1800's, scientists working with extremely cold temperatures had begun using the Kelvin scale, which was introduced in 1848. In 1886, English physicist James Dewar succeeded in lowering the temperature of oxygen to less than 55 K, causing it to freeze into a solid. And in 1898, he liquefied hydrogen by getting its temperature below 20 K.

Helium was the last gas to be liquefied. Using an expansion refrigerator, the Dutch physicist Heike Kammerlingh Onnes in 1908 lowered the temperature of helium gas to under 5 K, producing a cupful of liquid helium.

Liquefied gases were not just laboratory novelties—they soon found important applications in science and industry. For example,

How scientists achieve low temperatures

Low-temperature physics got its start in the late 1800's, when researchers learned how to liquefy gases by rapidly expanding them. In this century, scientists have developed new cooling techniques, using electromagnets and lasers, to push temperatures closer and closer to absolute zero.

Expansion cooling

Oxygen and the other gases in the atmosphere were first liquefied in laboratory experiments based on the principle of *expansion cooling*. In a rapidly expanding gas, the atoms or molecules must use some of their kinetic energy to overcome atomic forces tending to hold them together. The loss of energy causes the gas to become colder.

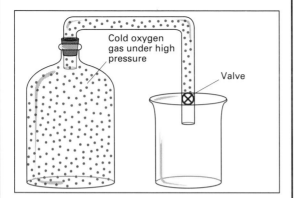

Cold oxygen gas under high pressure

Valve

Cold oxygen gas is held under high pressure in a sturdy container. A closed valve on the neck of the container prevents the oxygen from escaping.

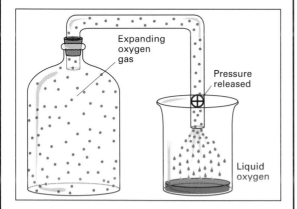

Expanding oxygen gas

Pressure released

Liquid oxygen

When the valve is opened, the oxygen rushes out of the container. As the gas rapidly expands, its atoms lose much of their kinetic energy and the gas's temperature plummets. This causes the gas to turn into liquid oxygen, which collects in a beaker.

Magnetic cooling

Magnetic cooling is based on the principle that making atoms or molecules more orderly makes them colder. The nuclear demagnetization refrigerator, *right,* reduces the random motion of atomic nuclei to almost nothing.

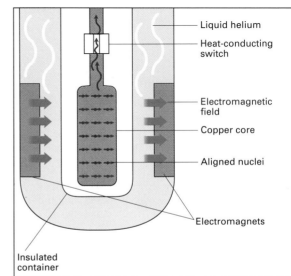

Liquid helium

Heat-conducting switch

Electromagnetic field

Copper core

Aligned nuclei

Electromagnets

Insulated container

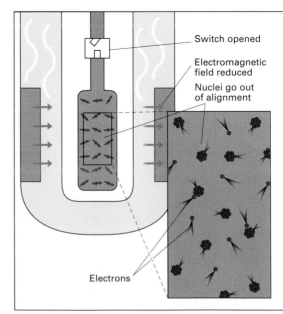

Switch opened

Electromagnetic field reduced

Nuclei go out of alignment

Electrons

Laser cooling
Laser beams can be used to slow the movement of atoms (red spot, *right*), thereby making them colder. With this technique, called optical molasses, scientists have achieved the lowest temperature yet, 0.000001 K.

A copper core within a highly insulated container is subjected to a strong electromagnetic field. This causes the nuclei of the copper atoms to align themselves with the magnetic lines of force, giving up much of their kinetic energy. The energy is absorbed by liquid helium through a special heat-conducting switch, lowering the temperature of the core to about 0.005 K.

When all the released energy has been removed from the core, the heat switch is opened, isolating the core from the outside. The magnetic field is then slowly reduced to a tiny fraction of what it had been. The copper nuclei slowly go out of alignment by absorbing energy from free electrons, thereby cooling the electrons. Repeating this process in successive stages can lower the temperature to about 0.00001 K.

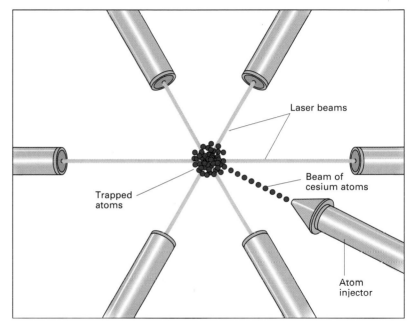

Laser beams

Trapped atoms

Beam of cesium atoms

Atom injector

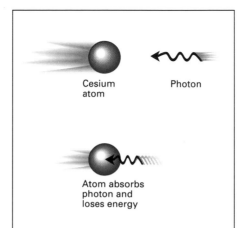

Cesium atom

Photon

Atom absorbs photon and loses energy

A beam of cesium atoms is injected toward the point where six laser beams intersect, *above*. The light beams confine the atoms so that they cannot move randomly. This effect is caused by *photons* (particles of light) striking individual atoms, *left*. Whenever an atom absorbs a photon, it loses kinetic energy and slows down.

the ability to liquefy air made it possible to obtain and store large quantities of oxygen for steelmaking, hospital uses, and other purposes. Today, the space program uses huge amounts of liquid oxygen and liquid hydrogen as propellants for rockets, and liquid nitrogen is commonly used as a coolant.

The discovery of superconductivity

Most of the pioneers of low-temperature physics expected gases to liquefy, but none of them predicted superconductivity. This phenomenon was discovered in 1911 by Onnes while he was studying frozen mercury. Onnes was puzzled to find that when the metal was cooled to a temperature of a few kelvins, its electrical resistance fell much faster than calculations predicted. When cooled below 4.1 K, it showed no resistance whatsoever. He trapped an electric current in a small ring of mercury kept below that temperature, and the current remained constant for days after the electrical source that initiated it was detached. Onnes concluded, correctly, that he had discovered a new property of matter. In later years, scientists found that many metals become superconductors, some at temperatures as high as 23 K. (Of course, that "high" temperature is still a very cold −250 °C [−418 °F].)

More than 40 years passed before physicists were able to offer an explanation for superconductivity. The accepted theory, developed in the 1950's, holds that the fundamental behavior of electrons changes at very low temperatures because of the effects of quantum mechanics. Electrons are tiny particles that make up the outer part of an atom, circling rapidly around the nucleus of the atom. In a regular *conductor*—a metal that conducts an electric current—the outermost electrons are not bound tightly to the atoms, and so they move around relatively freely. The flow of these electrons is an electric current.

At normal temperatures, a conductor's electrons cannot move completely freely through the metal because they are "bumped around" by the metal's atoms. But according to the leading theory of superconductivity, when a metal is very cold, electrons form pairs. Then, like couples maneuvering on a crowded dance floor but never colliding, the paired electrons are able to move unimpeded through the metal. In pairing up, it seems, the electrons are able to "blend together" and move in unison without resistance.

Higher-temperature superconductors

This explanation seems to account for superconductivity at extremely low temperatures, but in 1986 scientists in Switzerland found that some metal-containing ceramics are superconductors at much higher temperatures. By 1992, scientists had developed ceramics that become superconducting at more than 100 K, or −173 °C (−279 °F), and some researchers speculated that room-temperature superconductors may be possible. Scientists are still trying to formulate a theory for high-temperature superconductivity.

The new ceramic materials can be maintained at their superconducting temperatures with relatively inexpensive liquid nitrogen rather than the much colder and much more costly liquid helium required by metal superconductors. The cost difference could make superconductivity practical for many new technologies. For example, magnetically levitated trains, which require superconducting electromagnets, would be much cheaper to build than they are now. Superconducting devices might also be used for advanced power transmission lines and in new types of compact, ultrafast computers. But for the time being, superconductivity is finding application mostly in scientific research and in some kinds of medical imaging devices.

Another bizarre phenomenon: Superfluidity

Superconductivity was not the only strange new phenomenon encountered at low temperatures. Onnes and other experimenters also noticed that below about 2.2 K, containers of liquid helium suddenly sprang leaks. But it was not until 1938 that scientists in England and the Soviet Union explained why that had occurred. They reported the stunning news that helium at those temperatures has no *viscosity* (resistance to flow). The Soviet scientists named this phenomenon superfluidity.

If you stir superfluid helium with a spoon, it feels as though you are stirring air. What's more, the liquid, rather than spinning in one large circle like coffee in a cup, breaks up into numerous tiny *vortexes* (whirlpools). And if you pour superfluid helium through a fine-pored sponge, it flows as easily as through a hose. The reason the containers that Onnes and his colleagues were using to hold helium began to leak was that even microscopic holes let the helium run out when it reached superfluid temperatures.

During the 1930's, other investigators reported that heat flows almost instantly through liquid helium cooled to less than 2.2 K. Here was another strange and unexpected property. Liquid helium was a very puzzling fluid indeed at these low temperatures, and researchers were at a loss to explain its behavior.

Scientists now think that atoms of helium near absolute zero, just like the paired electrons in a superconductor, begin to merge and to "cooperate"

In a phenomenon known as the fountain effect, liquid helium jets from a bottle. At very low temperatures, liquid helium becomes a superfluid, flowing without friction and conducting heat very rapidly. Helium is the only gas that becomes a superfluid, because all other liquefied gases freeze at temperatures near absolute zero.

with one another. When that happens, the helium flows without friction and conducts heat with astonishing rapidity. Liquid helium is the only substance known that becomes a superfluid. Other liquid gases cannot be superfluids because they freeze first.

Toward new frontiers of cold

In search of other unusual properties of ultracold matter, scientists have developed techniques for pushing temperatures closer and closer to absolute zero. To get the temperature under 0.1 K, researchers in the 1960's developed the *dilution refrigerator*, a device using a mixture of the two *isotopes* (forms) of helium, helium-4 and helium-3. Helium-4, the much more common isotope, occurs naturally; helium-3 is produced by nuclear reactions. When mixed, the two isotopes tend to separate into two layers, one rich in helium-3 and the other consisting mostly of helium-4. But some helium-3 will migrate back into the helium-4, and when it does, the helium-3 it leaves behind is slightly colder. In this way, the migrating helium-3 exerts a cooling effect akin to that of an expanding gas. The dilution refrigerator uses pumps to keep moving the helium-3 back and forth, gradually reducing temperatures to below a millikelvin.

Imposing order on atoms

A process called *magnetic cooling*, invented in the 1920's and refined up to the present day, can achieve even lower temperatures. Magnetic cooling makes use of the idea that making things colder also means making them more orderly.

At one time, scientists thought that all atomic motion would cease at absolute zero. Now they know that while atoms do slow down as they get colder, they are never completely at rest, and even at absolute zero they would be in motion. But matter does become extremely orderly at low temperatures—all random motion comes to a stop. Completely cold atoms at absolute zero would move like members of a perfect marching band. In scientific terms, the atoms would have zero *entropy*. The entropy of a system is the amount of randomness or disorder it contains. Using a form of magnetic cooling called nuclear demagnetization, which was developed in the 1950's, physicists lower the entropy of atomic nuclei to almost zero and then use the nuclei to reduce the energy of electrons.

A nuclear demagnetization refrigerator consists of an encased metal core surrounded by a strong electromagnet. When the magnet is turned on, the nuclei of the core's atoms, which have a weak magnetic field of their own, align parallel to the electromagnetic lines of force. As they become orderly, the nuclei give up kinetic energy. This energy is transferred, by way of a special heat-conducting switch, from the core to liquid helium in a dilution refrigerator. When all the kinetic energy from the nuclei has been removed and the temperature of the core has dropped to about 5 millikelvins, the connection between the

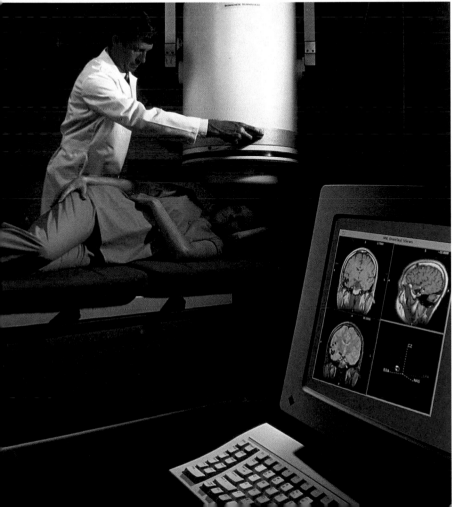

Practical applications of low-temperature research

An experimental magnetic train, *above,* rides on a cushion of air, held up and propelled by superconducting magnets. Already in widespread use are hospital medical imaging devices that employ superconducting coils to produce detailed images of the body, *left.*

core and the dilution refrigerator is severed. With the core now isolated from outside influences, the power of the magnetic field is gradually turned down, releasing the nuclei from its grip. This permits free electrons in the core (those that have become detached from atoms) to interact with the nuclei and gradually knock them out of alignment. The nuclei absorb energy from the electrons, which makes the electrons colder. But because the nuclei have a much greater heat capacity than electrons do, the nuclei become only slightly warmer. Thus, the average temperature of the core goes down. By repeating this process in successive stages, cooling the nuclei with each cycle and then waiting between cycles for the heat energy of the nuclei and electrons to even out, scientists have been able to drive temperatures down to about 10 microkelvins.

Laser cooling is the latest development in the quest for very low temperatures. Steven Chu, a physicist at Stanford University who helped pioneer the technique in the late 1970's and early 1980's, calls it "optical molasses," because the atoms being chilled are stuck in the laser beams like a spoon in cold molasses.

The optical molasses apparatus used by the University of Colorado experimenters consisted of six carefully aimed laser beams directed through the top, sides, and bottom of a small container. The beams were tuned to a precise frequency, or color. Inside the container was a gas of about 100 million atoms of the element cesium. The laser light exerted a force on the cesium atoms, pushing them into a tiny area in the center of the container and greatly reducing their random motions. The orderliness of the confined atoms corresponded to a temperature of one-millionth of a kelvin.

The Colorado researchers and their colleagues at other institutions think that further refinements in the optical molasses technique may lead to temperatures as low as one *nanokelvin*—one-billionth of a kelvin. Going from a millionth to a billionth of a kelvin may not seem like much, but a nanokelvin is 1,000 times smaller than a microkelvin.

Ordinarily, anything close to absolute zero should be a liquid or solid. The gas used in optical molasses, however, is quite thin, and so the atoms never get near enough to one another to freeze together and fall to the bottom of the container like a tiny rock. Some physicists say, therefore, that cooling a gas in optical molasses is a special case that may be of limited use in discovering new properties of matter. Thus, many researchers in low-temperature physics are continuing to concentrate on magnetic cooling.

Trillionths of a kelvin and beyond

In achieving ever lower temperatures, researchers face a dual challenge: Not only must they make things extremely cold, they must *keep* them that cold. And maintaining a temperature close to absolute zero is no easy task. Huge thermos bottles—called Dewar flasks after their inventor, James Dewar—are used to insulate equipment from heat. The tiniest vibration can warm things from the microkelvin to the millikelvin range by increasing the random motion of the cooled atoms. Physicist Robert Richardson of Cornell's low-temperature physics laboratory likes to say, with only a hint of exaggeration, that a fly doing a pushup on a Dewar flask can wreck an experiment. Even cosmic rays from outer space or the signals from commercial radio stations can add so much energy to a low-temperature physics apparatus that nuclear demagnetization refrigerators can't keep up with it. The closer temperatures approach absolute zero, the more disruptive such outside influences become. Richardson thinks that when experimenters start moving into the realm of nanokelvins—and beyond that, into *picokelvins* (trillionths of a kelvin)—they may have to move their equipment into caves deep underground to completely insulate it.

As they push temperatures closer to absolute zero, scientists expect to see matter behave in ways that are as strange and unexpected as superconductivity and superfluidity. At the University of Florida, physicists are trying to get free electrons so cold that they will orbit slowly through a small gold ring. Success in this experiment, the researchers think, could lead to a deeper understanding of magnetism. Magnetism ordinarily results when electrons in atomic orbits spin and move in such a way that their electric fields reinforce one another, giving the atoms north and south magnetic poles.

At the University of Colorado, the scientists experimenting with laser cooling think that if they can reach a temperature of 0.05 microkelvin, their cesium atoms may start to act like superfluid helium atoms or the electrons in a superconductor. In that state, the atoms would no longer be individual objects but would be "fuzzed together" into a sort of large quantum mechanical superatom, presumably with totally new properties.

But what are the limits of low-temperature research—just how cold can scientists make things? Physicists think it will be possible to continue almost indefinitely squeezing the entropy out of matter, achieving increasingly smaller fractions of a degree above absolute zero. Their calculations indicate, however, that absolute zero itself is a temperature that can never quite be attained.

How much remains to be learned about the nature of matter near absolute zero is anyone's guess. Although scientists exploring the frontiers of cold are already on the lookout for certain phenomena, they are also expecting the unexpected. They say it is possible that each additional step closer to the bottom of the temperature scale will bring new discoveries that cannot be predicted by current theory. Only one prediction seems like a safe bet: There are some surprises in store.

For further reading:

Chu, Steven. "Laser Trapping of Neutral Particles." *Scientific American,* February 1992.
Mendelssohn, Kurt. *The Quest for Absolute Zero.* McGraw-Hill, 1977.
Petit, Charles. "Vanishingly Close to Absolute Zero." *Mosaic,* winter 1990-1991.

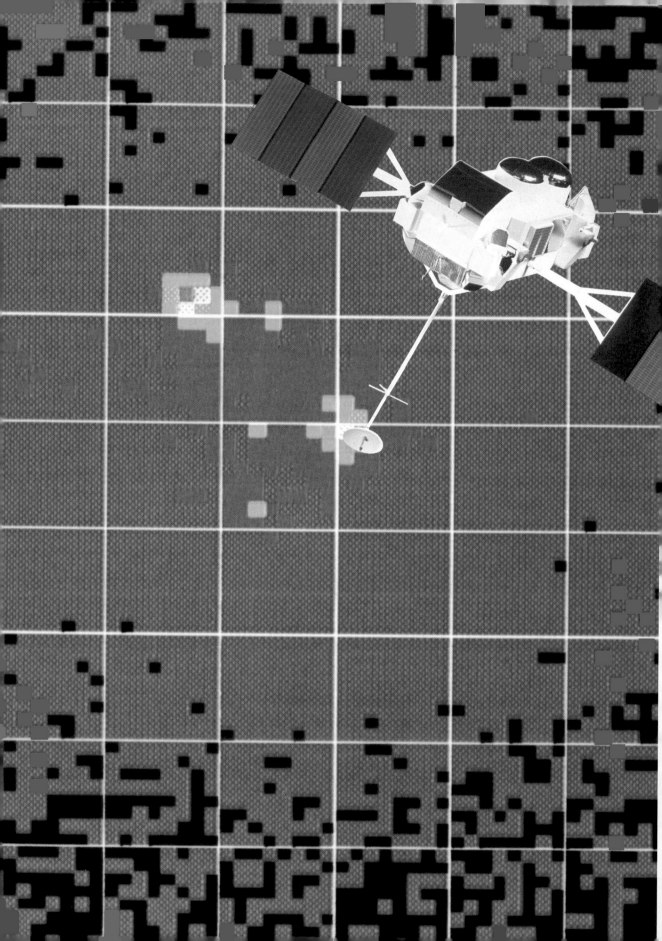

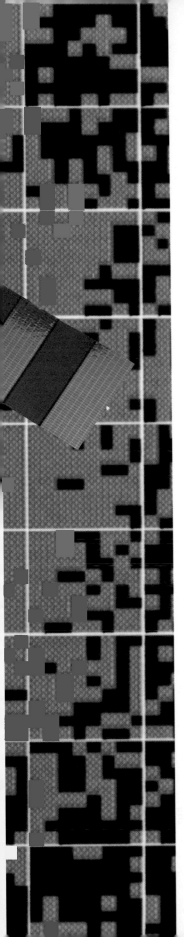

Early results from the Compton Gamma-Ray Observatory, launched in April 1991, offer tantalizing clues to some of the deepest mysteries of the universe.

Observing the Gamma-Ray Sky

BY DONALD A. KNIFFEN

The day was April 7, 1991. We had crowded into the control room at the Goddard Space Flight Center in Greenbelt, Md., a small group of scientists and engineers about to embark on a great venture. Two days earlier, the long-awaited launch of the Compton Gamma-Ray Observatory aboard the space shuttle Atlantis had followed an almost flawless countdown. It was now time to take the observatory out of the orbiting shuttle's cargo bay and to begin its scientific mission, a project sponsored by the United States National Aeronautics and Space Administration (NASA).

NASA was about to put into space the best telescopes ever made for observing gamma-ray emissions from such strange objects as, for example, black holes. Do black holes produce the energy that reaches Earth

Black hole: An object with such strong gravitational force that not even light can escape it.

Electromagnetic spectrum: The band of radiation that extends from extremely short gamma rays to long radio waves.

Gamma ray: The form of electromagnetic radiation with the shortest wavelengths.

Gamma-ray burst: A sudden, intense emission of gamma rays from an as-yet-unknown source. Also called *gamma-ray burster*.

Pulsars: Rotating, dense, collapsed cores of stars that send forth regular beams of radiation.

Quasars: Distant objects in the universe and sources of vast amounts of radiation.

Supernova: The explosion of a large star.

Wavelength: The distance between the crests of two successive waves.

The author:
Donald A. Kniffen, professor of physics at Hampden-Sydney College in Hampden-Sydney, Va., was Project Scientist for the Compton Gamma-Ray Observatory from 1979 to 1991.

from *quasars*—the most distant objects astronomers have ever detected? Closer to Earth, does a black hole fuel the enormous energies found at the center of the Milky Way? We hoped the telescopes would help us answer these and many other questions about the most violent and mysterious events in the universe.

Everything went beautifully as the observatory lifted out of the shuttle bay right on schedule and the solar panels that power it stretched out to their full 21-meter (70-foot) expanse. Next, we sent the command for the observatory's main communication antenna to unfold. The antenna would send the data from the observatory to a Tracking and Data Relay Satellite for relay to the ground.

The command went up, but nothing happened. Figuring we had sent the wrong command, we tried again. Then we varied the commands. But the antenna stayed locked in place. The hours wore on. As NASA Project Scientist for the Gamma Ray Observatory, I had been working on this mission since 1979. All of us involved with the observatory had dreamed for years of the discoveries that lay ahead. Now our hearts were in our throats. Would we have to settle for vastly inferior results than we had hoped?

Fortunately, the astronauts aboard the space shuttle—Jerry L. Ross and Jerome (Jay) Apt—had carefully practiced an emergency procedure that might solve the problem. At our request, they donned space suits, left the pressurized cabin, and ventured into the shuttle's cargo bay area. There, they worked to release the antenna by hand and crank it open. Suddenly, we heard the astronauts shout, and we saw on the control room monitor that the antenna had popped loose. The sigh of relief from the grateful project team was loud but brief as we turned to the remaining work of getting our mission underway.

Looking for gamma rays

The Compton Observatory's mission is so exciting because it gives scientists the opportunity to observe for the very first time large quantities of gamma rays with a sensitive set of instruments. Scientists are eager to detect gamma rays because they may help reveal the nature of some of the most interesting objects in the universe—and perhaps help us discover some new ones. Even a familiar object, such as the sun, might disclose some secrets through the gamma rays it produces.

Gamma rays themselves are not especially mysterious. We know their cousins well: radio waves, infrared radiation, visible light, ultraviolet light, and X rays. All these forms of radiation make up what we call the *electromagnetic spectrum*.

Electromagnetic radiation travels in waves, not totally unlike the waves we see at the beach. The waves may be characterized by their *wavelength*—the distance between the tops of two successive waves. Radio waves have the longest wavelength, more than one million times longer than the wavelengths of the light our eyes see. Gamma rays have the very smallest wavelengths—less than one millionth the wavelength of visible light. Gamma rays, whose wavelengths are comparable

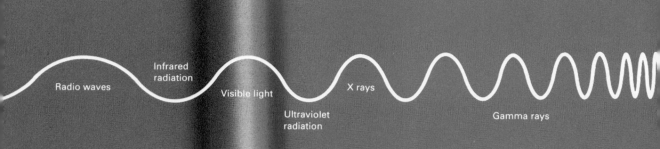

Radio waves

Infrared radiation

Visible light

Ultraviolet radiation

X rays

Gamma rays

to the diameter of an atomic nucleus or smaller still, are the last portion of the electromagnetic spectrum that astronomers have studied in detail.

The Compton Observatory was named after the American physicist Arthur H. Compton, who pioneered the study of high-energy radiation, including gamma rays. In 1927, Compton shared the Nobel Prize for physics for discovering a phenomenon named the *Compton effect,* which showed that high-energy rays sometimes behave as particles. Instruments aboard the observatory make use of his discovery in detecting gamma rays.

The Compton Gamma-Ray Observatory is the second of NASA's Great Observatories program, which will eventually place a total of four observatories in orbit for viewing different wavelengths of the electromagnetic spectrum. The first of these observatories, the Hubble Space Telescope, was launched in 1990 for viewing near infrared, visible, and ultraviolet light. Later in the 1990's, NASA plans to launch the Advanced X-Ray Astronomy Facility for studying X rays and the Space Infrared Telescope Facility for studying infrared radiation.

Radiation in different wavelengths helps astronomers get a better view of the universe. Imagine that your eyes could not see any green object. You could still see many things—but not the trees, the grass, or anything else that was green, such as lettuce, limes, or lily pads. You would be unaware of an important part of the world you live in. How could you understand it without knowing about the trees and the grass? We can think of gamma rays as also helping us see things in our universe that we could view in no other way and as giving us new information about objects we already know something about.

The extraordinary energy of gamma rays

What makes gamma rays so unusual is their extraordinary energy. This energy stems from their production by some of the most explosive events in our universe. To understand how gamma rays carry

Gamma rays are part of the electromagnetic spectrum, which also includes radio waves and visible light. Gamma rays have the shortest wavelengths of all electromagnetic waves.

Detecting gamma rays

Gamma rays are invisible and cannot be observed by ordinary telescopes because they pass right through glass and mirrors. An instrument for observing gamma rays must turn them into something detectable, such as flashes of light.

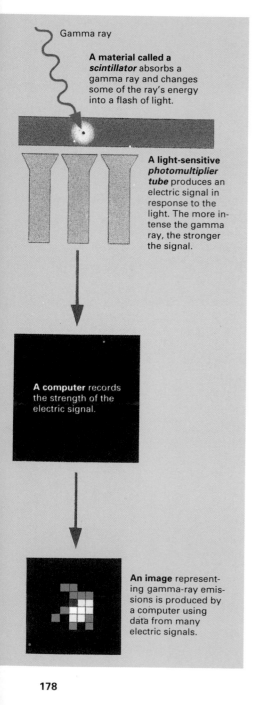

Gamma ray

A material called a *scintillator* absorbs a gamma ray and changes some of the ray's energy into a flash of light.

A light-sensitive *photomultiplier tube* produces an electric signal in response to the light. The more intense the gamma ray, the stronger the signal.

A computer records the strength of the electric signal.

An image representing gamma-ray emissions is produced by a computer using data from many electric signals.

greater energy than other radiation, return to the image of an ocean wave. Imagine counting the number of waves that hit the beach in an hour on a calm day. And suppose you did this on another day while a storm was blowing up. You would surely count many more waves on the stormy day. If you assume that the waves traveled at the same speed both times, you could count more waves the second day only if they came closer together. Waves that are closer together have a shorter wavelength. At the same time, their *frequency*—the number of waves counted in a fixed time—would be much greater.

Thus, the shorter the wavelength, the greater or higher the frequency becomes. This relationship holds true for electromagnetic waves because they all travel at the same speed—the speed of light. Because gamma rays have the shortest wavelengths, they also have the highest frequencies of any electromagnetic waves. A wave's energy increases along with its frequency, and this accounts for gamma rays' great energies.

Where gamma rays come from

It takes a lot of energy to generate such energetic waves as gamma rays and even more energy to produce them in numbers great enough that scientists far from the sources can detect them. To produce gamma rays we can observe on Earth, a distant object must release a tremendous amount of energy in a very short time. Only very violent and catastrophic events do this.

Let's consider some types of sources that meet this requirement. Very dense and massive objects—those that squeeze a tremendous amount of matter into a very small space—can provide the necessary energy. Black holes—objects with such strong gravitational force that nothing, not even light, can escape their surface—have an enormously dense concentration of mass. So do *neutron stars* (the leftover cores of dead stars), which squeeze about a billion tons of matter into each cubic centimeter (0.06 cubic inch).

The gravitational force of such dense bodies pulls in matter from stars, gas, dust, and other objects in space. The atoms that make up matter are sucked toward the massive object and accelerated to very high speeds. As the high-speed particles smash into one another, some of their energy is given off as gamma rays.

Other sources of gamma rays are *supernovae*—the dramatic explosions of large stars that run out of nuclear fuel and then collapse inward as a result of gravity. Scientists theorize that heavy radioactive elements are formed from lighter elements during supernovae, releasing gamma rays in the process. Each radioactive element emits gamma rays with a distinct energy, providing a "signature" by which scientists can identify the element. In a dramatic confirmation of the theory of how heavy elements form, scientists in 1987 observed gamma rays emitted from a radioactive form of cobalt in a supernova in a nearby galaxy called the Large Magellanic Cloud.

Catching some gamma rays

Detecting gamma rays is difficult. Gamma rays from space hardly ever reach Earth's surface because they collide with molecules of air in the thick atmosphere surrounding Earth. As a result, they lose all their energy before reaching Earth's surface. Thus, gamma-ray astronomy depends on putting instruments in space. But even an orbiting observatory may have difficulty detecting gamma rays, partly because of their extremely short wavelengths. These tiny wavelengths prevent gamma rays from being reflected by mirrors or focused by lenses, and so we cannot use ordinary telescopes to observe gamma rays.

Complicating the detection problem is the scarcity of gamma rays emitted by black holes, neutron stars, and other sources. Furthermore, gamma rays, like rays of light, spread out as they travel, so that the farther we are from the source, the fewer the gamma rays that reach us.

Scientists describe gamma-ray emissions as strong or weak, depending on the amount of radiation that reaches us. It's easier to understand these descriptions by thinking of the terms used for visible light: *bright* and *faint.* Large numbers of gamma rays produce a signal described as strong, bright, or intense, while small numbers produce a weak or a faint signal. A beam of light can be faint because little light is given off or because the source is very far away. So, too, with gamma-ray emissions. The term *energetic,* however, refers to frequency. High-frequency, short-wavelength gamma rays are more energetic than gamma rays with lower frequencies and longer wavelengths.

To collect enough gamma rays so that scientists can observe and locate their sources, gamma-ray detectors need a large surface area. All gamma-ray detectors share certain features. They first convert incoming gamma rays into something that can be more easily observed—usually, pulses of visible light. Most of the instruments aboard the Compton Observatory use special materials called *scintillators* that produce a flash of light as they absorb a gamma ray. In response to these flashes, light-sensitive photomultiplier tubes inside the detectors emit electric signals, which a computer can record. The more energetic the gamma ray, the brighter the pulse of light and the stronger the electric signal. Computers use the electric signals to construct an image that shows the strength and position of the gamma rays detected.

Besides determining the energy, intensity, and direction of incoming gamma rays, the detectors also need a way of filtering out other types of radiation, chiefly *cosmic rays* (high-energy particles that origi-

Surveying the gamma-ray sky

Orbiting high above Earth's atmosphere, the Compton Gamma Ray Observatory detects invisible gamma rays, which cannot penetrate Earth's atmosphere. Its four instruments—the largest and most sensitive ever to observe the gamma-ray sky—each cover a different range of gamma-ray wavelengths. Together, they map the sources of gamma-ray emissions in space.

Imaging Compton Telescope (Comptel) observes gamma rays produced by such sources as *neutron stars* (the dense cores of collapsed stars) and galaxies.

Solar panels power the observatory.

Energetic Gamma-Ray Experiment Telescope (EGRET) picks up gamma rays produced by the most violent events in the universe.

Burst and Transient Source Experiment (BATSE) consists of eight detectors that search for mysterious gamma-ray bursts.

Oriented Scintillation Spectrometer Experiment (OSSE) monitors emissions chiefly from radioactive elements, which scientists believe formed in the explosions of large stars.

Antenna transmits data to a Tracking and Relay Satellite for relay to scientists on the ground.

The Compton Observatory follows a circular path 380 to 450 kilometers (236 to 280 miles) above Earth. It completes an orbit every 93 minutes.

Equator

nate in outer space). Cosmic rays are at least 10,000 times more abundant in space than gamma rays. Scintillators surrounding gamma-ray detectors alert the detectors to incoming cosmic rays and prevent them from responding to these particles.

Early gamma-ray discoveries

Before the Compton Observatory, only a few small gamma-ray instruments had gone into space. Some orbited on spacecraft and others had been carried into the upper reaches of Earth's atmosphere by scientific balloons.

Satellites launched by NASA in the 1970's and the COS-B satellite, orbited by the European Space Agency from 1975 to 1982, established that many strong, high-energy gamma-ray sources are concentrated along the disk of the Milky Way galaxy. Scientists believe these emissions result primarily from collisions of cosmic rays with the gas and dust found between the stars.

Other gamma-ray sources previously observed include two *pulsars* (rapidly spinning neutron stars), which emit gamma rays in regular pulses. Astronomers have picked up radio waves from nearly 500 pulsars, and they believe many of these pulsars give off gamma rays as well. Previous instruments, however, lacked the sensitivity to detect gamma rays because pulsars are weak gamma-ray sources. Undetected gamma-ray pulsars may be contributing to the overall gamma-ray emission from the Milky Way.

Gamma-ray observations have also indicated that a black hole may lie at the center of the Milky Way. During the violent interactions believed to occur near black holes, negatively charged electrons, particles that orbit atomic nuclei, collide with their positively charged counterparts called *positrons*. In these collisions, the electrons and positrons annihilate one another, producing two gamma rays. According to theory, only a massive black hole can account for the tremendous amount of radiation observed at the center of the galaxy.

One other exciting discovery, first reported in 1973, was of short, extremely strong bursts of low-energy gamma rays coming from sources we have yet to identify. Gamma-ray bursts were first detected by satellites that monitored the testing of nuclear weapons in the atmosphere. Scientists soon realized that the gamma rays came from outside the atmosphere, not from nuclear explosions. The locations of the bursts do not correspond to any known celestial objects. The bursts may last from a fraction of a second to a few minutes. In that time, they give off more gamma-rays than the sun does in millions of years—if indeed they come from outside our galaxy, as many astronomers believe.

The Compton Observatory

All of the previous observations of gamma-ray sources had convinced us that we still had much to gain from the young field of gamma-ray astronomy. The observing capability of the Compton Gamma-

Searching for black holes

Scientists theorize that black holes form from the collapse of very massive stars, though they have yet to conclusively identify any black hole. By detecting intense gamma-ray emissions believed to occur just outside black holes, the Compton Observatory could pinpoint one of these elusive objects.

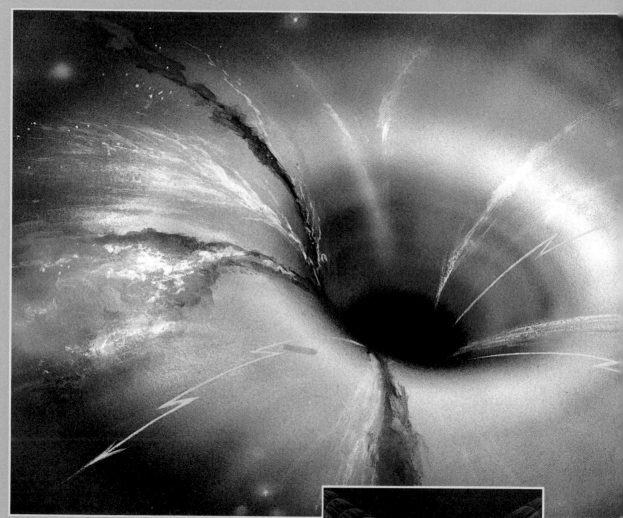

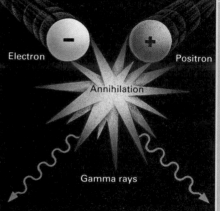

Scientists theorize that near black holes negatively charged particles called *electrons* collide with *positrons*, their positively charged counterparts. The two particles annihilate one another, emitting gamma rays.

Ray Observatory—far greater than that of any previous device—has shown already that we were correct.

The Compton Observatory is the largest set of gamma-ray detectors ever built. It weighs nearly 16,000 kilograms (35,000 pounds), making it the heaviest scientific satellite ever launched by the space shuttle. Compton carries four separate instruments that together cover more gamma-ray wavelengths than any previous devices. These instruments can detect gamma-ray sources 10 times fainter—and in much more detail—than those observed before.

Scientists designed the observatory and its instruments to operate for two years, but NASA plans to support the mission as long as the instruments last—possibly six years or more. The key to continuing the mission is a propulsion system built into the observatory. After Earth's atmosphere drags the observatory down to a lower orbit, commands sent to the propulsion system from the Goddard control room cause it to boost the spacecraft back to its initial orbiting altitude of 450 kilometers (280 miles).

Instruments on board the observatory record all of the information that scientists need to locate gamma-ray sources and determine their strengths and energies. These data are sent to the ground via the relay satellite about once every three hours. The data then go to Goddard, where technicians examine them to make sure the observatory and its instruments are operating safely and well. From Goddard, the data are forwarded to scientific teams for analysis.

The instruments on the Compton Observatory are attached to a platform that can be pointed at any source that scientists select. The plan calls for looking at 33 regions of the sky for at least two weeks apiece. Eventually, a survey of the entire sky will be completed during 18 months of orbiting. The data Compton gathers will give us our first-ever gamma-ray map of the sky.

Orchestrated instruments

Each of the four instruments aboard the Compton Observatory covers a different range of gamma-ray wavelengths and has its own set of scientific objectives:

■ *The Burst and Transient Source Experiment* (BATSE) consists of eight separate *modules* (units) placed at the four upper and lower corners of the observatory. This arrangement allows BATSE to examine the entire sky at once, except for the part blocked by Earth. The primary purpose of the instrument is to search for mysterious gamma-ray bursts. Because these bursts appear suddenly and randomly, BATSE must be able to scan the entire sky.

BATSE observes the low end of the gamma-ray energy range, where gamma rays from bursts lie. Four BATSE modules pick up each burst, measure the energy of the gamma rays coming from it, and together locate the direction of its source. When BATSE detects a burst, it also alerts the other three instruments aboard Compton so that they too can look at the burst. In addition to bursts, BATSE can monitor varia-

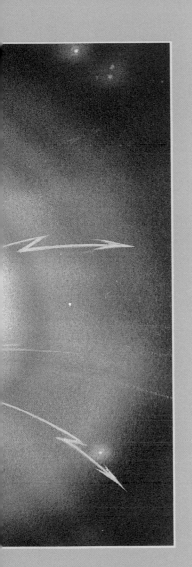

A black hole has such enormous gravitational force that it sucks in nearby matter and traps even light. Matter near the black hole may emit gamma rays (yellow arrows).

Quest for the energy of quasars

Quasars are the most distant and most energetic objects ever observed. These powerhouses radiate as much energy as a trillion suns, but scientists have much to learn about the processes involved.

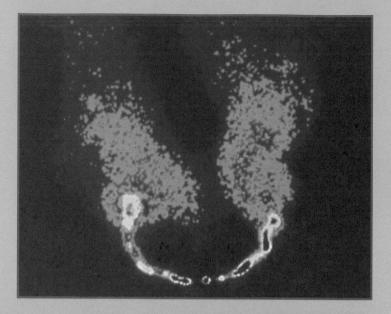

A quasar has such enormous gravitational force that it bends the radio waves streaming past it so that the waves appear to be coming from two sources rather than one, *right*.

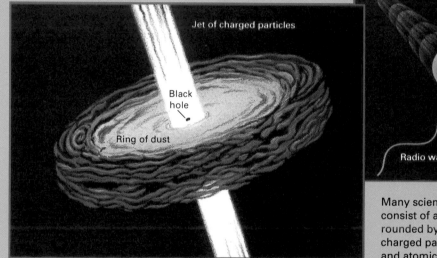

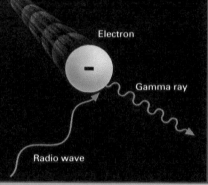

Many scientists believe that quasars consist of a central black hole surrounded by a ring of dust. A jet of charged particles—electrons, protons, and atomic nuclei—flows away from the black hole, *above left*. As the particles accelerate and interact, they generate radiation. When low-energy radiation, such as a radio wave, collides with a fast-moving electron, the radio wave is boosted to gamma-ray energy, *above right*.

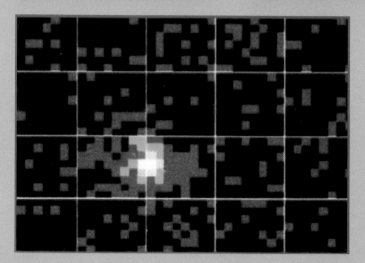

Quasar 3C279, *left*, was one of the brightest objects in the gamma-ray sky in June 1991, when Compton detected it. The quasar emitted thousands of times more energy in gamma rays than the entire Milky Way galaxy emits at all wavelengths. (Lighter colors indicate more intense gamma-ray emissions.)

tions over time in the intensity of the gamma-ray emissions from other strong sources, such as pulsars.

- *The Oriented Scintillation Spectrometer Experiment* (OSSE), like BATSE, detects low-energy gamma rays, but it can also pick up rays from very weak sources. OSSE has four identical detectors placed in one instrument at the front of the spacecraft. Each detector pivots independently, which helps OSSE pinpoint the location of gamma-ray sources and enables the instrument to look in a direction other than the direction in which the spacecraft is heading. Because many more gamma rays are emitted in the low-energy than the high-energy range, OSSE needs less observing time than the other instruments. It can normally observe at least two sources while the spacecraft points at just one target.

OSSE is especially suited for observing supernovae, the explosions that scientists believe create radioactive elements. Many of these elements emit gamma rays that fall within OSSE's energy-detecting range. Mapping the locations of radioactive elements in the universe will help scientists determine whether these elements formed in supernovae.

- *The Imaging Compton Telescope* (Comptel) detects medium-energy gamma rays, an important energy range that previous orbiting detectors missed. Comptel can view a large area at one time and will be used to produce a gamma-ray map of the entire sky.

- *The Energetic Gamma-Ray Experiment Telescope* (EGRET) covers the highest energy range of any instrument on the Compton Observatory. It was designed to observe gamma rays produced by some of the most energetic processes in the universe, including those that take place around black holes and quasars. EGRET's large size enables it to detect much fainter emissions than ever before measured. Like Comptel, it can view a wide area and will be used to map the entire sky. Both Comptel and EGRET were designed to look at gamma-ray producing events that last longer than the brief bursts observed by BATSE.

Mysterious bursts

The early findings from the Compton Observatory have surpassed our wildest expectations. Part of our excitement stems from how well the instruments have worked. Nature has done the rest, providing a bounty of explosive events directly revealed through their gamma-ray emissions.

To take advantage of these unexpected viewing opportunities, NASA scientists postponed a plan to survey the entire sky. The dramatic phenomena Compton viewed in its first months of operation include a very intense gamma-ray burst, several quasars spewing jets of gamma rays, massive gamma-ray-producing *solar flares* (tremendous discharges of energy from the sun), and three pulsars. Each of these discoveries is causing scientists to reconsider their ideas about the nature of the gamma-ray sources and the way they produce gamma rays.

The discovery that probably has excited and disturbed scientists the most concerns the mysterious sources of gamma-ray bursts. Since the observatory went into orbit, BATSE has detected bursts at the rate of

Puzzling over pulsars

Pulsars are the spinnng cores of stars that collapsed in violent explosions. Pulsars send out pulsed beams of electromagnetic radiation so regular that, when first observed in 1967, scientists thought they might be coming from extraterrestrial beings. Scientists hope gamma-ray observations will reveal the secret of how pulsars form and produce their enormous energy.

A pulsar (undetectable in visible light) lies near the center of the Crab Nebula, the remains of a *supernova* (exploding star) first seen in 1054.

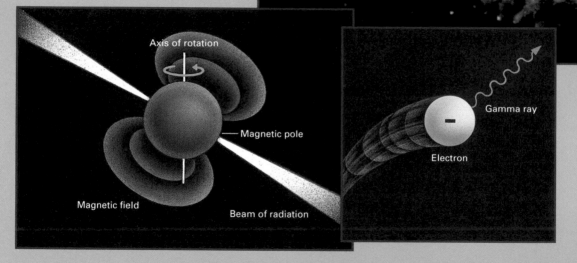

As a pulsar spins, its strong magnetic field also rotates, speeding electrons and protons on the pulsar's surface out from its magnetic poles. These particles emit gamma rays and all other forms of electromagnetic radiation as they accelerate, *above right.* The beams of radiation from the poles appear pulsed as they sweep the sky, *above left,* much like the beacon on a lighthouse.

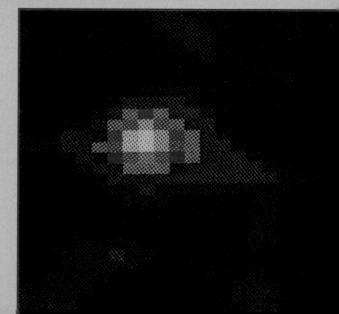

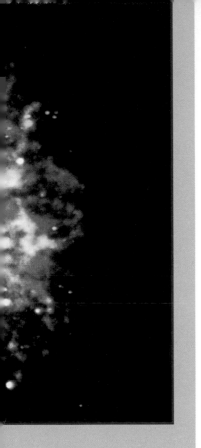

nearly one a day. By examining data on the positions of most of the bursts' sources, scientists have learned that gamma-ray bursts are distributed evenly across the sky.

This finding took us by surprise and cast serious doubt upon the prevailing theory that the bursts came from explosions on the surfaces of neutron stars. Neutron stars are scattered throughout our galaxy. Had they produced the gamma-ray bursts, these bursts would appear to be concentrated along the bright disk of the Milky Way. Although BATSE's observations show that the bursts do not lie along this disk, the Compton detectors cannot measure the distance to the sources of the bursts—or to the sources of any other gamma-ray emissions.

Scientists can explain the uniformity of the bursts across the sky only by assuming that the sources lie just beyond the solar system or that they lie quite far beyond our galaxy. Both explanations pose difficulties. If the bursts come from nearby, then scientists should have detected their sources at other wavelengths; but this has not happened. On the other hand, if the bursts come from very far away, they are triggered by more powerful sources than any celestial objects or events scientists yet know about. The unexpected findings have kept scientists busy formulating new theories.

All the Compton instruments detected one very intense burst on May 3, 1991. Comptel produced the first image of the event and fixed its position in the sky quite precisely with help from a small gamma-ray instrument aboard another spacecraft. The gamma rays that EGRET recorded from the burst had higher energies than scientists had ever before observed from a burst. More such observations should cast light (or at least gamma rays) on the nature of burst sources.

Dramatic flares and other sources

By mid-1992, EGRET had also observed gamma rays from 15 quasars and related, very energetic sources of gamma rays outside our galaxy. These observations should provide important clues to the mechanisms involved in these distant objects and thereby improve our understanding of them.

We know little about quasars, the brightest and the most distant celestial objects we can detect, though astronomers think of these strange distant bodies as resembling spinning pancakes. It remains a mystery how these powerhouses generate their tremendous energy, but scientists suspect a black hole may lie at the center of each quasar. Because radiation from quasars takes billions of years to reach Earth, detecting that radiation today provides information about events that occurred early in the universe.

While searching for a quasar labeled 3C273, which the COS-B mission had previously identified as a gamma-ray source, EGRET observed jets of gamma rays flaring from the center of another quasar, 3C279, nearly 6 billion light-years away. These jets emitted 10 million to 100 million times as many gamma rays as does the entire Milky Way galaxy. Because the COS-B mission would certainly have detected gamma-ray

The Crab Nebula and its pulsar, *left,* are visible as light-colored dots on an image created by the Compton Observatory in May 1991. The Compton observations show that the pulsar spins around its axis 30 times a second, producing two pulses of gamma rays with each revolution.

Baffled by bursts

Astronomers have detected intense bursts of gamma rays from space but do not know what produces them. Bursts typically last a few seconds but generate more energy than all other gamma-ray sources combined. By viewing bursts with the Compton Observatory, scientists hope to uncover a pattern that will help locate the sources of the bursts.

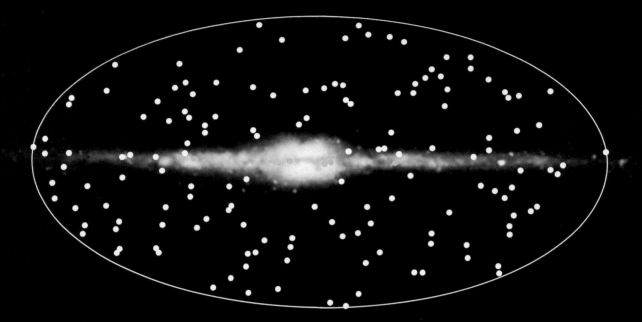

Compton revealed an even distribution of gamma-ray bursts across the sky. This finding stunned scientists and destroyed a prevailing theory that the flashes resulted from violent explosions on or around neutron stars in our Galaxy. If the bursts came from neutron stars, they would be clustered along the disk of the Milky Way.

emissions at this level, if the quasar had been producing them at the time, we assume that gamma-ray flares from quasars fluctuate in intensity. And when we looked again four months later, in October 1991, the quasar had stopped flaring.

EGRET found that the gamma-ray flares from 3C279 had extremely short wavelengths, so short that the other Compton instruments could barely detect the quasar. But not all emissions from quasars have such short wavelengths, and one possible explanation is that two separate mechanisms are involved in producing the gamma rays. Further studies of quasars should prove revealing.

All the Compton instruments have observed solar flares and measured the widest range of gamma rays ever recorded in such flares. The sun cooperated throughout 1991 by remaining very active and throwing off huge flares.

From observations of solar flares, we hope to learn more about the origins of cosmic rays. Scientists have theorized that some cosmic rays originate when electrically charged subatomic particles are accelerated in such events as solar flares and supernovae. Within the flares, the collisions of cosmic rays produce gamma rays, a process never observed before Compton.

The Compton observations confirmed the theory of cosmic-ray production by providing long-sought information about how the sun's strong magnetic fields accelerate the particles to very high cosmic-ray energies. Moreover, the gamma rays released by the particle collisions remained visible long after the flares had disappeared at other wavelengths. This finding indicated that the magnetic fields trap the cosmic rays temporarily after the flares die down.

Compton also helped solve a mystery that had puzzled scientists for more than 20 years: the identification of a gamma-ray source named Geminga, which has been nearly invisible at other wavelengths. Both EGRET and an orbiting X-ray observatory picked up pulsations from Geminga. The identical timing of the pulsations in X rays and in gamma rays convinced scientists that Geminga is a pulsar—only the fifth gamma-ray pulsar ever found.

Meanwhile, we continue to search for a black hole at the center of the Milky Way. A black hole emits gamma rays at varying intensities, depending on how much matter it is gobbling up. So far, OSSE has picked up only a low level of emissions from electron-positron annihilations in the general direction of our galaxy's center. Because these emissions may result from exploding stars in this region over the last 1 million years, we believe the black hole we seek may now be in a fairly inactive state. But we expect to learn much more as the data from Compton and from other observatories are analyzed and compared.

Gamma-ray astronomy remains in its infancy. Until Compton, we had few opportunities to observe gamma rays. But even these few opportunities taught us much about the most dynamic transfers of energy in our universe. With the great improvement in observing capability that Compton provides, we can confidently predict that the next few years will be rich in discoveries from deep in the universe and far back in time.

For further reading:

Kniffen, Donald A. "The Gamma Ray Observatory." *Sky & Telescope,* May 1991, pp. 488-492.

Neal, Valerie; Fishman, Gerald; and Kniffen, Donald. "The Gamma-Ray Observatory: The Next Great Observatory," *Mercury,* July/August 1990, pp. 98-111.

Talcott, Richard. "A Burst of Gamma Rays." *Astronomy,* October 1991, pp. 46-50.

Discoveries in basic genetic science, applied to the diagnosis and treatment of genetically caused diseases, are bringing about a major revolution in the practice of medicine.

The Evolution of Genetic Medicine

BY ROBERT H. TAMARIN

A landmark in the history of medicine was passed on Sept. 14, 1990, when scientists injected into a little girl with an incurable genetic disease cells that carried copies of the normal gene she lacked. This procedure, carried out at the National Institutes of Health (NIH) in Bethesda, Md., was the first officially approved attempt at *gene therapy*, the insertion of healthy genes into a person in the hope of curing or treating a disease caused by a genetic defect. By mid-1992, in the United States alone, about 20 clinical trials involving gene therapy were underway. These included experimental treatments for diabetes, rheumatoid arthritis, and various forms of cancer. A new era in medicine had begun.

Several times in the past 150 years, major discoveries have literally revolutionized the practice of medicine. In the 1800's, for example, anesthetics and antiseptics paved the way for extensive, lifesaving surgery. Before anesthetics freed patients from pain, surgeons were limited mainly to amputations and other operations that could be performed in a matter of minutes. And before the development of germ-killing antiseptics, surgical patients frequently died of postoperative infections. The widespread use of penicillin and other antibiotics since the 1940's saved many more lives that would otherwise have been claimed by infections. In addition, vaccines developed in the early to mid-1900's further revolutionized medicine by controlling infectious diseases, such as diphtheria, pneumonia, and polio, that once were major childhood killers. Now the application of genetic science to medicine promises health benefits at least as great as those brought about by anesthesia, antiseptics, and wonder drugs. It promises to provide relief for people suffering from once-untreatable genetic ills.

The beginning of genetic science

This new genetic medicine has grown out of the scientific study of *genes*, the basic units of heredity in all living organisms. It has its roots in the work of Gregor Johann Mendel, an Austrian monk who lived in the 1800's. Working for years in his monastery's garden, Mendel crossbred pea plants and observed how traits for height and other characteristics were passed from one generation to the next. Mendel theorized that these traits were determined by "hereditary units" passed on by each plant's male and female parents. From his observations, Mendel theorized that a parent has two hereditary units for each trait, but only one is passed on to an offspring. Mendel further concluded that among these units there were what he called dominant and recessive types. When an offspring inherits a dominant type from one parent and a recessive type from the other, the dominant hereditary unit will always "overrule" the recessive one. The offspring will exhibit the characteristics associated with the dominant type. An offspring could exhibit a trait associated with a recessive hereditary unit only by inheriting two recessive types—one from each parent.

Mendel's work laid the foundation for the modern study of genetics. But Mendel died in 1884 without having any idea about what his hereditary units actually were. And, the importance of his work was not recognized until the early 1900's, when three botanists studying heredity each rediscovered Mendel's work. These scientists—Carl Correns of Germany, Erich von Tschermak of Austria, and Hugo de Vries of the Netherlands—all conducted plant breeding experiments and independently obtained the same results as had Mendel. In 1909, Danish botanist Wilhelm Ludwig Johannsen proposed that Mendel's hereditary units be called *genes*, from a Greek word meaning *to give birth to*.

Discovering genes and how they work

Scientists then began to gain more detailed understanding of genes through plant and animal breeding experiments, by studying cells under the microscope, and by analyzing biochemicals found in cells. They learned that genes are located in the cell nucleus on structures called chromosomes. In most human cells, 50,000 to 100,000 genes are contained in 23 pairs of chromosomes. They discovered that genes not only pass traits from parents to offspring, but also control all the functions of cells. And by 1944, researchers had learned that genes are made of a molecule called DNA (deoxyribonucleic acid).

In 1953, a major discovery unlocked the secret of how genes work. American biologist James D. Watson and British biologist Francis H. C.

The author:
Robert H. Tamarin is professor of biology at Boston University and the author of *Principles of Genetics.*

Glossary

Chromosomes: Threadlike structures in the cell nucleus that carry the genes.

DNA (deoxyribonucleic acid): The molecule of which genes are made.

Gene: A section of DNA containing coded information for producing a protein. Genes are the basic units of heredity in all organisms.

Gene therapy: A technique for treating or curing diseases by implanting a normal gene in a patient's body.

Genetic engineering: Techniques that alter the genes or combinations of genes in an organism.

Proteins: Complex molecules that are produced by the body's cells and that are responsible for the cell's structure and functions.

Tracing diseases that run in families

Doctors had long observed that certain diseases tend to run in families. Genetic theory allowed them to predict the pattern of inherited disease.

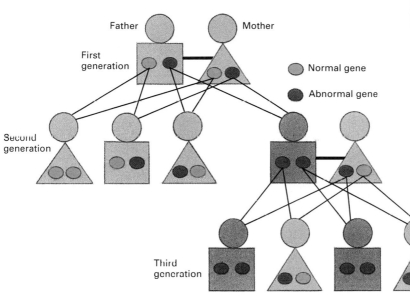

Gregor Mendel in the 1860's developed the theory of genetics by observing how traits were inherited in pea plants. The basic unit of inheritance later came to be called a gene, though scientists at first did not know what it was.

All offspring inherit two sets of genes, one from each parent. Most inherited diseases occur if a child inherits an abnormal gene from both parents. If each parent carries one normal gene and one abnormal gene responsible for a particular disease, each of their children has a 1 in 4 chance of inheriting two abnormal genes and, therefore, the disease. If the child with two abnormal genes marries someone with one normal and one abnormal gene, their children each have a 1 in 2 chance of inheriting the disease.

Selected inherited diseases

Cystic fibrosis is an often fatal disease of the lungs and digestive system. In the United States, it strikes 1 in 2,000 whites and 1 in 17,000 blacks.

Familial hypercholesterolemia is marked by very high levels of cholesterol in the blood. It affects 1 in 500 people.

Hemophilia is a disease in which the blood fails to clot normally. It affects 1 in 20,000 males.

Huntington's disease is marked by the progressive deterioration of the central nervous system. Its symptoms first appear in middle age. It strikes about 1 in 10,000 people.

Myotonic muscular dystrophy is the most common adult form of muscular dystrophy, a disease marked by the progressive weakening of the muscles. It occurs in 1 in 8,000 people.

Phenylketonuria (PKU) results in mental retardation unless treated early in infancy. It occurs in 1 in 12,000 people, mainly of western European descent.

Sickle cell anemia occurs mainly in blacks, of whom about 1 in 800 in the United States are affected. It can result in injury to many organs of the body, strokes, and dangerous infections.

Tay-Sachs disease is a nervous-system disorder. It occurs mainly among Jewish children of eastern European descent, afflicting about 1 in 3,000 of them.

Discovering genes and DNA

Beginning in the early 1900's, scientists learned that genes are carried on structures called *chromosomes*, located in the cell nucleus. During the 1940's, they discovered that genes are made of *deoxyribonucleic acid* (DNA).

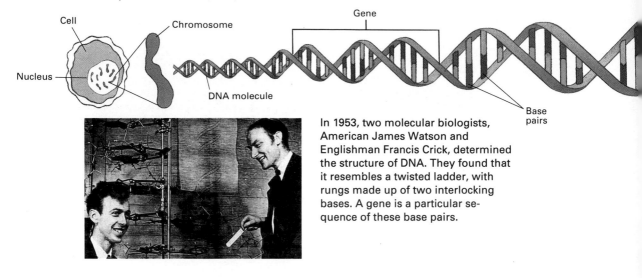

In 1953, two molecular biologists, American James Watson and Englishman Francis Crick, determined the structure of DNA. They found that it resembles a twisted ladder, with rungs made up of two interlocking bases. A gene is a particular sequence of these base pairs.

Crick announced that they had discovered the structure of DNA. They based their findings on the work of two other British scientists, Rosalind E. Franklin and Maurice H. F. Wilkins, who used X rays to study the DNA molecule. Franklin died in 1958. Watson, Crick, and Wilkins shared the 1962 Nobel Prize in physiology or medicine for this work.

Watson and Crick found that DNA is a very long molecule, shaped like a twisted ladder. The rungs of the DNA ladder are made up of chemicals called *bases*. There are only four of these bases, adenine (A), cytosine (C), guanine (G), and thymine (T). Two bases join together to form a *base pair*. Each base pair, in turn, forms a complete rung of the DNA ladder. When DNA replicates during cell division, the ladder "unzips" down the middle. Each half rung picks up another half rung and becomes a new rung following a simple rule: A always pairs with T and C always pairs with G. This is called the rule of complementarity, and it is a fundamental principle underlying all of genetic science and its medical applications. For example, the rule of complementarity ensures that each new strand of DNA becomes an exact duplicate of the original strand.

Researchers then discovered that a gene consists of a long *sequence* (series) of these base pairs. In fact, a gene often contains several thousand of them. The base-pair sequence codes for the production of *amino acids*, the building blocks of proteins, which carry out all the functions of the cell. When a protein is needed, the part of the DNA containing its code unzips so that other structures in the cell can "read" the DNA and then direct the construction of the protein from amino acids.

The role of genes in disease

Most genes *code for* (carry instructions for) the production of *proteins*, molecules that are essential to the structure and function of cells. The precise sequence of base pairs determines the particular protein that a gene codes for. The slightest variation in the base pairs may cause an abnormal gene that may result in the production of an abnormal protein. This protein, in turn, may cause a malfunction in the structure or function of the cells in which it operates.

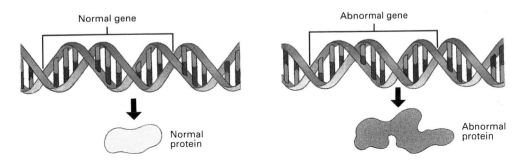

Normal gene

Normal protein

Abnormal gene

Abnormal protein

Genes and disease

While some scientists were deciphering the structure of genes, others became interested in the relationship between genes and disease. Doctors had long noted that certain diseases tend to run in families. In 1909, British physician Archibald Garrod proposed in his book, *Inborn Errors of Metabolism*, that these diseases are caused by particular genes. Since then, scientists have uncovered more specific information about inherited diseases. We now know that some diseases are caused by missing or extra genes or by *mutations* (changes) in a gene. A mutated gene will not code for the correct sequence of amino acids and thus makes a defective protein.

Scientists have also discovered that certain genes are linked to the development of cancer, the uncontrolled growth of cells that results in a tumor. Genes essential to controlling cell division and growth may mutate spontaneously or because of environmental factors—such as exposure to certain chemicals or radiation. People may also inherit a susceptibility to the genetic changes that lead to cancer.

The development of genetic engineering

The next major chapter in the genetic science story was the development of techniques for working with genes. These techniques, called recombinant DNA technology or genetic engineering, were to lead to a variety of medical applications. The first recombinant DNA techniques were developed in the early 1970's by molecular biologists Paul Berg and Stanley Cohen of Stanford University, in Stanford, Calif., and Henry Boyer of the University of California at San Francisco. They and other molecular biologists discovered how to cut a piece of DNA out of one organism and splice it into the DNA of another organism. Berg won the 1980 Nobel Prize in chemistry for his role in this work.

The earliest genetic engineering experiments involved splicing pieces of DNA from simple organisms into a *plasmid*, a circular piece of

The genetic revolution begins

In the 1970's, molecular biologists developed the "tools" of genetic engineering, which allowed them to manipulate individual genes. One of the first genetic engineering techniques, called *gene splicing*, enabled scientists to insert a gene from another species into the DNA of a bacterium. When the bacterium reproduced, the gene also reproduced.

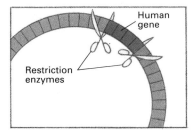

Chemical scissors called restriction enzymes snip out a human gene that codes for a particular protein.

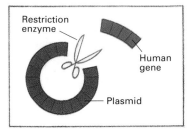

Restriction enzymes open a ring of bacterial DNA called a plasmid, allowing the human gene to be spliced in.

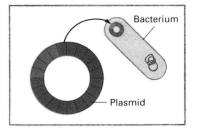

Genetically engineered plasmids are reinserted into bacteria, where they begin directing production of the protein for which the human gene codes.

Bacteria reproduce rapidly, so they are able to produce large numbers of the human gene, as well as huge quantities of the human protein that it codes for.

A new class of drugs

Through the use of gene-splicing techniques, scientists have used rapidly reproducing cells and organisms to produce a new class of drugs, consisting of natural human proteins.

Some human proteins used as drugs

Erythropoietin combats anemia by stimulating the creation of red blood cells.

Human insulin regulates the body's production of sugar. It is used to treat people with diabetes.

Human growth hormone stimulates growth in the human body. It is used to treat dwarfism in children.

Interferon is used for treating certain viral diseases, leukemia, Kaposi's sarcoma, and the liver diseases hepatitis B and C.

Neupogen increases the production of white blood cells. It is used by cancer patients undergoing *chemotherapy* (treatment with strong anticancer drugs).

Tissue plasminogen activator dissolves blood clots. It is used to save the lives of people suffering heart attacks caused by blood clots blocking the coronary arteries.

DNA found in bacteria. For these experiments, the scientists used *restriction enzymes*, a kind of "biochemical scissors," that cut strands of DNA at specific base pair sequences. The scientists could cut a gene from one organism, open a bacterial plasmid, and insert the "foreign" gene.

From the very beginning, recombinant DNA technology raised a number of questions regarding ethics and safety. Scientists, environmentalists, and political leaders feared the accidental creation of a deadly strain of microorganism. In 1974, a number of distinguished scientists, including Berg, Cohen, and Watson, called for a voluntary ban on gene-splicing experiments until safeguards could be established. Many of the scientists involved in this work met for a conference at Asilomar, Calif., in 1975 to discuss potential dangers and propose research guidelines. In 1976, the National Institutes of Health set standards requiring that laboratories in which these experiments took place be designed to prevent any microorganisms from escaping. Although ethical concerns about potential abuses of genetic technology continue to this day, the fears about potential dangers of gene splicing proved to be largely unfounded.

Eventually, scientists learned how to splice human genes into plasmids and insert the plasmids into fast-growing bacteria. Whenever the bacteria reproduced, so did the plasmid and the human gene that had been inserted. This process, called gene cloning, made it possible for scientists to create billions of copies of a particular human gene.

Genetically engineered drugs

Molecular biologists realized that it would be possible to use this technique to create "biological factories" consisting of bacteria, yeast, or other fast-growing cells for the production of a needed human pro-

Probing for defective genes

Genetic engineering techniques are allowing researchers to identify, or map, human genes. This has already led to tests for several inherited diseases through the use of gene probes.

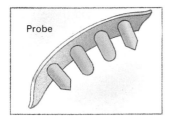

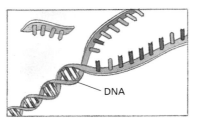

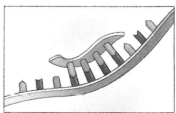

A gene probe is a DNA segment that has been tagged with a radioactive compound. Probes attach to regions of DNA near a defective gene.

The probe is mixed with a sample of a person's DNA that has been treated to cause the rungs of the DNA ladder to separate, much as a zipper does.

If the DNA sample contains the defective gene, the probe will attach to the related region and give off a radioactive "glow" when the sample is analyzed.

tein, which could then be administered as a drug. Such genetically engineered drugs provided the first large-scale medical benefits of genetic science.

By 1992, biotechnology companies were producing several important human proteins, including *hormones* (substances that regulate certain bodily functions). The first of these commercially produced bioengineered drugs was human *insulin*, a hormone that helps the body store sugar. In 1982, the Food and Drug Administration approved genetically engineered insulin for commercial use, and Genentech Incorporated, a California biotechnology company, manufactured it to treat diabetes.

Other drugs consisting of human proteins soon followed. Genetically engineered human growth hormone, for example, is used to treat children whose growth is well below average. Other genetically engineered drugs include *tissue plasminogen activator*, used to treat heart attacks by breaking up blood clots; *interferon*, used for halting the spread of viruses from cell to cell; and *erythropoietin*, a hormone for combating anemia in patients with kidney diseases.

The search for disease-causing genes

Meanwhile, efforts began to map the locations of human genes. In 1990, the U.S. government committed $200 million a year to a program called the Human Genome Initiative. Scientists working on this project in the United States, along with scientists in other countries, hope to map the locations of all human genes by 2005.

Molecular biologists since the late 1970's have also been searching for the genes that are responsible for particular diseases. To locate particular genes, scientists often rely on various kinds of restriction enzymes that cut DNA at different sites and thus chop it into smaller and smaller pieces.

The first disease truly understood at the level of the DNA sequence was sickle cell anemia, a disease that mainly affects people of African or Mediterranean descent. Red blood cells sickle, or deform, clogging small blood vessels and causing fever, pain, and sometimes fatal organ damage. The sickle cell gene is a recessive gene, so a parent without symptoms can be a carrier. If a child inherits two copies of this reces-

Damaged genes and cancer

Generally, cancer, the uncontrolled growth of cells, is not an inherited disease, but it does have a genetic component. Using the tools of genetic engineering, scientists have learned that potential cancer genes predispose people who have them to developing cancer. If these genes or related genes are damaged or shifted around on the chromosomes, the result can be wild cell growth that produces tumors. Tests designed to detect potential cancer genes might one day be used to identify those people who are most likely to get cancer. They could then take steps to avoid exposure to the cancer-causing agents that increase their cancer risk.

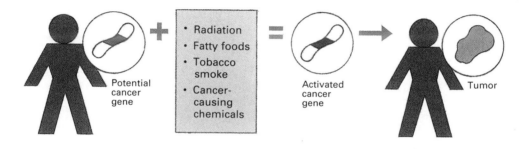

Potential cancer gene + • Radiation • Fatty foods • Tobacco smoke • Cancer-causing chemicals = Activated cancer gene → Tumor

sive gene, one from each parent, the child will develop sickle cell anemia, which is caused by a defect in the oxygen-carrying protein hemoglobin. In 1977, molecular biologists at Yale University in New Haven, Conn., traced the abnormal hemoglobin to a mutation involving a single base pair in the hemoglobin gene. Since then, researchers have discovered the genes responsible for a number of ills, including cystic fibrosis, an often fatal lung disease; myotonic muscular dystrophy, a disease in which a person's muscles gradually waste away; and, in April 1992, the gene responsible for a common type of diabetes.

Finding the cystic fibrosis gene

The search for the cystic fibrosis gene provides an excellent example of this kind of biochemical detective work. People with cystic fibrosis produce abnormally thick mucus that can form plugs in the lungs and intestines. Complications from infections and damage to the heart, lungs, or other organs are often fatal. The search for the gene responsible for this disease began in the early 1980's, when geneticist Lap-Chee Tsui of the University of Toronto in Canada and his colleagues began comparing DNA samples of members of families in which the disease had occurred frequently. Tsui knew that members of the same families would have a great number of identical genes. What Tsui was looking for, however, were differences between the DNA of family members who have the disease (or who were known carriers of it) and the DNA of those who did not have it. Tsui and his colleagues figured that if they could find one particular variation that always appeared in the DNA of every family member with cystic fibrosis, they would be close to finding the gene responsible for the disease itself.

Tsui's search for the cystic fibrosis gene stretched through most of the 1980's. In November 1985, he announced that his team had discovered a consistent pattern of variations in his patients' DNA. These variations led him to believe that the cystic fibrosis gene was located somewhere on chromosome 7. That same month, other scientists in the United States and Europe reported similar evidence of a variation on chromosome 7.

Then, for the next three years, Tsui closed in on the gene, gaining an ever more precise understanding of the location of the gene on chromosome 7. In 1988, he began working with Francis Collins, a geneticist at the University of Michigan in Ann Arbor. Finally, on Aug. 24, 1989, Tsui and Collins announced that they had located the gene responsible for cystic fibrosis.

After Tsui and Collins located the cystic fibrosis gene, they determined the exact order of base pairs making up the gene. They found that the gene is about 250,000 base pairs long, but the defect that causes most cases of cystic fibrosis involves only three base pairs. These base pairs are missing in the abnormal version of the gene. The normal version of the gene codes for a protein that helps maintain a normal balance of salt and water in the cell. The tiny variation in the abnormal gene creates an abnormal version of the protein, which allows salt to build up in the cell. The excess salt draws water into the cell and away from the mucus lining, causing the mucus to become abnormally thick.

Tests for disease-causing genes

As soon as Tsui and Collins had discovered the sequences of the healthy and mutant genes that are associated with cystic fibrosis, it became possible to create diagnostic tests for the disease. By the early 1990's, there were diagnostic tests available for a number of genetic ills. Most of these diagnostic tests involved tools called genetic probes.

Probes are segments of DNA that search out and attach themselves to specific regions in or near a known gene. Doctors can probe for a defective gene if at least part of the base-pair sequence of that gene is known. The technique of probing is based on the rule of complementarity. For example, if one strand of the DNA making up a gene has the sequence CCCGGTTA, then the complement has the sequence GGGCCAAT. A DNA probe made of the sequence of GGGCCAAT would be tagged with a radioactive compound and used to find the probe's complement in a sample of DNA that was chemically treated to make it unzip.

With tests of this sort, it became possible to identify carriers who do not have symptoms but who could pass the disease to their children. Genetic tests can also be used to see if a young person has a genetic disease that manifests symptoms only later in life, such as Huntington's disease, a fatal nervous system disorder whose symptoms generally appear when a person is between 35 and 40 years old. It may also become possible to detect genetic *predispositions* (susceptibilities) to certain diseases, such as heart disease or various types of cancer, so that a susceptible person can avoid certain practices, such as eating high-fat food, that make the disease more likely to occur.

The first gene therapy experiments

The frontier of genetic medicine today involves the challenges of getting normal genes into patients and getting those genes to function permanently. Scientists hope that if they can meet these challenges, they will be well on the way to creating cures for people with certain inherited diseases.

For the first U.S. government-approved gene therapy treatment in 1990, NIH researchers W. French Anderson and his colleagues used a virus to transport copies of a normal gene into a 4-year-old girl with *adenosine deaminase* (ADA) *deficiency*. This genetic disease results in a weak immune system. People with ADA deficiency are often unable to fight off infections, and they generally die at an early age. The NIH researchers removed some of the girl's blood and isolated from it the white blood cells, which play a crucial role in the immune system. The doctors then spliced copies of a normal ADA gene from a healthy donor's cells into harmless viruses and mixed the viruses with the girl's

Gene therapy: The frontier of genetic medicine

A major challenge facing genetic medicine is that of finding safe ways to insert into patients new genes that will survive, function, and thereby treat or cure not only inherited diseases, but also such other ills as cancer and heart disease. One method being explored involves the use of viruses to carry new genes into the cells.

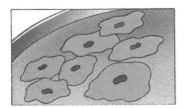

Cells removed from a patient are grown in a laboratory culture. These may be white blood cells or cells from an organ, such as the liver.

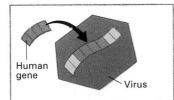

A human gene coding for the desired protein is spliced into the genetic material of a harmless virus.

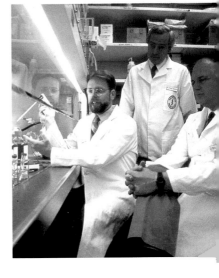

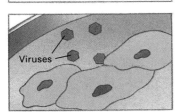

The genetically engineered viruses are mixed with cells in the laboratory culture, and the viruses "infect" the cells.

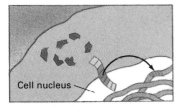

Inside the cells, the viruses transfer copies of the normal gene to the cells, so that when the cells are injected back into the patient, the normal gene will code for the production of the normal protein.

Gene therapy's early landmarks

September 1990: Researchers at the National Institutes of Health perform the first officially approved gene therapy experiment, treating an immune system defect called ADA deficiency in a 4-year-old girl.

January 1991: National Cancer Institute (NCI) scientists use genetically engineered white blood cells to treat patients with *melanoma*, a deadly form of skin cancer.

October 1991: NCI researchers treat cancer patients with genetically altered cells from their own tumors. The altered cells contain additional genes for a tumor-destroying substance.

February 1992: The Recombinant Advisory Committee of the NIH approves the first commercial gene therapy project to be carried out by Targeted Genetics Corporation of Seattle. The first experimental treatment involves injecting modified white blood cells into AIDS patients.

April 1992: Scientists in Milan, Italy, carry out the first experiment to treat ADA deficiency using stem cells, immature cells found in bone marrow. Stem cells give rise to all other blood cells, including white blood cells, and thus could provide a permanent cure.

white blood cells in the laboratory. The viruses infected the white blood cells and inserted the normal ADA genes into the white blood cell's chromosomes.

The scientists injected the genetically altered white blood cells into the girl through blood transfusions. After nearly a year of regular transfusions, the scientists found that the girl's immune system had noticeably improved. By July 1991, the researchers reported that the girl's body was producing surprisingly high levels of the ADA enzyme needed to keep her immune system functioning.

Nevertheless, the NIH team acknowledged some drawbacks to this particular approach to gene therapy. Most important was the fact that white blood cells die off quickly, making it necessary to repeat the transfusions on a regular basis. So, in effect, this technique is a sophisticated drug-delivery system that provides the girl with regular doses of ADA. For diseases of the blood and immune system, scientists would prefer to use genetically altered *stem cells* (immature cells in the marrow that become red or white blood cells). Stem cells give rise to many generations of blood cells, and inserting a normal gene into stem cells would, for all practical purposes, provide a cure. In April 1992, Italian researchers led by Claudio Bordignon at the San Raffaele Research Institute in Milan began a study using stem cells to treat ADA deficiency. However, stem cells are very hard to identify and isolate, and there are many questions about their use and safety.

The frontiers of genetic medicine

A number of other attempts at human gene therapy were underway by 1992. Steven Rosenberg, also of the NIH, is leading several of these projects. In January 1991, Rosenberg's team began treating two patients with *melanoma*, a deadly type of skin cancer. They transfused into the patients copies of a human gene that codes for the production of *tumor necrosis factor* (TNF), a powerful antitumor protein. Although the patients did not lack the normal TNF gene, Rosenberg hoped that additional copies would help the patients' bodies destroy the tumors. In July 1991, Rosenberg reported that the therapy had apparently prolonged the lives of both patients.

Another experiment, designed to treat patients with familial hypercholesterolemia (FH), called for inserting normal genes into liver cells rather than blood cells. People with FH do not have the normal gene that enables their liver to remove *cholesterol,* a fatlike substance, from the blood. As a result, people with FH develop life-endangering amounts of cholesterol that can clog blood vessels and cause strokes or heart attacks.

Researchers are also experimenting with other methods to introduce modified cells into the body. In 1991, for example, a team of scientists at the NIH led by Ronald G. Crystal sprayed into the lungs of laboratory rats viruses carrying the normal gene that in its abnormal form causes cystic fibrosis. The rats were soon producing the normal protein in their lung tissues. The scientists hope that they will be able to use spray inhalers for transmitting normal genes to human cystic fibrosis patients.

Meanwhile, scientists at Stanford University and the Howard Hughes Medical Institute at the University of Michigan are working on techniques for delivering normal genes through immature muscle cells, called *myoblasts*. The scientists hope that myoblasts will prove to be an effective means for transmitting the normal genes for inherited muscular diseases, such as muscular dystrophy, into human patients.

The future of genetic medicine

While genetic medicine promises many future "miracle cures," it is still surrounded by social and ethical concerns. One concern focuses on whether gene therapy should be confined to body cells, whose DNA is not passed on to subsequent generations, or whether it should also be extended to sex cells. Sex cells—eggs and sperm—contain the DNA inherited by a person's offspring. Altered sex cells would be passed on through the generations. For the time being, most genetic scientists agree human gene therapy experiments should be confined to body cells. But altering sex cells is one way to eliminate certain inherited diseases, so the issue is likely to remain a matter for debate.

Another concern involves the potential misuse of information about individuals' genetic makeup. For example, some people fear that an insurance company might decide not to sell life or health insurance to people with genes that make them prone to cancer or some other medical condition. Employers might also gain access to information about job-seekers' DNA and make employment decisions based on their genetic makeup.

Questions such as these will be debated for years to come. Some may be settled by courts of law, others by legislators. But for thousands of sufferers of inherited diseases, the blossoming revolution in genetic medicine offers hope where before there was none.

For further reading:

Bishop, Jerry E., and Waldholz, Michael. *Genome.* Simon & Schuster, 1991.
Montgomery, Geoffrey. "The Ultimate Medicine." *Discover,* March 1990, pp. 60-68.
Verma, Inder M. "Gene Therapy." *Scientific American,* November 1990, pp. 68-84.
Watson, James D. *The Double Helix.* NAL-Dutton, 1969.

Science Studies

Global Change

BY GEORGE M. WOODWELL

From creating a "hole" in the ozone layer to causing the extinction of plant and animal species, humanity is unintentionally changing the environment of the Earth. Understanding the causes and effects of the world's environmental crisis is the first step toward developing solutions.

Introduction

Scientists around the world believe that human activities are threatening the *biosphere*—the thin skin of Earth where life occurs. The biosphere extends from a few inches below the surface of the deepest ocean trenches, where microbes exist, to Earth's upper atmosphere, where pollen spores are carried by the wind. It includes the human habitat, the only one we know or will know in any time of interest to us, our children, or our children's children.

The biosphere offers an incredible richness and variety of plants and animals and, in the process of maintaining itself, has maintained a habitat suitable for people. The biosphere does not need humanity's presence to continue, but people need nature and the organisms within it to sustain an environment suitable for human life. Despite this fact, humanity in the final decades of the 1900's is destroying the natural systems upon which it depends.

Many factors contribute to this destruction. They include the growth of the human population and the progressive poisoning of nature with the chemical by-products of modern agriculture, industry, power generation, and transportation. Scientists warn of a potentially catastrophic warming of Earth's climate, the depletion of Earth's protective layer of ozone in the upper atmosphere, and the loss of plants and animals.

For human beings, these problems may create an increase in human diseases from cancer to cataracts. But they may also lead to dwindling supplies of safe air, water, and food, putting greater and greater strains on governments to protect people's basic needs.

The situation raises issues that are large and complex but far from insolvable. The solutions will rely on scientific and technical research, on developing clear definitions of the problems, and on creating equally clear political and economic solutions.

In June 1992, the leaders of 178 nations convened in Rio de Janeiro, Brazil, to try to set the world on a new course. The meeting, called the United Nations Conference on Environment and Development or simply the Earth Summit, was designed to forge agreement between nations on how to combat such environmental problems as global climatic change, the destruction of forests, and the loss of plant and animal species. Although most scientists were disappointed that the summit delegates did not agree to more forceful solutions, the process itself was an important recognition of the problem of global environmental change.

The author:
George M. Woodwell is president and director of the Woods Hole Research Center in Woods Hole, Mass.

Human Population Growth

At the beginning of 1992, Earth supported about 5.4 billion people, a dramatic rise since 1900, when Earth contained about 1.6 billion people. The United Nations estimates that by the year 2000, the world population will be around 6.4 billion people.

Each day, the world's human population increases by about 250,000 people, or more than 90 million each year. This annual increase is approximately equal to the population of Mexico. The rate at which the human population is growing can be illustrated by how little even catastrophic natural disasters slow it down. For example, the June 1990 earthquake in Iran killed an estimated 40,000 people. Within six hours, new births worldwide replaced the number of people lost from this immense tragedy.

Population growth is not due simply to an increase in births but to the excess of births over deaths. Improvements in public health and medicine around the world propel population growth by enabling people to live longer. The growth feeds itself as greater numbers of young women survive to childbearing age and start to have children.

The rate of population growth

These advances are causing the world's population to double at a much faster rate than ever before. In the year 1000, the human population grew at a rate so slow that—had it continued—the world population would not have doubled for 575 years. By 1825, the doubling time had decreased to about 100 years. Today, the world's population is doubling in 35 to 40 years.

For Earth as a whole, the rate of population growth in 1991 was 1.7 per cent. This means that the population at the end of the year was 1.7 per cent larger than at the beginning.

But the growth rate varied greatly from country to country. In the richer, industrialized nations—such as the United States, Canada, Japan, and the countries of Western Europe—population growth averaged 0.5 per cent. Germany and Hungary had rates that were slightly less than zero, meaning that their populations were declining. In the developing nations, however, population growth was higher, averaging 2.1 per cent. The highest growth rates occurred in Africa and in Arab states on the Persian Gulf. The populations of Kenya, Tanzania, Zambia, and Uganda grew by 3.7 to 3.8

per cent, as did those of Ivory Coast, Saudi Arabia, and Oman.

Although such percentages may seem insignificant, the difference between a worldwide 1 per cent rate of growth and a 3 per cent rate is the difference between adding 54 million people and adding 200 million people to Earth each year. A sustained worldwide growth rate of 3.7 per cent, for example, would cause Earth's population to double in only 20 years.

Poverty and population growth

Many economists and social planners believe that economic development is the key to slowing population growth. The sharp difference between the rates of population growth in richer, economically developed nations and the rates in developing nations seems to support this view.

In developing nations, where many people farm for a living, there is an economic advantage to having several children who can help with the work and provide for the parents in old age. When societies become economically and technologically advanced, however, modern agricultural techniques enable the production of the same amount of food using the labor of fewer people. In such societies, large families are unnecessary and may be costly. As a result, family size drops. This so-called *demographic transition* has helped reduce the growth of populations in the wealthier, industrialized nations.

Unfortunately, a rapidly expanding population can by itself prevent a developing nation from improving its economy. A nation's people can become poorer when its population growth outstrips its economic growth. Kenya, for instance, with a 1992 population of 24 million, will have 48 million people in 2012 if the current population growth rate continues. Few experts believe that Kenya's economic circumstances can improve sufficiently during that time to provide adequately for so many people. The nation may be doomed to worsening poverty unless it can limit its population growth.

Other causes of overpopulation

The human population is expanding in many regions simply because people lack awareness of birth control or the ability to limit the size of their families. Recent United Nations statistics indicate that 90 per cent of women in 10 African nations have not heard of contraception.

In other cases, people in developing countries who want to limit the growth of their families lack access to contraception. Family planning methods are simply not available in large sections of the world. According to a study by the International Statistical Institute in The Hague, the Netherlands, as many as 500 million women in developing countries live too far from health centers to obtain contraceptives.

But attempts to slow population growth confront more than economic or educational problems. Human reproduction is a matter of great religious and cultural importance as well. The religious teachings of many people prohibit or discourage contraception. And some cultures traditionally value large families as a sign of prestige and power.

China's birth-control experiment

The problem of uncontrolled population growth prompted the government of China in 1955 to begin a program that restricts families to having only one child. China is one of the most densely populated nations of the world. It has the largest population, estimated at more than 1.1 billion people. China's 9.6 million square kilometers (3.7 million square miles) gives it a population density of about 119 people per square kilometer (309 people per square mile). But because the land is not all habitable, the density in inhabited places is much higher.

By comparison, the United States, whose 250 million people live on a land area approximately equivalent to that of China, has a population density of only 27 people per square kilometer (70 people per square mile).

Experts say that China's population control program has not been a clear success. The government's rules are modified for special groups, such as ethnic minorities, within the larger population. Also, families often desire male children—a wish that in practice may lead to the killing of female newborns or simply a disregard for governmental restrictions. Thus, there are more births than officially allowed in order to produce males.

In 1991, despite several years' experience with the program, the population of China was still increasing by about 1.4 per cent annually. At this rate, the nation's population will double in about 50 years.

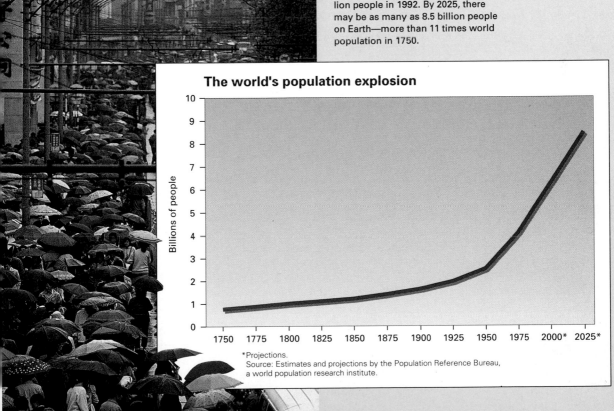

Since 1750, the world's population has grown dramatically—to about 5.4 billion people in 1992. By 2025, there may be as many as 8.5 billion people on Earth—more than 11 times world population in 1750.

The world's population explosion

Billions of people

10 9 8 7 6 5 4 3 2 1 0

1750 1775 1800 1825 1850 1875 1900 1925 1950 1975 2000* 2025*

*Projections.
Source: Estimates and projections by the Population Reference Bureau, a world population research institute.

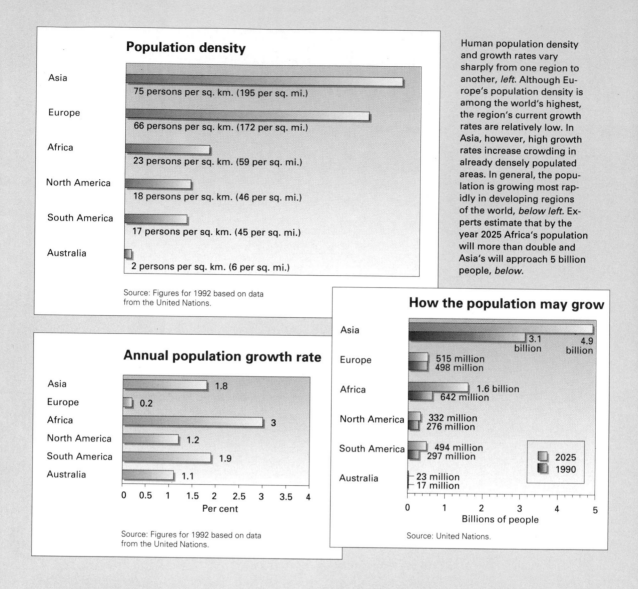

Population density

Asia	75 persons per sq. km. (195 per sq. mi.)
Europe	66 persons per sq. km. (172 per sq. mi.)
Africa	23 persons per sq. km. (59 per sq. mi.)
North America	18 persons per sq. km. (46 per sq. mi.)
South America	17 persons per sq. km. (45 per sq. mi.)
Australia	2 persons per sq. km. (6 per sq. mi.)

Source: Figures for 1992 based on data from the United Nations.

Human population density and growth rates vary sharply from one region to another, *left*. Although Europe's population density is among the world's highest, the region's current growth rates are relatively low. In Asia, however, high growth rates increase crowding in already densely populated areas. In general, the population is growing most rapidly in developing regions of the world, *below left*. Experts estimate that by the year 2025 Africa's population will more than double and Asia's will approach 5 billion people, *below*.

Annual population growth rate

Asia	1.8
Europe	0.2
Africa	3
North America	1.2
South America	1.9
Australia	1.1

0 0.5 1 1.5 2 2.5 3 3.5 4
Per cent

Source: Figures for 1992 based on data from the United Nations.

How the population may grow

Asia	3.1 billion / 4.9 billion
Europe	515 million / 498 million
Africa	1.6 billion / 642 million
North America	332 million / 276 million
South America	494 million / 297 million
Australia	23 million / 17 million

2025
1990

0 1 2 3 4 5
Billions of people

Source: United Nations.

Billions of mouths to feed

One of the problems of having an increasing world population is the difficulty of feeding everyone. As many as 13 million people die every year from malnutrition and starvation, despite the fact that global food production continues to increase and total world food supplies are adequate.

Experts say that complex political and economic factors lead to poverty and hunger in various regions. But some scientists fear that current demands for agricultural resources already exceed Earth's capacity to supply the population on a continuing basis. From 1950 until 1984, world agricultural production nearly tripled. In the mid-1980's, however, world agricultural production began to level off, and, in certain places, production declined.

Loss of farmland is a major cause of the decline in agricultural production. Usable farmland is lost for many reasons, but the major causes are erosion and salinization. Erosion occurs when wind and water rob land of its nutrient-rich soil. Salinization is the accumulation of salts on the soil, a problem common in regions where irrigation is used. Finally, as cities grow, they take over land once available for agriculture. The result of all these factors is that less and less land must feed more and more people.

Dwindling farmland is not the only problem, however. Across the entire globe, overpopulation continues to deplete croplands, fisheries, water resources, and energy supplies. Some scientists fear that uncontrolled population growth will thus produce dangerous conflicts among nations and regions over access to Earth's natural resources.

Polluting the Earth

As the human population grows, pollution from human activity also increases. Many activities—such as driving automobiles, farming, manufacturing, and power generation—release pollutants into the air, water, or soil. Common results of such pollution are changes in the chemistry of the environment.

These chemical changes affect not only the nearby environment—and the people who live there—but also areas hundreds or even thousands of kilometers from the place of release. For example, substances released into the air may be carried by the wind and be deposited far away by rain. Currents in rivers, lakes, and oceans spread pollutants that are dumped into water. Pollution in soil can seep into ground water and appear later in wells. Scientists have found evidence of pollution everywhere on Earth, from the largest cities to the remote and isolated South Pole.

Plant and animal life is sensitive to changes in the chemistry of the environment. For example, scientists have discovered extreme sensitivity in animals and plants that communicate by releasing biochemical compounds called pheromones. Some species can detect and respond to pheromone concentrations of as little as one part in a trillion—the equivalent of one teaspoonful in a lake that is 1 square kilometer (0.4 square mile) in area and 1 to 2 meters (3 to 7 feet) deep.

Such chemical sensitivity suggests to scientists that organisms may be easily affected by small but sudden changes in the chemistry of air, water, and land. Plants and animals may be able to adapt to changes as they evolve over thousands or millions of years. But in time periods measured in a few decades or even centuries, such changes may prove highly disruptive to many forms of life, including human beings.

Studying the effects of pollutants

There are many *toxic* (poisonous) pollutants, but the most well studied are radioactive elements and certain chemical compounds used to kill insects. Radioactive elements give off radiation that is harmful to plants and animals. They have been well studied because scientists can measure and track them easily with instruments that detect the radiation they give off. Such radioactive elements as strontium 90 were distributed worldwide in nuclear-bomb testing in the 1950's and early 1960's.

Strontium 90 chemically resembles the mineral calcium. Plants and animals absorb and store strontium 90 in tissues where calcium normally accumulates. In animals, strontium 90 accumulates in bone and *marrow*, the blood-cell-forming tissue, and can cause *leukemia*, a cancer of the blood. Small amounts of strontium 90 in the environment are a direct hazard to people.

Certain chemical pesticides used to control insects have also been well studied. Scientists can trace the chemicals' effects because some of the compounds remain in the environment for a long time. In addition, they have been used in large amounts in many parts of the world.

Studies of radioactive and chemical contaminants have taught scientists a great deal about the hazards of toxins and their threat to people and nature. One of scientists' most important discoveries was that toxins released into the environment not only circulate widely in air and water, but also may appear in living creatures in concentrations that are tens, hundreds, thousands, or hundreds of thousands of times higher than those measured in the air, water, or soil.

The concentrations may be increased or decreased as toxins are passed up the food chain. For example, a single plant may retain only a small amount of a toxin on its leaves. A rabbit eating many such plants may absorb the toxin in all the plants. And when a wolf eats many rabbits over the course of its lifetime, it absorbs the toxin in all the rabbits. In this way, the concentrations of a pollutant that is stored in animal tissues and not excreted may be dramatically larger in the tissues of some animals at the top of a food chain. This process is called biomagnification.

The case of DDT

A group of insecticides called chlorinated hydrocarbons illustrate this effect. These insecticides include DDT (dichloro-diphenyl-trichloroethane), a compound banned in the United States in 1972. DDT sprayed into the air kills mosquitoes and other insect pests. Scientists have found, however, that some of the compound remained in the air and was carried far away and sometimes fell with precipitation into bodies of water. DDT dissolves in fat but not water, so if the toxin contaminated a lake, river, or stream, it would bond to the fatty tissue in fish. In predators that ate the fish, the chemical accumulated. Farther up the food chain, in human beings or other animals that eat meat-eaters, the compound could reach concentrations hundreds to thousands or more times greater than the concentration in the general environment.

In this way, DDT—before it was banned—reached levels high enough to seriously disrupt the reproduction of many birds in North America, especially hawks, owls, and eagles. The chemical affected the development of the birds' eggs. DDT caused the birds' eggshells to be extremely thin and fragile, so that the young died before they could hatch. The use of DDT caused the peregrine falcon to become extinct throughout much of its normal range throughout the Eastern United States.

Many countries, especially in the tropics, still

Polluting the air

There are many sources of air pollution, *below right,* and their effects range from health problems in people to damage to forests, *photo below.* One of the most serious results of air pollution is acid rain, which forms when certain chemicals—mostly sulfur dioxide and nitrogen oxides—combine with moisture in the atmosphere to form weak acids. These acids reach Earth in rain, snow, or fog. The major sources of sulfur dioxide and nitrogen oxides are electric power generation, industrial processes, and transportation, *right.*

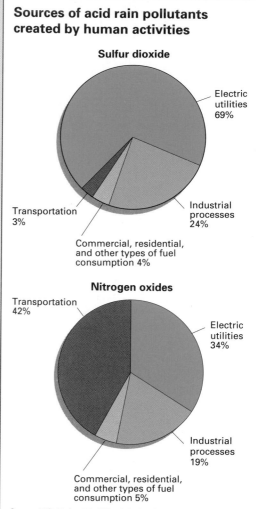

Sources of acid rain pollutants created by human activities

Sulfur dioxide

Electric utilities 69%

Industrial processes 24%

Commercial, residential, and other types of fuel consumption 4%

Transportation 3%

Nitrogen oxides

Transportation 42%

Electric utilities 34%

Industrial processes 19%

Commercial, residential, and other types of fuel consumption 5%

Source: U.S. National Acid Precipitation Assessment Program.

Air pollution

Major sources:

- Emissions from motor vehicles, aircraft, power plants, and factories
- Burning of garbage, plant material, and fossil fuels
- Industrial emissions

Major effects:

- Respiratory disorders and other human health problems
- Damage to livestock, crops, and other plants and animals
- Damage to Earth's atmosphere
- Acid rain

Soil pollution

Major sources:

- Agricultural chemicals and animal waste
- Solid waste in garbage dumps and landfills
- Industrial toxic waste dumps
- Nuclear fallout

Major effects:

- Damage to plants and soil
- Health problems in human beings and other animals
- Water pollution from soil runoff

Polluting the land

Many human activities pollute soil, *left.* Discarded solid waste fills landfills and may release harmful chemicals into the environment. Toxic waste from industry, agriculture, and nuclear testing can also cause damage to animals and plants. A plane sprays pesticides to control crop-damaging insects, *photo left.* Some chemicals that enter food and water supplies cause such visible effects as a deformed bird's beak, *above.*

permit the use of DDT. The compound continues to cause worldwide problems, because winds deposit it far from the place of use. As recently as 1991, researchers reported finding DDT and other U.S.-banned pesticides in U.S. lakes.

Ecologists consider DDT and radioactive substances such as strontium 90 to be representative of contaminants as a whole. Radioactivity such as that of strontium 90 causes health problems in people even at low levels. Plants and animals will be protected if the amount of radioactivity released into an area is low enough to be safe for human beings. Small amounts of toxins such as DDT and other poisons, on the other hand, may not be a direct threat to people. Yet scientists have learned that this type of pollutant can accumulate through biomagnification, contributing to the loss of plant and animal life and ultimately threatening the health of human beings.

From air pollution to acid rain

Scientists are continuing to amass data concerning the effects of many other types of toxic pollutants. Air pollution, for example, can cause breathing difficulties and other health problems in people, aggravating diseases such as asthma and pneumonia and contributing to the development of cancer and emphysema. Air pollution also harms plants and animals.

Two of the most serious air pollutants are oxides of sulfur and of nitrogen. A major source of these compounds is the burning of *fossil fuels* (coal, oil, and natural gas) in industry and in transportation. The pollutants often occur with high levels of other toxins such as lead, zinc, and ground-level ozone, a component of smog formed by chemical reactions between car exhausts and sunlight.

Sulfur dioxide and nitrogen oxides also cause acidic precipitation, commonly called *acid rain.* Acid rain results when the airborne pollutants combine with moisture in the air to form sulfuric and nitric acids that fall back to Earth, usually in rain or snow. Since the late 1960's, numerous scientific studies have demonstrated acid rain's effects on the environment. These studies have shown that acid rain hinders plant *photosynthesis* (the process by which plants make food from water, sunlight, and carbon dioxide). Acid rain also contributes to the death of trees, destroys life in lakes and rivers, and damages statues and other structures.

The weighty problem of heavy metals

Other pollutants under study include the metallic elements called *heavy metals.* These contaminants can pollute air, water, and soil. They include lead, mercury, silver, zinc, iron, copper, nickel, chromium, and cadmium. Some coal is rich in heavy metals, and burning it in electric power stations, incinerators, steel mills, and motor vehicles may produce air pollution containing the metals. The elements enter the atmosphere as extremely small particles called *particulates*. These particulates then fall to Earth and contaminate soil and water.

Scientists are accumulating evidence of the effects of heavy metals in the environment. Studies show that exposure to lead in soil or water can cause nervous-system damage in children, for example, and that if human beings eat mercury-poisoned fish, the effects can be deadly. In March 1991, Joel Schwartz, a scientist with the U.S. Environmental Protection Agency, reported that as many as 60,000 people in the United States may die prematurely each year as a result of particulate pollution. In August 1991, measurements of mercury levels in fish caught in several U.S. lakes prompted officials in 20 states to warn consumers against eating fish from those waters. Heavy metals also threaten the growth of forests by disrupting the supply of nutrients in the soil.

Other water pollutants

Acid rain and heavy metals are only a few of the many pollutants that contaminate rivers, lakes, streams, seas, and oceans. Waste from industries is a particularly important cause of water pollution. Factories may dump waste containing toxic chemicals directly into bodies of water or into sewerage systems. Sewage itself is another major contaminant of water that can cause ecological problems and such human diseases as cholera and dysentery. Marine life is also harmed by agricultural waste, chiefly runoff containing chemical fertilizers and pesticides. Finally, oil and other petroleum products that are spilled into bodies of water foul beaches and kill sea birds and mammals, such as dolphins and whales.

Solid waste

Chemical pollutants released into water or spread through the air are often invisible to the human eye. But the growing masses of solid waste that people produce are an all-too-visible pollutant in the form of trash.

The EPA estimates that by 2000, the United States will generate about 175 million metric tons (193 short tons) of solid waste per year. According to the U.S. National Solid Wastes Management Association, an organization of businesses that collect, dispose of, and recycle trash, about 83 per cent of U.S. solid waste goes into landfill dumps.

In most landfills, operators spread earth over the most recent garbage to keep rats, flies, and

Polluting water
Untreated sewage, agricultural chemicals, and toxic industrial emissions are common pollutants that damage life in rivers, lakes, and oceans, *below.* Oil spills, *photo below,* are one of the most dramatic examples of water pollution. Oil spills kill fish and other marine life, *below right.*

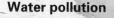

Water pollution

Major sources:

- Agricultural chemicals and animal wastes
- Industrial wastes
- Untreated sewage
- Oil spills
- Acid precipitation

Major effects:

- Damage to plants and animals
- Cancer and other diseases in human beings
- Disruption of the ecology of lakes, rivers, and other aquatic ecosystems

Selected common pollutants

Chemical	Sources	Effects
Benzene	A component of gasoline; used as a solvent in inks and paints; used to make synthetic rubber, styrofoam, and detergents.	Can pollute air, land, and water; has been shown to cause cancer in human beings.
Chlorofluorocarbons (CFC's)	Gases used as industrial solvents and as refrigerants.	Destroys ozone in Earth's upper atmosphere.
Vinyl chloride	Used in the production of polyvinyl chloride, a common plastic.	Pollutes air and can cause cancer in human beings.
Mercury	Used to make chemicals, paint, batteries, and electrical switches; emitted by power plants and incinerators.	Pollutes air, water, and land; accumulates in animals and humans; can kill wildlife; at high doses, causes nervous-system damage in human beings.
Lead	Leaded gasoline; lead-based paint; batteries.	Pollutes land and air; can cause mental impairment in children; at high doses, decreases the human body's ability to make hemoglobin, a substance in blood that carries oxygen; can cause nervous-system damage and digestive problems.
Polychlorinated biphenyls (PCB's)	Once used as an insulator in electrical transformers, as hydraulic fluid, and to make paint and adhesives. Banned in the United States since 1979.	Pollutes land and water; at high concentrations, may cause liver damage and cancer in human beings.
Sulfur dioxide	Combustion of fossil fuels in power plants and industry.	Pollutes land, air, and water; helps cause acid rain, which can kill vegetation and marine life.
Nitrates	Fertilizers.	Excessive use can cause water pollution when fertilizers run off into lakes and rivers; can decrease oxygen-transporting capacity of hemoglobin in human beings.

other vermin away. But landfills still pose a widespread pollution hazard.

Apart from the land that landfills pollute, they can also poison underground reservoirs of water with metals and dangerous chemicals from packaging materials and other debris. This happens when rain seeps through garbage, dissolves the metals and chemicals, and carries them into the soil. Once in the ground, the compounds slowly filter down to enter water supplies—which are often used for drinking water. As solid wastes fill more and more landfills, this form of water pollution is an increasing concern.

Clearing the water, land, and air

To protect people and the environment, most developed nations have placed limits on the amount and types of pollution that can be released into the environment. But laws and political boundaries cannot stop the spread of pollution through the air or through the water. Therefore, nations and states with high levels of pollution can adversely affect those with the strictest pollution laws.

Another difficult question involves what level of pollution is safe. Many laws require that pollution levels not exceed those found to be harmful to people. But, as scientists have learned through the study of DDT and other pesticides, it may be necessary to protect plant and animal life in order to protect people. Doing so would require much more restrictive standards than those based simply on protecting people from direct contamination. Yet experts say that enacting such tough standards is the only way to assure the protection of people from the poisoning of the environment that is now underway.

Earth's Threatened Ozone Layer

One of the most disturbing aspects of the changes in Earth is the rate at which chemical pollutants produced by human activity are destroying the protective layer of ozone in Earth's upper atmosphere. Ozone is a molecule that consists of three oxygen atoms. An oxygen gas molecule consists of two oxygen atoms. Reactions between oxygen and ultraviolet radiation from the sun create a layer of ozone throughout Earth's *stratosphere* (upper atmosphere).

Although ground-level ozone is considered a harmful pollutant, the ozone layer in the stratosphere is beneficial. The layer normally absorbs 95 to 99.9 per cent of the ultraviolet radiation from the sun, protecting life on Earth from this biologically damaging form of energy.

Ultraviolet radiation causes skin cancer—including *malignant melanoma*, a form of the disease that can be fatal—and other health problems. Ultraviolet radiation increases the risk of cataracts, which cloud the lens of the eye and can cause blindness. It may also weaken the human body's disease-fighting immune system. Scientists fear that the continued depletion of the ozone layer in the upper atmosphere will thus cause widespread health problems.

Ultraviolet radiation threatens other forms of life as well. It may interfere with plant photosynthesis, causing ecological damage and reducing agricultural production. Ultraviolet radiation may also damage marine life by killing one-celled

An October 1991 measurement of ozone levels in the upper atmosphere above Antarctica, *below*, shows the extent of the loss of ozone. (Pink and white areas represent the lowest ozone concentrations.) The levels were the lowest since scientists first reported an ozone "hole" above Antarctica in the mid-1980's.

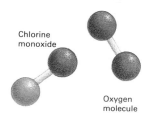

How chlorofluorocarbons destroy ozone

Chlorofluorocarbons (CFC's) are commonly used chemicals in industry. Many refrigeration systems and air conditioners also contain CFC's. Because CFC's are gases, they can escape into the atmosphere. In the upper atmosphere, ultraviolet radiation breaks down CFC molecules, beginning a chain of events that leads to the destruction of ozone molecules.

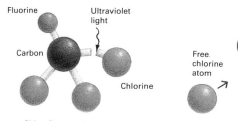

Fluorine

Ultraviolet light

Carbon

Chlorine

Chlorofluorocarbon molecule

Free chlorine atom

Ozone molecule

Chlorine monoxide

Oxygen molecule

Atoms of chlorine, fluorine, and carbon make up CFC molecules. Ultraviolet radiation breaks chlorine atoms free from the CFC molecule.

A free chlorine atom can react with other molecules in the atmosphere. When a chlorine atom reacts with an ozone molecule, it steals one of the ozone molecule's three oxygen atoms.

The oxygen atom combines with the chlorine atom to form a molecule of chlorine monoxide. The remaining two oxygen atoms form an oxygen molecule.

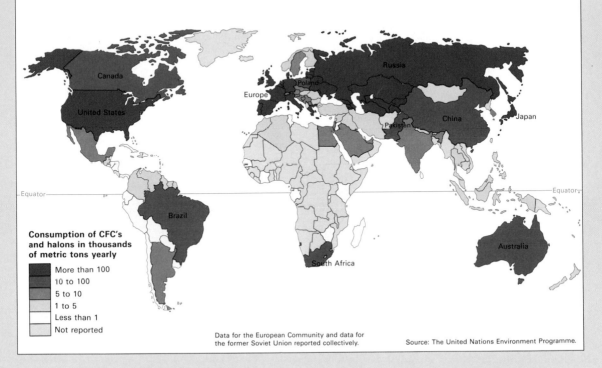

Worldwide consumption of CFC's and halons

The United States, Europe, the Commonwealth of Independent States, and Japan have consumed most of the world's CFC's and halons—the two most important ozone-destroying chemicals. Most of the world's industrialized nations have agreed to stop producing CFC's by 2000 in an attempt to halt the destruction of the ozone layer in Earth's upper atmosphere.

Consumption of CFC's and halons in thousands of metric tons yearly

- More than 100
- 10 to 100
- 5 to 10
- 1 to 5
- Less than 1
- Not reported

Data for the European Community and data for the former Soviet Union reported collectively.

Source: The United Nations Environment Programme.

---

plants called phytoplankton, which form the base of the ocean's food chain. *Krill* (small, shrimplike animals) feed on phytoplankton. Krill, in turn, are a major source of food for many sea animals, including penguins, seals, and whales.

Ozone-destroying chemicals

In 1974, scientists first proposed the idea that manufactured chemicals could threaten the ozone layer. A group of widely used gases called chlorofluorocarbons (CFC's) posed the greatest chemical threat.

These gases have a variety of uses. Electronic equipment manufacturers use CFC's to clean metal, and CFC's are commonly used as refrigerants and to make foam insulation. Aerosol sprays may also contain the compounds. The United States banned the use of CFC's in aerosol sprays in 1978, but many other countries still permit this use. Finally, halon gases, which are used in fire extinguishers, are also CFC's.

Each year, the world uses approximately 750,000 metric tons (827,000 short tons) of CFC's. Much of those gases are sealed in refrigerators and air conditioners, where they do not threaten the environment. However, some CFC's escape from leaking, poorly serviced, or discarded appliances. Industrial processes such as electronics and insulation manufacturing also release CFC's into the atmosphere.

Once in the upper atmosphere, CFC's react with ozone to destroy it. First, ultraviolet light breaks down CFC molecules. One of the products of this breakdown is the element chlorine. As a single chlorine atom or when combined with one oxygen atom as chlorine monoxide, this element breaks down ozone molecules. Scientists estimate that one chlorine atom can destroy as many as 100,000 ozone molecules.

The frigid temperatures and atmospheric conditions above Antarctica favor the destruction of ozone. Scientists believe that tiny ice crystals of nitric acid in Antarctica's upper atmosphere are directly involved. These crystals may help begin the chemical changes that result in the destruction of ozone.

In 1985, British scientists confirmed that chemi-

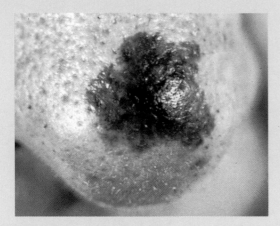

Skin cancer, *above,* may become more prevalent as a result of damage to the ozone layer. The layer blocks much of the sun's dangerous ultraviolet radiation, which can cause skin cancer and other harmful effects.

cal reactions had begun to damage the ozone layer above Antarctica. They reported results from ozone measurements taken with instruments on the ground, in airplanes, and put aloft in scientific balloons during the previous 27 years. Their measurements showed a 40 per cent reduction in ozone concentrations over Antarctica from the mid-1970's to 1984. This thinning occurred during September and October—springtime in the Southern Hemisphere. Media reports dubbed the annual thinning a "hole" in the ozone layer.

Many groups of scientists quickly began monitoring the Antarctic ozone layer. In 1986, U.S. National Aeronautics and Space Administration (NASA) scientists confirmed the British findings and found that the hole in the ozone layer was nearly as large as the entire continent of Antarctica. In 1987, scientists reported that the hole was wider and deeper than in 1986, and that it lasted longer. In 1991, scientists reported that, during 1990, Antarctic ozone levels had dropped to their lowest recorded level.

The danger of ozone destruction is not limited to Antarctica, however. In April 1991, the U.S. Environmental Protection Agency (EPA) reported that atmospheric ozone concentrations above the United States decreased by 4 to 5 per cent during the 1980's, three times faster than during the 1970's. The EPA report fueled concerns that cases of skin cancer and deaths due to melanoma would rise dramatically in the United States in future decades.

In October 1991, United Nations scientists reported that ozone losses above the United States and other temperate areas of Earth between the tropics and the poles was taking place during summertime. This alarmed many experts, who feared that the summer decrease in the protective ozone layer could cause even more cases of skin cancer.

In February 1992, NASA scientists announced that levels of chlorine monoxide resulting from the breakdown of CFC's were at record levels above the Northern Hemisphere near the Arctic and that these conditions could cause an ozone hole to develop over much of Europe, Canada, Russia, and northern portions of the United States by the year 2000.

For an ozone hole to form, proper weather conditions must also exist. In April 1992, NASA scientists reported that ozone-layer depletion above the Arctic was not as extensive as expected because of unusually warm weather. The weather helped break up a pattern of strong, cold winds called the circumpolar vortex. These winds help trap chlorine monoxide and speed ozone destruction. But scientists said that if the circumpolar vortex lasts longer than usual in future years, a large ozone hole can be expected to develop above the Arctic.

Protecting the ozone layer

Scientists and politicians worldwide are working to slow the destruction of the ozone layer. In September 1987, 24 nations, including the United States, signed an agreement in Montreal, Canada, to limit the production of CFC's. The agreement, called the Montreal Protocol, froze CFC production at 1986 levels, beginning in 1989. The 24 nations also agreed to reduce CFC production by 50 per cent by 1999.

Since the Montreal Protocol, however, most nations have agreed that an even quicker phase-out of CFC's is needed. In June 1990, the world's industrial nations agreed to halt all production of CFC's by the year 2000. Some countries have adopted an even more rapid phase-out schedule. Most European nations plan to stop producing CFC's by the end of 1995, and the United States announced in February 1992 that it would also stop making the chemicals by the end of 1995.

But CFC's remain in the atmosphere for at least 75 years before natural processes break them down and the chlorine washes out of the atmosphere as hydrochloric acid in rain. So even if all CFC production stopped immediately, the threat of ozone depletion would continue for more than a century. And the CFC's needed for industry are not easily replaced. There are, however, substitutes for most uses, including refrigeration. The challenge for scientists and chemical engineers is to find substitutes that will be as effective as CFC's—and that will not have some other group of harmful effects.

The Global Warming Issue

Since the early 1970's, Earth's average surface air temperature has increased rapidly—more rapidly than at any time in recorded history. In itself, a change in Earth's climate is nothing new. Throughout the planet's history, warm periods have alternated with *ice ages*, spans of tens of thousands of years during which large areas of Earth were covered by glaciers.

In the past, global climatic changes have been the result of changes in geological and biological processes, cloud cover, ocean currents, and even the amount of radiation the sun produces. These factors continue to affect the Earth. But many scientists fear that the current warming is the result of human activities that produce carbon dioxide and other so-called *greenhouse gases* that accumulate in the atmosphere and trap heat from the sun. These scientists believe that warming from the continued accumulation of greenhouse gases may cause serious environmental, social, and economic problems for people around the world.

The greenhouse effect

Heat-trapping gases such as carbon dioxide, water vapor, and methane are responsible for the natural *greenhouse effect:* They keep the Earth substantially warmer than it would be otherwise.

The Earth is bathed continuously in radiant energy from the sun in the form of light and heat. Some of the heat is absorbed by heat-trapping gases in the atmosphere, and this warms Earth's atmosphere. Some of the light energy from the sun that strikes Earth's atmosphere is reflected back into space. The surface of the Earth absorbs the rest of the light energy and radiates it back again as heat. Some of this heat can be absorbed by the heat-trapping gases.

The carbon cycle

Carbon dioxide is a major greenhouse gas. Natural cycles ordinarily keep the levels of carbon dioxide in the atmosphere from changing rapidly. Some carbon is removed from the atmosphere through plant photosynthesis. An equivalent amount of carbon is released into the atmosphere by animals and plants, including organisms that cause decay. These organisms give off carbon dioxide during a process called respiration. The respiration of decay organisms also releases methane, another heat-trapping gas, into the atmosphere. Throughout most of the planet's recent history, the concentration of carbon dioxide in the atmosphere has not changed from year to year as long as the processes of carbon release and absorption were in balance.

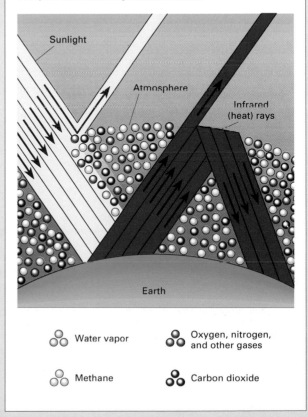

The greenhouse effect
Carbon dioxide, methane, and water vapor are gases that occur naturally in Earth's atmosphere. They allow sunlight to enter the atmosphere but trap some of the *infrared* (heat) rays from Earth's surface. This heat trapping makes Earth warm enough to support life. In this way, the gases act somewhat like greenhouse windows and are thus called *greenhouse gases*. The process by which greenhouse gases trap heat in Earth's atmosphere is called the *greenhouse effect*.

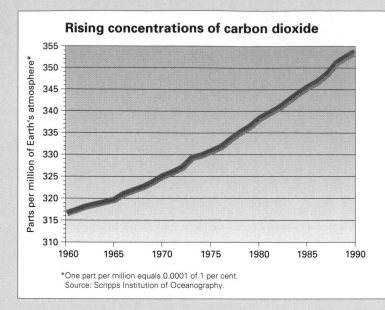

Rising concentrations of carbon dioxide

*One part per million equals 0.0001 of 1 per cent.
Source: Scripps Institution of Oceanography.

The concentration of carbon dioxide in the atmosphere rose dramatically between 1960 and 1990, according to scientists at the Scripps Institution of Oceanography in La Jolla, Calif., who have been monitoring the yearly increases since 1958. Experts say that burning *fossil fuels* (coal, natural gas, and oil) has produced most of the excess carbon dioxide.

A build-up of carbon dioxide

Today, however, humanity releases large quantities of carbon dioxide into the atmosphere through the burning of *fossil fuels* (oil, coal, and natural gas). Before the Industrial Revolution began in the mid-1700's, this release of carbon dioxide was gradual enough that the oceans could absorb any excess and there was little noticeable accumulation in the atmosphere.

The oceans have a very large capacity for holding carbon dioxide. At the surface, the gas dissolves in water. Through complex chemical processes, some of the carbon becomes part of the tissues of marine organisms. Carbon-containing sea shells eventually settle to the ocean floor, forming carbonate sediments such as limestone.

Since the Industrial Revolution, the combustion of fossil fuels has soared. At the same time, the human population has increased, and people have cleared more and more forestland to make room for agriculture and other enterprises. This *deforestation* (destruction of forests) leads to still higher levels of carbon dioxide in the atmosphere. When trees are burned, carbon dioxide is released. If the plants are not burned, the branches, leaves, bark, roots, and organic material in the soil decay, releasing carbon dioxide and methane.

About 6 billion metric tons (6.6 billion short tons) of carbon are released into the atmosphere each year through the combustion of fossil fuels. About 3 billion tons are released from deforestation, and an unknown additional quantity comes from the accelerated decay of organic matter.

Scientists have been monitoring carbon dioxide levels in the atmosphere since 1958. That year, the first precise measurements of the levels of carbon dioxide in Earth's atmosphere were developed by Charles David Keeling at the Scripps Institution of Oceanography in La Jolla, Calif. He and his colleagues set up measuring devices 3,300 meters (11,000 feet) above sea level on Mauna Loa in Hawaii. Since then, Keeling has measured a steady rise in carbon dioxide levels in Earth's atmosphere. These levels can be compared with the concentrations found in bubbles of air trapped in glacial ice up to 160,000 years ago. For example, in 1990, atmospheric carbon dioxide levels were about 25 per cent higher than those measured in air trapped in ice that formed in 1880.

Scientists believe that the largest source of the increase is the combustion of fossil fuels, which produced about 160 billion metric tons (176 billion short tons) of carbon from 1850 to 1980. Experts estimate that deforestation has released a somewhat lesser amount.

The controversy over global warming

Some data are not in question: The carbon dioxide content of the atmosphere is now higher than at any time in the past 160,000 years. The causes are human activities—deforestation and the burning of fossil fuels. The effect of adding carbon dioxide and other heat-trapping gases to the atmosphere will be to make Earth warmer than it would have been otherwise.

But many other uncertainties surround the issue of global warming. Chief among them is when the heat-trapping gases, among the various factors that affect the temperature of the Earth, will dominate and cause a rapid warming.

Most scientists say that the rising levels of carbon dioxide have already caused an increase in Earth's average surface temperature. To establish such a link, the scientists compare the rising carbon dioxide levels with temperature measurements taken during the past 100 years. Until the early 1900's, Earth's average surface temperature was warming slowly. In the 1980's and 1990's, record high annual global temperatures have been recorded, with 1991 being the warmest year on record. The rate of warming since 1980 has been about 0.2 degree Celsius (0.4 degree Fahrenheit) per decade.

These scientists fear that global warming will cause temperatures to increase by as much as 0.5 degree Celsius (0.9 degree Fahrenheit) per decade sometime between 2000 and 2030, perhaps more in the higher latitudes. The temperature increase could severely affect the world's major agricultural regions. Crops could no longer be grown in the Midwestern United States, and the major food-producing regions would shift to Canada and Siberia. The higher temperatures could also melt polar ice, flooding low-lying areas—such as the deltas of Egypt's Nile River, India's Ganges River, and North America's Mississippi River, as well as cities along seacoasts.

Although there is a consensus within most of the scientific community as to the seriousness and causes of the problem, a smaller number of scientists question whether Earth will warm in response to the increasing levels of heat-trapping gases or whether the warming will be a problem for human beings. Their reasons differ. They range from assertions that the warming will be checked by an increase in cloud cover to predictions that

plants will grow better on a warmer Earth. The discussion is made more complex by the assertions of U.S. government officials that taking action to curb the use of fossil fuels would be too costly. Many scientists and international leaders dispute this point as well.

Predicting the course of global warming

For ecologists, one crucial question is the effect of higher temperatures on plants and on microorganisms that cause decay. Evidence shows that higher temperatures will have little effect on rates of photosynthesis, a process that removes carbon dioxide from the atmosphere. But the warming will increase rates of respiration among some organisms, thus releasing more carbon dioxide.

A 1 degree Celsius (1.8 degree Fahrenheit) increase in temperature often increases rates of respiration in some organisms by 10 per cent to 30 per cent. Warming will thus speed the decay of organic matter in soils, peat in bogs, and organic debris in marshes. Indeed, the higher temperatures of the last few decades appear to have accelerated the decay of organic matter in the Arctic tundra.

Warming will also change patterns of rainfall and other aspects of climate. Scientists think that such changes destroy large, long-lived plants such as trees and favor small plants with short lifetimes and rapid reproduction. Thus, forests may be destroyed and replaced by shrubs or grassland. The death of some plants and their decay will release more stored carbon into the atmosphere.

Another important question involves the effect of rising levels of carbon dioxide coupled with the higher temperatures. Together, these factors may

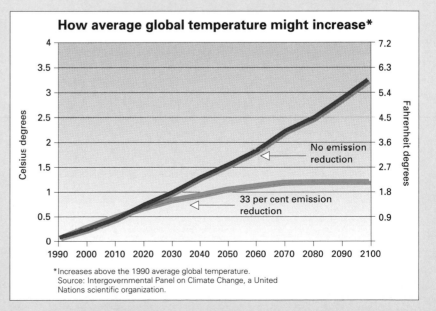

Some atmospheric scientists estimate that continued high levels of greenhouse gas emissions will by 2100 cause average global temperatures to rise by more than 3.0 Celsius degrees (5.4 Fahrenheit degrees) above the 1990 global average. If greenhouse gas emissions fall by 33 per cent, temperatures will not rise as quickly or as much and, by about 2075, would level off at about 1.2 Celsius degrees (2.2 Fahrenheit degrees) higher than the 1990 average.

How average global temperature might increase*

*Increases above the 1990 average global temperature.
Source: Intergovernmental Panel on Climate Change, a United Nations scientific organization.

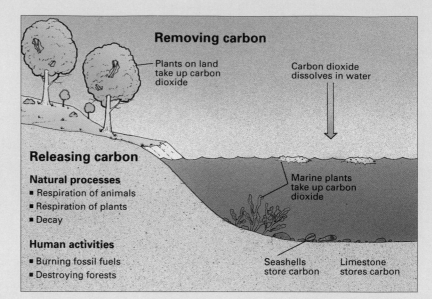

Removing carbon

Plants on land take up carbon dioxide

Carbon dioxide dissolves in water

Releasing carbon

Natural processes
- Respiration of animals
- Respiration of plants
- Decay

Human activities
- Burning fossil fuels
- Destroying forests

Marine plants take up carbon dioxide

Seashells store carbon

Limestone stores carbon

increase the amount of carbon plants take in and may increase plant growth, at least under certain circumstances. Abundant evidence from studies of plants in greenhouses seems to confirm this.

Increased plant growth would be beneficial, because plants would remove carbon dioxide from the atmosphere for photosynthesis. But ecologists fear that the stimulation of plant growth must be small. There is no evidence, for example, that the higher temperatures and rising carbon dioxide levels of recent decades has increased the growth of trees worldwide. Although controversy surrounds this point, many experts believe that a rapid warming will lead to the rapid loss of carbon from plants and soils and thus to an acceleration of the warming.

To gather more evidence, researchers analyze air in glacial ice to compile a record of carbon dioxide and methane concentrations in the atmosphere. The data show that as temperatures rose in the past, the concentrations of carbon dioxide and methane also rose. As temperatures fell over thousands of years, the concentrations also fell, though not always in perfect unison.

The pattern is consistent with, but does not prove, the theory that a warming releases carbon stored in vegetation and soils and that a cooling results in storage of carbon there. The processes involved in such transitions are complex, however. Such relatively simple explanations may ultimately need to be changed.

Preventing global warming

How might we stabilize the composition of the atmosphere? That question looms large in the eyes of scientists and political leaders as the levels

of carbon dioxide grow. Carbon dioxide and methane have long lives in the atmosphere and, once they are there, Earth may be destined to become warmer. If we find that the climate is becoming too warm, there is no easy or rapid way to remove the gases and return to an earlier climatic pattern.

We may be able to control fossil fuel use and rates of deforestation, but there is no direct way to control the acceleration of decay except by stopping the warming. To stabilize the composition of the atmosphere immediately, we would have to cut present releases by about 4 billion tons of carbon annually. It is not now possible to accomplish this without reducing both deforestation and our consumption of fossil fuels.

Most scientists believe that if immediate global action is not taken, the rapid increases of atmospheric carbon from decay will exceed the reductions possible through control of fossil fuel use and management of forests. In 1990, the United Nations gathered many scientists from around the world to review these issues. This group, the Intergovernmental Panel on Climate Change, concluded that an immediate 60 per cent reduction in fossil fuel use would be necessary. But by April 1992, no nation had accepted that goal, though several had recognized a need for reducing emissions by 20 per cent.

At the Earth Summit in June 1992, leaders from most industrialized nations agreed in principle to return to earlier levels of carbon dioxide emissions—though opposition from the United States prevented them from agreeing to specific targets for emissions, as many scientists had hoped. The leaders also agreed to assist developing nations in limiting their releases of greenhouse gases.

The Endangered Web of Life

Human beings are only one of millions of organisms sufficiently different from one another to be recognized as species. Until the 1980's, scientists estimated that there were between 3 million and 10 million species on Earth. Then, scientists began to examine populations of insects living in the high foliage of trees in tropical forest, and the experience caused them to increase their estimate to 30 million species. After scientists began to consider the populations of microorganisms in the tropics, the upper limit of their estimates rose to 100 million species. We shall probably never have an accurate count of the different kinds of organisms that share our planet.

We do know, however, that these species— plants and animals together—keep the planet functioning as a habitat suitable for all. Scientists call the variety of life forms Earth's *biological diversity* or *biodiversity*. We also know that human activities are reducing both the numbers of species on Earth and the potential of land and water for supporting them. This process is commonly called *biotic impoverishment*—the loss of the rich biological potential of Earth.

Biotic impoverishment is the result of chronic disturbance of the surface of Earth on land or sea. The result, no matter what its cause, is a reduction in the complexity of the form and structure of nature. Ecologists have found that large-bodied organisms that reproduce slowly are lost most readily. Small-bodied organisms with short reproductive times often survive. These rapidly reproducing, small organisms are the life forms that compete with human beings most effectively and are regarded as "pests," such as mice and insects.

The threat of extinction

The loss of biological diversity has become most spectacularly noticeable in the extinction or decline of populations of large and well-known animals. Many animal species have become extinct since the 1700's, among them the California grizzly bear, the dodo, and the passenger pigeon. Hundreds of other animal species are threatened. In North America, endangered species include the black-footed ferret, the California condor, the desert tortoise, and the whooping crane.

Most species in danger of extinction anywhere in the world are suffering from the encroachment of human beings. The Asian elephant, for example, has become an endangered species due to the expansion of the human population throughout its range in southern Asia. In Africa, the African elephants are being killed off for their tusks. Monkeys and other primates throughout the world are threatened by hunting, capture for medical use, and the destruction of their habitats. And the rhinoceroses, lions, and other large mammals of the African *savanna* (grassy plains with scattered trees) compete for land and life with some of the most rapidly growing human populations in the world.

The loss of biological diversity is most severe, however, in the tropical rain forests. The forests of the tropics are particularly vulnerable to disturbance because the soils have a low capacity for retaining nutrients. Most of the forests' nutrient elements are held in the tissues of plants. When loggers and farmers destroy existing plant cover, the nutrients are washed from the land into streams, and the land itself becomes less able to support life. Destruction of these forests destroys the habitat of hundreds, sometimes thousands, of species—from such creatures as the howler monkey and indigo macaw, to less visible species of plants, insects, and microbes, many of which are not yet known to science.

Smaller and smaller habitats

The apparently sudden surge of threats to species has brought a parallel surge of interest in what can be done to stop the losses. Scientists and conservationists have been primarily interested in determining how large a park or other reserve must be to prevent a decline in the number of species there. In the case of the large migrating animal populations of the African savannas, the required area is obviously very large. But even the bird populations of the tropical forests in South America's Amazon region require thousands of hectares of intact habitat to avoid rapid losses.

Animals need large habitats for reasons that are complex and not always easily defined. Each species, however, is dependent on many others. Birds, for example, may depend on the fruit of several different species of trees, each of which may bear fruit at a different time.

Scientists' understanding of habitat size has borrowed from the observations of Charles Darwin, a British naturalist of the 1800's. Darwin showed that the number of different kinds of plants and animals on islands varies with the size

of the islands and their distance from continents. The larger the island and the closer it is to a continent, the more species it will have.

Darwin's observation takes on special importance in our time because some human activities are cutting apart the natural landscape. When people build roads or extend cities, the effect is to create "islands" within the once-continuous plant and animal communities of a region. Within these islands, the number of species drops. The amount of the decline depends on how small the island is and its degree of isolation.

Expansion of agriculture

Even modern farming methods may lead to a loss of biological diversity. Chemical fertilizers can cause *eutrophication,* a process that upsets the balance of life by encouraging the abundant growth of certain species to the exclusion of others. In a lake, for example, fertilizer runoff can cause the overgrowth of algae. As the larger amounts of algae die, bacteria and other decay-causing organisms thrive. They use up so much oxygen that fish and other marine organisms begin to die. Despite the chemical "enrichment," such lakes support fewer species of plants and fish.

The process works in reverse as well. Irrigation, for instance, almost always leads to *salinization,* the accumulation of salts on the land's surface. Salinization occurs because irrigation water evaporates, leaving behind minerals dissolved in the water. This alters the soil chemistry and renders the land less capable of supporting plant life. Finally, agricultural practices may also contribute to soil erosion if croplands are left barren after harvest and before planting.

These problems, though often ignored, are widespread. Officials in India, for example, say that one-third of that nation's land area is so impoverished that it supports no plants. The need to replace agricultural land lost to impoverishment is one of the most important causes of deforestation. Farmers abandon their barren land, clear trees from a forest, and begin the cycle of land impoverishment anew.

Effects of pollution

If we were simply interested in preserving known species, a system of extensive parks and reserves around the world involving both land and water might solve it. But the threats to species arise not simply from hunting and the encroach-

ment of people, with their cities and farms, but also from the general pollution of Earth. The pollution causes an often irreversible series of changes in the environment that reduce its potential for supporting plant and animal life.

What are the changes and how threatening are they? The most noticeable evidence on land appears downwind of copper and zinc smelters and other heavily polluting industries. The barren landscapes around Copper Hill, Tenn.; Sudbury, Canada; and now on dozens of sites in the former Soviet Union and in Eastern European countries reveal the progressive effects of pollution with oxides of sulfur and various toxic metals such as copper and zinc.

In the most extreme instances, the areas consist of barren soil, too toxic for any plant to grow in. In some places, severe damage extends over many square kilometers around the industrial plant that is the source of the pollution. These areas are so stark that the landscape appears moonlike. U.S. astronauts preparing to visit the moon in the 1970's practiced navigating their small moon rover on the barren landscape downwind of the smelters at Sudbury. Such environmental changes are underway over vast areas of Earth.

Establishing the link between a particular pollu-

tant and its effect on the landscape can be difficult, however. One of the clearest examinations of the patterns of biotic impoverishment was an experiment at Brookhaven National Laboratory that began in 1961 and ended 15 years later. Here, radiation from the radioactive element cesium 137 caused damage to a forest of oaks and pines.

Less than 200 meters (220 yards) from the source of the radiation, the full range of effects was clearly visible. Areas of plant growth formed ringlike patterns around the source of pollution. Immediately next to the source, no plants survived. Outside that zone, where radiation exposures were still very high, there was a zone where only certain mosses and lichens survived. Farther away was a ring of *herbaceous* (green) plants. Farther still, there was a ring of low shrubs, then one of taller shrubs. The most subtle effects occurred farther from the source of pollution, where the forest appeared intact. Pines proved to be the most vulnerable of the tree species. They died off before noticeable effects appeared in the several species of oaks.

Oak forests without pines are common in central Long Island and elsewhere in North America where oak and pine trees once grew together. Even an experienced ecologist might overlook

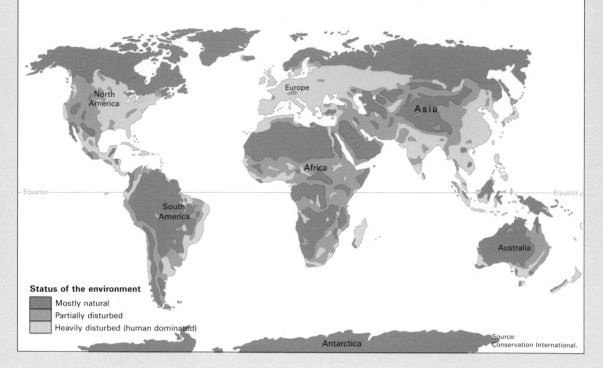

Threatened environments around the world
Human activity has seriously damaged natural environments over wide areas of the world. Antarctica, the Arctic regions, large areas of South America, the Sahara in Africa, and much of Australia remain largely undisturbed by human activity, but humanity threatens plants and animals in nearly every other region of the world.

North America

Europe

Asia

Africa

Equator

South America

Australia

Status of the environment
- Mostly natural
- Partially disturbed
- Heavily disturbed (human dominated)

Antarctica

Source:
Conservation International.

this change and assume that nothing had happened to a forest that had actually lost its pines. Such are the difficulties of determining the effects of chronic human disturbance at low levels.

Preserving biological richness

In the United States, the need to protect plant and animal species has become a highly controversial and sharply political issue since the passage of the Endangered Species Act in 1973. The act, designed to protect species, in effect requires the preservation of the species' habitats, and policies that preserve land and forests compete with economic interests. In the 1990's, for example, the loggers of forests in the Western United States were challenged legally in their attempt to cut trees for lumber in the Cascade Mountains. The challenge was mounted to protect the endangered spotted owl, whose remaining population occupies these forests and requires the intact, ancient forest for survival. The dilemma pitted the interests of environmentalists against those of corporations and of individuals who stood to lose jobs. After months of debate and legal battles, the

fate of the loggers—and the owls—was still undecided in mid-1992.

Similar tensions exist between the developed and the developing nations. Many people in industrialized nations, for example, believe that developing nations in tropical regions should do more to protect their rain forests and other natural areas. But the developing countries may be impoverished, with populations growing so rapidly that using the land is a means to temporarily avoid worsening poverty and starvation.

Many of the changes to Earth that concern scientists have the potential to rob the planet of its biological richness. The destruction of Earth's ozone layer, for example, could contribute to the general process of impoverishment by allowing ultraviolet rays to harm plants and animals. And global warming could wipe out species unable to quickly adapt to changing climates. Clearly, protecting Earth's biodiversity is a complex problem. But solutions to humanity's current problems will come only through coordinated international efforts to control human population, stabilize the composition of the atmosphere, and preserve intact Earth's complex web of life.

Reading and Study Guide

For further reading:

Bilger, Burkhard. *Global Warming*. Chelsea House, 1992.

Biodiversity. Ed. by E. O. Wilson. National Academy Press, 1988.

Ehrlich, Paul R. and Anne H. *The Population Explosion.* Simon & Schuster, 1990.

Malthus, Thomas R. *An Essay on the Principle of Population.* Penguin, 1983. First published in 1798.

Mann, Charles C., and Plummer, Mark L. "The Butterfly Problem." *The Atlantic.* January 1992.

Schneider, Stephen H. "The Greenhouse Effect: Science and Policy." *Science.* Feb. 10, 1989.

White, Robert W. "The Great Climate Debate." *Scientific American.* July 1990.

Worldwatch Institute. *State of the World.* Norton, 1990: "Feeding the World in the Nineties," pp. 59-78.

For more information:

The U.S. Department of Agriculture offers a free information package on global climatic change. Send requests along with a self-addressed mailing label to: National Agricultural Library; Room 111; Reference; 10301 Baltimore Blvd.; Beltsville, Md.; 20705-2351.

Questions for thought and discussion:

1. What are some of the effects of human population growth on solid-waste disposal, air and water pollution, and global warming?

2. Pretend you are the president of a chemical manufacturing company whose factory is emitting unsafe levels of air pollution. An environmental group is pressuring the local government to pass an ordinance requiring your company to shut down the factory or reduce the level of pollution it emits by 80 per cent in one year. Modernizing the factory so that it does not pollute will be very expensive, however. If the company pays for it, you will have to fire 700 workers. What would you do? What alternatives would you explore?

3. Your state legislature is considering passing a law that would ban CFC's in auto and home air conditioners and refrigerators. CFC's are responsible for destroying the protective ozone layer in Earth's atmosphere. But the use of a CFC alternative in air conditioners and refrigerators would make the devices more expensive, and they may not cool as well.

Two groups are asking citizens to write letters to their representatives. One group urges that the legislation to ban CFC's be passed. The other group wants representatives to vote against the measure. Which letter would you write? Why?

4. Ozone can be either beneficial or harmful to people depending on where it is in the atmosphere. Explain how this can be so.

5. Burning fossil fuels may lead to a warming of Earth's climate. Name five things you can do to reduce your use of fossil fuels.

6. Pretend you are the manager of a nature preserve that contains rare trees scientists want to cut down in order to obtain a lifesaving drug. The trees are endangered, and disturbing the area might also threaten several endangered animals. What would you do? Why?

7. Give two or three specific examples of how species depend on each other. In these examples, what would be the consequences of eliminating one of the species?

8. Much of the world's threatened rain forests are in Brazil. A group of industrialized nations is pressuring Brazil to stop destroying the rain forest, because the forest is the "lungs" of the world, taking carbon dioxide from the atmosphere and releasing oxygen. Cutting and burning the trees releases more carbon dioxide, and excess carbon dioxide may be causing the planet to warm.

Many Brazilians believe they have the right to clear the forests for their economic benefit. They point out that the industrialized nations are still the greatest carbon dioxide producers as a result of burning fossil fuels.

Should other countries have the right to tell Brazil how to use its land when such use provides food and jobs for the Brazilian people? Why or why not?

9. How many of your daily activities directly or indirectly cause pollution? How could you reduce the amount of pollution that your activities are responsible for?

Science News Update

Science Year contributors report on the year's major developments in their respective fields. The articles in this section are arranged alphabetically.

Page 238

Page 248

Page 257

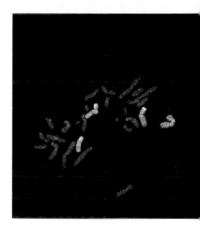

Page 290

Page 338

In May 1992, the United States Food and Drug Administration (FDA) announced that most genetically altered foods would not be subject to special standards for safety testing and other regulations different from those used for ordinary food products. Gene-altered foods that contain ingredients not usually found in the product would be subject to special review, however.

Foods developed by biotechnology are not currently on the market, but companies are conducting extensive research in this area, and some products are nearly ready for sale. Manufacturers have sought such a statement of how products would be regulated so that they could develop appropriate marketing plans. Critics of the new FDA policy argued that genetically engineered products could pose new safety risks and should undergo the same extensive testing that food additives are subject to.

Gene-altered tomatoes. In October 1991, scientists from Washington State University in Pullman announced a major discovery about fruit ripening that may greatly increase the storage life of fruit. Scientists have long known that ethylene, a gas that occurs naturally in fruit, is somehow involved in the ripening process. But the Washington State scientists discovered that ethylene is the trigger that starts the ripening process.

The scientists used genetic engineering to develop tomato plants that did not produce ethylene. Fruit from these plants ripened only after they were treated with the gas.

Experts say such fruit could be stored for long periods of time without refrigeration, and then ripened just before people want to eat it. Scientists estimate development of this technology could ultimately save hundreds of millions of dollars in storage costs, result in higher-quality fruit for consumers, and enable farmers and orchard growers to develop new markets for fruit in countries where refrigeration is unavailable.

Milking by computer. Agricultural researchers at the Maryland Agricultural Experiment Station in College Park installed the first fully automated milking system in North America in autumn 1991. In a milking room, the system's computer identifies each cow through radio signals from a device hanging from a chain around the cow's neck. If computer records show that it is time for the cow to be milked, the computer instantly sends an electronic command that opens a gate to a milking stall.

In the stall, a robotic arm swings in from behind the cow to clean its udder, which helps maintain milk quality and the animal's health. A milking unit, which consists of four teat cups, then slides into position and automatically attaches to the cow's udder.

While the cow is milked, feed is automatically dispensed to a trough in the stall. When milking is completed, the computer records the amount of milk produced and calculates the next milking time. The milking unit then detaches from the udder, allowing the cow to leave the stall.

Device "hears" bugs eat. A new device detects ultrasonic sounds made by insect larvae as they feed inside seeds, grains, and vegetables. The larvae produce high-frequency sound waves well outside the range of human hearing, yet clearly recordable on the device, called the Purdue Insect Feeding Monitor. Entomologist Richard Shade and his colleagues at Purdue University in West Lafayette, Ind., demonstrated the monitor in Indianapolis in February 1992.

Shade reported that the new device could be installed on a ship to monitor the grain in the hold while the ship is at sea. If an insect infestation were discovered, the grain cargo could be fumigated immediately to prevent major loss.

The laboratory model of the device includes a computer and a 16-channel ultrasonic monitor. The sound waves produced by the larvae as they eat are picked up by the monitor, which automatically processed by the computer, which automatically records and graphs the level of activity. The scientists report that the monitor is so sensitive that it can detect signals from 1 infected seed in 4,000.

Keeping up with Chinese pigs. A sow of the Meishan breed of China usually produces three to five more piglets in a litter than a does a sow of most breeds that are common in the United States. The hormone estrogen may be the reason, according to an announcement in October 1991 by animal scientists at Iowa State University of Science and Technology in Ames.

During the first two weeks of pregnancy, pig embryos—unlike the embryos of most other mammals—are not nourished through a *placenta* (an organ attached to the inner wall of the mother's uterus). Instead, secretions from the uterus enable the embryo to survive. The composition of those secretions is triggered by the level of estrogen that the embryos produce.

University researchers found that embryos in the uterus of a Meishan sow produce estrogen at a slowly increasing rate during the first two weeks after conception. In contrast, the estrogen production by embryos of Yorkshire pigs, a common U.S. breed that the scientists studied, increases rapidly as the piglets develop during this period.

Every litter of pigs has some large embryos and some smaller ones. The Iowa scientists speculated that the larger embryos in U.S. sows may quickly produce enough estrogen to change the environment in the uterus enough to kill the smaller embryos. Because the increase in estrogen production is slower in Chinese pig embryos, the environment in the uterus may change more gradually, enabling more embryos to survive.

Profitable organic farming. Farmers who refrain from using manufactured chemicals to fertilize crops and control weeds and insect pests usually find that crop yields suffer. But in autumn 1991, a new survey suggested that organic farming can be profitable despite reduced yields. Agricultural economists at Ohio State University in Columbus compared the production costs and farm income of Ohio farmers who grew crops using organic farming methods and those of farmers practicing conventional farming techniques. The economists found that Ohio's organic farmers were holding their own economically.

Economist Marvin Batte said that organic growers had lower costs and received higher prices for their crops than conventional farmers. These factors boosted their profits near to those of conventional farmers, despite lower average yields per acre for the organically grown crops. For example, corn grown organically needed only about $1.17 per acre for organic agents to suppress insects, weeds, and diseases, compared with $16 to $17 per acre for chemicals

Technicians demonstrate a portable laser scanning system to detect soil erosion. A camera transmits to a computer the changing positions of the end of a laser beam as it moves over soil surfaces. The computer then creates a map of the surface. Maps created at different times are compared to detect erosion. The system was developed by U.S. Department of Agriculture scientists in West Lafayette, Ind., in 1991.

New mulching technique for growing tomatoes

Tomato plants grown in a common groundcover called hairy vetch were greener, bigger, and yielded more tomatoes in a 1991 experiment, *bottom,* than plants in plots mulched with plastic or paper or not mulched, *below.* The vetch, planted by U.S. Department of Agriculture researchers in plots in Beltsville, Md., was mowed just before the tomatoes were planted. The vetch also reduced the need for fertilizer, herbicides, and pesticides. Bordering plots mulched with plastic and paper were severely infested with insects.

Agriculture Continued

used on corn grown with conventional methods.

Although organically grown corn yielded 27 bushels per acre less than the conventional average, organic growers could charge $3.50 to $4 per bushel for their product if it was specially marketed as organically grown. That price compared with $2.16 per bushel for conventionally grown corn. Batte planned to gather data for several more years, because prices and yields fluctuate from year to year.

Pilotless plane controls pests. A radio-controlled airplane outfitted with a satellite guidance system and cameras to detect *infrared* (heat) radiation spread biological agents on Iowa fields in 1991 to control insects, parasites, and diseases that attack crops. Biological agents are organisms that are natural enemies of the insects and weeds that can overwhelm crop plants.

Agricultural researchers at Iowa State University found that radio-controlled planes could fly more slowly and target pests more accurately than could full-sized, piloted planes. The researchers also found that applying biological-control agents with a radio-controlled airplane costs 80 per cent less than using a full-sized aircraft. The pilotless airplane is about one-third to one-fourth the size of full-sized piloted planes that are used to spread pesticides.

The equipment on one plane studied included a highly accurate satellite system that is used to guide ships and to assist in surveying land. The satellite relayed the plane's location to a computer, which guided the plane on a preprogrammed course. If a plane lost radio contact, it was programmed to return to its starting point or shut down and, aided by a parachute, descend gently to the ground.

Infrared cameras mounted on the plane transmitted video images of planted fields to a monitor on the ground. The images revealed any crop damage from heavy weed and insect infestations. That information would enable a farmer to treat only the problem areas instead of entire fields, saving time and money. [Steve Cain and Victor L. Lechtenberg]

In WORLD BOOK, see AGRICULTURE.

Anthropology

A 13-million-year-old fossil from an ancient creature that may be a candidate for the shared ancestor of African apes and human beings was described in March 1992 by a team of scientists led by anatomist Glenn C. Conroy of Washington University Medical School in St. Louis, Mo. The fossil—a piece of a lower jaw—was found in the Otavi Mountains in Namibia in southwestern Africa.

The Namibian fossil represents one of at least six types of ancient apes that existed from 20 million to 10 million years ago. Paleontologists agree that *hominids* (human beings and their prehuman ancestors) evolved from an extinct apelike creature that also may have been an ancestor of modern chimpanzees and gorillas. Determining which ape was this common ancestor, however, has been difficult because of the lack of fossils and the number of possible candidates.

The newly discovered fossil consists of a single fragment from a lower jaw with four complete teeth and sockets for seven other teeth. Conroy and his team believe that the fossil belonged to a previously unknown species, which they have named *Otavipithecus namibiensis* (the Otavi ape of Namibia). The size of the jaw indicates that an adult *Otavipithecus* weighed from 14 to 20 kilograms (30 to 44 pounds), about half the weight of living chimpanzees. The form of the jaw and teeth indicates that *Otavipithecus* ate mostly soft plant foods such as berries, buds, flowers, and leaves.

Because of the scarcity of fossils from *Otavipithecus*, paleontologists cannot yet determine its relationship to other ancient apes or to hominids. But the discovery in Namibia is important because it provides additional evidence for the theory that favorable climatic conditions from 20 million to 10 million years ago permitted apes to spread widely and to evolve into many different species. During this period, the world climate was warmer and wetter than it is now, and forests—needed by apes for food and shelter—sprang up in many areas, including northern Namibia.

Early hominid evolution. A 2.4-million-year-old fossil found near Lake Baringo in Kenya in 1965 but not identified until early 1992 is the oldest known fossil of the genus *Homo,* which includes all living people and their direct prehistoric ancestors. The identification of the fossil—a piece of a skull from near the right ear—was made by anthropologist Andrew Hill of Yale University in New Haven, Conn., and anatomist Steven Ward of Northeastern Ohio Universities College of Medicine in Rootstown. The fossil is about 500,000 years older than the oldest previously known *Homo* fossil.

The identification of the *Homo* fossil strengthens the theory that another hominid, *Australopithecus afarensis,* gave rise to two hominid lines between 3 million and 2.5 million years ago. *A. afarensis* lived between 4 million and 3 million years ago. It is the only known hominid species from that time. Scientists think one line produced the "robust" australopithecines, creatures that walked upright on two legs but were probably apelike in many other aspects of their behavior. The other line led to the *Homo* genus and, eventually, to modern human beings.

DNA and human origins. A landmark genetic study that traced the origin of modern human beings to one woman living in Africa about 200,000 years ago was fatally flawed, according to two reports published in February 1992. The studies were conducted by molecular biologist Alan R. Templeton of Washington University and by a team of scientists at Pennsylvania State University in University Park that included one of the authors of the original study. The scientists contended that many thousands of equally valid "family trees"—indicating other geographic origins for modern human beings—could be constructed from the data used in the genetic study, published in 1987.

Anthropologists agree that modern-looking human beings appeared within the last 200,000 years, but they disagree on how this evolution occurred. By about 200,000 years ago, groups of *archaic* (nonmodern) human beings had spread throughout Africa and much of Europe and Asia. Some anthropologists theorize that each group evolved into modern human beings at about the same time. Other scientists argue that modern human beings evolved first in

Oldest known human fossil

A 2.4-million-year-old skull-bone fossil, *right,* is the oldest known fossil of the genus *Homo,* which includes all modern people and their direct prehistoric ancestors. Anthropologist Andrew Hill of Yale University in New Haven, Conn., *below,* uses another skull to show that the piece came from near the ear. The fossil, found in Kenya in 1965, was identified by Hill and a colleague in 1992.

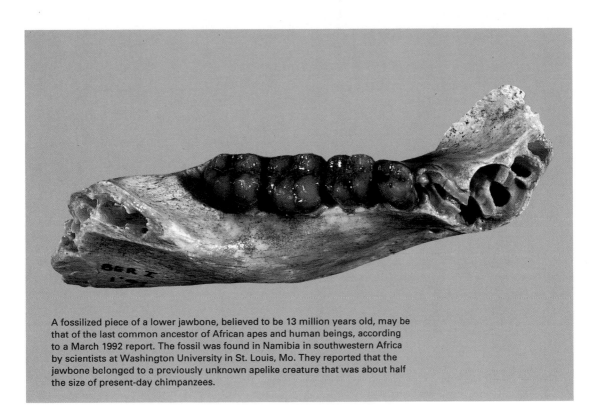

A fossilized piece of a lower jawbone, believed to be 13 million years old, may be that of the last common ancestor of African apes and human beings, according to a March 1992 report. The fossil was found in Namibia in southwestern Africa by scientists at Washington University in St. Louis, Mo. They reported that the jawbone belonged to a previously unknown apelike creature that was about half the size of present-day chimpanzees.

Africa and then spread out, replacing archaic groups elsewhere.

The 1987 study provided strong evidence for the African origins theory. In that study, scientists from the University of California, Berkeley, analyzed mitochondrial DNA (deoxyribonucleic acid) from living women from around the world.

Most DNA—the complex molecule of which genes are made—is inherited from both male and female parents. But mitochondrial DNA, which is found outside the nucleus of the cell, is inherited only from females and so is unaltered by genetic mixing from generation to generation. Differences in mitochondrial DNA thus represent random genetic changes that have occurred over time, and shared mitochondrial types can reveal common ancestry.

Analysis of the mitochondrial DNA data led the Berkeley scientists to construct a human family tree with two main branches. The first was made up exclusively of living Africans. The second included some Africans and everyone else. The simplest explanation for the form of this tree seemed to be that all human mitochondrial DNA types found today originated from a single type that existed in Africa within the last 200,000 years. This theory became popularly known as the "African Eve hypothesis." Although the conclusions of the Berkeley study were controversial, they were supported by the fossil record and, later, by other genetic studies.

The February 1992 studies did not show that the tree constructed by the Berkeley scientists was wrong, but they revealed that many different trees could be constructed by using the same data. Some of these other trees could easily indicate a non-African origin for modern human beings.

Despite the ambiguity of the mitochondrial DNA research, many anthropologists still believe modern people originated in Africa. The fossil record and some other genetic evidence support this position.   [Richard G. Klein]

In the Special Reports section, see WHO WERE THE NEANDERTHALS? In WORLD BOOK, see ANTHROPOLOGY; PREHISTORIC PEOPLE.

Widespread warfare may have led to the collapse of Maya civilization, according to reports published in 1991. The findings came from ongoing excavations at the ancient Maya city of Dos Pilas in what is now Guatemala. In the spring, archaeologist Arthur A. Demarest of Vanderbilt University in Nashville had reported the discovery at Dos Pilas of the tomb of a Maya king known to archaeologists as "Ruler 2." This warrior king, who reigned from A.D. 698 to 725, was one of several kings of Dos Pilas who engaged in a campaign of expansion that led to the formation of this militaristic city-state.

Additional exploration at Dos Pilas and the surrounding area revealed the remains of walls, moats, and fortifications stretching for many kilometers and dating from about 760 to 820, the end of Maya civilization in this region. According to Demarest, the extent of the fortifications suggests that after 760, the entire region around Dos Pilas was wracked by intense, economically devastating warfare. This conflict may have led to the collapse of Maya civilization.

Columbus' first landfall. New archaeological findings and historical research reported in January 1992 may have provided the definitive solution to a centuries-old puzzle: Where did explorer Christopher Columbus make his first landfall in the New World? Archaeologist William F. Keegan of the Florida Museum of Natural History in Gainesville reported that Columbus first set foot in the New World on Oct. 12, 1492, on San Salvador Island, as many historians have believed.

In 1982, Keegan began an archaeological survey of islands in the Bahamas to identify villages of the Lucayan Indians that were mentioned by Columbus in his ship's log. While working at the site of a former Lucayan village on the western side of Acklins Island (which Columbus had named La Isabela), Keegan's team unearthed abundant shellfish remains along with fire pits, trash deposits, and many pieces of pottery that had been imported from what are now Cuba and Hispaniola.

The presence of the pottery and the size of the village—six times that of an

Oldest New World pottery
Pottery fragments, *right,* discovered near Santarém in northeastern Brazil, *below,* are the oldest known pottery found in the Western Hemisphere, according to a December 1991 report. The fragments are from 7,000 to 8,000 years old.

average Lucayan site—led the archaeologists to conclude that they had found the city of a king mentioned in Columbus' log as being the ruler of San Salvador and neighboring islands. Columbus landed on the eastern side of Acklins Island on Oct. 19, 1492, but shallow water prevented his ships from reaching "the city of the king."

Keegan then began to retrace the earlier part of Columbus' route through the Bahamas. On nearby Long Island, Keegan's survey recorded two Lucayan sites at locations described by Columbus on October 17 and 18. Sites on Rum Cay, 32 kilometers (20 miles) east of Long Island, matched those described by Columbus in his second landfall, on October 15. San Salvador Island lies a short distance northeast of Rum Cay.

While Keegan was conducting his research, archaeologists led by Charles Hoffman of Northern Arizona University in Flagstaff were digging on the western side of San Salvador. There they found a huge number of European-made objects, including glass beads, pottery, brass belt buckles, and other objects that had been described by Columbus in his log. Hoffman also found that the location and characteristics of San Salvador match the description of the site of Columbus' first landfall in his log. Together, Hoffman's excavations and Keegan's survey and retracing of Columbus' route provide strong evidence that Columbus first set foot in the New World on San Salvador.

Archaeology in Costa Rica. Archaeologist Payson Sheets of the University of Colorado in Boulder reported in December 1991 on archaeological excavations around the Arenal volcano in northwestern Costa Rica. Sheets and his team explored an area that has been populated for more than 11,000 years despite numerous volcanic eruptions. The ashfall from the eruptions had covered and helped preserve campsites, homes, and artifacts.

The oldest object found in the area was a spearpoint that was dated to about 11,000 years ago. The next oldest objects—a campsite, cooking areas, and stone tools—were unearthed in *geological strata* (layers of earth) dating from about 6,000 years ago, the time of the first known eruption of the volcano. The people of this period lived by hunt-

ing wild game and gathering wild plants.

The next major eruption occurred about 3,750 years ago, when the people in the area had begun to farm and were becoming increasingly settled in villages. At one site, the ash from this eruption preserved the contents of five circular houses that were from 5 to 8 meters (16 to 26 feet) in diameter. In the houses, archaeologists uncovered chipped stone tools and areas where baskets of water had been heated by placing hot stones in them. No domesticated plants were found. This suggested that although the people lived a settled life, they relied largely on the abundant plants and animals of the rain forest.

During the period from about 2,500 to 1,450 years ago, the population of the area reached its height. Also at this time, the people began to bury their dead in large cemeteries near their villages. Two major eruptions occurred during this period.

Another major eruption occurred between 1,100 and 1,000 years ago. The archaeologists found that thick layers of ash devastated the area, smothering massive numbers of plants, including crops. At this time, the people retreated to a refuge in the Rio Piedre Valley where the ashfall was not so heavy. Despite the destruction—and a decline in population that began about 1450 years ago—civilization progressed. The people began to make more elaborate pottery and to build aboveground stone tombs in cemeteries set apart from the villages.

The most violent volcanic eruption occurred about 500 years ago, just before Spaniards conquered the area. The archaeologists linked this eruption to a continuing decline in population that occurred between 650 and 450 years ago. During this period, the people of the area lived mainly in small hamlets scattered across the countryside, rather than in the large villages of the previous period.

Sheets concluded that people were able to live around the Arenal volcano despite the volcanic eruptions, because, in part, they relied on both crops and wild food sources throughout their history. In addition, the population of the area remained small, which meant that the people did not overexploit the area's natural resources. Finally, the

Royal Maya tomb

Recent discoveries made at the ancient Maya city of Dos Pilas in western Guatemala, *below,* have provided additional evidence of the warlike nature of the city's rulers. Pottery vessels decorated with hieroglyphic inscriptions, *right,* were among the artifacts found in the tomb of a warrior king, known to archaeologists as Ruler 2. The glyphs have helped archaeologists identify the neighboring city-states conquered by Dos Pilas.

In a palace near Ruler 2's tomb, archaeologists unearthed a stairway decorated with more than 100 hieroglyphic blocks, *below.* The stairway text describes Dos Pilas' military campaigns, its defeat of the great Maya city-state of Tikal, and the torture and decapitation of the captured king of Tikal. The text is one of the largest Maya stairway texts found in the 1900's.

people often escaped the most devastating effects of the eruptions by moving to areas where the ashfall was lighter.

First Americans? Archaeological artifacts found in southern New Mexico may be up to 38,000 years old, according to a February 1992 report. Some confirmation of the artifacts' age would strengthen the theory that the ancestors of modern Native Americans reached the New World tens of thousands of years earlier than most scientists believe they did. However, many archaeologists expressed doubts about the findings.

The discovery was made at a cave near the town of Orogrande by scientists led by archaeologist Richard S. MacNeish of the Andover (Mass.) Foundation for Archaeological Research. MacNeish reported finding in the cave what appears to be a cooking pit that may be 16,400 years old, several possibly older cooking pits dated to about 25,000 years ago, and stone tools and animal bones dated to about 38,000 years ago. According to MacNeish, many of the bones had been shattered, apparently to get at the bone marrow. Finally, the archaeologists found with the bones broken pieces of limestone that they identified as tools used to butcher the animals.

MacNeish reported that some of the limestone came from sources that were more than 24 kilometers (15 miles) away. He argued that this finding alone indicates that people transported the stones into the cave. Also cited as evidence of a human presence is what appears to be a handprint impressed in the side of a baked clay fire pit. Investigators radiocarbon-dated the pit to about 28,000 years ago.

Many archaeologists expressed skepticism about MacNeish's findings, suggesting that some of the scientist's discoveries—such as the possible cooking pits—are the remains of ancient pack rat nests. Others asserted that the stones were not tools at all but probably rocks that had fallen from the roof of the cave.   [Thomas R. Hester]

In the Special Reports section, see THE RISE OF ANDEAN CIVILIZATION. In WORLD BOOK, see ARCHAEOLOGY; COLUMBUS, CHRISTOPHER; INDIAN, AMERICAN; MAYA.

Archaeology, Old World

The preserved body of a man who died as long as 5,300 years ago was found on a glacier in northeastern Italy in September 1991. The corpse—the oldest naturally preserved human body ever discovered—represents the most intact archaeological find from the late Neolithic Period (New Stone Age), which lasted from 8,000 to 4,000 years ago.

Most of the man's clothing decayed. But scientists located parts of one boot, which was lined with straw. They also unearthed a bow, a leather quiver, 14 arrows tipped with bone, a flint and dried mushrooms for making fires, and an ax with a copper head and wooden shaft.

The man, who was about 25 or 30 years old at the time of his death, may have been a shepherd who died of exposure, according to scientists at the University of Innsbruck in Austria, where the corpse is being studied. In addition to establishing an age for the corpse, scientists were conducting a partial autopsy to try to determine how the man died. They were also analyzing the man's DNA (deoxyribonucleic acid), the molecule of which genes are made, to learn more about the genetic relationship between late Neolithic Age people and modern Europeans.

Dead Sea Scrolls. The first radiocarbon tests conducted on the Dead Sea Scrolls confirmed that the documents date from the mid-100's B.C. to the late first century A.D., as many scholars had contended. The findings were reported in September 1991. Some scholars had questioned the authenticity and age of the documents.

The Dead Sea Scrolls are a collection of some 2,000 manuscripts that were found in caves along the shore of the Dead Sea in the late 1940's and early 1950's. They contain a variety of religious texts, including all the books of the Old Testament except Esther.

Previously, the Israeli Antiquities Authority, which oversees scholarship on the original scrolls, had refused to permit radiocarbon testing because large pieces of the documents would have been destroyed in the process. (Radiocarbon dating measures the relative amount of a radioactive form of carbon in material to provide an estimate of its

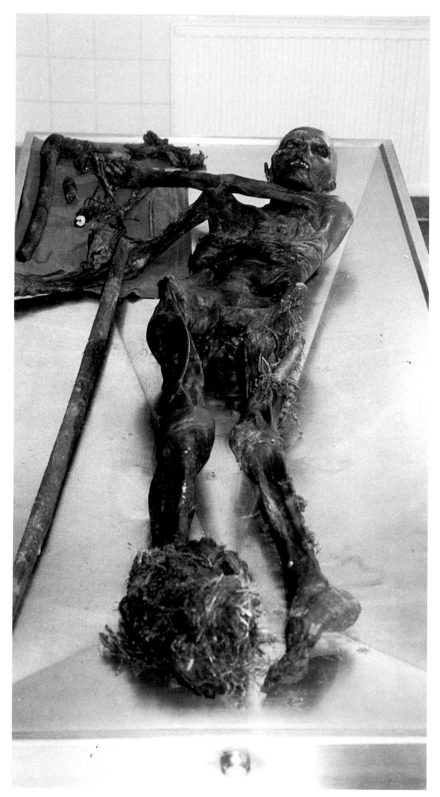

The preserved body of a man who died as long as 5,300 years ago was found on a glacier in Italy in September 1991. The remains are the oldest naturally preserved corpse ever found and the most complete archaeological find from the Neolithic Period (New Stone Age). Although most of the man's clothing had disintegrated, parts of a boot remained attached to one foot.

age.) As a result, scholars had relied on analyses of handwriting styles used in the scrolls to determine their age. The new tests were conducted using a sophisticated form of radiocarbon dating in which only minute amounts of the documents had to be destroyed.

Gulf War aftermath. Archaeologists who study the ancient Near East spent much of 1991 and early 1992 trying to assess the damage to archaeological sites and museums in Iraq caused by bombing during the Persian Gulf War of early 1991 and by the subsequent civil uprisings. In May 1992, two United States archaeologists reported that the damage to Iraq's ancient archaeological sites did not end with the cease-fire.

Archaeologists Elizabeth C. Stone of the State University of New York at Stony Brook and Paul Zimansky of Boston University visited Iraq in early 1992 as part of a humanitarian delegation. At the ancient Sumerian city of Ur, they found four bomb craters as well as bullet holes on a side of Mesopotamia's best-preserved *ziggurat* (pyramid). The two archaeologists also saw photographs of massive ditches, which the Iraqis said had been made by U.S. bombs, at an ancient unexcavated site.

According to Stone and Zimansky, the director of Iraq's Department of Antiquities and Heritage reported that repairs had been completed at the Iraq Museum and several other Islamic buildings in Baghdad, Iraq's capital, and on a 1,500-year-old arch at Ctesiphon. Both structures were cracked and weakened by bomb blasts. But the director also noted that new cracks continued to appear in ancient buildings and monuments in Baghdad.

One of the greatest threats to Iraq's ancient heritage, however, may be new irrigation canals and farm fields. Skyrocketing food prices and the continuing international economic boycott against Iraq, imposed by the United Nations in August 1990, led the government to greatly increase the amount of land under cultivation. According to Stone and Zimansky, Iraq's Department of Antiquities was unable to determine whether these projects were damaging archaeological sites and unable to excavate sites before they are damaged.

Lost city found. Radar images of buried tracks made thousands of years

ago by caravans helped lead a team of U.S. archaeologists in November 1991 to the lost city of Ubar in southern Arabia. Religious and historical documents describe Ubar as the powerful center of a highly profitable trade in frankincense, a fragrant tree resin. An analysis of pottery from the site indicated that the city was occupied from about 2800 B.C. to about A.D. 100. Many scholars had doubted the existence of the city, which nevertheless had been the object of several previous searches.

The archaeologists found the buried tracks using ancient maps as well as images made by ground-penetrating radar carried on the U.S. space shuttle Challenger and on U.S. and French Earth-orbiting satellites. The scientists followed the tracks to a water well, where they found the ruined walls and towers of an ancient city they concluded was Ubar.

According to Islamic writings, Ubar was destroyed because of the wickedness of its people. The archaeologists reported that the city was built over a large limestone cavern, which eventually collapsed, destroying the city.

In April 1992, the scientists reported finding the ruins of a second major hub in the ancient frankincense trade. Pottery and other artifacts found at Saffara Metropolis, located in southern Oman along the coast of the Indian Ocean, indicate that it existed at the same time that Ubar did. The discovery of these two trading centers promised to shed new light on the once-thriving incense trade, an important part of the economy of the ancient Near East.

Mummy family. The discovery of six ancient Egyptian mummies, believed to be from a single family, was announced in March 1992 by Egyptologist Neguib Kanawati of Macquarie University in Australia. Kanawati found the mummies, which date from about 2130 B.C., at Al Hagarsa, about 400 kilometers (250 miles) south of Cairo. After analyzing the mummies' DNA, the scientists concluded that the six were two grandparents, a son and daughter-in-law, and two children, perhaps aged 10 and 12 at the time they died.

The discovery of the mummies is significant because scientists know of only three other mummies from this period. The mummies have also provided scientists with a rare opportunity to study the

An archaeologist examines a plaster cast of a victim of the eruption of Mount Vesuvius that destroyed the ancient Roman town of Pompeii in A.D. 79. The mummified bodies of eight people—the first new remains found since 1961—were unearthed in August 1991. Archaeologists made casts of some of the bodies by injecting plaster into cavities left by the remains in the volcanic ash that buried the town.

genetic links between three generations of an ancient Egyptian family.

Ancient Egyptian bakery. The discovery of a 4,500-year-old bakery that may have provided bread for ancient Egyptian kings and the workers who built the pyramids at Giza was reported in March 1992 by archaeologist Mark Lehner of the University of Chicago. The discovery of the bakery, part of a complex of storerooms and administrative offices, provides support for the theory that a sizable, permanent town probably existed at the site, which was occupied from about 2600 to 2100 B.C.

The bakery appears large enough to have produced bread for thousands of workers. Lehner and his co-workers found the remains of baking pots weighing 12 kilograms (26.5 pounds) and measuring 30 centimeters (12 inches) high. To bake the bread, the ancient bakers placed the pots in large vats and covered them with hot coals.

Archaeologists also discovered a massive stone wall—9 meters (30 feet) thick and 9 meters high—surrounding part of the site. Lehner theorized that the wall separated an area used by royalty from that used by workers.

According to Lehner, the findings suggest that Giza was a permanent city, of perhaps as many as 200,000 residents, and not just a seasonal labor camp for workers building the pyramids. He also concluded that Egypt's rulers lived near the construction site much of the time.

Ancient Eskimo colony. The discovery of 520 crude circular dwellings on an uninhabited island off the northeast coast of Greenland was reported in August 1991 by Danish explorers and archaeologists. The dwellings date from 500 B.C.—nearly 1,500 years before the Viking invasion of the island—to A.D. 400. The scientists believe the site represents a colony established by a virtually unknown group of ancient Eskimos, perhaps from North America or Greenland. The colony's economy apparently was based on seal and whale hunting.

[Robert Wenke and Nanette Pyne]

In the Special Reports section, see THE RISE OF ANDEAN CIVILIZATION. In WORLD BOOK, see DEAD SEA SCROLLS; EGYPT, ANCIENT; ESKIMO.

Astronomy, Milky Way

Two United States astronomers reported in January 1992 that they had discovered the strongest evidence yet of planets circling another star. Alexander Wolszczan of Cornell University and Dale A. Frail of the National Radio Astronomy Observatory in Socorro, N. Mex., made the discovery through radio-telescope observations of a pulsar. A pulsar is a collapsed, rotating star whose powerful beam of radio energy is detected as a radio pulse each time it sweeps past Earth. Data from the pulsar indicate that the star is orbited by two, and perhaps three, large planets. (See CLOSE-UP.)

Probable black holes. New evidence for the existence of black holes in our Galaxy was reported in 1991 and 1992 by several teams of astronomers in Europe. One group, at Cambridge University and the Royal Greenwich Observatory in England and at the Institute of Astrophysics in Spain's Canary Islands, announced in February 1992 that a star called V404 Cygni almost certainly has a partner star that is a black hole. The other team, at institutions in Italy, France, and Russia, reported in December 1991 that they had found a probable black hole near the center of the Milky Way galaxy.

Black holes are usually the collapsed remnants of stars at least three times as massive as our sun. During the collapse, matter is squeezed into such a small volume that the object's gravitational field becomes enormous. The force of gravity is so strong near a black hole that nothing, not even light, can escape from it. Thus, a black hole cannot be seen with a telescope.

The only way to detect a black hole is to observe its gravitational effects on matter near it. Such effects are sometimes apparent in *binary* (double-star) systems in which a normal star is found to be orbiting an invisible companion. Astronomers have detected several such systems since the late 1980's, but the evidence supporting the presence of a black hole has not been conclusive. V404 Cygni is the best candidate so far for a star whose binary companion is a black hole.

By measuring V404 Cygni's orbital

speed, the researchers determined that the star has an unseen partner whose mass is at least eight times that of the sun. If astronomers' calculations are correct, a body that massive emitting no detectable light can only be a large star that has collapsed into a black hole.

The Italian, French, and Russian scientists used instruments aboard a rocket and a satellite to study a source of powerful X rays and *gamma rays* (a very-high-energy form of electromagnetic radiation) near the center of the Milky Way. They found that the emissions from the source, called 1E 1740.7-2942, are similar in their intensity and pattern of variability to those of another black hole candidate known as Cygnus X-1. Cygnus X-1, thought to be a binary system, was identified as the site of a probable black hole in the 1980's.

The black heart of the Galaxy. Astronomers have known for years that a source of intense energy emissions lies at the center of the Milky Way galaxy, obscured from view by vast clouds of dust and gas. In February 1992, researchers at the Max Planck Institute in Garching, Germany, reported evidence that the mysterious energy source is a gigantic black hole.

Observations have shown that many strong energy sources lie at the heart of the Milky Way. One of them, called Sagittarius A, is thought to be the actual center of the Galaxy, the point about which the great spiral of stars rotates. Sagittarius A is a powerful emitter of radio waves and X rays.

Astronomers have considered two possible explanations for the identity of Sagittarius A. They theorized that it is either a compact cluster of normal stars or a supermassive black hole containing as much mass as a million or more suns. The German scientists reported that they found strong evidence in support of the black hole explanation.

The astronomers used a new telescope high in the Andes Mountains of Chile to obtain the sharpest images ever made of the region around Sagittarius A. The images showed that Sagittarius A is a single, small object rather than a cluster of stars.

The researchers also found that a

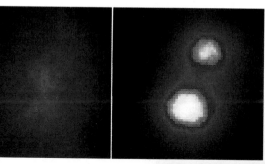

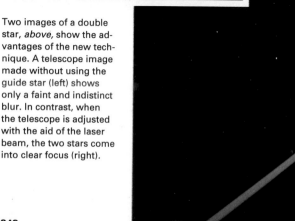

Two images of a double star, *above,* show the advantages of the new technique. A telescope image made without using the guide star (left) shows only a faint and indistinct blur. In contrast, when the telescope is adjusted with the aid of the laser beam, the two stars come into clear focus (right).

A laser-beam "star"

At a New Mexico observatory, a laser beam is bounced off the upper atmosphere to create an artificial "guide star" for astronomers. An instrument measures distortions of the beam caused by the motion of the atmosphere. Using this data, a computer can adjust the curvature of a telescope mirror to counteract the atmospheric turbulence, according to a September 1991 report.

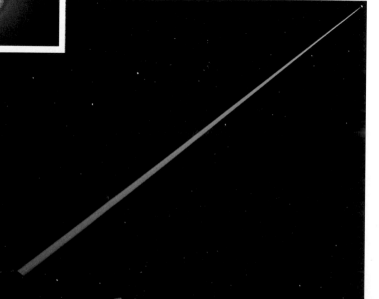

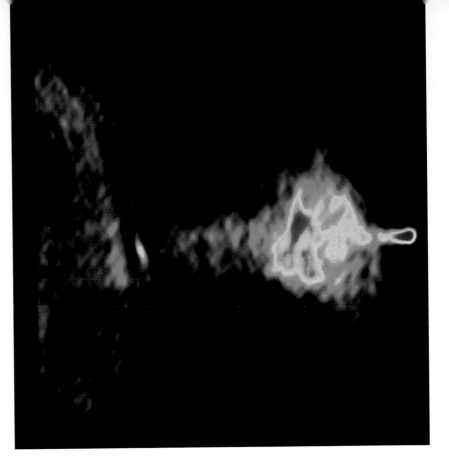

A pulsar, red spot at right, speeds through the gaseous remains of a *supernova* (exploding star) in a radio image taken by the Very Large Array radio telescope near Socorro, N. Mex., and released in August 1991. The pulsar, a small and extremely dense body, is the remaining core of the star. When the star exploded an estimated 15,000 years ago, the gaseous shell was moving faster than the pulsar. Gradually, however, the gases slowed down, and the pulsar caught up and passed through them.

bubble of gas is expanding outward from Sagittarius A. This expanding gas is similar in temperature, density, and composition to the jets of gas that astronomers have observed flowing away from the centers of many other galaxies. Such jets are thought to be generated by accretion disks surrounding enormous black holes. Accretion disks are vast, swirling masses of gas and dust that give off titanic amounts of energy as they are sucked into the black hole. The similarity between the jets emitted by some galaxies and the gas bubble surrounding Sagittarius A supports the idea that Sagittarius A is a supermassive black hole.

Brown dwarfs. A decade-long search for *brown dwarfs*—objects less massive than stars but more massive than planets—may have finally met with clear success in 1992. In March, astronomer Claia Bryja and her colleagues at the University of Minnesota in Minneapolis reported finding several possible brown dwarfs in a cluster of stars called the Hyades.

Astronomers think that brown dwarfs

form in the same way stars do, through the gravitational contraction of a large cloud of gas and dust. If a cloud contains a sufficient amount of mass, gravitational compression will eventually generate enough internal heat to trigger nuclear reactions, and a star is created.

If the mass of the cloud is too small, however—less than about 8 per cent of the sun's mass, according to theoretical calculations—the internal temperature of the contracting mass never gets hot enough to start the nuclear reactions. Although such an object may become hot enough to glow a dull red, it is called a brown dwarf.

Some theories of star formation hold that there should be many brown dwarfs in the Galaxy—perhaps hundreds of billions. Yet astronomers had long been frustrated in their attempts to find one. Such small, dim objects are very hard to detect.

The probable brown dwarfs reported by Bryja's research team showed up when the astronomers were making a routine examination of photographs of the Hyades region. They were analyzing

Planetary Clues from a Collapsed Star

One of the most profound questions confronting astronomers is whether planetary systems like our own solar system are rare or whether many other stars in the universe are orbited by planets. This has been a difficult question to answer, because even the nearest stars are so far away that it is very difficult to tell if planets are circling them.

Nevertheless, astronomers have continued the quest, and in 1992 their efforts were rewarded. In January, astronomers at Cornell University in Ithaca, N.Y., and the National Radio Astronomy Observatory in Socorro, N. Mex., reported finding the first strong evidence of a planetary system outside the solar system. But the newly discovered planets orbit not a star like our sun but rather the collapsed core of an exploded star.

The search for planets beyond the solar system had long been confined to small or medium-sized stars that, like the sun, are in the most stable part of their life cycle. These stable stars are known as *main-sequence* stars.

Astronomers have used several techniques to search for planets around main-sequence stars. For some nearby stars, they have simply tried to see planets directly, using high-powered optical telescopes to detect the faint light that would be reflected from any planets circling the stars. But even the best telescopes have been unable to detect planets, whose light would be no more than one-billionth as bright as the star they orbit.

Another technique depends on the fact that, strictly speaking, planets do not orbit their parent star. Rather, the planets and the star orbit the system's common center of mass, the point around which the mass of the system is balanced. The center of mass is likely to be located some distance from the star's center, and may even lie beyond its surface in space. Like a mother whose arm is being tugged by her child, the star will wobble slightly around the center of mass as it responds to the gravitational pull of the moving planets.

One way of detecting these small wobbling motions is by measuring a star's *radial velocity*, its movements toward or away from Earth. Astronomers can measure a distant star's radial velocity by making use of the *Doppler effect*, the apparent shift in the wavelength of a star's light as the star moves toward or away from an observer. When a star is moving toward Earth, its light is shifted toward the shorter-wavelength, or blue, end of the visible spectrum. When it is moving away from us, its light is shifted toward the longer-wavelength, or red, end. To date, however, neither of these techniques has enabled astronomers to find planets around a main-sequence star.

Astronomers have concentrated on main-sequence stars because they are the ones most likely to have planets. Most researchers thought that it would be all but impossible to find planets around stars in their final stages, when they become unstable and may destroy their planets.

The most extreme cases are massive stars that run out of nuclear fuel and blow apart in a supernova explosion, in which the star's outer layers are blasted into space and only a small, collapsed core remains. That core, in many cases, is a *neutron star,* an extremely dense body made almost entirely of subatomic particles called neutrons. Although a supernova would probably have vaporized any planets that had been orbiting the star, some planet hunters decided to study neutron stars anyway. That research paid off: It was around a neutron star that the first persuasive evidence of a planetary system beyond our own was found.

The astronomers who made the discovery—Dale A. Frail of the National Radio Astronomy Observatory and Alexander Wolszczan of Cornell—studied the radial velocity of a type of neutron star called a *pulsar*. A pulsar is a rapidly spinning neutron star that emits a strong beam of radio waves. Each time the beam sweeps past the Earth, it is detected by radio telescopes as a brief pulse of radio energy.

This pulse rate is extremely precise. But the spacing of the pulses can vary slightly if the wavelength of the radio beams is altered by the Doppler effect, which causes shifts in radio wavelengths just as it does in wavelengths of visible light. Such a Doppler shift could occur if a pulsar has planets that are tugging it to and fro. Using highly accurate timing instruments, astronomers can detect these tiny variations in the spacing of signals from a pulsar.

Frail and Wolszczan were not the first scientists to announce the discovery of planets around a pulsar. In July 1991, astronomers at the University of Manchester in England reported that they had detected a shifting pattern of radio waves from a pulsar known as PSR1829-10. Their observations indicated that the star had a planet with a mass at least 10 times that of Earth. But in January 1992, the researchers issued a retraction, explaining that they had erred in their data analysis.

Just a week earlier, however, Frail and Wolszczan had announced their finding, and it appeared that this time a new planetary system had indeed been discovered. The two astronomers used the Arecibo radio telescope in Puerto Rico to study a pulsar called PSR1257+12.

"Listening" for signs of planets

An unusual pattern of radio signals from a *pulsar,* a collapsed star that emits a constant beam of radio waves, may indicate the presence of planets in orbit around the pulsar. A pulsar rotates rapidly on its axis, and the radio beam turns with it. Each time the beam sweeps past Earth, it is detected by radio telescopes as a pulse of radio energy. Variations in the time between each pulse suggest that the pulsar's position in space is changing because it is orbiting a common center of mass with one or more planets.

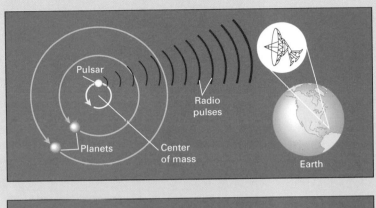

At times, the intervals between the pulses of radio energy from the pulsar grow slightly longer. The lengthening intervals indicate that the pulsar is moving away from Earth. This would occur when the pulsar's motion about the center of mass, due to the gravitational pull of the planets, is away from Earth.

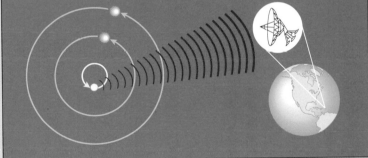

At other times, the intervals between radio pulses become shorter. This would occur when the pulsar's motion, because of the pull of its planets, is toward Earth.

PSR1257+12 pulses—and hence rotates—162 times a second. Very slight changes in the intervals between the pulses indicated that the star is orbited by two planets with masses about three times the mass of the Earth. The data suggested that a third planet might also exist.

The discovery of two planets orbiting a neutron star raised fascinating questions about how planets are formed. Both of PSR1257+12's planets are in nearly circular orbits at approximately the same distance from the star as Mercury is from the sun. This is a curious finding, because the supernova that created the neutron star would almost certainly have destroyed planets so close in. At the very least, it would have thrown them into highly *eccentric* (noncircular) orbits.

For these reasons, astronomers believe that PSR1257+12's planets must have formed after the supernova explosion. Another important clue pointing to that conclusion is the star's fast rate of rotation. Astronomers theorize that a rapidly spin-ning neutron star has gained momentum by attracting matter from a companion star. Since no other star has been detected around PSR1257+12, the onetime companion probably became unstable, and it too exploded. The explosion may have formed a disk of material around the pulsar, the scientists theorize, and that matter eventually came together to form two or three planets.

But even assuming this scenario is correct, we still do not know whether planetary systems exist around main-sequence stars other than the sun. Nonetheless, the discovery that planets can apparently develop from the rubble of an exploded star, along with numerous observations showing disks of gas and dust around young stars, is valuable information. Together, these findings support the view that the formation of planets may be a common phenomenon. Furthermore, if astronomers detect other planets around pulsars, it will be a reminder that, in nature, different means may lead to the same end.   [Jonathan I. Lunine]

the photographs with a machine known as an automated plate scanner. This is a computer-driven device that scans a photographic plate, locating all objects on it and measuring their brightness.

The scanner typically detects a large number of faint objects. Each such object could be anything from a nearby brown dwarf to a faraway normal star. In order to determine the nature of a particular object, it is thus necessary to find out how far away it is.

The distances to many star clusters, including the Hyades, have been well established. The main problem when looking for brown dwarfs in a cluster is determining whether a particular object that might be a brown dwarf is actually a part of that star group. An object that is located far beyond a certain cluster might appear to belong to the cluster simply because it is located along the same line of sight.

One way to prove that an object is in fact a member of a cluster is to show that the object moves with the other stars in the group. But measuring the motions of stars is difficult because stars are so far away. But if astronomers compare photographs taken at widely separated times, they can often measure small shifts in the positions of stars.

Bryja and her colleagues studied photographs of the Hyades cluster taken several years apart. They found that a number of objects they had identified as probable brown dwarfs are moving across the sky with the Hyades cluster and so must be part of the cluster. Thus, there seems little doubt that these objects are brown dwarfs.

Many researchers are excited about the possibility of finding brown dwarfs, because brown dwarfs could account for much of the *dark matter*—matter that is not part of stars or gas clouds—that astronomers have been looking for. Observations of the Milky Way indicate that at least 90 per cent of its mass is in the form of dark matter. If the Galaxy does indeed contain hundreds of billions of brown dwarfs, their total mass would be enormous.   [Theodore P. Snow]

In the Special Reports section, see OBSERVING THE GAMMA-RAY SKY. In WORLD BOOK, see MILKY WAY.

Astronomy, Solar System

That rare event in the heavens, a total eclipse of the sun, awed millions of people in Hawaii, Mexico, and Brazil on July 11, 1991. Astronomers made detailed observations of the sun during the eclipse, concentrating especially on the *corona,* the sun's thin, extremely hot outer atmosphere. Data from those observations were still being evaluated in mid-1992.

A total eclipse of the sun occurs when the moon passes directly in front of the sun as seen from Earth and blots it out completely. This sort of alignment occurs less than once a year on the average. Moreover, a total eclipse visible at any one particular place on Earth is an extremely rare event. If you were to stand in one spot and wait for a total eclipse, you would have to wait an average of 400 years for the moon's shadow to blot out the light from the sun at that location.

The July 1991 eclipse was special for two reasons. The period of totality—the time during which all of the sun's disk was blocked by the moon—lasted 6 minutes 53 seconds along part of its path, the longest for any eclipse since one in 1973 that lasted a little over 7 minutes. The 1991 event was also the longest total eclipse until the year 2132, when an eclipse with 6 minutes 55 seconds of totality will occur. (The maximum possible length for totality is about 7 minutes 40 seconds.)

The 1991 eclipse was noteworthy for another reason as well: The path of totality crossed over a major complex of astronomical observatories on Mauna Kea, Hawaii. That fortunate occurrence gave scientists a once-in-a-lifetime opportunity to carry out observations of a total eclipse with large, stationary astronomical instruments.

The eclipse enabled astronomers to get a good look at the corona, which is normally obscured by the blinding light from the sun's surface. The corona puts on a dazzling display, with bright loops and streamers of gas moving under the influence of the sun's magnetic field. Astronomers think these phenomena may be linked in some way to the behavior of the *solar wind*—a flow of charged particles from the sun—which can affect

Earth's upper atmosphere and disrupt radio and television transmissions. So coming to a better understanding of the corona is of considerable interest to researchers.

During the July eclipse, astronomer Serge Koutchmy of the French Institute of Astronomy obtained the most detailed images of the corona ever made, using a large Canadian-French-United States telescope on Mauna Kea. Other researchers in Hawaii obtained the first images of the corona ever taken in the infrared part of the light spectrum. Astronomers expect to present the conclusions from their eclipse observations by 1993.

Galileo encounters an asteroid. The U.S. unmanned space probe Galileo, on its way to Jupiter, made the first-ever close-up study of an asteroid in October 1991. The spacecraft, launched in October 1989 by the National Aeronautics and Space Administration (NASA), passed within 1,600 kilometers (1,000 miles) of the asteroid Gaspra.

Asteroids are small bodies, none more than 800 kilometers (500 miles) across.

Gaspra, a potato-shaped hunk of rock, is much smaller than that—about 20 kilometers (12.5 miles) in length. More than half of the asteroids in orbit around the sun inhabit a "belt" between Mars and Jupiter. Most astronomers think that asteroids are leftover fragments from the period of planet formation early in the history of the solar system but were never part of a large planet themselves. (In the Special Reports section, see STONES FROM SPACE.)

Galileo made more than a dozen images of Gaspra and radioed them to Earth. The spacecraft's electronic camera was able to record details as small as 160 meters (525 feet) across on the surface of the asteroid.

Galileo also analyzed the asteroid's surface using a device called a near-infrared mapping spectrometer, which breaks up light into its component wavelengths. The amount of light coming through the instrument at each wavelength provided data that will help researchers determine the asteroid's surface composition.

Astronomer Michael Belton of the

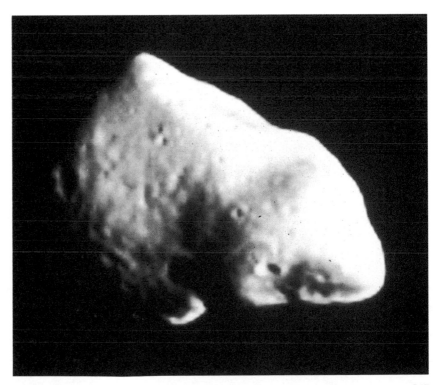

The first close-up photograph of an asteroid was taken in October 1991 by the U.S. unmanned space probe Galileo from a distance of about 1,600 kilometers (1,000 miles). The rocky asteroid, named Gaspra, is about 20 kilometers (12.5 miles) long, and orbits the sun between Mars and Jupiter. This and other images of Gaspra taken by Galileo's camera showed the asteroid to have smooth edges, indicating that it is covered with a deep layer of dust.

Total eclipse

Observatories atop Mauna Kea, a volcanic peak on the island of Hawaii, are shrouded in darkness on the morning of July 11, 1991, *below,* as a total eclipse of the sun by the moon turns day to night. The eclipse, which lasted almost 7 minutes at the midpoint of its path across the Pacific Ocean and Latin America, was one of the longest total eclipses of the century and the first to occur over a major group of observatories. Astronomers made many images of the sun's corona—its thin and extremely hot outer atmosphere—while the sun's disk was blocked by the moon, including the first such pictures taken in the infrared portion of the spectrum, *right.*

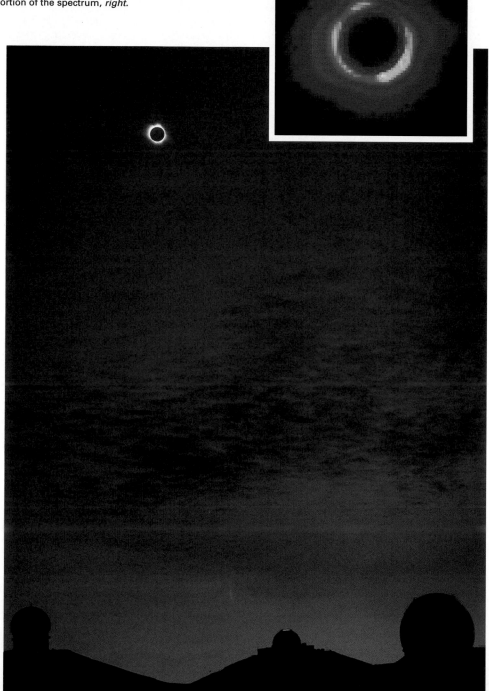

National Optical Astronomy Observatories in Tucson, Ariz., headed a team that analyzed the photographic images. They found that Gaspra has few craters and rather smooth edges. Both those observations suggested that the asteroid is covered with a deep layer of dust.

Mapping Venus. The U.S. space probe Magellan completed its second cycle of mapping the surface of Venus in January 1992. The latest series of images brought to 95 per cent the amount of the planet's surface that has been mapped by the unmanned spacecraft, which was launched in May 1989.

Venus, the second planet from the sun, is our nearest planetary neighbor. It is nearly the same size as the Earth, and the two planets are similar in mass. But Venus is perpetually shrouded in clouds, which trap heat from the sun and keep the planet's surface temperature at about 462 °C (864 °F).

Planetary geologists have long wondered whether a planet so similar in size and mass to the Earth would have the same kinds of geologic features. Magellan was designed to help answer that question by sending back highly detailed images of Venus' surface. Surveying the planet with radar signals—able to "see" through the dense cloud cover as though it is not there—Magellan can discern features on the surface as small as a football field.

The first mapping cycle of Venus was completed in May 1991. In October 1991, NASA's Jet Propulsion Laboratory (JPL) in Pasadena, Calif., released the first detailed global map of Venus, compiled from that series of radar images.

JPL planetary scientist R. Stephen Saunders led the team analyzing the data from both mapping cycles. Saunders and his colleagues learned that Venus is every bit as geologically active as Earth. It is a world covered with volcanic flows, which have spread out to create continents that rise above vast, dry plains.

In the third mapping cycle, scheduled for completion in October 1992, Magellan has made radar surveys of areas previously studied, but from different angles. These data will enable researchers to produce accurate three-dimensional images of the surface. The first two mapping cycles also yielded three-dimensional images of surface features, but

those measurements were made with an instrument called an altimeter. The altimeter could determine the height of broad areas of the surface but not of every small feature seen by the radar.

A fourth cycle will provide information on Venus' gravitational field. Magellan's instruments will detect any slight changes in the spacecraft's orbit caused by variations in gravity over different parts of the planet. Such variations would be caused by differences in the planet's density.

Ice on Mercury? Despite its closeness to the sun, Mercury may have water ice at its poles, planetary scientist Duane Muhleman of the California Institute of Technology (Caltech) in Pasadena reported in November 1991. Muhleman and his colleagues at Caltech and the JPL bounced radar signals off Mercury and detected a feature near the north pole that may be a large ice deposit.

Mercury is the innermost planet of the solar system. Its average distance from the sun is only 58 million kilometers (36 million miles), about one-third of Earth's distance from the sun. Because Mercury is so close to the sun, most of its surface is extremely hot—up to 700 °C (1,290 °F), a temperature at which water cannot exist as a liquid. The poles of Mercury, however, are almost exactly at right angles to the orbit of the planet, so they receive only a small amount of sunlight. The poles thus remain very cold, making it theoretically possible for ice to exist there.

The scientists used a large antenna to beam a powerful radar signal at Mercury. The radar echoes that bounced back from the planet were picked up by the Very Large Array, a group of radio telescopes near Socorro, N. Mex. The image created from the signals showed a bright spot at Mercury's north pole.

The researchers said the bright spot could be echoes from deposits of sodium or other minerals but most likely shows the presence of frozen water. If that result is confirmed, it raises another mystery: How did ice form on a planet in the hottest part of our solar system? The scientists said the ice might have come from comets that sometimes strike Mercury.   [Jonathan I. Lunine]

See also SPACE TECHNOLOGY. In WORLD BOOK, see ASTEROID; ECLIPSE; MERCURY; SOLAR SYSTEM; VENUS.

Astronomers in the United States reported in April 1992 that they had detected traces of the first clumps of matter to form in the universe. The finding, made by a research team headed by astrophysicist George Smoot of the University of California at Berkeley, capped a nearly 30-year search by astronomers for clues to the origin of the structures in the universe.

Scientists have long theorized that the universe began with a tremendous explosion called the big bang, which occurred several billion years ago. After the big bang, according to the theory, the universe expanded and cooled. Clouds of gas collected into vast clumps that slowly contracted, forming galaxies, clusters of galaxies, and even larger structures.

Smoot and his colleagues used the Cosmic Background Explorer (COBE) satellite to measure variations in the *cosmic background radiation,* a faint hiss of radio waves coming from every point in the heavens that represents the remaining afterglow of the big bang. The investigators reasoned that if matter had indeed clumped together soon after the big bang, those regions of higher density would appear as "cold spots"—slightly cooler areas—in the background radiation. Areas of lower density would appear as "hot spots," parts of space where the temperature is a bit higher.

The satellite's instruments made hundreds of millions of readings of the cosmic background radiation and did detect a number of cold spots and hot spots, which had the appearance of vast ripples across space. The temperature variations that COBE detected were just a few millionths of a degree higher or lower than elsewhere. The readings were combined into maps of the universe showing its state about 300,000 years after the big bang. (See PHYSICS [CLOSE-UP].)

Youthful star clusters. In January 1992, a group of astronomers led by Jon Holtzman of the Lowell Observatory in Flagstaff, Ariz., and Sandra M. Faber of the University of California at Santa Cruz announced that they had discovered clusters of newly formed stars in a galaxy named NGC 1275. The astron-

A computer image of what a black hole might look like was created by researchers at Stanford University in California in June 1991. Although a black hole itself (center) would give off no light, it could be revealed by a disk of glowing gases being sucked into the hole and by a ring of *photons,* or particles of light (dotted line).

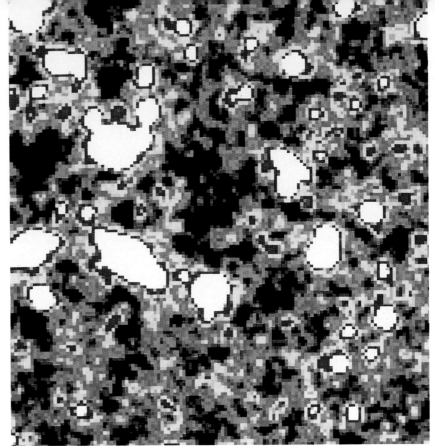

White spots on an image made by the New Technology Telescope in Chile in June 1991 may be the most distant galaxies ever observed. Astronomers estimated that the galaxies are 10 billion to 18 billion *light-years* from Earth. (A light-year is the distance light travels in one year, about 9.5 trillion kilometers [5.9 trillion miles].) The galaxies are more than twice as faint as any object ever seen before.

omers, using a camera on the Hubble Space Telescope, noted about 50 large blue dots of light surrounding the galaxy, which is located about 200 million *light-years* away. (A light-year is the distance light travels in one year, about 9.5 trillion kilometers [5.9 trillion miles].) These dots appear to be *globular clusters,* ball-shaped collections of up to 10 million stars.

Similar globular clusters surrounding our own Milky Way galaxy contain only very old stars, 10 billion to 15 billion years old. The light of these stars is red. The blue color of the stars in the newly discovered globular clusters, on the other hand, indicates that the stars are young, no more than a few hundred million years old.

Until now, astronomers thought all globular clusters were among the oldest objects in the universe, formed not long after the galaxies themselves. So Holtzman and Faber were almost as surprised at finding these relatively young globular clusters as a paleontologist would be to discover a living dinosaur.

By studying the young clusters in

NGC 1275, astronomers hope to learn more about how the stars in galaxies form. They think that the globular clusters in NGC 1275 may have formed from huge clouds of gas that were forced together when two galaxies collided. NGC 1275 has a peculiar shape, and astronomers have suspected for some time that it is actually two galaxies that have merged.

Galactic black holes. Astronomers have theorized since the 1980's that many large galaxies, including our own Milky Way, have supermassive black holes at their center. In early 1992, astronomer Tod R. Lauer of the National Optical Astronomical Observatories in Tucson, Ariz., reported that two nearby galaxies seem to contain enormous black holes.

A black hole is a dense concentration of matter so tightly packed that its gravity prevents anything, even light, from escaping from it. Astronomers think black holes may form in the centers of galaxies when massive stars collide, merge, and then collapse under their own weight.

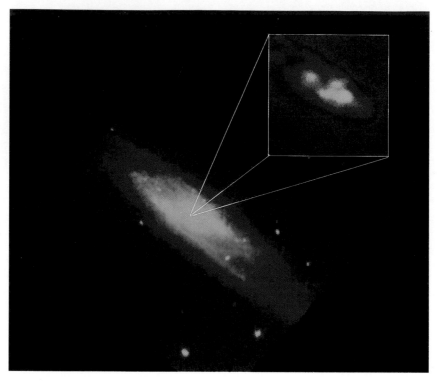

An infrared image of a galaxy called NGC 253 shows four "hot spots" (inset) at the galaxy's center. Three of the hot spots form a large cluster separate from the fourth. Astronomers think hot spots are caused when *supernovae* (exploding stars) compress surrounding clouds of gas and dust, heating them up. Because hot spots continue to glow long after a supernova has faded, they should help astronomers determine where these tremendous explosions have occurred, according to an October 1991 report.

Astronomy, Universe Continued

In January 1992, Lauer, leader of the Hubble imaging team, reported that M87, a galaxy about 52 million light-years away, may contain a black hole. Lauer said pictures from the Space Telescope showed that stars near the center of M87 are packed a thousand times more densely than are stars in the vicinity of the sun. Such a dense concentration of stars would be a likely site for an enormous black hole.

In April 1992, Lauer's team released pictures of another galaxy, M32, which, at a distance of 2.3 million light-years, is one of the Milky Way's closest neighbors. Because M32 is so near, the astronomers got an even clearer view of its center than of M87's. The stars at the middle of M32 appear to be jammed together even more densely than those of M87. But M32 is a smaller galaxy than M87, so its black hole—if indeed there is one—probably contains much less matter than the black hole in M87.

Most distant quasar. The discovery of a quasar more distant from Earth than any previously known was reported in September 1991 by a research team led by astronomer Donald Schneider of the Institute for Advanced Study in Princeton, N.J. Quasars, which look like tiny points of light through a telescope, are the most distant objects known in the universe.

Because quasars are visible from so far away, they must emit enormous amounts of light. Astronomers search for quasars in an effort to learn what the universe looked like billions of years ago, when the light from these mysterious energy sources began its long journey to Earth. Schneider and his colleagues determined that the newly discovered quasar is 12 billion to 14 billion light-years from the Earth. If the universe is no more than 15 billion years old, the quasar must have been formed within a billion or so years after the big bang.

A younger universe? In the past, estimates for the age of the universe ranged from 15 billion to 20 billion years. In 1991 and 1992, however, several astronomers announced findings suggesting that the universe may be considerably younger, only about 10 billion years old.

The new evidence, first reported in June 1991 by astronomer Robert McClure of the Dominion Astrophysical Observatory in Hawaii, is based on a revised estimate of the distance to a group of galaxies called the Virgo Cluster. Using a telescope equipped with a special camera designed to remove the blurring effects of Earth's atmosphere, McClure and his colleagues were able to make out individual stars in the galaxies of the cluster.

Going on the assumption that the brightest stars in the cluster are no more luminous than the brightest stars in the Milky Way galaxy, the researchers calculated how far away the Virgo Cluster stars must be to have their observed brightness. They concluded that the cluster is no more than 50 million light-years away—much closer to us than many astronomers had thought.

The Virgo Cluster is used as a yardstick against which the distances to other galaxies are determined. Therefore, determining that the Virgo Cluster is nearer to Earth implies that the entire universe is smaller than astronomers had thought. If that is the case, the universe must also be younger than had been thought, because the universe's size is related to the amount of time that it has been expanding.

Other astronomers reported results similar to those of McClure and his colleagues. However, many astronomers were not convinced by the new findings. They hoped that repairs to the flawed mirror of the Hubble Space Telescope, scheduled for 1993 or 1994, will permit investigators to make more precise galactic-distance measurements that will settle the issue.

Will the universe expand forever? Evidence from the Hubble telescope indicates that the universe will continue to expand forever, astronomer Jeffrey Linsky of the Joint Institute for Laboratory Astrophysics in Boulder, Colo., reported in January 1992. Earlier observations had shown that the expansion of the universe is slowing because of the mutual gravitational attraction of the galaxies. Because of that finding, some astronomers have speculated that the universe will eventually contract in a "big crunch."

The universe will expand indefinitely unless the total amount of mass in all the galaxies exceeds a certain "critical" amount. If there is more than that amount, gravity will eventually begin to draw matter together again. If there is less than the critical amount, the expansion can never quite stop, and the matter in the universe will simply become more and more thinly distributed as time goes on.

Linsky and his colleagues made their observations with an instrument on the Hubble Space Telescope called the High Resolution Spectrograph, which analyzes the light from stars and other celestial objects. The researchers used the spectrograph to examine light from a bright star called Capella. As the starlight passed through gas clouds on its way to Earth, various elements in the clouds absorbed particular wavelengths of light. The absorbed wavelengths showed up as dark lines on a spectrum of the light from the star. By studying the lines, the researchers could tell what elements were in the gas clouds, and in what proportions.

The investigators were especially interested in learning how much deuterium, a form of hydrogen, is in the gas clouds. Although most elements were forged in the interiors of stars, astronomers think that nearly all the deuterium in the universe was created soon after the big bang, along with large amounts of hydrogen and helium.

The amount of deuterium created depends on how much matter was present to form elements just after the big bang. By determining the abundance of deuterium in ancient gas clouds, astronomers can thus infer the total amount of mass that was created at the birth of the universe.

The researchers found that the clouds contain just 15 atoms of deuterium for every 1 million atoms of ordinary hydrogen. That ratio, Linsky noted, indicates that the universe contains no more than 10 per cent of the amount of matter required to stop the expansion—if the mass in the universe is made up only of ordinary matter. Unless some other type of matter makes up the other 90 per cent of the needed mass, he said, the universe appears to be on a one-way trip outward.   [Laurence A. Marschall]

In the Special Reports section, see OBSERVING THE GAMMA-RAY SKY. In WORLD BOOK, see COSMOLOGY; UNIVERSE.

Here are 22 outstanding new science books suitable for the general reader. They have been selected from books published in 1991 and 1992.

Archaeology. *Fantastic Archaeology: The Wild Side of North American Prehistory* by Stephen Williams examines some of the archaeological hoaxes perpetrated by people in search of fame. A number of the fraudulent "discoveries" were made in the 1800's, often to make the claim that people of a particular nationality discovered the New World. (University of Pennsylvania Press, 1991. 407 pp. illus. $28.95)

Astronomy. *Chandra: A Biography of S. Chandrasekhar* by Kameshwar C. Wali is an account of the many contributions this Nobel Prize-winning, Indian-born scientist made to astronomy. At the age of 19, Chandrasekhar discovered that stars of a certain mass must ultimately collapse as a result of their own gravitation. (University of Chicago Press, 1991. 341 pp. illus. $29.95)

How the Shaman Stole the Moon: In Search of Ancient Prophet-Scientists from Stonehenge to the Grand Canyon by William H. Calvin looks at ancient ruins, such as Stonehenge in England and Chaco Canyon in New Mexico, and considers how they may have been used by early cultures to achieve and preserve knowledge of astronomy. (Bantam, 1991. 223 pp. illus. $21.50)

Biology. *One Long Argument: Charles Darwin and the Genesis of Modern Evolutionary Thought* by Ernst Mayr explores the complexity of Darwin's evolutionary theories, the frequent misunderstanding and misinterpretation that has surrounded them, and the continuing significance of the issues he identified and studied. (Harvard University Press, 1991. 195 pp. illus. $19.95)

The Triumph of the Embryo by Lewis Wolpert describes the development of cells and embryos and how their growth and differentiation give rise to the mature adult. Wolpert discusses the development of the brain, explains the processes of regeneration, growth, and aging; and suggests that cancer is a deviation from the normal controls of development. (Oxford University Press, 1991. 211 pp. illus. $22.95)

Viruses by Arnold J. Levine. Viruses, the smallest, simplest life forms, are unable to reproduce outside the cells of the higher organisms they infect. Levine explains how studies have led to the creation of vaccines for controlling viral illnesses and describes the significance of these studies for our understanding of the origins of cancer. (Scientific American Library, 1991. 239 pp. illus. $32.95)

Chemistry. *Discovering Enzymes* by David Dressler and Huntington Potter tells how the attempt to understand alcoholic fermentation led to the discovery of enzymes, substances that control chemical reactions without taking part in the reactions themselves. The authors show how enzymes help create biologically useful molecules from other substances. (Scientific American Library, 1991. 263 pp. illus. $32.95)

From Caveman to Chemist: Circumstances and Achievements by Hugh W. Salzberg is a history of chemistry from earliest times until the end of the 1800's. (American Chemical Society, 1991. 294 pp. ill. $24.95)

Earth science. *Fire Under the Sea: The Discovery of the Most Extraordinary Environment on Earth—Volcanic Hot Springs on the Ocean Floor* by Joseph Cone concentrates on the study of sea-floor hot springs that occur in many places near the chain of underwater mountains known as the mid-ocean ridge. The springs were unknown before 1977. Their exploration in manned submersibles has resulted in new discoveries about our planet, about the existence of life under extreme conditions, and about the complex relationships between the inner heat of the Earth and the oceans that cover it. (Morrow, 1991. 285 pp. illus. $25)

Engineering. *Flying Buttresses, Entropy, and O-Rings: The World of an Engineer* by James L. Adams includes a history of technology and the engineering profession. The book surveys the engineer's world, describing the importance of design and invention in the generation of new ideas, the role of mathematics in engineering, and the need for experiment and testing. (Harvard University Press, 1991. 264 pp. illus. $24.95)

General science. *Basic Nature* by Andrew Scott concisely summarizes the scientific view of nature, explaining the most fundamental concepts of science, from space time, gravity, and energy to the origins of life, evolution, and human thought. Its stated goal is "to convey the essence of the scientific view of nature in as few pages as possible." (Blackwell, 1991. 192 pp. illus. $17.95.)

Charles Darwin: A New Life by John Bowlby provides a new look at the great English naturalist whose theory of evolution and 1859 book, *The Origin of Species*, forever changed the study of living creatures. Bowlby's biography also offers a new explanation for the chronic illness Darwin suffered for most of his adult life. (Norton, 1991. 511 pp. illus. $24.95)

The Natural History of the Universe from the Big Bang to the End of Time by Colin A. Ronan is a richly illustrated survey of the universe, containing current scientific knowledge of what we know about its origin. Ronan covers such topics as space, relativity, galaxies, black holes, the planets, and theories about hidden dimensions of the universe. (Macmillan, 1991. 212 pp. illus. $39.95)

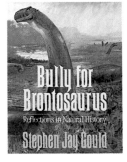

Mathematics. *Prisoner's Dilemma: John von Neumann, Game Theory, and the Puzzle of the Bomb* by William Poundstone tells the story of the invention of *game theory* (the mathematical study of competition) by mathematician John von Neumann in the late 1930's and early 1940's. The book also discusses the importance of game theory in the development of United States nuclear weapons policy and the influence of game theory on modern public policy. (Doubleday, 1992. 290 pp. illus. $22.50)

Beyond Numeracy: Ruminations of a Numbers Man by John A. Paulos is a collection of mathematical essays, some quite unconventional, ranging from summaries of whole disciplines to biographical and historical asides, and tidbits of mathematical folklore. The book is written for a lay audience. (Knopf, 1991. 290 pp. $22)

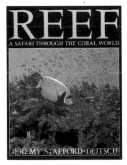

Meteorology. *Watching the World's Weather* by W. J. Burroughs shows how weather satellites have transformed the science of meteorology. Burroughs explains how satellites are playing increasingly important roles in monitoring Earth for a possible global warming, the depletion of ozone in the upper atmosphere, and climatic change. (Cambridge University Press, 1991. 196 pp. illus. $24.95)

Natural history. *Bully for Brontosaurus* by Stephen Jay Gould is the fifth collection of essays from Gould's column in the magazine *Natural History.* The book contains more than 35 articles that explore various aspects of evolutionary change and demonstrate the elegant adaptations of organisms to their environments. (Norton, 1991. 540 pp. $22.95)

Madagascar: A Natural History by Ken Preston-Mafham surveys the inhabitants of the world's fourth largest island. Included are the island's plant life, amphibians and reptiles, birds, and lemurs and other mammals. The book contains pictures of animals whose portraits have never before appeared in print. (Facts on File, 1991. 224 pp. illus. $45)

Living Fossil: The Story of the Coelacanth by Keith S. Thomson focuses on a primitive type of fish found in the western Indian Ocean. Scientists have found fossils of the coelacanth that are more than 300 million years old. They believed the coelacanth was extinct until one was found in 1938. The author tells how the coelacanth lives, where it lives, and how it has managed to avoid extinction. (Norton, 1991. 252 pp. illus. $19.95)

The Miner's Canary: A Paleontologist Unravels the Mysteries of Extinction by Niles Eldredge. Observing the disappearance of once common songbirds from his backyard, Eldredge began to develop the general theory of species extinction presented here. Eldredge discusses the causes of extinction, explores whether human activity accelerates extinction, and distinguishes between the simple workings of nature's order and the omens of ecological disaster. The book's title refers to the birds that once alerted coal miners to the presence of odorless, poisonous gases in the mines. (Prentice Hall, 1991. 256 pp. $19.50)

On Methuselah's Trail: Living Fossils and the Great Extinction by Peter D. Ward discusses how a number of still-living organisms have survived the massive extinctions suffered by other similar life forms. Among them are the familiar dragonfly and magnolia. (W. H. Freeman, 1992. 212 pp. $18.95)

Reef: A Safari Through the Coral World by Jeremy Stafford-Deitsch contains beautiful photographs and text describing the nature and behavior of reef inhabitants and explaining the pressing need to conserve them. (Sierra Club Books, distributed by Random House, 1991. 200 pp. illus. $25)

[William Goodrich Jones]

255

A fungus that was called the world's largest known organism was discovered in a forest near Crystal Falls, Mich., according to an April 1992 report by researchers at the University of Toronto in Canada and Michigan Technological University in Houghton. The fungus is a member of the species *Armillaria bulbosa,* which typically grows by sending out stringlike hyphae under the surface of a forest floor. Occasionally, it sends up edible mushrooms.

The researchers performed genetic testing on a fungal network that extended across 15 hectares (37 acres) of the Michigan forest and discovered that the entire growth was genetically identical. They concluded that it was a single individual. The researchers estimated that the fungus weighed more than 10,000 kilograms (22,000 pounds) and had been growing for more than 1,500 years.

Then in May, researchers at the Rocky Mountain Forest and Range Experiment Station in Fort Collins, Colo., and at the Washington State Department of Natural Resources reported that for 20 years they had been studying a fungus, *Armillaria ostoyae,* that was 40 times as large as the Michigan fungus. It grows in a pine forest in southwestern Washington and covers more than 600 hectares (1,500 acres). The researchers estimated that the fungus was 400 to 1,000 years old. They and the Michigan researchers said that even larger, yet undiscovered fungi could exist.

Botanists say, however, that there is no way to be certain that all the hyphae underground are attached to each other. If they have become detached, and the researchers suspect that this may be the case, then the giant "organism" would be a group of genetically identical individuals that arose without sexual reproduction from a single parent. That is, the detached individuals would be *clones,* not unlike the world's many plant varieties produced by horticultural cloning techniques. Many biologists thus dispute the reports that the fungi are the world's largest organisms.

New tomato hormone. One defense mechanism plants have against insect enemies is the ability to produce substances that give the insects indigestion.

The *calyx,* a star-shaped cluster of leaves that surrounds a cherry tomato, unexpectedly ripened into fruit in an experiment by a U.S. Department of Agriculture scientist in Albany, Calif. In the experiment, reported in January 1992, tiny immature tomatoes with attached calyxes had been placed in nutrient-filled test tubes for a study of fruit ripening. In mid-1992, investigators were trying to discover the mechanism that triggered the calyx into becoming fruit.

Communicating with color

More plants than previously thought—74 plant families—have the ability to change color to attract insect pollinators to fertile blossoms. Experiments in 1991 by a scientist at the University of California at Berkeley showed that many plants use color cues to help insects recognize young, pollen-filled flowers.

The first day they open, the flowers of *Androsace lanuginosa, above,* display yellow centers. Such flowers are fertile—ready for pollination by visiting insects. Within several days, the centers change to orange and, finally, to red, which indicates that the flower has little or no nectar or pollen to offer.

A showy cluster of *Lantana camara* flowers, *above,* attracts insects from afar, but only the newly opened yellow flowers contain nectar and pollen. The University of California researcher found that young butterflies quickly learned to prefer the plant's yellow flowers over its older reddish blooms. *Lupinus nanus, right,* uses different color cues. The white center of a flower indicates fertility, while a purple center tells insects that the flower contains no more pollen or nectar.

A hormone in tomato plants that is far more effective in controlling production of such compounds than any substance previously known was isolated and identified in August 1991. Scientists at Washington State University in Pullman and Harvard Medical School in Boston reported this finding.

The researchers call the substance *systemin.* They reported that it is the first known plant hormone that is a *polypeptide* (a compound consisting of many amino acids, which are the building blocks of proteins). Polypeptide hormones such as insulin are common in animals, but other known plant hormones are simpler compounds.

The researchers isolated only a tiny amount of systemin from 27 kilograms (60 pounds) of tomato plant leaves and identified its chemical structure. They then created synthetic systemin and applied it to cuts on tomato leaves to discover if the artificial hormone would also cause the plants to make the indigestion-causing substances, called proteinase inhibitor I and proteinase inhibitor II.

The scientists found that only a tiny amount of the hormone, about 1 part in 10 trillion, made the leaf produce the inhibitors. And when the researchers traced a radioactive form of systemin applied to a small part of a leaf, they found systemin throughout the leaf within 30 minutes and throughout the plant within two hours.

One gene makes flowers. Activating just one gene causes a snapdragon plant (*Antirrhinum majus*) to develop flowers, reported researchers at the Agriculture and Food Research Council's Plant Science Laboratory in Norwich, England, in July 1991. Botanists have long known that many plants respond to environmental factors, such as the relative lengths of day and night, by producing flowers. The Norwich researchers discovered the gene that is activated by these environmental factors.

The scientists screened 50,000 snapdragon plants to find a plant that did not flower. The lack of flowers in this plant was caused by a *jumping gene*, a gene that has moved during cell division from one place on a chromosome to another. There, it may interfere with the normal function of the neighboring gene. By examining the position of the jumping gene, the scientists were eventually able to track down the gene that causes the snapdragon to flower.

A botanical bonanza. A tree native to Africa and Asia, called the neem tree, bears seeds that contain an insecticide that can kill at least 200 species of insects, including such destructive pests as aphids, cockroaches, gypsy moths, locusts, and medflies. Yet, according to a February 1992 report by the National Research Council in Washington, D.C., neem seed insecticide is much less toxic to such beneficial insects as ladybugs, which eat crop-destroying bugs, than are conventional insecticides. One reason for this apparent selectivity is that neem compounds penetrate plants and thus are deadly to insects that eat the plants. Insects that feed upon the plant-eating insects are apparently unharmed.

Plants that grow plastic. Plants can be genetically engineered to produce granules of biodegradable plastic within their roots, leaves, and stems. That was the finding reported by researchers at Michigan State University in East Lansing and James Madison University in Harrisonburg, Va., in April 1992.

The scientists engineered a plastic-growing plant by transferring genes from a species of soil bacteria that naturally produces the plastic. The species of plant used in the experiment, *Arabidopsis thaliana,* naturally contained one of the three genes needed to produce the plastic. The researchers inserted each of the other two genes into two groups of the plants. Crossbreeding the two groups yielded a hybrid plant that contained all three genes and produced plastic granules.

The researchers reported that the experiment was the first to alter a plant so that it created a compound other than proteins. But scientists must conquer other obstacles to grow usable amounts of plastic inside plants. *Arabidopsis,* widely used for laboratory tests, is a tiny plant with a short life cycle, and the plants that produced the plastic were stunted compared with normal plants. Botanists will have to genetically engineer larger and more productive plants, such as the potato or tobacco, before growers can "farm" plastic from plants in amounts large enough to be profitable.   [Frank B. Salisbury]

In WORLD BOOK, see BOTANY.

Chemists at the Massachusetts Institute of Technology (MIT) in Cambridge disclosed in February 1992 that they had created molecules that mimic some of the essential features of living things. In particular, they showed for the first time that it may be possible for compounds made in the laboratory to reproduce in solution. This is a significant step that may eventually lead to more complex chemical compounds that can reproduce in the same manner as DNA (deoxyribonucleic acid), the molecule of which genes are made. Genes are the units of heredity in cells.

The compounds—prepared by organic chemist Julius Rebek, Jr., and his colleagues—behave in much the same way as DNA. The synthetic molecules, which are carbon compounds containing nitrogen, oxygen, and hydrogen, combine in a fashion similar to that of DNA, which forms a double *helix* (spiral). And like DNA, the synthetic molecules can make copies of themselves when placed in solutions containing their chemical ingredients.

Perhaps most startling of all, and again like natural DNA, the synthetic molecules display the ability to *evolve* (develop and change into a more organized state). For example, bombarding the compounds with ultraviolet radiation causes them to change their structures into new forms that are more successful at reproducing than the original molecules.

Rebek's molecules are different from DNA in important ways, however. They are not truly living and have structures quite different from DNA. Many scientists consider the ability to continuously evolve into new forms a sign of life. Unlike the DNA in living cells, however, the synthetic molecules have only a limited ability to evolve into new forms or to store information. But the MIT work could lead to other compounds that possess these traits.

A better propellant. Reports in January 1992 described a new aerosol spray propellant system that is more effective than the once widely used chlorofluorocarbon (CFC) propellants. Unlike CFC's, however, the new aerosol propellant system does not damage Earth's

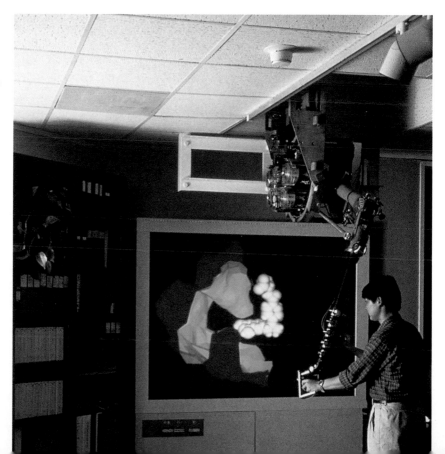

A computer system that enables users to "feel" molecular interactions was being refined by scientists at the University of North Carolina in Chapel Hill in 1991. The user manipulates a "docking arm" to move computer images of molecules toward each other. The computer signals motors in the arm to resist or accelerate movement, mimicking the repulsive and attractive forces between atoms. Biochemists plan to use the system to help design better drugs.

The New Game in Chemistry: Buckyball

Chemists released a flood of reports during late 1991 and early 1992 about the behavior of *fullerenes*—amazingly versatile molecules made up of 60 or more carbon atoms. These accounts suggested that buckminsterfullerene, as the 60-carbon-atom (C_{60}) molecule is known, and its larger relatives could have a wide range of practical uses.

Buckminsterfullerene, which scientists first prepared in large quantities in 1990, received its name because the soccer-ball-shaped molecule resembles the geodesic domes popularized by the American architect R. Buckminster Fuller. Noteworthy discoveries about the molecule, dubbed the buckyball, came so fast that *Science* magazine named it "Molecule of the Year" for 1991.

Fullerenes can be made *superconducting*—able to conduct electricity with no resistance. A record high temperature at which mixtures of C_{60} and C_{70} (70-carbon-atom) fullerenes become superconducting was announced in November 1991 by chemist Ray H. Baughman of Allied-Signal, Incorporated, in Morristown, N.J. When he added *ions* (electrically charged atoms) of the metals thallium and rubidium, the fullerenes became superconducting at −228 °C (−378 °F). The previous record was −245 °C (−409 °F).

Although still very low, this temperature was significant. Cooling is expensive, so the less cooling a material needs to become superconducting, the greater its chances of finding an application. Some researchers speculate that extra-large fullerenes containing hundreds or even thousands of carbon atoms—molecules not yet made—might require no cooling at all to become superconducting. Superconducting materials may someday be used in transcontinental power lines that carry electricity with practically no loss of power or in lightweight, highly efficient electric motors.

Fullerenes also may make it easier to deposit a synthetic diamond coating on drill bits, knives, and other tools, according to a November report by researchers Robert P. H. Chang and Manfred M. Kappes of Northwestern University in Evanston, Ill. Diamond, a superhard form of carbon, boosts the tools' durability. Scientists currently grow synthetic diamond coatings from the carbon deposited by a carbon-rich gas. But the coating adheres only if the metal surface has been polished beforehand with a diamond powder.

The Northwestern researchers first sprinkled C_{70} fullerenes on the surface to be coated and then bombarded it with a gas of carbon and hydrogen ions. The fullerenes caused the diamond coating to adhere readily, eliminating the need for a prior diamond polish.

Fullerene magnets entered the realm of the possible, thanks to a discovery announced by chemist Fred Wudl of the University of California at Santa Barbara in July 1991. Wudl disclosed that fullerenes become magnetic at very low temperatures when combined with certain *organic* (carbon-containing) molecules and exposed to a magnetic field. Although the fullerenes' magnetism disappears when the field is withdrawn, Wudl believes his finding may eventually lead to permanent magnets made from fullerenes, paving the way for a new generation of lightweight magnets.

Superstrong fibers are another possible outgrowth of fullerene research. In October, Japanese chemist Sumio Iijima of the Fundamental Research Laboratories at NEC Corporation near Tokyo revealed that he had prepared microscopic, tube-shaped fullerenes. Scientists believe that long strands of fullerenes would rank among the strongest fibers known.

New *polymers* (long, chainlike molecules) that incorporate fullerenes in their structure came

The versatility of molecules built of 60 carbon atoms, dubbed buckyballs, intrigued chemists in late 1991 and early 1992. A computer created the image of stacked buckyballs, *above.*

closer to realization, several chemists announced at a December meeting of the Materials Research Society (MRS) in Boston. Wudl told of his laboratory's successful efforts to attach various groups of chemicals to the outside of the C_{60} molecule. The chemical groups could serve as anchors for other chemicals in building carbon-based polymers.

Douglas Loy and Roger A. Assink of Sandia National Laboratory in Albuquerque, N. Mex., also announced in December that they had formed a simple polymer composed of buckminsterfullerene and a compound of carbon and hydrogen related to benzene. Although the powder that resulted had few useful properties, useful polymers might be formed in the future by attaching fullerenes to chemical groups that react readily with other substances. Such polymers could someday serve as strong coatings that conduct electricity or be used in chemical *catalysts* (substances that speed up chemical reactions).

Richard E. Smalley of Rice University in Houston, one of the chemists who discovered buckminsterfullerene in 1985, disclosed in late 1991 that he had trapped atoms of the metal lanthanum inside hollow fullerene molecules. The ability of fullerenes to be "carbon cages" holding atoms or smaller molecules may prove quite useful. For example, they could serve as delivery systems that slowly release medications inside the body or as containers for molecules that store high-density electronic data.

Information about the optical properties of fullerenes was reported in late 1991 by research groups from Du Pont de Nemours and Company in Wilmington, Del.; the U.S. Naval Research Laboratory in Washington, D.C.; Northwestern University; and elsewhere. The groups reported that light waves passing through fullerenes increased in *frequency* (the number of waves that pass a fixed point each second). Materials with this optical property have the potential to act as high-speed on/off switches in computers and telecommunications equipment. Someday, fullerenes might even form the basis of ultra-high-speed optical computers, which would use pulses of light to transmit and encode information, rather than the electrons that today's computers rely upon.

A March 1992 report disclosed that solutions of C_{60} fullerenes transmit low-intensity light but block light at higher intensities. This finding, by Lee W. Tutt and Alan Kost of Hughes Research Laboratory in Malibu, Calif., suggested a role for fullerenes as *optical limiters*—materials that could be coated on goggles to protect the eyes of workers exposed to intense light or coated on windows to protect light-sensitive instruments from powerful bursts of light. This finding and the flurry of others made it likely that fullerenes will grab headlines for some time. [Gordon Graff]

Chemistry Continued

protective layer of ozone in the upper atmosphere.

Ozone molecules consist of three oxygen atoms. The ozone layer in Earth's upper atmosphere absorbs most of the sun's damaging ultraviolet radiation before it reaches Earth's surface, but CFC's destroy ozone in Earth's upper atmosphere. Although the United States banned CFC's in aerosols in the 1970's, some countries still permit use of the chemicals.

The new aerosol system, developed by Scottish inventor Bernard D. Frutin, consists of a solution of carbon dioxide dissolved in *acetone* (a colorless, flammable liquid widely used as a solvent). The solution is forced into the microscopic holes of porous beads. The beads are made of a *polymer* (a long chainlike molecule made of simpler molecules). Because the beads are so porous, a large quantity of dissolved gas can be stored in them.

Pressing the button of an aerosol-spray can loaded with the polymer beads causes the pressure inside the can to drop. This, in turn, causes the beads to release the gas, which forces the contents of the can out of the nozzle. According to Frutin, the new spray system is completely harmless to ozone.

Superdense data storage. In a continuation of research that began in the 1970's, a scientist in March 1992 suggested that clusters of tiny beads of plastic containing small droplets of light-emitting dyes might someday be used to create data-storage devices. These devices could be capable of holding thousands of times more information than can today's computer chips, according to a report by physicist Stephen Arnold of New York City's Polytechnic University.

The dye molecules used in the beads can absorb laser light at very precise frequencies, depending on the sizes of the beads in which the dye droplets are trapped. When the dyes absorb light, they *fluoresce* (give off light). But when a very intense laser beam is used, the dye molecules break up into forms that no longer fluoresce.

Arnold called these nonfluorescing dye molecules "holes," and reported that a pattern of holes or a lack of holes in the dye molecules could mimic the "0" and "1" patterns used to store data on computer chips. If the dyes were trapped in plastic beads in a wide range of sizes, then an array of such beads could store information in a very wide range of distinct but closely spaced laser frequencies. The very narrow spacing of laser frequencies could conceivably allow very dense data storage.

Clays as catalysts. A new way to open up the normally tightly packed flat crystal layers of clay minerals was described in September 1991 by chemist Thomas J. Pinnavaia of Michigan State University in East Lansing. The process involves chemically inserting microscopic "pillars" between the layers. Such chemically modified clays, he said, may someday be used as *catalysts* (substances that speed up chemical reactions without themselves being changed). The clay catalysts could be used to create high yields of fuels and other chemicals from crude oil, to remove pollutants from water, and to form a variety of heat-resistant coatings.

Clay is made of chemically reactive minerals containing aluminum, silicon, and oxygen. Normally, the layers of clay are too closely spaced to allow the minerals to participate in chemical reactions. But Pinnavaia propped open these layers by inserting pillars made of connected groups of metal, oxygen, and hydrogen atoms. Various molecules—for example, those found in crude oil—can fit inside these spaces and react with the clay minerals. Similar but more expensive catalysts now used in industry can convert crude oil to useful products. Pinnavaia also reported that poisonous compounds in water could fill the spaces and react with the catalysts to form harmless by-products.

Better oil cleanups. Experiments reported in April 1992 suggest that it may be possible to use chemically coated, hollow glass beads to clean up oil spills more quickly and cheaply than traditional methods. Engineers usually clean large oil spills—such as the March 1989 *Exxon Valdez* accident in Alaska's Prince William Sound—by using special detergents to break up oil slicks on the surface of water.

Chemical engineer Adam Heller of the University of Texas at Austin developed the new technique using glass beads coated with a *photocatalyst* (a substance that causes chemical changes when exposed to sunlight). The photocatalyst consisted of the metal palladium and the relatively inexpensive white pigment titanium dioxide, which is often found in paint. The beads are hollow and float on the surface of water, where their coatings interact with sunlight. This creates a chemical reaction in which the *hydrocarbons* (carbon and hydrogen compounds) in spilled oil form smaller molecules that can be broken down by bacteria in the water.

Based on laboratory models, Heller estimated that the coated beads could disperse an oil spill the size of the *Exxon Valdez* accident in two weeks at about 1 per cent of the cost of the *Valdez* cleanup. Cleanup of the *Valdez* spill took two years and cost about $4 billion.

Controlled reactions. Chemists have long wished they could break and reassemble a molecule's chemical bonds in highly specific places so that they could obtain certain rare drugs, industrial chemicals, and other useful products in much higher amounts than is possible by traditional methods of chemical synthesis. Several reports in early 1992 showed how lasers may someday make this goal a reality.

In January, chemist Ahmed Zewail of the California Institute of Technology in Pasadena reported that he made molecules of iodine and the rare gas xenon react to form exceptionally large quantities of xenon iodide. Zewail aimed two beams of ultrafast laser pulses at the iodine molecules. Each pulse lasted about a millionth of a billionth of a second. One of the beams excited and weakened the bond between the two iodine atoms that make up an iodine molecule, and the other beam actually broke the bonds, allowing the two atoms to fly apart and react with the xenon.

Chemist Richard Zare of Stanford University in Stanford, Calif., in April 1992 revealed another way of selectively breaking chemical bonds with lasers. He reported that he produced reactions at selected portions of ammonia molecules. Zare bombarded the molecules with laser beams carefully tuned to frequencies that matched the natural vibrating frequencies of selected bonds in the molecules. This increased the energy supplied to those bonds and broke them. [Gordon Graff]

In WORLD BOOK, see CHEMISTRY.

Computer Hardware

Personal computers in late 1991 and early 1992 increased in performance while dramatically decreasing in price. Many popular computer models for both home and office were built around Intel Corporation's 80386 and 80386SX microprocessors, which made possible the increased computing power and speed. Such computers have the ability to run software requiring large amounts of *random access memory* (RAM), the working memory into which programs and data are loaded from disks. The ability to run large programs is important to people who use *graphical user interfaces*—software that is activated by selecting items displayed as pictures or in simple menus rather than by typing commands.

From 1991 to mid-1992, the prices of powerful 80386 and 80386SX computers dropped as much as 70 per cent. Prices on some models had fallen as low as $1,500 by spring 1992. The lower prices enabled computer users to buy more-powerful machines for less money—while manufacturers earned smaller profits on each machine sold.

Notebook computers, about the size of this volume of *Science Year* (and, in some cases, weighing even less), displayed more dramatic growth than any other category of computer hardware in late 1991 and early 1992. Several powerful models were introduced, and sales of notebook computers grew nearly 25 per cent during the period, according to some industry observers.

Notebook computers weigh as little as 1.4 kilograms (3.1 pounds), yet their computing speed, power, and data storage match those of much heavier machines. Like other portable computers, notebook computers rely on batteries for operation. Some notebook computers offered colored screens.

In autumn 1991, Zenith Data Systems of Buffalo Grove, Ill., introduced MastersPort 386SL, a notebook computer that uses an Intel microprocessor specially designed to maximize battery life. The MastersPort 386SL, which carries a suggested price of $4,999, includes a 60-megabyte hard disk drive for storing data and 2 megabytes of RAM. (Computer memory is measured in units

A wearable computer that straps around the hand was introduced by Grid Systems in March 1992. PalmPad, which sells for $2,895, is designed for people who need to record data while on the move. Users enter information by writing directly on the computer screen with an electronic pen.

Taking it with you
Lightweight, portable computers became more powerful than ever in late 1991 and early 1992. Many new laptop and notebook models packed the same computing power as larger desktop personal computers.

IBM's PS/2 laptop computer, *left,* features a color screen and weighs 5 kilograms (11 pounds). It lists at $5,995. The PowerBook 170, *above,* the most powerful of three notebook computers from Apple Computer, weighs 3.1 kilograms (6.8 pounds) and sells for $4,599.

The T4400SX notebook computer from Toshiba America Information Systems, *above,* weighs 3.4 kilograms (7.5 pounds) and, like other notebook models, fits handily in a briefcase. Its list price is $5,599.

Computer Hardware Continued

called bytes. A computer with 1 million bytes—1 megabyte or MB—of memory can hold the equivalent of about 500 double-spaced typed pages.)

Dell Computer Corporation of Austin, Tex., introduced its Dell System 325NC, priced at $3,999, in December. This notebook computer includes a 16-color screen, a 60-MB hard disk, and 4 MB of RAM. The computer can be used up to three hours before the battery needs recharging.

Apple Computer, Incorporated, of Cupertino, Calif., unveiled its Power-Book series in November. These notebook computers run Macintosh software and can also read disks from IBM-compatible computers. The PowerBook comes in three models that are priced from $2,299 to $4,599 and offer from 20 MB to 40 MB of hard-disk storage, depending on the model.

All the new Apple models can record and play back sound, giving them the capability to run multimedia software. Multimedia software combines text, sound, graphics, animation, and in some cases full-motion video, producing an experience that more closely resembles watching television than it does traditional computing.

The top-end Apple PowerBook can transmit data over telephone lines, using a facsimile (fax) machine or a device called a modem. This enables notebook users to transfer files, for example, to a computer in a distant office.

Compaq Computer Corporation of Houston, Tex., joined competitors in January 1992 with two lightweight models priced at $2,900 and $4,600. The Compaq LTE Lite/20 and LTE Lite/25 have batteries that run more than four hours before they need recharging—longer than rival notebook computers. They provide 40 MB and 80 MB of hard-disk storage, respectively.

Multimedia machines. Various manufacturers introduced personal computers that are designed to use multimedia software, as well as standard computer programs, in late 1991 and early 1992. Multimedia software, which allows users to both see and hear materials, is expected to find applications in education and business.

Operating multimedia software requires a powerful computer with a hefty amount of memory for storing sound and pictures. Multimedia systems also require a sound card to handle the software's audio output and a CD-ROM (compact disc, read-only memory) drive to handle compact discs, which store even more material. The drop in hardware prices has made multimedia systems more affordable.

In October 1991, Tandy Corporation of Fort Worth, Tex., introduced its 2500SX multimedia personal computer. Priced at about $4,950, the 2500SX comes equipped with a 105-MB hard disk, a CD-ROM drive, Windows software, and audio output.

Also in October, International Business Machines (IBM) of Armonk, N.Y., unveiled the PS/2 Ultimedia M57 SLC personal computer. This multimedia system is built around Intel's 386SLC microprocessor and includes a 160-MB hard disk, a CD-ROM drive, and features for recording sound and playing it back. The PS/2 Ultimedia computer is priced at about $6,000.

"Wearable" computers debuted in 1992, made possible by the continued miniaturization of computer parts. Wearable computers are computing devices that the user can strap around the hand or wrist or hang from the shoulder. People who move around as they work or need their hands free for other tasks are expected to find these computers especially useful.

The first wearable computer was introduced by Grid Systems Corporation of Fremont, Calif., in March. PalmPad, a computer to hold in the hand or strap on, is intended for people who take inventories or do other jobs that require them to collect and enter data while on foot. It offers users the opportunity of writing directly on the computer screen with an electronic pen called a stylus. PalmPad is priced at $2,895.

Some industry observers see wearable computers as a first step in the spread of computers into every aspect of life. They envision a time when microprocessors can be built into clothing and even into books and magazines.   [Keith Ferrell]

In WORLD BOOK, see COMPUTER.

Computer Software

A destructive computer virus dubbed Michelangelo created a scare in early March 1992. The virus was timed to destroy all data and programs stored on computer hard disks on March 6, the 517th anniversary of the birth of Italian artist Michelangelo.

Computer viruses are programs designed to attach to computer software, copy themselves, and spread from one computer to another through shared disks. Some viruses are essentially harmless, perhaps delivering a message to the computer screen at a specified time. But other viruses, including Michelangelo, damage computer data.

Despite its reputation as one of the most widely distributed viruses in the world, Michelangelo wreaked little actual havoc. By the time March 6 arrived, extensive media coverage had alerted people to the risk the virus posed. Software that detected computer viruses and protected against their spread enjoyed brisk sales. In the end, only a few hundred computers worldwide felt Michelangelo's destructive effects. Even so, the existence of the virus reminded computer users of the vulnerability of computer data and the potential for acts of "computer terrorism."

Going for the GUI. Sales of software for personal computers continued to climb in 1991 and 1992, spearheaded by the growing popularity of graphical user interfaces (GUI's). GUI's typically make use of symbols called *icons* and of menus written in straightforward language. Rather than typing commands, GUI users activate programs and functions by moving a pointing device—usually a mouse—to the appropriate icon or word on the screen and then clicking a button on the mouse.

Apple Computer, Incorporated, of Cupertino, Calif., has always employed a GUI in its popular Macintosh line of personal computers. The new GUI's are intended for use in computers manufactured by International Business Machines Corporation (IBM) of Armonk, N.Y., and in IBM-compatible machines.

The best-selling GUI is Microsoft Windows, produced by Microsoft Corporation of Redmond, Wash. In April 1992, Microsoft released Windows 3.1, an up-

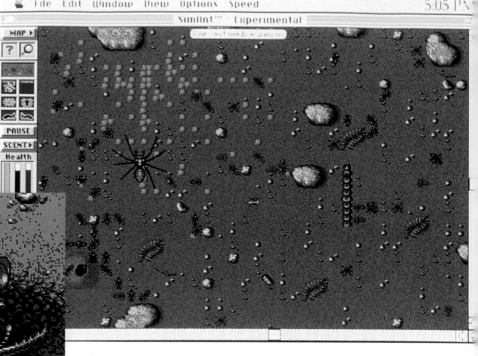

SimAnt™ - Experimental

MAP ▸

? 🔍

PAUSE

SCENT ▸

Health

"Edutainment"
Computer software intended to educate as well as entertain, dubbed "edutainment" by the industry, gained in sophistication during 1991 and 1992. Noteworthy new titles included SimAnt and Civilization.

SimAnt, produced by Maxis, offers an opportunity to run an ant colony, complete with queens, soldiers, and worker ants, *above,* and predators, *left*. Players can vary the number of ants of each type and make decisions about hoarding food or attacking another colony. While competing, players learn about ant behavior. Civilization, released by MicroProse Software, challenges players to take a band of hunter-gatherers and, through a series of decisions, move through various stages of civilization, *below*.

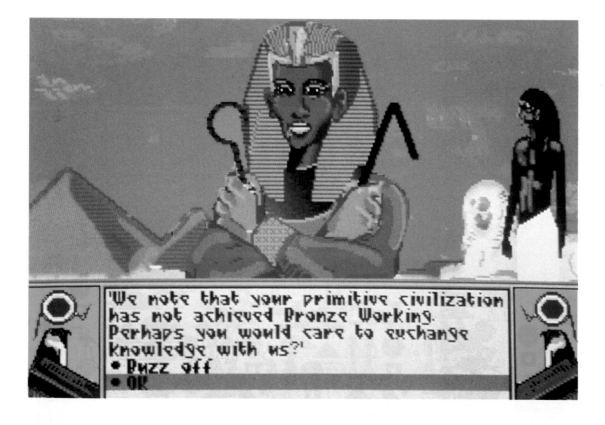

'We note that your primitive civilization has not achieved Bronze Working. Perhaps you would care to exchange knowledge with us?'
• Buzz off
• OK

dated, speedier version of its popular Windows 3.0. Priced at $150, Windows 3.1 can run multimedia software—software that combines text, graphics, sound, and full-motion video.

Windows also met its first strong competition in April, when IBM released the latest version of OS/2, a graphical operating system that sold for $195. An operating system is the master program that manages a computer's resources, controlling such operations as the transfer of data from disks to working memory. Windows is not a true operating system, unlike the Macintosh GUI, which is part of the Macintosh operating system. Instead, Windows requires an operating system, such as Microsoft's MS-DOS, to run.

IBM had developed OS/2 in cooperation with Microsoft. But the two parted ways in 1990, when Microsoft brought out Windows. IBM then went ahead with the development of OS/2 on its own. One strength of the new OS/2 is its ability to perform two or more operations simultaneously, an ability called *multitasking*. Users can, for example, work on word processing and spreadsheet programs at the same time. Additionally, OS/2 makes it simpler to move data from one application to another.

Disputed icons. A long-running lawsuit took an unexpected turn in April 1992, when a California judge dismissed charges brought by Apple Computer against Microsoft in 1988. Apple had charged that Microsoft had violated copyright laws by using movable icons and other aspects of the Macintosh graphical interface in Microsoft's Windows software.

The lawsuit raised the question of whether a manufacturer could "own" the appearance of software as well as its functions and capabilities. The dismissal of Apple's charges was expected to have a large impact on other so-called look-and-feel lawsuits.

Conversational computing. Automatic speech recognition (ASR) software, under development in early 1992, may provide what many software developers believe is the ultimate computer interface. The new software accepts spoken commands, translating them into forms recognized by the computer.

Late in 1991, Kurzweil Applied Intelligence, Incorporated, of Waltham, Mass., demonstrated an experimental ASR program designed for the Japanese language. Because Japanese has more than 7,000 separate characters, typing in Japanese on a computer can be time-consuming. Software that recognizes speech thus sharply reduces the amount of time required to generate reports and send messages.

When speech-recognition software becomes available, many applications should follow, including voice annotation of written reports. A teacher receiving a student's report on a computer disk, for example, might record spoken comments on the disk for the student to review later. In anticipation of ASR software, a number of computers, including some Macintoshes, now come equipped with microphones and built-in recording devices.

Apple-IBM alliance. IBM and Apple, two of the computer industry's largest companies and fiercest competitors, joined forces in 1992. In January, they announced an agreement to work together on the next generation of operating-system software.

The rivals expected their collaboration to result in computers better able to share software, communicate with one another, and link up in networks. Industry analysts also saw the alliance as an attempt by Apple and IBM to hold onto their leadership in the industry, a position increasingly threatened by low-priced computers from other manufacturers. By joining forces on software, the companies hoped to reap sales benefits on their hardware.

Multimedia software became more salable in late 1991 and early 1992, thanks to a dive in the prices of the powerful computers needed to run the software. (See COMPUTER HARDWARE.)

Notable new multimedia software included MediaMaker, released by Macro-Mind Paracomp Incorporated of San Francisco in September 1991. The program, priced at $695, enables Macintosh users to assemble their own multimedia presentations, using material from compact discs, laser discs, videotapes, and other formats. Apple introduced another multimedia product, QuickTime, in May 1992. QuickTime, like MediaMaker, allows users to coordinate sound and video on a Macintosh computer. It sold for $169.　　　　[Keith Ferrell]

Deaths of Scientists

Notable scientists and engineers who died between June 1, 1991, and June 1, 1992, are listed below. Those listed were Americans unless otherwise indicated in the biographical sketch.

Anderson, Thomas F. (1911-Aug. 11, 1991), biophysical chemist and geneticist who pioneered the use of the electron microscope to study viruses. An electron microscope uses a beam of electrons, rather than visible light, to magnify objects. Anderson's studies with such microscopes helped show how viruses affect cells.

Asimov, Isaac (1920-April 7, 1992), Russian-born biochemist and author who helped popularize science and technology in many of the nearly 500 books he wrote; former contributor and contributing editor to *Science Year*.

Avigad, Nahman (1905-Jan. 28, 1992), Ukrainian-born Israeli archaeologist known for his excavations in the walled Old City of Jerusalem and his discovery there of the Upper City.

Barrett, Alan H. (1927-July 3, 1991), radio astronomer who detected the first molecule to be discovered in *interstellar space* (the space between the stars) at radio wavelengths.

Birch, Francis (Albert Francis Birch) (1903-Jan. 31, 1992), geophysicist known for his studies of how materials respond to the extremely high pressures found in Earth's interior. Birch also worked on the atomic bomb project during World War II (1939-1945).

Dodington, Sven H. M. (1912-Jan. 13, 1992), Canadian-born engineer who invented the navigation system used globally in which radio beacons guide airplanes to airports.

Elsasser, Walter M. (1904-Oct. 14, 1991), German-born geophysicist credited with being among the first to recognize that motions within Earth's iron core could be responsible for the magnetic field that surrounds the planet.

Feinberg, Gerald (1933-April 21, 1992), physicist who predicted the existence of two kinds of *neutrinos* (subatomic particles).

Goertz, Christoph K. (1944-Nov. 1, 1991), German-born astrophysicist known for his theoretical investigations into Saturn's rings, Jupiter's magnetic field, and the sun's hot ionized gases.

Good, Ralph E. (1937-Dec. 10, 1991), biologist whose studies of the ecology of the New Jersey Pine Barrens helped lead to the preservation of 445,000 hectares (1.1 million acres) of tidal marshes and wetlands known as the Pineland National Reserve.

Gürsey, Feza (1921-April 13, 1992), Turkish-born American physicist who specialized in the study of fundamental particles and made important theoretical contributions to the ideas of symmetry and supersymmetry.

Hamburger, Jean (1909-Feb. 1, 1992), French physician who was considered one of the founders of *nephrology* (the branch of medicine dealing with the kidney) and a pioneer in the field of kidney transplants. In 1962, Hamburger directed a team of physicians and surgeons who performed the first successful kidney transplant between individuals who were not twins.

Hopper, Grace M. (1906-Jan. 1, 1992), mathematician who pioneered in the development of computer programming. Hopper was instrumental in helping create COBOL, the first computer language widely used by business; and in programming the first large-scale computer, the Mark I, and the first commercial computer, the UNIVAC I. Hopper was a retired rear admiral in the United States Navy.

Kalman, Sumner M. (1918-Jan. 11, 1992), pharmacologist noted for his role in campaigning against the use of the pesticide DDT.

Kaplan, Joseph (1902-Oct. 3, 1991), physicist known for his studies of atmospheric phenomena, such as *auroras* (displays of light in far northern and southern regions) and *airglows* (faint illuminations in the night sky).

Lawrence, John H. (1904-Sept. 7, 1991), physician who helped develop the field of nuclear medicine and who founded the Donner Laboratory, the first research laboratory devoted to nuclear medicine. Lawrence pioneered the use of radioactive *isotopes* (different nuclear forms of the same element) and high-energy particle beams to treat cancer and other diseases.

MacVicar, Margaret L. A. (1943-Sept. 30, 1991), Canadian-born metallurgical engineer and educator who helped shape science education policies in public schools. She was dean of undergraduate education at the Massachusetts Institute of Technology in Cambridge and a

Isaac Asimov

Grace M. Hopper

Margaret L. A. MacVicar

former member of the editorial advisory board of *Science Year*.

Mark, Herman F. (1895-April 6, 1992), Austrian-born chemist who became one of the world's leading authorities on *polymers,* large molecules made of smaller molecules linked in a chain. Mark's research into the chemical structure of rubber, a natural polymer, led to the development of the first synthetic rubber products.

Martin, John L. (1953-Jan. 17, 1992), psychologist and AIDS researcher who began one of the first major surveys on the sexual behavior of homosexual men.

McMillan, Edwin Mattison (1907-Sept. 7, 1991), physicist and pioneer in modern chemistry who shared the Nobel Prize in chemistry in 1951 for his codiscovery of the elements plutonium and neptunium. During World War II, McMillan worked on the development of radar, sonar, and the atomic bomb. Following the war, McMillan developed a device called the synchrotron that greatly expanded the capacities of particle accelerators. From 1958 to 1973, he headed the Lawrence Berkeley Laboratory in Berkeley, Calif.

Nicholson, Dwight R. (1947-Nov. 1, 1991), astrophysicist who headed the physics and astronomy department at the University of Iowa in Iowa City. Nicholson was a specialist in *plasma physics,* the study of hot, electrically charged gases.

Paine, Thomas O. (1921-May 4, 1992), engineer who headed the National Aeronautics and Space Administration during the first manned missions to the moon.

Parr, Albert E. (1901-July 17, 1991), marine biologist and oceanographer and director of the American Museum of Natural History in New York City from 1942 to 1959.

Perlman, Isador (1915-Aug. 3, 1991), chemist who discovered several *artificial isotopes* (isotopes produced in particle accelerators). He also pioneered in the use of subatomic particles called neutrons to date ancient pottery.

Racker, Efraim (1913-Sept. 9, 1991), Polish-born biochemist whose research on energy storage in living cells had implications for cancer research.

Revelle, Roger R. D. (1909-July 15, 1991), oceanographer and geologist who in the 1950's was among the first to predict that the build-up of carbon dioxide in the atmosphere due to the burning of fossil fuels might lead to global warming. While head of the Scripps Institution of Oceanography at La Jolla, Calif., from 1951 to 1964, Revelle and his colleagues discovered that unusually hot material flowed below the ocean floor, a finding that helped develop the theory of plate tectonics, which explains why Earth's surface continually changes. Revelle was a former member of *Science Year*'s editorial advisory board.

Salk, Lee (1926-May 2, 1992), child psychologist who was the author of several popular books on raising children.

Schreiber, Edward (1930-Nov. 11, 1991), geologist who was an expert on the geology of the moon.

Shemin, David (1911-Nov. 26, 1991), biochemist whose research shed light on how *hemoglobin* (a pigment in the blood) carries oxygen from the lungs to all parts of the body.

Smith, Harlan J. (1924-Oct. 17, 1991), astrophysicist who was known as an expert on *quasars* (extremely energetic objects that may be at the centers of extremely distant galaxies).

Stoller, Robert J. (1925-Sept. 6, 1991), psychoanalyst who was regarded as a leading theorist on problems of human sexuality.

Stommel, Henry M. (1920-Jan. 17, 1992), oceanographer and a leading theoretician on ocean circulation. In 1958, Stommel and a colleague proposed that cold dense water in northern polar regions sinks to the ocean floor and flows southward, setting up a global circulation pattern that causes water near Antarctica to flow northward.

Williams, Carroll M. (1916-Oct. 11, 1991), biologist who discovered how hormones control the development of insects from eggs through various larval stages and who also pioneered the study of how insects communicate with each other through chemical signals.

Wilson, Allan C. (1934-July 21, 1991), New Zealand-born biochemist who was among the first to apply findings from molecular genetics to the study of human evolution.

Zumberge, James H. (1923-April 15, 1992), geologist and famous explorer of Antarctica; president of the University of Southern California in Los Angeles from 1980 to 1991. [Rod Such]

Edwin M. McMillan

Roger R. D. Revelle

Henry M. Stommel

A simple and rapid technique for measuring sulfides related to *halitosis* (bad breath) could be incorporated in the dental office, according to an August 1991 report by researchers at Tel Aviv University in Israel and at Israel's Ministry of Health. The technique could help dentists diagnose and treat halitosis, which affects most adults, and it could also provide evidence of change in a patient with *periodontal disease* (gum disease), another cause of bad breath.

In most cases, halitosis is due to decay of food debris normally found in the mouth. The decay process gives rise to hydrogen sulfide and methyl mercaptan, the primary gases responsible for the bad odor. There have been no satisfactory methods for measuring halitosis in the dental office. Previous methods for studying halitosis have relied primarily on subjective scoring by human judges or on the use of *gas chromatography,* an analytical technique requiring special equipment. However, subjective judging cannot scientifically measure odor-causing gases, and gas chromatography can be time-consuming and expensive. It only identifies substances in the breath sample without determining the amount of each substance.

The Israeli researchers used a portable industrial hydrogen sulfide monitor to analyze breath. This device is ordinarily used to measure levels of hydrogen sulfides in the environment. The researchers investigated the breath of 75 volunteers, ranging in age from 11 to 77 years, and compared the monitor's measurements of the amount of hydrogen sulfide in the volunteers' breath with breath-odor ratings given the volunteers by a panel of judges. Although there were large variations in ratings by individual judges, their average ratings were significantly similar to the measurements of the sulfide monitor. The case of halitosis rated worst by the judges registered the highest amounts of hydrogen sulfides on the monitor.

Chewing reduces decay. Frequent gum-chewing causes salivary glands to increase the production of saliva, which may prove beneficial because saliva may limit decay caused by *plaque,* a sticky, acidic film containing bacteria. These results were reported in December 1991 by researchers at the University of Texas Health Science Center in San Antonio.

An adequate flow rate of saliva is important for the maintenance of oral health because saliva decreases the acidity of plaque coating the teeth after eating foods containing sugar. In plaque, bacteria break down trapped food particles, forming acids that can dissolve tooth enamel and cause tooth decay. Researchers have previously shown that chewing influences the rate that saliva flows from the *parotid gland,* which produces saliva. For example, the flow rate decreases in individuals placed on a liquid diet for one week.

The University of Texas researchers instructed 11 healthy young adults to chew sugarless gum for 10 minutes of each waking hour for two weeks. At the beginning and end of the study, the participants rinsed their mouths with a solution of water and 10 per cent *sucrose* (table sugar). Researchers then measured saliva flow and plaque acidity.

The results of the study indicated that frequent gum-chewing increased saliva flow and reduced acid levels in plaque. Whether similar results would be obtained with less frequent gum-chewing or whether individuals who habitually chew gum have increased salivary flow rates needs to be explored.

New therapy for gum disease. Thin fibers that slowly released the antibiotic tetracycline for 10 days helped reduce infection when placed under the gums of people who had periodontal disease. This was the finding of researchers at five dental institutions in the United States who compared the effects of three techniques: placing fibers containing tetracycline under the gums, placing fibers without tetracycline under the gums, and the thorough *scaling* (scraping) of teeth below the gums to remove the bacterial plaque that causes periodontal disease. A total of 113 volunteers participated in the trials, which were reported by researchers from the Forsyth Dental Center in Boston and the Micro Probe Corporation in Bothel, Wash., in September 1991.

Tetracycline fiber therapy and scaling significantly reduced the number of infected sites. In contrast to thorough scaling alone, tetracycline fibers also reduced the depth of *pockets* (areas of the gum separated from the teeth) resulting from gum disease.   [Paul Goldhaber]

In WORLD BOOK, see DENTISTRY.

The United States Food and Drug Administration (FDA) attempted to speed up its process of reviewing new drugs in 1991. The agency approved 30 new prescription drugs during the year. In the past, about 20 drugs were approved each year. Among the new drugs the FDA approved was flumazenil, the first antidote for life-threatening overdoses of sedatives called *benzodiazepines,* which include Ativan, Halcion, and Valium.

The changes in the approval process were sparked by public concerns about the high cost of newly developed drugs. The costs are partly linked to the long time it takes a pharmaceutical company to research and develop a drug and then to obtain FDA approval for its use. According to current estimates, developing a new drug and seeking FDA approval takes an average of 12 years and costs more than $200 million.

President George Bush's Council on Competitiveness, chaired by Vice President Dan Quayle, reviewed the drug development process in 1991 and recommended ways to streamline it. Among the council's suggestions was that the

FDA use outside experts not employed by government or the pharmaceutical industry to review applications for drug approval and make appropriate recommendations. The council also suggested that the FDA rely more heavily on research conducted as part of trials in nations outside the United States and ultimately develop a multinational process for the approval of drugs. On Nov. 14, 1991, the FDA announced plans to implement the council's recommendations, saying it would use outside experts only for well-established categories of drugs, such as painkillers, in which a backlog of applications is most likely to occur.

New AIDS drug approved. After a near-record review time of only six months, the FDA on Oct. 9, 1991, approved dideoxyinosine (DDI) to treat AIDS. The rapid review was spurred in part by pressure from AIDS activists and physicians who care for AIDS patients. DDI slows the progression of AIDS and was approved for patients who cannot tolerate AZT (zidovudine, the only other drug approved for the treatment of

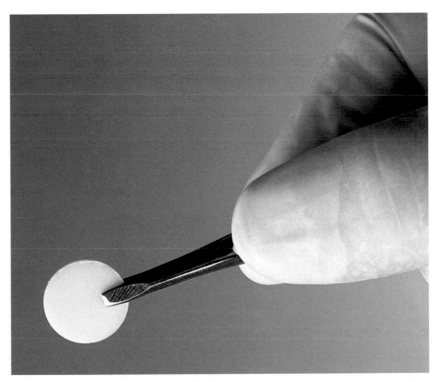

A plastic wafer filled with a cancer-killing drug is no bigger than a thumbnail. The wafer was designed to be implanted on the human brain to treat brain cancer after tumor surgery. Up to eight of the small wafers can be placed beneath the skull, where they slowly dissolve, releasing the drug over a period of four weeks. Trials were underway in 1992 to discover whether the wafers can prevent brain tumors from recurring.

A Cancer Drug that Grows on Trees

Medical researchers and environmentalists have come face-to-face with what may be one of the most difficult questions regarding human use of natural resources versus conservation. Thousands of rare Pacific yew trees in forests in the Western United States will fall in 1992 to give some cancer patients a longer lease on life. In a unique agreement with the U.S. Forest Service, Bristol-Myers Squibb Company, a New York City pharmaceutical manufacturer, will oversee an annual harvest of these slow-growing evergreen trees from government lands. The company will use the bark to make the drug taxol to treat hundreds of cancer patients in 15 clinical trials conducted by the National Cancer Institute (NCI).

Taxol is the latest in a long line of drugs to emerge from the plant kingdom. For example, digitalis, used to treat heart failure, is purified from foxglove, and quinine, used to treat malaria, comes from the cinchona tree. Inspired by these examples, the NCI in 1958 launched a program to test thousands of plants for compounds that had anticancer properties. In 1963, chemists began testing a crude taxol concentrate from yew tree bark. Taxol did not directly kill cancer cells growing in laboratory culture. Instead, the drug prevented cancer cells from dividing. Because the cancer cells stopped multiplying, cultures treated with taxol would stop growing and soon die off. This was a key effect, because cancer is the uncontrolled growth of cells.

Researchers later found that taxol arrests cell division by attaching to *microtubules,* microscopic passageways within the cells. Microtubules regulate the formation of *spindles,* structures that organize the cell's contents in preparation for division. By interfering with microtubule function, taxol prevents spindle formation and makes it impossible for a cell to divide.

In the early 1980's, trials began on human volunteers. In one trial, taxol treatment eliminated tumors in 12 of 40 women with advanced ovarian cancer, and rendered 3 of 25 women with advanced breast cancer free of the disease for at least a year. Furthermore, the drug had few side effects beyond reducing the number of white blood cells. In 1990, NCI researchers decided that the only way to get a better idea of the drug's effectiveness was to test it on a large number of cancer patients.

However, large-scale testing meant producing large amounts of the drug, which was a daunting prospect. Taxol purification is a 50-step process, and it takes 27.2 kilograms (60 pounds) of bark—the amount harvested from several 100-year-old trees—to yield enough taxol to provide several weeks of cancer treatment for a single patient. To get enough taxol for hundreds of cancer patients would mean that thousands of yews must be chopped down.

Wholesale harvesting of yews would have severe environmental consequences. There are about 29.5 million yew trees scattered among 6.7 million hectares (16.6 million acres) of old-growth forest, mainly in national forests in Washington and Oregon. Because the trees grow slowly, they could not be easily replaced. Ecologists were also concerned that the spotted owl, which shares the trees' habitat and already is designated an endangered species, would be in even greater jeopardy if the trees were harvested.

In 1990, the NCI asked pharmaceutical companies to propose plans for producing taxol without harming the forests. In January 1991, NCI signed an agreement with Bristol-Myers Squibb,

The Pacific yew, a relatively rare and slow-growing evergreen found in Western U.S. forests, contains taxol in its bark. The natural compound is a promising anticancer drug.

who agreed to supply the drug in return for exclusive rights to data resulting from taxol's use in clinical trials. The drug company would then submit the data to the U.S. Food and Drug Administration to support its application for approval to market taxol commercially.

Bristol-Myers Squibb contracted with Hauser Northwest, a Boulder, Colo., company, to harvest enough trees to supply the 340,000 kilograms (750,000 pounds) of bark required for the first year's research. Hauser followed U.S. government guidelines, cutting trees selectively and leaving stumps behind to sprout. Bristol-Myers Squibb also signed an agreement with Weyerhaeuser Company, a commercial forester and paper manufacturing firm, to grow yew seedlings to replace the harvested trees. Weyerhaeuser planned to plant 5 million seedlings in 1992.

Even with a new generation of yews, the demand for the drug will far outstrip the supply of bark if taxol lives up to its promise. Therefore, Bristol-Myers Squibb is funding several groups who are searching for alternative sources of taxol. Two plant biotechnology companies have developed processes for extracting taxol from yew cells grown in culture. Researchers at the University of Mississippi in University have extracted taxol from needles pruned from an ornamental yew, a shrublike cousin of the Pacific yew. Still other research teams are trying to bypass the yew trees altogether by synthesizing the complex taxol molecules in the laboratory.

Instead of attempting the difficult task of synthesizing taxol, some researchers are looking for substitute molecules that have some of the characteristics of a taxol molecule. In April 1992, researchers at Stanford University in California reported that they had found the basis of such a molecule in pinene, a substance harvested from pine trees that is a primary ingredient in turpentine and other paint thinners.

Other researchers think that it may not be necessary to craft a twin of taxol to duplicate its cancer-stopping action. Teams at the University of Kansas in Lawrence and Virginia Polytechnic Institute and State University in Blacksburg are looking at compounds that are not identical to taxol but that disrupt the function of microtubules in cancer cells. In 1992, an estimated 100 groups of scientists worldwide were working on taxol-related research. Meanwhile in the United States, processing bark has yielded enough taxol to treat approximately 1,000 people enrolled in clinical trials, a fraction of the 50,000 to 100,000 cancer patients who might benefit from treatment. "For the short term, we will be living with inadequate supplies of this drug," said NCI director Samuel Broder, "but in the long term, the problem is going to be solved." [Beverly Merz]

Drugs Continued

AIDS) or who failed to respond to AZT treatment.

Tamoxifen and breast cancer. In an unusual effort, researchers from the Imperial Cancer Research Fund in London pooled the results of 133 treatment trials worldwide on more than 75,000 women with early-stage breast cancer. Their analysis of this data, published in January 1992, showed that, after surgery, treatment with either cancer-killing drugs or tamoxifen, a hormonelike drug, was very effective in preventing recurrence of the disease.

For women over age 50, a group that includes 75 per cent of all breast cancer patients, drug therapy after surgery improved their 10-year survival rate by 5 per cent over that of patients who had surgery alone. The 10-year survival rate for women who took tamoxifen for two years after surgery improved by 8 per cent over that of women treated only with surgery. And women who were given both the cancer-fighting drugs and tamoxifen after surgery had a 12 per cent greater survival rate compared with patients having only surgery.

Many U.S. doctors have been reluctant to use these treatments on women who have early-stage breast cancer, in which the cancer has not spread out of the breast. Doctors were concerned that cancer-killing drugs might not be effective, and even if the treatment worked, there was a possibility that the drugs might actually cause a new cancer to develop in the future.

Doctors are also beginning to study the use of tamoxifen to prevent the development of breast cancer in groups of women who are at very high risk to develop the disease. It will take many years to establish if this drug is effective in these women.

Heart drug reduces deaths. Patients with mild or moderately severe congestive heart failure felt better and lived longer by taking a drug called enalapril, according to the results of two federally sponsored research studies reported in August 1991. The drug had been used in patients with severe congestive heart failure, but the new studies are the first to indicate that enalapril helps patients in earlier stages of the disease.

Congestive heart failure is an illness in which the heart is unable to maintain the normal circulation of blood in the

Radio-controlled drug delivery

A high-tech system for delivering medications to specific areas in the gastrointestinal tract was tested in human beings in 1992. In developing the system, scientists at the State University of New York at Buffalo combined a special computer-generated map of the patient's intestinal tract, a radio transmitter in a drug-containing capsule, and a radio receiver in a special vest to track the capsule as it travels through the body. The system was designed to deliver drugs that otherwise would be broken down by digestive juices.

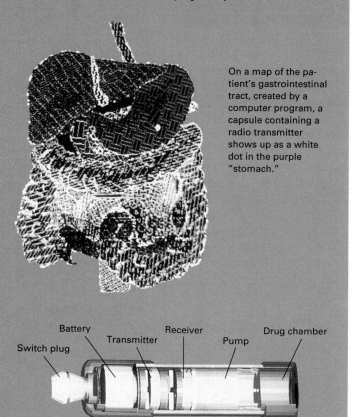

On a map of the patient's gastrointestinal tract, created by a computer program, a capsule containing a radio transmitter shows up as a white dot in the purple "stomach."

Switch plug | Battery | Transmitter | Receiver | Pump | Drug chamber

The capsule, slightly more than 2.5 centimeters (1 inch) long, carries a single dose of medication. A silicone rubber plug inserted into one end of the capsule before it is swallowed acts as a switch to activate the battery. The battery provides power to the electronic mechanisms, including a transmitter that emits radio signals as the capsule moves through the patient's intestinal tract. When the receiver gets the proper signal from the researchers, it activates a pump to eject the drug.

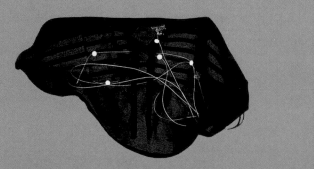

The vest worn by the patient contains a receiver and several antennae that detect radio signals from the capsule as it moves through the gastrointestinal tract so that the researchers can tell when the capsule reaches the area in the body where the drug is needed.

Drugs Continued

body. The lungs and liver become congested with blood, causing breathlessness and weakness. Without treatment, the condition is fatal. Doctors estimate that from 2 million to 3 million people in the United States suffer from congestive heart failure.

Enalapril is one of a group of drugs called *vasodilators*. Vasodilators cause blood vessels of the body to relax and *dilate* (enlarge). These dilated blood vessels offer less resistance to blood flow, and the decrease in resistance allows the heart to pump blood more easily.

The two studies included more than 3,000 patients with mild or moderately severe congestive heart failure—most of them from 50 to 70 years old—from hospitals in the United States, Canada, and Belgium. The larger study, involving more than 2,500 patients, found that those taking enalapril were 16 per cent less likely to die during the study period than patients taking *placebos* (pills containing no active ingredients). Also, patients taking enalapril were 26 per cent less likely to be hospitalized for heart failure during the study period than those in the placebo group.

Reducing calcium loss. Vitamin D supplements appear to help prevent the loss of calcium in women past the age of menopause better than calcium tablets, concluded a New Zealand study published in February 1992. Menopause is the time in a woman's life when menstruation ceases. The loss of calcium in bone, called osteoporosis, occurs mainly in older women after menopause. The disease can lead to severe pain, bone fractures, and major disability.

The study involved 622 postmenopausal women age 50 to 79 who were given either *calcitriol* (a vitamin D supplement) or calcium tablets. During a three-year period, the patients who received calcitriol had one-third as many spinal fractures as the patients who received calcium tablets.

Tamoxifen also appears to prevent loss of calcium in bone, according to researchers at the University of Wisconsin in Madison. In December 1991, they reported that breast cancer patients receiving tamoxifen for two years had 3 per cent greater bone density in the spine than patients who did not receive the drug.   [B. Robert Meyer]

In WORLD BOOK, see DRUG.

Ecologists focused much energy in 1991 and 1992 on the topic of chaos. Chaos theory is based on the idea that random variations control the behavior of natural systems that change with time, such as the weather and ecosystems. The theory predicts, in essence, that science cannot predict the changes in some systems.

Scientists believe that chaotic systems, such as the weather, are those in which very small changes produce unexpectedly dramatic results. Small changes in temperature, air pressure, or wind speed or direction, for instance, may produce weather wildly different five days later than if that change had not occurred. Because of a shortage of precise data from long-term studies of ecological systems, however, it has been difficult to determine where and when chaos is occurring.

In October 1991, ecologists David Tilman and David Wedin of the University of Minnesota in Minneapolis reported the results of a five-year study showing that growth patterns of *Agrostis scabra*, a common prairie grass, exhibit many properties of chaotic systems. The scientists planted different groups of the plants in soils with varying degrees of nutrients.

The scientists found that plants in nutrient-rich soils grew more unpredictably than the plants in the poorer quality soils. Plants in the better soil grew better during the first two years of the experiment, but their growth became unpredictable in the third year and remained unpredictable for the rest of the experiment. These plants' populations dropped wildly compared with plants in poorer soils.

The researchers attributed this drop to the accumulation of *litter* (dead plant material) at the end of the previous growing season. As litter accumulated, the scientists discovered, it blocked light to the plants. Plant growth thus varied most in the most favorable conditions, suggesting that plants with the most luxurious growth may be susceptible to unpredictable changes.

Prairie dogs and ranchers. Human attempts to improve on nature or to control pests have created many ecological

An ecologist at Cornell University in Ithaca, N.Y., displays a newly discovered, hardier species of zebra mussel, left, along with the species already causing ecological havoc in the Great Lakes, right. Ecologists found about 50 of the hardier zebra mussels in Lake Ontario in October 1991 and reported that the newcomers could cause damage to a wide geographic region. Since the mid-1980's, zebra mussels in the United States have been multiplying rapidly in lakes and rivers, depriving other marine organisms of food and damaging industrial plants and boats.

problems. In August 1991, biologist Jake Weltzin reported the results of a study he performed while at Texas A&M University in College Station, Tex., showing the outcome of one such attempt. Weltzin reported that ranchers in Western grasslands have been trying to eliminate *prairie dogs* (large, squirrellike rodents) because they compete with cattle for food. The ranchers' program has resulted in the widespread extermination of prairie dogs. Now, however, ranchers have a new problem with mesquite. This prairie shrub decreases the amount of grass available to the cattle and makes roundups difficult.

According to Weltzin, prairie dogs may actually help ranchers by controlling mesquite. Prairie dogs feed on mesquite, and Weltzin concluded that the successful removal of prairie dogs has probably removed the major control on mesquite, allowing its growth to increase and causing problems for the ranchers.

Can iron slow global warming? In July 1991, scientists from the American Society of Limnology and Oceanography (ASLO) rejected another idea that would involve tampering with ecosystems without adequate knowledge of the consequences. This idea, first proposed in May 1990 by John Martin, an oceanographer at the Moss Landing Marine Laboratory in Salinas, Calif., would involve dumping large quantities of powdered iron into Earth's southern oceans in an attempt to reduce a possible global warming.

Although some warming of Earth's atmosphere is natural, scientists fear that humanity has begun to warm the atmosphere beyond normal levels by releasing excess heat-trapping gases into the atmosphere. These gases, called *greenhouse gases,* act like the windows of a greenhouse to let sunlight in and trap some of the heat radiating from Earth's surface. Burning *fossil fuels* (coal, oil, and natural gas) produces carbon dioxide, a major greenhouse gas. The build-up of carbon dioxide, scientists warn, could warm Earth enough to disrupt global agriculture and melt polar icecaps, flooding low-lying coastal areas.

According to Martin, the increased growth of tiny plantlike organisms

A hungry bug
An agricultural biologist, *right,* holds a melon damaged by the poinsettia sweet potato whitefly in southern California in November 1991. The bug destroyed millions of dollars of crops in southern California, western Arizona, and northern Mexico in autumn 1991. The sweet potato whitefly, *above,* feeds on many fruits and vegetables and has no natural predators in the devastated areas.

called *phytoplankton* in Earth's southern oceans could reduce carbon dioxide levels in the atmosphere. Because plants convert carbon dioxide, sunlight, and water to sugar and oxygen during photosynthesis, more phytoplankton may thus absorb the excess carbon dioxide.

Because iron is a plant nutrient, Martin has proposed dumping it into the southern oceans to determine whether it increases phytoplankton growth. Much of Earth's southern oceans have low concentrations of phytoplankton compared with other oceans, according to Martin. Although traces of iron occur naturally in seawater, low phytoplankton concentrations correspond to low iron levels in southern waters, leading Martin to the conclusion that adding iron may boost phytoplankton growth.

Despite some initial support for this idea, ASLO scientists doubt its potential effectiveness in reducing global warming and fear the effects of iron dumping upon the ocean's ecology. Mathematical climate models disagree as to how much carbon dioxide iron dumping would lead phytoplankton to absorb. But most oceanographers agree that even a successful large-scale iron fertilization would remove only about 5 per cent of atmospheric carbon dioxide at best, not enough to affect global warming.

Scientists also fear how iron fertilization would affect the ocean's ecology. There are different types of phytoplankton, and scientists are unsure whether all of them would benefit from extra iron. Changes in phytoplankton populations may also affect animals that feed on phytoplankton, such as whales, penguins, and squid.

Scientists are still interested in adding iron to ocean waters, but on a smaller scale. Martin plans to continue testing how iron concentrations affect phytoplankton populations near the equator in the Pacific Ocean in late 1993. This may solve one of the mysteries of our oceans—why some areas with adequate nutrients such as nitrogen and phosphorus produce relatively small amounts of phytoplankton.   [Robert H. Tamarin]

In the Science Studies section, see GLOBAL CHANGE. In WORLD BOOK, see ECOLOGY.

Electronics

A new generation of consumer electronics technology began to emerge between June 1991 and June 1992. Many long-anticipated products finally came on the market, and research and development moved ahead in several areas.

CD products. The electronics giant N. V. Philips of the Netherlands introduced its compact disc-interactive (CD-I) players on Oct. 16, 1991, in New York City. CD-I plays compact discs (CD's) that store digital sound, text, graphics, and video. The machine, which also plays standard audio CD's, had a list price of about $1,000. The launch of CD-I had been awaited—and repeatedly postponed—since 1986.

About 50 CD's came out at the same time as the players, and Philips expected to bring out another 50 discs by December 1992. The discs offer games, museum tours, and sports information.

Sony Corporation of Japan introduced the Data Discman in November 1991. This handheld CD player displays the text of various dictionaries, guidebooks, encyclopedias, and other reference works stored on CD's. The Discman listed for about $550, and the discs sold for about $40 each.

The Eastman Kodak Company of Rochester, N.Y., planned to begin selling its Photo-CD player during summer 1992. The machine displays on a television screen photographic images stored on a CD. The company planned to sell the players for about $400 and to charge about $20 to store 24 slides or 35-millimeter negatives on a disc. Photo-CD players play audio discs as well.

TV service. A new subscription television service was launched in April, when Skypix took to the airwaves. Skypix broadcasts directly into viewers' homes by satellite, offering subscribers the opportunity to choose from 80 channels carrying motion pictures. The service offers most of the movies on a pay-per-view basis, meaning that subscribers pay only for movies they watch. To receive the broadcasts, subscribers also must purchase an $850 satellite dish. If successful, Skypix could pose a challenge to cable television and video rental stores.

VideoPhone. A long-time staple of science fiction, the VideoPhone, was intro-

New products to view

A telephone that lets you see the person on the other end of the line and an electronic device that displays text were among the new consumer electronics products manufacturers introduced in late 1991 and early 1992.

The VideoPhone, introduced by American Telephone & Telegraph Company, has a color screen measuring 8.4 centimeters (3.3 inches) across. It sells for about $1,500.

The Data Discman from Sony Corporation displays the text of books stored on compact discs. It sells for about $550. Discs carrying reference material are priced at about $40.

Electronics Continued

duced in a consumer version by American Telephone & Telegraph (AT&T) of Parsippany, N.J., in January. The phone enables people to see one another on an 8.4-centimeter (3.3-inch) screen as they speak, though the video's fuzzy images and slow motion resemble old-time movies in quality. VideoPhones cost about $1,500 and can be used only with other VideoPhones manufactured by AT&T. They plug into standard telephone outlets.

Digital recording. Progress continued on two systems that will give consumers the ability to record sound digitally: the digital compact cassette (DCC) from Philips and the Mini Disc from Sony. DCC is an audiotape that provides the same sound quality as a compact disc. DCC players, which will play standard audiotapes as well, were scheduled to appear in September 1992 and to cost about $600. Mini Discs, recordable CD's measuring 6.4 centimeters (2.5 inches) in diameter, and players were expected to appear soon afterward.

Interactive TV. As early as 1993, Americans could begin using their tele-

vision sets to perform such tasks as shopping, banking, and paying bills without the use of a computer or telephone. The go-ahead for interactive television came on Jan. 16, 1992, when the United States Federal Communications Commission (FCC), which regulates radio and TV broadcasting, allocated part of the radio band for interactive video and data services. Radio waves will link the TV sets via satellite to the services.

Soon after the FCC decision, TV Answer, a leader in wireless interactive technology, announced that Hewlett-Packard Company of Palo Alto, Calif., had agreed to manufacture its home units. These will consist of a remote control unit and a control box to be placed on top of the TV set. Viewers will use the controls to transmit information to the satellite, enabling them to order merchandise or transfer funds from their bank to pay bills. Hewlett-Packard said it planned to build more than 1.5 million units in 1993 and to sell them for about $700.   [Elliot King]

In WORLD BOOK, see COMPACT DISC; ELECTRONICS; TAPE RECORDER.

The first controlled fusion experiment to combine tritium with deuterium—both *hydrogen isotopes* (forms of hydrogen that have different numbers of neutrons)—took place on Nov. 9, 1991, in the Joint European Torus (JET) experimental fusion reactor near Oxford, England. The experiment produced a two-second burst of 1.7 megawatts (1.7 million watts).

Nuclear fusion is the process that fuels the sun and other stars. Fusion occurs when the *nuclei* (cores) of elements *fuse* (combine) under extremely high temperatures and pressures.

When a deuterium nucleus and a tritium nucleus combine, the reaction produces helium, energy, and a neutron. By contrast, nuclear fission reactors produce energy by breaking apart the atoms of heavy elements such as uranium and plutonium.

If fusion proves practical, it would be more desirable than fission because deuterium, fusion's main fuel, is commonly found in seawater. Fission fuels, on the other hand, are difficult to obtain. Fusion also produces far less radioactive waste than fission does, and fusion is considered safer because an uncontrolled chain reaction cannot occur.

The 10.7-meter- (35-foot-) tall JET reactor weighs almost 3,600 metric tons (4,000 short tons). It is a doughnut-shaped vacuum vessel lined with graphite and surrounded by strong electromagnets. The electromagnets accelerate the deuterium and tritium to high speeds. This heats the elements so that the electrons, which orbit the nuclei of atoms, separate from the nuclei. This creates a *plasma*—a gas made of free electrons and nuclei. The magnetic fields also help confine the extremely hot plasma to the center of the reactor, where the nuclei are more likely to collide and fuse.

In the experiment, the JET reactor heated a mixture of 11 per cent tritium and 89 per cent deuterium gas to about 200,000,000 °C (360,000,000 °F)—nearly 15 times hotter than the center of the sun. Although the experiment was a major breakthrough because it was the first to use tritium as well as deuterium, it did not achieve the crucial break-even point where the fusion power produced equals the power used to heat the plasma. The JET reactor produced only 10 per cent of the power required to heat the plasma. (See also PHYSICS.)

Fuel cell start-up. In June 1991, the Pacific Gas and Electric Company's (PG&E) Technology Center in San Ramon, Calif., began testing a new, 100-kilowatt, molten carbonate fuel-cell power plant. The plant is the first in the world to generate electricity using a molten carbonate fuel cell and deliver it for use to an electric utility.

Unlike conventional electrical power plants, which burn *fossil fuels* (coal, oil, and natural gas), fuel cells use electrochemical reactions to release the energy in natural gas and convert it to electricity. Fuel cells work in a manner similar to a car battery.

Hundreds of power cells make up a fuel-cell power plant. The cells include positive and negative electrodes and an *electrolyte* (a conductive material) between the two electrodes. An electric current is created when chemical reactions release electrons at one electrode and absorb them at the other. Fuel cells can use different types of electrolytes. PG&E's San Ramon plant uses an electrolyte of molten carbonate, a form of carbonic acid.

Pumps inject natural gas and steam through one electrode (the anode), where chemical reactions re-form the gases into hydrogen and carbon dioxide. Oxygen and carbon dioxide are fed to the other electrode (the cathode) and, together with available electrons, react to form carbonate *ions* (charged atoms). The ions travel through the molten carbonate electrolyte to the anode, where they react with hydrogen, liberating electrons and forming carbon dioxide and water. The freed electrons then flow to the cathode, completing an electrical circuit.

The environmental benefits from fuel-cell power plants would be substantial. Conventional power generation produces pollutants, including nitrogen oxides and sulfur dioxide, which cause acid rain. Acid rain kills marine life and destroys forests. According to the Gas Research Institute in Chicago, fuel-cell power plants emit no sulfur dioxide and as much as 250 times less nitrogen oxide than conventional power plants. Fuel-cell power plants are expensive, however—as much as five times the cost of current power stations. But energy researchers expect fuel-cell prices to fall as the technology develops.

Cleaner diesel fuel. A plant designed to convert naturally occurring gases in landfills into diesel fuel that contains reduced amounts of sulfur began operation in January 1992. The United States Clean Air Act, passed in November 1990, requires that, starting in October 1993, diesel engines give off less sulfur, a major air pollutant.

The Synhytech (*Syn*thetic *Hy*drocarbon *Tech*nology) plant is in a landfill in Pueblo, Colo. Plant operators drilled wells into the core of the landfill to collect methane-containing gas, one of the products of garbage decomposition. The gas contains 52 per cent methane plus carbon dioxide, nitrogen, and water vapor.

The Pueblo plant is designed to convert the methane gas into high-grade naphtha and wax. Naphthas are used to manufacture many items, including paint, adhesives, perfumes, and glues. Wax is also used in many products—from adhesives to lipsticks.

Operators pump the methane gas through a bed of zinc oxide, which chemically removes the sulfur. The sulfur-free gas is combined with oxygen and fed into a device called a steam reformer, which converts it to carbon dioxide and *synthesis gas*, a mixture of hydrogen and carbon monoxide. In a special reactor, the hydrogen and carbon monoxide combine. The resulting gas is condensed and distilled into waxes, diesel fuel, and naphtha.

Hydrogen burns more completely than carbon. Because sulfur-free synthetic diesel fuel contains more hydrogen and less carbon than conventional diesel fuels, it burns more cleanly. The synthetic fuel produces fewer particulates, a result of incomplete carbon combustion that can form smog. Also, the reduced carbon results in fewer hydrocarbons being produced during combustion. Hydrocarbons are a family of compounds often found in fossil fuels that contain hydrogen and carbon. They can be released during combustion and cause serious health problems in people if inhaled for extended periods.

"Natural" solar cell
An inexpensive but efficient solar cell—whose design is related to the principle by which green plants capture energy from sunlight—powers a small fan, *below left*. The new cell, reported by Swiss and American researchers in October 1991, uses a special dye coating to trap solar energy. The energy causes dye molecules to transfer electrons to a transparent semiconductor, *below right*. The semiconductor in turn transfers the charge to a layer of conducting material, creating a useful electric current.

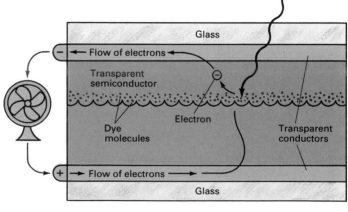

Sunlight

Glass

← Flow of electrons ←

Transparent semiconductor

Electron

Dye molecules

Transparent conductors

→ Flow of electrons →

Glass

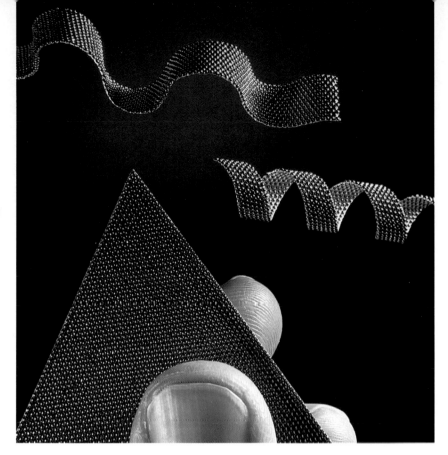

A new type of solar cell made of impure silicon beads imbedded in aluminum can be manufactured at a cost that is about 35 times less than that of similar conventional solar cells. The Southern California Edison Company in Rosemead, Calif., and Texas Instruments Incorporated in Dallas joined efforts to begin making the cells for test installations in December 1991.

Vehicle emission tests performed by the Environmental Test Center in Aurora, Colo., showed that the sulfur-free fuel reduced particulates by 35 per cent, reduced hydrocarbons by 53 per cent, and reduced carbon monoxide by 41 per cent compared with emissions from engines using commercially available diesel fuels.

A new light bulb. Researchers announced a new light bulb in June 1992 that uses radio waves to produce light. The new bulb—called the E-lamp—uses about 75 per cent less energy than an incandescent bulb giving off the same amount of light but lasts about 20 times longer, according to Intersource Technologies of Sunnyvale, Calif., the new lamp's manufacturer. However, the E-lamp costs $15—about 20 times more than a standard 100-watt incandescent bulb. The E-lamp is suitable for residential and commercial use and should be available in early 1993, according to Intersource Technologies.

A magnetic coil in the E-lamp transforms electricity into high-frequency radio waves. The radio waves excite a mixture of gases inside the lamp, which produce light outside the visible spectrum. This light causes chemicals called phosphors on the inside of the lamps to emit visible light.

GM debuts Ultralight. The General Motors Corporation unveiled its newest experimental car, Ultralight, at the 1992 North American International Auto Show in Detroit in January 1992. The 635-kilogram (1,400-pound) sedan achieved an efficiency of 161 kilometers per gallon (100 miles per gallon) in highway driving at 80 kilometers per hour (kph) (50 miles per hour [mph]). The Ultralight can accelerate from a standing start to 97 kph (60 mph) in less than eight seconds. A 1.5-liter, three-cylinder engine powers the Ultralight. The all-aluminum engine weighs 79 kilograms (174 pounds), 40 per cent less than a conventional engine producing equivalent power.

[Marian Visich, Jr.]

In the Special Reports section, see CLEARING THE AIR WITH CLEANER CARS. In WORLD BOOK, see ENERGY SUPPLY; SOLAR ENERGY.

Leaders from 178 nations met in Rio de Janeiro, Brazil, in June 1992 at the United Nations (UN) Conference on Environment and Development, also called the Earth Summit. The leaders addressed a wide variety of global environmental problems and signed several treaties, including measures designed to preserve the world's species and combat global climate change.

Persian Gulf War aftermath. The environmental effects of the Persian Gulf War in early 1991 continued well into 1992. On Oct. 25, 1991, the United States Environmental Protection Agency (EPA) reported that Iraqi troops ignited or damaged 732 oil wells in February 1991, resulting in 650 uncontrolled well fires. As of June 1991, those fires still emitted about 2 million metric tons (2.2 million short tons) of carbon dioxide into the atmosphere daily, or about 3 per cent of the total global emissions from all fossil fuel sources, according to the EPA. Fire fighters capped the last burning oil well in November 1991.

The environmental consequences of smoke from the burning oil well fires were not as severe as some scientists had predicted, however. Some scientists had predicted that the smoke would block sunlight and dramatically cool Earth's climate, possibly damaging agriculture. But most of the smoke hovered 400 to 460 meters (1,300 to 1,500 feet) aboveground—too low, say experts, to cause climate change.

The massive amount of smoke apparently did not cause the increase in respiratory problems that some health officials had expected. Because of the oily, dustlike particles in the smoke, the air in and around Kuwait City exceeded U.S. air quality standards for particulates. If inhaled, air containing too many particulates can cause respiratory problems. Through July 1991, however, there was no documented increase in the number of people who visited Kuwaiti hospital emergency rooms for acute upper and lower respiratory infections or asthma, compared with a similar period before the oil well fires, according to the EPA.

The EPA's October report estimated that oil spills resulting from the war

February 15, 1991　　　　October 29, 1991

Aftermath of the Persian Gulf War
A February 1991 image from the scientific satellite Landsat, *right,* shows smoke streaming from Kuwaiti oil wells set ablaze during the Persian Gulf War in early 1991. The smoke did not cause as much environmental damage as scientists had feared, in part because most of the fires were extinguished by October, *far right.*

caused heavy environmental damage, however. The EPA estimated that Iraq's late January 1991 sabotage of Kuwait's oil production facilities discharged between 6 million and 8 million barrels of oil into the Persian Gulf. The oil formed numerous lakes in the desert, some as long as 1.6 kilometers (1 mile) and as deep as 1 meter (3 feet). The oil damaged salt marshes, mangrove swamps, and intertidal creeks and streams. These ecosystems support fish, shellfish, and birds, including endangered species such as the cormorant and the flamingo.

Ozone depletion. Satellite measurements of ozone concentrations in the *stratosphere* (upper atmosphere) over Antarctica in October 1991 were the lowest on record, according to scientists from the United States National Aeronautics and Space Administration (NASA). This marked the third year in a row that concentrations of ozone—a molecule made up of three oxygen atoms—have fallen low enough that a severe "hole" has formed in the ozone layer over Antarctica.

Ozone in Earth's stratosphere protects people and other organisms by absorbing most of the damaging ultraviolet radiation from the sun. This radiation can cause skin cancer and *cataracts* (clouding of the lens of the eye), weaken the human immune system, disrupt plant growth, and kill marine organisms called *phytoplankton,* which form the base of the ocean's food chains.

Scientists say that chemicals called chlorofluorocarbons (CFC's) are destroying the ozone layer. CFC's are widely used as industrial cleaning agents and in refrigeration systems. Most industrialized countries have agreed to stop making CFC's by the end of 1999.

In October 1991, a UN panel of scientists reported that ozone problems are not limited to the Antarctic. The UN scientists reported evidence showing that, for the first time, ozone depletion was occurring over the United States and other middle latitude regions of the world during summer. Scientists had thought that ozone depletion took place only over Earth's poles and middle latitude areas during winter.

Workers drain an oil lake in the Kuwaiti desert in April 1992. Numerous lakes of oil were created when Iraqi troops destroyed Kuwaiti oil wells during the Persian Gulf War. The lakes—which were up to 1.6 kilometers (1 mile) wide and 1 meter (3 feet) deep—threatened wildlife in many areas of Kuwait.

If this pattern of ozone destruction continues, it could have serious health and environmental effects. The UN panel estimated, for instance, that a 10 per cent decrease in the ozone layer, which the scientists said is likely by the year 2000, will cause as many as 300,000 additional cases of skin cancer and an additional 1.6 million cases of cataracts each year worldwide.

Arctic ozone worries. Scientists detected record-high concentrations of chlorine monoxide, an ozone-destroying molecule that is derived from CFC's, over New England and Canada on Jan. 20, 1992. An international team of 40 scientists reported in February that chlorine monoxide concentrations were higher than ever seen before, even in the Antarctic ozone hole. The scientists estimated that, given the right conditions, the recorded chlorine monoxide levels were high enough to destroy ozone at a rate of 1 to 2 per cent per day in the presence of sunlight.

Scientists caution that high levels of chlorine monoxide do not necessarily mean that an ozone hole will develop over the Arctic, however. For an ozone hole to develop, a cold air mass called a *polar vortex*, which traps chlorine monoxide, must persist into March, when sunlight reaches the Arctic region again after its winter absence. Sunlight begins the chemical reactions with chlorine monoxide that destroy ozone molecules. But, normally, the polar vortex breaks up before March. In April, NASA scientists said that the polar vortex above the Arctic did not last long enough for an ozone hole to develop.

Scientists cannot predict with absolute certainty whether such conditions will occur, but some believe they are likely to happen by the year 2000. An Arctic ozone hole would expose Canada and parts of the United States, Europe, and Asia to dangerous levels of ultraviolet radiation. In response to worsening news on ozone depletion, U.S. President George Bush on Feb. 11, 1992, called on U.S. manufacturers to end production of virtually all chemicals that destroy the ozone layer by Dec. 31, 1995, slightly accelerating the international schedule for banning CFC's.

Global lead levels. Lead concentrations in air and land around the world appear to be falling, according to a September 1991 report by Claude F. Boutron of Grenoble University in Grenoble, France. His study of ice samples from a remote area in Greenland indicates that lead levels dropped more than 85 per cent between 1967 and 1989, reversing the dramatic rise during the 1950's and 1960's caused primarily by the increasing use of lead additives in gasoline. In the United States, the use of lead additives has declined 90 per cent since the late 1960's. Lead has been shown to impair nervous system function in human beings, and it may cause elevated blood pressure and heart disease in men.

Ozone and asthma. Degrees of ground-level ozone pollution currently acceptable under U.S. environmental guidelines may be responsible for a dramatic rise in *asthma*, a disease in which spasms and mucus build-up in the body's airways make breathing difficult, and, in severe cases, can cause death. That was the conclusion of a report by respirologist Noe Zamel of the University of Toronto in Canada in July 1991.

Ground-level ozone is present in most urban areas as a component of smog. It is produced in a complex series of chemical reactions involving sunlight and common pollutants called volatile organic compounds and nitrogen oxides. Both types of pollutants are released as a result of fuel combustion in automobiles, factories, power plants, and other sources.

Zamel and his colleagues examined asthma patients who inhaled air containing 0.12 parts per million of ozone, the maximum safety limit set by the EPA. One part per million is roughly equivalent to one grain of salt in a glass of water. When inhaling ozone-containing air, patients were twice as sensitive to ragweed or grass pollen, which can trigger asthma attacks in some individuals, as they were when they inhaled clean air.

In the United States, the rate of diagnosis for asthma has tripled since 1970. According to the EPA, at least 98 U.S. cities exceeded the agency's ozone safety limit in 1991.

Controlling urban smog. In October 1991, the governors of nine Eastern states and the mayor of Washington, D.C., agreed to adopt smog control measures similar to those previously enacted by the state of California. The measures will require cleaner emissions from gasoline-powered vehicles and the introduction of cars powered by alternative fuels such as methanol.

A December 1991 report by the U.S. National Research Council (NRC) noted that despite two decades of massive and costly efforts, many areas of the country have made little progress in reducing ground-level ozone. The major problem, according to the NRC report, is that flawed measuring methods underestimated the amount of volatile organic compounds in the atmosphere. Most ozone-control efforts have concentrated on reducing volatile organic compounds. Control methods have thus been less effective than anticipated.

The NRC said that in many regions, nitrogen oxides may also play a more important role than previously thought in ozone formation. Control of nitrogen oxide emissions may thus reduce ground-level ozone more effectively, according to the NRC.

Indoor air pollution. A preliminary study suggests that nonsmokers face in-creased risks of contamination from *radon* (a naturally occurring radioactive gas) if they live or work with smokers. Physicists Raymond H. Johnson, Jr., of Key Technology Incorporated in Lebanon, Pa., and Eric Geiger of Radon QC in Palmer, Pa., performed tests in which they found that the level of airborne *radon decay products* (radioactive atoms formed as radon decays) increased dramatically in the presence of cigarette smoke.

Within five hours of lighting a cigarette in a nonsmoking family's basement, the researchers detected about 25 per cent more radon decay products than before. A cigarette lit 24 hours after the first increased the levels of decay products by 40 per cent. The scientists believe that the increase results when radioactive atoms bind to *particulates* (small particles suspended in the air) in the smoke.   [Daniel D. Chiras]

In the Special Reports section, see WETLANDS: MIRED IN CONTROVERSY. In the Science Studies section, see GLOBAL CHANGE. In WORLD BOOK, see ENVIRONMENTAL POLLUTION.

Fossil Studies

One of the oldest known species of amphibians apparently still spent most of its time in the water, according to research reported in July 1991 by zoologists M. I. Coates and J. A. Clack of Cambridge University in England. The finding supports the theory that the limbs of *tetrapods* (land-dwelling vertebrates with four legs) evolved first for use in the water rather than for walking on land.

Animals began to emerge from the water and live on land about 365 million years ago, in the Late Devonian Period. One of the oldest known amphibian tetrapods—a distant relative of modern frogs, toads, and salamanders—was a small creature called *Acanthostega*. Scientists had assumed that because *Acanthostega* had lungs and four limbs with feet, it was mainly a land-dwelling creature that breathed air.

When Coates and Clack analyzed the bone structure of *Acanthostega* fossils, however, they discovered that this ancient amphibian also retained gills inherited from its fish ancestors and so was probably still largely aquatic.

Additional support for the theory that limbs possessing *digits* (fingers or toes) evolved first for use in water was reported in November 1991 by paleontologist Pere E. Ahlberg of Oxford University in England. Ahlberg determined that 370-million-year-old fossils previously identified as the remains of fish are actually those of the oldest known amphibian. Ahlberg reported that the still-unnamed fossil had limbs with at least five digits.

Paleontologists have suggested that ancient amphibians' limbs, which resembled flippers, may have evolved for moving about in ponds choked with vegetation. Later, the limbs evolved into legs for walking on land.

Permian extinction. One of the largest volcanic eruptions in Earth's history may have been responsible for Earth's greatest mass extinction, according to a July 1991 report. Geologists Asish R. Basu of the University of Rochester in New York and Paul R. Renne of the Institute of Human Origins in Berkeley, Calif., reported that a vast outpouring of lava in Siberia occurred about 248 million years ago. This was approximately the time when up to 95 per cent of all marine animal species died out. This mass extinction marks the end of the Permian Period.

Basu and Renne determined that the volcanic activity in Siberia lasted less than 1 million years—a short time, geologically speaking. During this period, Siberian volcanoes threw out about 1.6 million cubic kilometers (384,000 cubic miles) of lava. The now-hardened lava covers an area spanning 337,000 square kilometers (130,000 square miles). The scientists theorized that the Siberian eruptions may have produced huge amounts of ash that darkened the skies, blocking out sunlight and lowering temperatures around the world.

To determine the time of the Siberian eruptions, the scientists measured the ratio of argon to a particular radioactive form of potassium in the rock. Because the potassium atoms change to argon atoms over time at a known rate, the ratio can be used to determine the age of the rock. The scientists concluded that the volcanic activity in Siberia began about 248.3 million years ago and end-ed about 247.5 million years ago.

Triassic extinction. The impact of three large meteorites or comets on Earth's surface may have resulted in a mass extinction that occurred about 208 million years ago, at the end of the Triassic Period. That conclusion was announced in January 1992 by a team of geologists led by David M. Bice of Carleton College in Northfield, Minn. During the Triassic extinctions, numerous species of *invertebrates* (animals without backbones), including about 92 per cent of European clam species, died off.

The geologists' evidence for the impacts consists of small bits of so-called *shocked quartz* found in sediments in northern Italy dated to the Triassic Period. Shocked quartz grains display a distinctive pattern of microscopic fractures produced only when rock is subjected to great pressure, such as during an impact by a meteorite.

Bice and his colleagues reported finding shocked quartz grains at three levels in the sediments. This suggests, they said, that the three objects collided with Earth within a short time at the end of

The skull of the largest and best-preserved skeleton of a *Tyrannosaurus rex* bears evidence of the injury that killed the dinosaur in old age, according to an October 1991 report by scientists who unearthed the fossil in South Dakota. In May 1992, federal officials seized the skeleton after Cheyenne River Sioux Indians charged that the scientists had illegally taken it from tribal land.

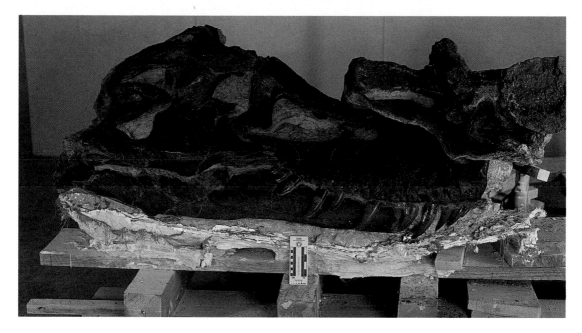

the Triassic. The site or sites where the objects struck are unknown. (In the Special Reports section, see STONES FROM SPACE.)

Out with a bang. Two studies reported in 1991 provided support for the theory that another mass extinction, which occurred about 65 million years ago at the end of the Cretaceous Period, happened suddenly. During this extinction, many plant and animal species, including many marine organisms and the last of the dinosaurs, died out.

Many scientists believe the extinction resulted from the collision of one or more asteroids with Earth. According to this theory, the impact ejected immense amounts of dust into the atmosphere. This triggered a series of environmental disasters, including a dramatic cooling of Earth's climate. Some scientists, however, argue that the Cretaceous extinctions occurred gradually, perhaps as the result of volcanic activity or a changing climate.

In August, geologist Jack Wolfe of the United States Geological Survey in Denver, Colo., reported on his study of fos-silized vegetation from an ancient lily pond dating from the end of the Cretaceous Period. Wolfe saw distinctive wrinkles in the fossilized leaves. He was able to re-create the wrinkles in modern lily leaves in a laboratory environment by freezing them quickly. Wolfe concluded from this experiment that the ancient lily pond had also been rapidly chilled and frozen.

In November, paleontologists led by Peter M. Sheehan of the Milwaukee Public Museum in Wisconsin reported on an extensive survey of dinosaur fossils in rocks dating from the last 2.5 million years of the Cretaceous Period. The fossils were found in parts of Montana and North Dakota. Sheehan and his colleagues discovered about 4,100 dinosaur bones representing 8 taxonomic families. The group reported finding fossils from all eight families in all levels of the rocks. This evidence indicated that the dinosaur populations had not dwindled gradually over time but had died off suddenly.   [Carlton E. Brett]

In WORLD BOOK, see AMPHIBIAN; DINOSAUR; PALEONTOLOGY; VOLCANO.

Genetic researchers during 1991 and 1992 continued to identify genes that are responsible for several diseases, including forms of deafness, muscular dystrophy, and colon cancer. In addition, geneticists debated the accuracy of deoxyribonucleic acid (DNA) analysis, or DNA fingerprinting, in identifying perpetrators of a crime.

DNA fingerprinting. A controversy erupted in the scientific community in early 1992 over the use of DNA fingerprinting in criminal investigations. DNA fingerprinting was introduced in 1987 as a method to identify individuals based on a pattern seen in their DNA, the molecule of which genes are made. DNA is present in every cell of the body except red blood cells. DNA fingerprinting has been used successfully in various ways, such as to determine paternity where it is not clear who the father of a particular child is. However, it is in the area of criminal investigations that DNA fingerprinting has potentially powerful and controversial uses.

DNA fingerprinting and other DNA analysis techniques have revolutionized criminal investigations by giving investigators powerful new tools in the attempt to prove guilt, not just establish innocence. When used in criminal investigations, a DNA fingerprint pattern from a suspect is compared with a DNA fingerprint pattern obtained from such material as hairs or blood found at the scene of a crime. A match between the two DNA samples can be used as evidence to convict a suspect.

The controversy in 1992 stemmed from a report published in December 1991 by population geneticists Richard C. Lewontin of Harvard University in Cambridge, Mass., and Daniel L. Hartl of Washington University School of Medicine in St. Louis, Mo. Lewontin and Hartl called into question the methods used to calculate how likely it is that a match between two DNA fingerprints might occur by chance alone. In particular, they argued that the current method cannot properly determine the likelihood that two DNA samples will match because they came from the same individual rather than simply from two different individuals who are members of the same ethnic group. Lewontin and Hartl called for better surveys of DNA patterns within ethnic groups in order

to determine whether the DNA fingerprinting methods are adequate.

In response to their criticisms, population geneticists Ranajit Chakraborty of the University of Texas in Dallas and Kenneth K. Kidd of Yale University in New Haven, Conn., argued that enough data are already available to show that the methods currently being used are adequate. In January 1992, however, the Federal Bureau of Investigation and laboratories that conduct DNA tests announced that they would collect additional DNA samples from various ethnic groups in an attempt to resolve some of these questions. And, in April, a National Academy of Sciences panel called for strict standards and a system of accreditation for DNA testing laboratories.

Deafness gene identified. Identification of the gene responsible for Waardenburg's syndrome, an inherited form of deafness, was announced simultaneously in February 1992 by two groups of scientists—one from Manchester, England and the Max Planck Institute in Germany and the other from Boston University and the Federal University of Puernambuco in Brazil. Deafness in humans has many causes, but Waardenburg's syndrome is responsible for more than 2 per cent of the cases.

Waardenburg's syndrome is known to take one of two forms, both of which involve white hair. In one form, the deaf individuals often have a white streak of hair, white eyelashes, or both. In the other form, patients have these characteristics along with an eye abnormality.

In the search to identify the responsible gene, the researchers studied a family in Brazil that had information available for more than 100 of its members stretching over six generations. Almost half of the members of this extensive family have Waardenburg's syndrome. Using genetic information from this and other families, researchers narrowed the location of the gene to a small region of one chromosome. They then found that one of the genes in this region has a configuration that is known as a *paired box*. Genes with a paired box play crucial roles in the earliest stages of embryonic development.

Another important clue to the cause of Waardenburg's syndrome was the identification of a mutation in mice known as Splotch. Mutations are changes in genes. In the case of Splotch mice, the mutation causes neurological defects and unusual white spots in several places on their bodies. The scientists were aided in their work by earlier gene mapping efforts, which showed that the mutant genes responsible for Splotch mice and for Waardenburg's syndrome were in similar locations on mouse and human chromosomes. The researchers then found that the mutant mouse and human genes are almost identical. In addition, the Splotch gene contains a paired box and so is involved in embryonic development.

The identification of this gene may help scientists understand a whole group of inherited diseases that may be due to problems occurring during the development of human embryos. In addition, the Splotch mouse can be used as a model system for studies of the defect causing Waardenburg's syndrome.

Expandable genes. The gene responsible for myotonic dystrophy can grow longer as it is passed from one generation to another. This surprising finding was announced in February 1992 by re-searchers from the United States, Great Britain, Sweden, and the Netherlands.

Myotonic dystrophy is the most common adult form of muscular dystrophy and causes progressive weakening of the muscles. This disease affects about one in 8,000 adults worldwide.

To identify the actual defect responsible for myotonic dystrophy, the scientists used artificial chromosomes, which have only been recently developed in the laboratory for handling very large pieces of DNA. The researchers found one particular segment of DNA that had unusual features. Not only was this segment of DNA always larger in people with myotonic dystrophy, it could also vary in size even between members of the same family that had the disease.

In addition, the size of the DNA segment seemed to be directly related to the severity of the disease. In some families the segment of DNA would get larger as it was passed from parents to children to grandchildren, and at the same time, the symptoms of the disease would worsen.

The scientists did not know whether

Genetically engineered *myoblasts* (immature muscle cells) appear blue when viewed under the microscope, revealing that they have become part of the muscle tissue into which they were inserted. This experiment, reported in December 1991, showed that myoblasts can be used for gene therapy. They could carry normal genes for treating diseases such as muscular dystrophy.

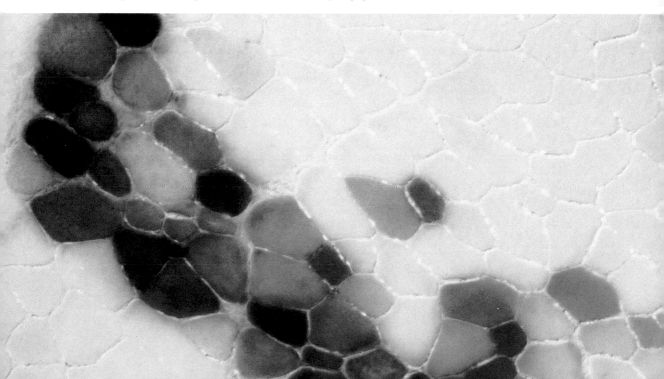

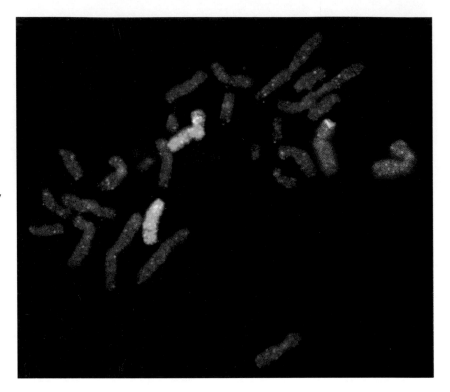

Fluorescent dyes developed by Lawrence Livermore Laboratories in California and reported in October 1991 cause chromosomes to glow in different colors when examined under a powerful microscope. The red tip on a green chromosome and the green tip on a red one reveal an abnormality caused by the chromosomes exchanging material. The ability to see such abnormalities will help in the diagnosis of some cancers and other diseases.

Genetics Continued

the changes in DNA segment size were the cause of the disease or just an effect of it. Similar "unstable" or changeable segments of DNA have been found in an inherited form of mental retardation, called fragile X syndrome, and in a rare neurological disease. Genetic scientists are now exploring expandable genes as the cause of other inherited ills.

Treating muscular dystrophy. A possible new treatment for another type of muscular dystrophy, called Duchenne muscular dystrophy, was reported in August 1991 by scientists at the University of Wisconsin in Madison and two hospitals in England. The gene, which in its defective form is responsible for this type of muscular dystrophy, had been identified in 1987.

The researchers injected copies of the normal version of this gene directly into muscles of a type of mouse that has muscular dystrophy. Genes ordinarily direct the production of proteins, which carry out the functions of cells. An abnormal protein coded for by a defective gene causes Duchenne muscular dystrophy.

After injecting copies of the normal

gene, the researchers found that the correct human protein was being produced in the mice. Although in this experiment the protein was produced at levels too low to be of great help, the scientists believe that if they can boost the levels about 10 times, they may have an effective treatment for this disease.

Genes and hypertension. Using two different types of rats, an international group of researchers from the United States, France, Belgium, Germany, and Japan in October 1991 announced important findings about genes involved in high blood pressure, or hypertension. Hypertension is believed to be a major cause of both strokes and heart disease.

These researchers mated hypertensive rats with normal rats and then mated the offspring of these rats, producing what was in effect the "grandchildren" of the original rats. Some of the "grandchild" rats had hypertension and some did not. By carefully comparing gene segments called markers found in those rats with hypertension to those without, the scientists were able to identify two genes that seemed to make the difference. One of these genes appeared to be the same as, or at least very close to, another gene already identified and named the ACE gene. The ACE gene produces an *enzyme* (a type of protein) known to play an important role in controlling blood pressure in humans. So the ACE gene may play a major role in hypertension.

Even if this can be verified in future studies, control of this disorder is not likely to be a simple matter. Researchers know that there are other genes involved and that environmental factors, such as stress, diet, and smoking habits, play a critical role.

Genes and cancer susceptibility. In August 1991, research teams at Johns Hopkins University in Baltimore, the Tokyo Cancer Institute in Japan, and the University of Utah in Salt Lake City announced finding what appears to be the gene responsible for familial adenomatous polyposis (FAP), which represents an inherited susceptibility to colon cancer. A tendency or susceptibility to develop certain types of cancer—rather than the disease itself—is passed from generation to generation. FAP, one of the most common examples of a genetic tendency for cancer, affects about 1 person in every 5,000 in the United States.

Finding this gene was a difficult task, partly because researchers have found mutations in other genes that cause cases of colon cancer that are not inherited. However, the researchers were particularly interested in finding the gene for FAP because of its tendency to occur in several members of the same family. The gene ultimately identified has been designated APC for adenomatous polyposis coli. This gene appears to be mutated in members of families that have FAP, suggesting that this gene is of a type known as tumor-suppressor genes. Normal tumor-suppressor genes prevent the formation of tumors. When these genes are mutated, a tumor develops. Although scientists do not yet know the exact function of the APC gene, identification of this gene will make it possible to design a test that will detect a tendency to develop this type of cancer.

Commercial genes. The National Institutes of Health (NIH) in Bethesda, Md., in October 1991, announced it would begin applying for patents on fragments of genes its researchers dis-

covered while working on the worldwide project to map all human genes. The British government then announced it would do likewise. In April 1992, biologist James D. Watson, head of the NIH gene-mapping effort, resigned, saying that patenting unknown DNA fragments would undermine international cooperation to map genes.

Permission for the first commercial testing of gene therapy—medical treatments involving genetically altered cells—was granted to Targeted Genetics Corporation of Seattle in February by the NIH. The first tests will be aimed toward developing genetically engineered white blood cells that might be able to fight the virus that causes AIDS.

Stem-cell gene therapy. A new method to correct genetic defects in human beings by replacing defective genes in a special type of cell called a stem cell was tested in 1992. Stem cells, found in the bone marrow, produce all other blood cells of the body. If the gene is successfully put into a stem cell, all of the white blood cells produced by that stem cell should also have a copy of the necessary gene.

The first officially approved gene therapy experiments, conducted at the NIH in Bethesda, Md., beginning in September 1990, involved genes inserted into mature white blood cells of two young girls with defective immune systems. The defect was caused by a missing enzyme. As of 1992, the experimental genes were directing the production of the critical enzyme. But, because white blood cells die off and must constantly be replaced, the scientists knew that using white blood cells would not be the best long-term approach.

An experiment to treat the same immune-system defect by inserting normal versions of the gene into stem cells began in Italy in April 1992. In the United States in February, an advisory committee of the NIH approved stem cell experiments proposed by NIH scientists. If these stem cell experiments work, it could mean that many genetic diseases might be cured using gene therapy.

[David S. Haymer]

In the Special Reports section, see THE EVOLUTION OF GENETIC MEDICINE. In the Science News Update section, see MEDICAL RESEARCH. In WORLD BOOK, see CELL; GENETICS.

Natural disasters continued to make headlines in 1991 and 1992. Mount Etna, Europe's most active volcano, erupted on Dec. 14, 1991. Lava from the eruption, which lasted until spring 1992, threatened a village at the foot of the volcano. Mount Etna has erupted at least 260 times since its earliest known eruption in about 700 B.C.

Several moderately large earthquakes shook California in April 1992. A pair of quakes measuring 4.6 and 6.1 on the Richter scale struck about 2½ hours apart in an region near Desert Hot Springs in southern California on April 22. The quakes occurred along an unnamed fault 9 kilometers (5.6 miles) from the San Andreas Fault, an enormous break in Earth's crust that extends more than 1,200 kilometers (750 miles) through California.

The quakes provided the United States Geological Survey (USGS) with its first opportunity to test a new system for estimating the likelihood that any quake along the southern end of the San Andreas Fault would be followed by a major quake—one with a magnitude of at least 7.5. After the first quake, the USGS estimated there was a 1 to 5 per cent chance that a major quake would occur within 72 hours. The second quake increased the chances to from 10 to 25 per cent. However, no additional earthquakes took place.

An unrelated earthquake and several strong aftershocks struck near Petrolia in northern California on April 25. The quakes, which measured 6.9, 6.0, and 6.5, occurred near the junction of the Gorda, North American, and Pacific plates, three of the huge tectonic plates that make up Earth's outer shell.

Then, in late June, earthquakes measuring 7.4 and 6.5 shook southern California. The first quake, whose epicenter was near the town of Landers, east of Los Angeles, was the strongest earthquake to hit the state in 40 years.

Cretaceous extinction. The theory that the collision of an asteroid with Earth 65 million years ago caused the extinction of many species, including the last of the dinosaurs, continued to stimulate both scientific research and debate in 1991 and 1992. A buried impact crater on the northern coast of the Yucatán Peninsula in Mexico may be the strongest candidate yet discovered for the impact site, according to research published in September 1991 by scientists led by planetologist Alan R. Hildebrand of the University of Arizona in Tucson.

The precise age of the crater, called the Chicxulub crater, is unknown. However, petroleum engineers who were drilling at the site in the early 1980's unearthed fossils dating from the Cretaceous-Tertiary (K-T) boundary at the bottom of the crater. The K-T boundary marks the end of the Cretaceous Period 65 million years ago and the beginning of the Tertiary Period, the time of the mass extinction.

Hildebrand and his co-workers were led to the crater in 1990 after finding a layer of rocky debris in rock samples from the K-T boundary in Cuba and the western Caribbean area. The debris is similar to that deposited by *tsunamis* (huge tidal waves) as they pass through shallow water. If the asteroid had landed in the ocean, it would have created a tsunami several kilometers high. From the arrangement of the debris, the scientists concluded that the impact probably occurred in the Caribbean region.

The Chicxulub crater, which extends into the Gulf of Mexico, lies about 500 meters (1,640 feet) beneath the surface of the Yucatán Peninsula. To determine its size and shape, the scientists relied chiefly on studies of variations in Earth's gravity in the rocks in the area and on information obtained from oil wells drilled there.

The gravitational studies revealed three concentric circular areas where the attraction of Earth's gravity is less than average. The innermost area has a diameter of 70 kilometers (43.5 miles); the outermost, a diameter of 180 kilometers (112 miles). Geologists believe such areas of lessened gravitational attraction are caused by fractured rock, such as that found in impact craters. The density of fractured rock is less than that of solid rock and so it has a smaller mass and a weaker gravitational field.

The crater also contains rock typical of that found at meteorite impact sites. Rock samples obtained during drilling operations revealed that the crater is filled with *breccia* (rock made of angular fragments). The thickness of the breccia and other rock in the crater indicates that the crater was more than 1,000 me-

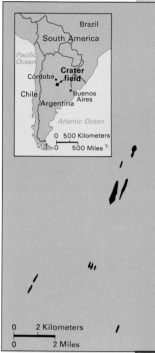

Crater hop

Oblong impact craters, *right,* mark the path of a meteorite that skipped across part of central Argentina, *inset above,* about 2,000 years ago, according to a January 1992 report. The meteorite apparently crashed into Earth at a shallow angle and then broke into pieces that bounced 50 kilometers (30 miles) across the landscape, creating almost a dozen craters, *above.*

ters (3,280 feet) deep at the time it was created.

Support for a Yucatán impact was provided in research reported in October 1991 by two teams of scientists led by volcanologist Haraldur Sigurdsson of the University of Rhode Island in Narragansett. They reported on their efforts to determine the kind of rocks the asteroid struck.

Earlier in 1991, Sigurdsson and one of the teams had reported that the geologic characteristics of deposits from the K-T boundary in Haiti—one of the most complete geologic records of this period known—were similar to those of only two known impact sites, the Manson crater in Iowa and the Chicxulub crater. The scientists then analyzed the chemistry of the Haitian deposits and found that they were related to the deposits in the Chicxulub crater, indicating the impact there was the source of the Haitian deposits.

Effects of the impact. Sigurdsson and Hildebrand also explored the possible environmental effects of a Cretaceous impact. Sigurdsson and his fellow re-

searchers estimated that the impact *vaporized* (turned to gas) and ejected into the atmosphere about 6.4 billion metric tons (7 billion short tons) of sulfur. This is 100 times the amount of sulfur discharged by the 1815 eruption of the Tambora volcano in Indonesia, Earth's largest recorded volcanic explosion.

According to these scientists, the sulfur was ejected as particles of sulfur and as sulfur dioxide gas. Sulfur dioxide in the atmosphere combines with water to form sulfuric acid. The scientists believe the sulfur particles and sulfuric acid droplets remained suspended in the upper atmosphere for many years, blocking sunlight. Their effect was to lower the temperature at Earth's surface by 4 Celsius degrees (7 Fahrenheit degrees). The scientists also theorized that the sulfur produced widespread acid rain, which killed numerous marine plant and animal species.

Hildebrand's group disagreed with the conclusion that the impact might have lowered global temperatures. They calculated that the impact would have vaporized the limestone rock that un-

Ribbons of glowing lava illuminate the southeastern side of Mount Etna in Sicily during an eruption that began on Dec. 14, 1991. Italian officials unsuccessfully attempted to halt the flow by erecting earthen barriers, bombing side streams that fed the main lava stream, and dumping concrete slabs into the surface opening from which the lava was pouring. The lava flow destroyed orchards and threatened a village.

California quakes
A man works to repair damage caused by a large earthquake and several strong aftershocks that rocked northern California on April 25 and 26, 1992. The quakes, the strongest of which registered 6.9 on the Richter scale, occurred along a fault near the junction of three of the huge tectonic plates that make up Earth's outer shell.

Medford,
Oregon
Eureka
Ferndale,
Epicenter
Nevada
California
North
Pacific
Ocean
Carson City,
Sacramento,
0   100 Kilometers
0   100 Miles
San Francisco

derlies the Chicxulub crater, releasing the carbon dioxide it held. The estimated rise in atmospheric carbon dioxide—to as much as 10 times its present level—could have caused a rise in global temperatures of 10 Celsius degrees (18 Fahrenheit degrees) that may have lasted up to 100,000 years.

Abrupt ocean warming. A major extinction of deep-sea creatures about 57 million years ago, just before the end of the Paleocene Epoch, resulted from a sudden increase in ocean temperatures. That conclusion was reported in September 1991 by paleontologists James P. Kennett of the University of California at Santa Barbara and Lowell D. Stott of the University of Southern California in Los Angeles.

To determine the temperature of the ocean during the Paleocene, the scientists analyzed the ratio of light and heavy *isotopes* (forms) of oxygen—normally found in seawater—incorporated in the shells of plankton and *foraminifera* (single-celled creatures) from that period. The shells were found in cores that were drilled as part of an exploration of the floor of the Weddell Sea in Antarctica.

The relative proportions of the two isotopes in shells depends on several factors, including the temperature of the seawater. Shells forming in warmer water have higher levels of the light isotope. In contrast, shells forming in colder water have increased levels of the heavier isotope.

The scientists found that the temperature of the water increased suddenly between 57.3 million and 57.2 million years ago. According to their analysis, the temperature of the surface water at the drill site rose from about 13 °C to about 21 °C (55 °F to 70 °F). The temperature of the deep water increased from about 10 °C to about 16 °C (50 °F to 61 °F). The scientists concluded that many bottom-dwelling species died out because of the warming of the deep water. The cause of the sudden temperature rise is not known.

Gondwanaland reorganized. Gondwanaland, the supercontinent out of which the modern continents of the Southern Hemisphere formed, may have formed originally from blocks of

295

continental crust left over from the breakup of another, older supercontinent. That conclusion was reported in June 1991 by geologist Paul F. Hoffman of the Geological Survey of Canada in Ottawa.

Most geologists accept that Gondwanaland first formed between 2.5 billion and 570 million years ago, during the Proterozoic Eon. But questions about how this occurred have puzzled geologists for 20 years. Hoffman theorized that Gondwanaland was created about 600 million years ago as the central section of the older, unnamed continent broke away and the remaining blocks were completely reorganized.

Hoffman theorized that 700 million years ago, Laurentia (what are now North America and Greenland) and Baltica (what are now Scandinavia and Russia east of the Ural Mountains) were part of a yet-unnamed supercontinent. Also included in this supercontinent were the continental blocks that later formed Gondwanaland. But their configuration in this supercontinent was very different from their known arrange-

ment in Gondwanaland, Hoffman said.

To account for this change, Hoffman suggested that near the end of the Proterozoic, about 600 million years ago, Laurentia and Baltica separated from the supercontinent. The remaining continental fragments also broke apart. But instead of drifting apart, these fragments closed together like a fan. In the process, Hoffman argued, the blocks were reorganized into their known configuration in Gondwanaland.

About 200 million years ago, Gondwanaland, Laurentia, and Baltica collided to form the supercontinent Pangaea. About 180 million years ago, Pangaea broke in two, and Gondwanaland once again became a separate supercontinent. Then within about 10 million or 20 million years, Gondwanaland itself began to split into what are now the continents of South America, Africa, Australia, and Antarctica, and the continental blocks of Arabia, Madagascar, and India. [William W. Hay]

In the Special Reports section, see STONES FROM SPACE. In WORLD BOOK, see DINOSAUR; OCEAN; PLATE TECTONICS.

Materials Science

The Administration of United States President George Bush announced in January 1992 the Advanced Materials and Processing Program. The initiative includes a proposed 10 per cent increase in federal funding for materials science research.

Some experts said the initiative's symbolic value is more important: It shines a spotlight on the often little-noticed field of materials science, which has played a pivotal role in the development of products ranging from airliners to pantyhose.

Shining silicon. At the December 1991 meeting of the Materials Research Society (MRS) in Boston, more than 100 scientists from around the world shared new findings on silicon's ability to emit light. Harnessing silicon's light-emitting capacity may facilitate an emerging realm of *optoelectronics* (technologies based on light as well as electronic signals).

Silicon, an abundant nonmetallic element, is a *semiconductor*, a material that conducts electricity better than insulators but less well than conductors. For

decades, silicon crystals have been recognized as crucial materials for their ability to turn on, turn off, delay, amplify, and otherwise affect currents of electrons flowing through them. Silicon chips are at the heart of electronic microprocessors.

The new findings suggest that engineers might be able to design silicon chips that communicate with each other by sending light signals. Light travels faster than electronic signals, so light-based communication presumably would be faster as well. Before the luminous silicon came along, more complicated and expensive materials such as gallium arsenide seemed the only option for combining electronic and optical features on the same chip.

Scientists previously had observed hints that silicon is able to emit light, but the light was too faint for practical applications. In April 1991, Leigh T. Canham and his colleagues in the electronics division of the Royal Signals and Radar Establishment in Malvern, England, reported that silicon crystals processed to have countless tiny *pores* (holes) emitted surprisingly bright visible light when laser light was shined on it. The scientists had used acid and other techniques to etch the minuscule pores into the silicon crystal. A group from the University of Grenoble in France then confirmed Canham's finding and presented preliminary evidence that porous silicon might emit light when stimulated electrically.

In late 1991 and early 1992, hundreds of researchers joined the effort to understand how porous silicon emits light and how to harness it for optoelectronic technologies. At the December MRS meeting, several researchers reported processing the material into experimental devices somewhat like the light-emitting diodes commonly used in commercial electronic products.

Numerous scientists speculated that the light emission derives from electrons confined in minuscule silicon structures produced when pores are etched in the crystals. Others reported in May at another MRS meeting that siloxene—a molecular structure made of silicon, oxygen, and hydrogen and long known to emit light when stimulated—was responsible for the light emission. Nevertheless, researchers remain uncertain about what precise physical processes and which tiny structures in the porous crystals are responsible for silicon's light-emitting properties.

Buckyball season. Throughout 1991 and 1992, scientists devoted an extraordinary amount of attention to *fullerenes*, molecules made exclusively of carbon atoms arranged in a spherical shape. The most famous of these molecules—buckminsterfullerene, also known as C_{60} or buckyball—is made of 60 carbon atoms bonded together in the shape of a soccer ball. There was also a great deal of interest in how fullerenes might affect the field of materials science. (See CHEMISTRY [CLOSE-UP].)

Smart materials. A meeting on Active Materials and Adaptive Structures held in Alexandria, Va., in November 1991 focused attention on "intelligent" materials. Such materials may be equipped with sensory mechanisms that detect emerging weaknesses or failures and with active components similar to muscles or glands. Smart materials that can repair problems they detect in themselves are also under development.

Raymond Measures, director of the Fiber Optic Smart Structures Laboratory at the University of Toronto in Canada, described efforts to implant smart optical fibers in airplane wings. These fibers, which Measures calls "nerves of glass," would relay regular signals to the cockpit. The fibers are designed to break if the wing begins to change shape too rapidly. The snapped fiber stops sending a regular signal to the cockpit, alerting the crew to the problem.

Materials scientist Carolyn Dry of the University of Illinois reported on her efforts to develop concrete that will detect and repair cracks as they are created. Dry designed fibers that contain an adhesive filler and can be implanted in freshly poured concrete. When the concrete develops cracks, the fibers also split apart, spilling the adhesive filler into the cracks.

Space shuttle experiments. In January 1992, an international team of seven astronauts flew the space shuttle Discovery into orbit. They brought with them the reusable International Microgravity Laboratory, in which they carried out dozens of life science and materials science experiments. Many materials scientists believe that the low-gravity environment of space will prove ideal for growing crystals and for processing other materials. Such materials often develop many imperfections in ground-based laboratories or factories, due to the greater pull of gravity on Earth.

The experiments included tests of different methods for growing crystals of compounds such as mercury iodide, which is used in X-ray and gamma-ray detectors. Other experiments focused on growing crystals made of proteins such as bacteriorhodopsin, a light-sensitive biochemical that could be used in optoelectronics.

Shuttle scientists also performed studies of how fluids behave in low-gravity conditions. The strength of a piece of metal depends partially on the size and arrangement of its constituent grains—which form from hot metallic liquid as it cools. Because of this, materials scientists hope that the low-gravity experiments will help researchers find methods of processing metals into stronger forms.   [Ivan Amato]

In WORLD BOOK, see MATERIALS SCIENCE; PHYSICS.

Replacing the female hormone estrogen in women who have undergone *menopause* (the time in a woman's life when menstruation ceases) may reduce their risk of heart disease. Researchers at Harvard Medical School in Boston reported this finding in September 1991.

The Harvard group analyzed questionnaires completed by 121,700 nurses enrolled in a long-term health study begun in 1976. The questionnaires, which asked for information on the women's health habits and illnesses, were sent to the women every two years.

After reviewing all the questionnaires, the researchers selected those of 48,470 women who, over the course of the study, were between the ages of 30 and 63. These women had reported being free of cancer and heart disease when they entered the study. The women also had undergone either *hysterectomies* (removal of the female reproductive organs) or natural menopause between 1976 and 1986.

The researchers studied the health questionnaires of three categories of these women. Those taking estrogen in 1986 were classified as current hormone users and comprised 22 per cent of the total. Women who had taken estrogen for a year at some time during the 10-year period were labeled former hormone users, and they made up 25 per cent of the total. The third category was composed of the remaining women, who had never used estrogen.

The researchers looked for evidence of *cardiovascular* (heart and blood vessel) disease, such as heart attack or stroke, that had required treatment. They found that among the group of women who had never used estrogen, 250 had major, but not fatal, heart disease; 129 had died of heart disease; and 123 had suffered strokes. For women designated current estrogen users, 45 had major heart disease, 21 had suffered fatal heart disease, and 39 had had strokes. For former estrogen users, 110 had suffered major heart disease; 55, fatal heart disease; and 62, strokes.

The researchers computed the number of years each woman had been in the study and added the figures for all the women in each group to get each group's total number of "person years." Calculating the number of person years per group enabled the researchers to adjust their findings to take into account the rising risk of cardiovascular disease as a person ages.

After taking age and other risk factors into consideration, the researchers compared the heart disease risk of the three groups. They concluded that the group designated current estrogen users had a 44 per cent lower risk of developing major heart disease and a 39 per cent lower risk of fatal heart disease than did women who had never taken estrogen. Former estrogen users had a 17 per cent lower risk of major heart disease compared to nonestrogen users, and a 21 per cent lower risk of fatal heart disease. The three groups showed no major differences in the risk of suffering a stroke.

There was no evidence that the women who took estrogen had a higher death rate from cancer—which past studies had linked to the hormone supplements—or other diseases. Thus, the researchers concluded that estrogen therapy appears to reduce the risk of heart disease in postmenopausal women without increasing the risk of death from other causes.

Aspirin and colon cancer. Regular low doses of aspirin may reduce the risk of fatal colon cancer, according to a December 1991 report. Researchers at the American Cancer Society in Atlanta, Ga., announced this finding, which supported previous studies suggesting that aspirin and certain other pain relievers may protect against colon cancer.

The researchers analyzed reports from 662,424 adults over age 30 who had been enrolled in 1982 in the American Cancer Society's Cancer Prevention Study II. The study, which required participants to answer questions on their health, was designed to reveal habits that seemed either to prevent or to increase the risk of developing cancer.

The study included only those people who thoroughly answered the questions on aspirin use. The researchers divided this group into four categories according to the number of aspirins each person took monthly. The researchers then computed the person years for each of the four groups and the number of deaths from colon cancer in each group between 1982 and 1988. After adjusting for the increasing risk of colon cancer with age, the researchers computed an age-adjusted death rate (the number of

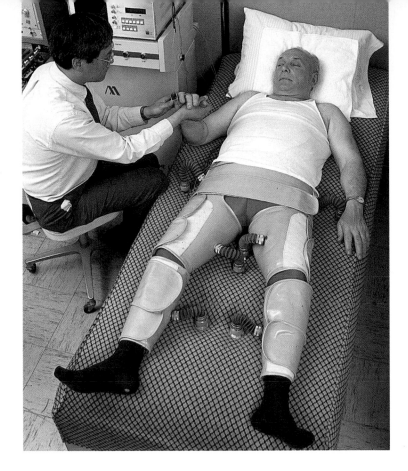

A patient undergoes an experimental treatment for coronary artery disease in 1992 at the Health Sciences Center at Stony Brook, N.Y. In the procedure, air-filled cuffs wrapped around the patient's legs and hips rhythmically inflate. This forces blood—which diseased arteries otherwise could not deliver—to the heart. In some patients, several sessions of the treatment reduced the symptoms of their disease.

deaths per 100,000 person years) for each group.

They found that among the men who took no aspirin, the death rate from colon cancer was 58.3 per 100,000 men. Among men who took less than 1 aspirin per month, the death rate decreased to 44.8. For men who took from 1 to 15 aspirins per month, the death rate was 40.5. And for those who consumed 16 or more aspirins per month, the death rate sank to 34.8.

Among women, those who took no aspirin had a colon cancer death rate of 40.8 per 100,000. Women who took less than 1 aspirin per month had a death rate of 29.8. Those who took 1 to 15 aspirins per month showed a death rate of 26.5, and those who took 16 or more aspirins a month had a death rate of 23.5.

The researchers then compared the risk of dying of colon cancer for people who took aspirin regularly and for those who did not. The researchers determined that men who took less than 1 aspirin per month had a 23 per cent lower risk of dying of colon cancer than did those who took no aspirin. The men

who took from 1 to 15 aspirins had a 31 per cent lower risk. And those who consumed 16 or more aspirins slashed their risk by 40 per cent.

For women who took less than 1 aspirin each month, the risk of dying of colon cancer was 27 per cent lower than that of women who did not take aspirin. For those who took from 1 to 15 aspirins, the risk dropped by 35 per cent, and for those who took 16 or more, it fell by 42 per cent.

The researchers speculated that aspirin inhibits the growth of colon tumors. But the aspirin may also have caused stomach or intestinal bleeding, which could have led to blood in the stool, a symptom of colon cancer that might have prompted some people to seek medical attention. In these cases, cancerous or precancerous conditions could have been found and treated before they progressed to a fatal stage.

"Parent" blood cell identified. Researchers in October 1991 announced that they may have isolated *stem cells,* a type of blood cell that is responsible for giving rise to the different types of red

299

and white cells of the human blood system. Molecular biologist Irving Weissman and his colleagues at Stanford University School of Medicine in Stanford, Calif., and SyStemix Incorporated in Palo Alto, Calif., said that identification of the stem cell theoretically makes it possible to reproduce an entire human blood system from a single cell. A stem cell eventually gives rise to oxygen-carrying red blood cells, infection-fighting white blood cells, and clot-forming platelets.

Researchers have been unable to find stem cells because they make up only about 1 in 2,000 immature blood cells, and they look no different from other immature blood cells. The scientists set out to test a series of blood cells to see which one, after dividing several times, could not only give rise to all blood cells, but reproduce itself as well—the unique ability of a stem cell. The researchers believed they could identify molecules on this cell that would differentiate it from other blood cells.

To find the cell, the researchers used SCID mice, which naturally lack the ability to produce white blood cells that defend the body against invading organisms and transplanted tissue. The researchers transplanted human thymus tissue into the mice. Thymus tissue is necessary to turn immature white cells into mature immune-system cells that produce antibodies, substances that can recognize foreign invaders. Because the mice lacked an immune system and therefore could not reject human cells, the researchers could study the development of human blood cells in them.

The researchers isolated several groups of immature human blood cells according to identifying molecules on the cell surface. They then injected different groups of cells into different groups of SCID mice. After several days, the researchers withdrew blood samples from the mice and checked to see which samples showed a full complement of human blood cells. The scientists isolated those groups of cells that had succeeded in creating each type of blood cell, and then they repeated the procedure. Finally, they were left with a group of cells that produced all blood-cell

Changing muscle into bone

Bone tissue, *below,* was created from muscle in a 1991 experiment on rats at Washington University School of Medicine in St. Louis, Mo. Scientists first created a tiny mold using a model bone, *right.* Then they placed a flap of rat muscle in the mold, added biochemicals, and implanted the mold into a live rat. When the researchers removed the mold 10 days later, the muscle had become bone.

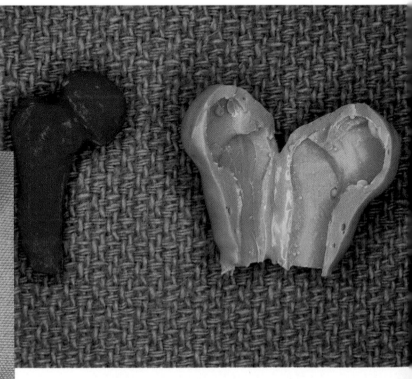

types and also reproduced themselves.

If the California researchers can reproduce their results in human tests, the cell they identified might be used to treat several conditions. For example, stem cells would greatly improve the success of bone-marrow transplants in cancer patients, and they might restore the infection-fighting white blood cells of AIDS patients. The cells could also be used in gene therapy to carry normal genes into the body where they would replace defective genes. (In the Special Reports section, see THE EVOLUTION OF GENETIC MEDICINE.)

Muscle turned into bone. Researchers in October 1991 reported that they had transformed rat muscle tissue into bone. Reconstructive surgeon Roger K. Khouri and his colleagues at Washington University School of Medicine in St. Louis, Mo., speculated that such newly formed bone might eventually replace bone transplants or synthetic bone substitutes currently used in reconstructive surgery. The new bone can be molded to the required shape and created from the patient's own tissue, assuring that the body will not reject it.

The researchers removed small flaps of muscle from the thighs of 23 rats. The researchers injected the flaps from 18 rats with a solution containing a hormone that promotes bone growth. They also coated the muscle flap with powdered bone, which contains substances that foster bone growth. They then placed each muscle flap into a bone-shaped mold and implanted it in the rat's abdomen, near the thigh. They repeated the process in the other five rats, but did not add either the hormone or the bone powder to the mold.

Ten days later, the researchers removed the molds and examined the flaps. They found that all of the treated flaps, but none of the untreated flaps, turned into bone that exactly matched the shape of the mold.

Stress and colds. People who feel under psychological stress may catch more colds than people with lower anxiety levels, according to a study reported in August 1991. Researchers at Carnegie Mellon University in Pittsburgh, Pa.; the Medical Research Council Common Cold Unit in Salisbury, Great Britain; and the University of Wales in Cardiff tested the theory that psychological

stress depresses the human immune system, making the body more vulnerable to infection.

The researchers selected 420 volunteers—154 men and 266 women, all between the ages of 18 and 54—who agreed to spend nine days in Britain's Common Cold Unit. Each of the volunteers was in good health and taking no medication at the start of the study. Each volunteer completed questionnaires that allowed the researchers to measure the number of experiences that had had a negative psychological impact on the volunteers in the past year, the person's perception of his or her ability to cope with stress, and the person's current negative feelings. The researchers then ranked each person's stress level on a scale of 3 to 12.

On the third day, the volunteers were given nose drops. The drops given to 394 people contained viruses responsible for the common cold. The remaining 26 people received saltwater drops. At the time, neither the volunteers nor the researchers knew which drops contained viruses.

During the volunteers' remaining time in the unit, doctors examined them daily and noted whether they showed such cold symptoms as coughing, sneezing, runny nose, and watery eyes. Technicians examined mucus from the nose and blood to see if they contained antibodies to the cold viruses.

The researchers analyzed the volunteers' symptoms and the laboratory tests to determine how many of the volunteers had caught colds. Those who had both cold symptoms and the virus or antibodies to the virus were classified as having colds. None of the volunteers who were given saltwater nose drops got colds, but 148—or 38 per cent—of the volunteers who had received virus-laden drops did.

When the scientists compared the volunteers' scores on the stress evaluation with the results of the physical examinations and laboratory tests, they found that the chances of getting a cold corresponded to the level of stress. For example, 90 per cent of those with a stress score of 11 to 12 became infected with a virus, while only 74 per cent of those with a stress score of 3 to 4 were infected. Moreover, only 27 per cent of those who scored 3 to 4 on the stress tests exhibited cold symptoms, in contrast to 47 per cent of those who scored 11 to 12.

The researchers concluded that when psychological stress increased, so did the risk of contracting a cold. At the same time, they found no evidence that stress resulted in more-severe colds.

Tiny transplants control diabetes. A new transplant technique allows pancreas cells to produce insulin in diabetic mice, according to a study published in December 1991. Researchers at Washington University School of Medicine in St. Louis developed the new technique, which could eventually replace the daily insulin shots that many diabetics must receive.

Many medical researchers think that transplanted islet cells, the insulin-producing cells of the pancreas, can also do a better job of controlling blood-sugar levels than can insulin injections. Unlike shots, islet cells continually release insulin, the hormone that regulates how the body uses sugar.

Islet cells had been transplanted in the past, but the body would reject the transplants as foreign tissue. Drugs could prevent rejection by suppressing the immune system, but this made transplant recipients vulnerable to infections, which can be difficult to treat in diabetics. Previous transplant techniques also caused blood clotting or allowed the islet cells to clump together, which prevented them from releasing insulin.

To overcome these problems, the St. Louis researchers embedded rat islet cells in a gel that prevented them from clumping together. They inserted the cell-laden gel into a fiber—a plastic, tubelike device about 2.5 centimeters (1 inch) long—which had not provoked an immune reaction in earlier studies.

The researchers implanted the fibers in untreated diabetic mice. In some of the mice, the fibers were inserted under the skin. In others, they were implanted in the abdomen.

The blood-sugar levels of the mice had, on average, been five times higher than the levels of nondiabetic mice. But their levels began to fall steadily after the islet cell transplants and reached normal levels within one week. With the transplants, more than 80 per cent of the mice maintained normal blood-sugar levels until the researchers removed the transplants 60 days later. Then the mouse blood-sugar levels rose sharply and returned to their former high levels within 10 days.

Upon examining the removed fibers, the researchers determined that the transplants had not provoked an immune reaction and that the islet cells were still functioning. The researchers believe the approach might be useful in human beings with diabetes—not only because it succeeded in mice, but also because the fibers can be removed easily if the transplant fails.

Help for premature infants. A type of sugar found in breast milk helps premature babies survive and protects them from some diseases. Researchers at the University of Helsinki Children's Hospital in Finland and at the University of California in Irvine reported in May 1992 that the compound inositol protected against certain diseases of the lung and eyes that are common among premature infants. Inositol is a sugar that seems to be necessary for the formation of natural surfactants, compounds that increase the lung's ability to absorb oxygen.

The study included 221 premature babies with breathing problems. All were fed *intravenously* (through a vein) and were on mechanical ventilators to aid breathing. The researchers randomly assigned the infants to two groups. During the first five days of life, one group of 114 babies received standard feedings supplemented with the amount of inositol they would have received if they had been fed breast milk. The other 107 babies received standard feedings without inositol.

At the end of 28 days, 24 per cent of the infants who had not received inositol had died, while only 11 per cent of those who had received the supplement had died. In addition, 18 per cent of the babies receiving inositol suffered lung damage, compared with 24 per cent of the babies who were not receiving the compound.

Inositol also seemed to protect the infants against retinopathy, a serious eye disorder thought to result from a lack of oxygen to the eye. Retinopathy occurred in 13 per cent of the infants on inositol and in 26 per cent of those not on inositol. [Beverly Merz]

In WORLD BOOK, see CANCER; DIABETES; HEART.

In November 1991, scientists at the Lamont-Doherty Geological Observatory in Palisades, N.Y., confirmed the appearance of El Niño in tropical waters of the Pacific Ocean. El Niño is a warming of an enormous area of surface water in the central and eastern tropical Pacific combined with a cooling of surface waters in the far western tropical Pacific. It occurs every three to five years. The 1991 El Niño was the third occurrence in less than a decade.

El Niño has a major impact on worldwide weather patterns. According to David Rodenhuis, director of the U.S. National Weather Service's Climate Analysis Center in Camp Springs, Md., El Niño is the most important recurring event affecting world climates, apart from the change of seasons. Some of El Niño's effects include a reduction in the frequency of monsoons in the Indian Ocean, a cooling of summer temperatures in the western Pacific, and a great increase in midwinter rainfall in the central Pacific and along the west coast of South America. El Niño also increases the frequency of typhoons that strike the Philippines and Japan. Past El Niños have strongly affected North America, bringing abnormally heavy rains to California and Texas and perhaps reducing the frequency of Atlantic hurricanes.

The first sign of El Niño is usually a weakening of the steady winds over the central and western Pacific. This is quickly followed by rising sea-surface temperatures, which intensify storm activity over the central Pacific. Stronger storms pump additional heat and moisture high into the atmosphere. This heating and moistening of the high atmosphere modifies winds there, which changes weather patterns around the world.

By January 1992, sea-surface temperatures in the eastern Pacific and along the west coast of South America had risen 2.2 to 2.6 Celsius degrees (4 to 4.7 Fahrenheit degrees) above average. The warming was expected to peak in early spring 1992 but remain noticeable through the summer.

To help forecast and study El Niño, the U.S. National Weather Service in 1991 had set up more than 300 buoys

January 1992 measurements of the upper atmosphere show high levels of chlorine monoxide (orange areas) in the Northern Hemisphere. Chlorine monoxide—which results from the breakdown of chlorofluorocarbons (CFC's)—can destroy ozone in Earth's upper atmosphere, but wind patterns apparently prevented such destruction in 1992.

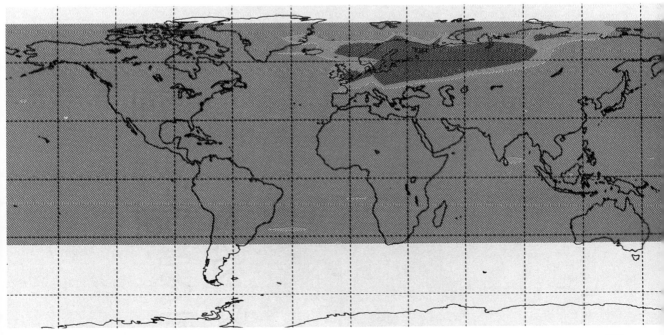

Global Effects of a Volcanic Eruption

Millions of tons of gases, ash, and lava were expelled into the atmosphere when Mount Pinatubo in the Philippines erupted in a series of explosions in June 1991. It was the most violent volcanic eruption of the 1900's, and scientists around the world in 1991 and 1992 were monitoring its far-reaching effects on Earth's atmosphere.

Much of the ejected material immediately descended the slope of the volcano in superheated flows of gas, mud, and lava, or fell nearby in a rain of ash and *pumice* (light, glasslike rock). But the volcano also ejected a plume of between 15 million and 18 million metric tons (17 million to 20 million short tons) of material 24 kilometers (15 miles) or more into the air. The plume thus reached into the part of the atmosphere called the lower tropical stratosphere. Carried east by stratospheric winds that averaged 120 kilometers per hour (75 miles per hour), Pinatubo's volcanic plume spread into a belt of gases, droplets, and dust 5,000 kilometers (3,000 miles) wide north to south. These gases had circled Earth around the equator by July 8, 1991, according to the United States National Center for Atmospheric Research in Boulder, Colo.

Scientists from the U.S. National Aeronautics and Space Administration (NASA) began work in early July to determine the spreading cloud's contents. Flying in a research aircraft, the scientists found the gases sulfur dioxide, hydrogen chloride, nitrogen oxide, and nitric oxide in the cloud. In the stratosphere, much of these gases combined with oxygen and condensed into droplets of sulfuric acid.

Stratospheric winds in Earth's middle latitudes continued to spread the Mount Pinatubo debris north and south in late summer 1991, and by midwinter, the debris had covered nearly the entire globe. The most visible sign of this high-altitude volcanic cloud was the coloring of evening skies in many regions of the world. On clear days, Mount Pinatubo's global effects were visible in the red, pink, and orange colors in the sky 30 to 60 minutes after sunset. These colors formed as light was filtered and reflected through the high-altitude sulfuric acid droplets formed from the volcanic gases. The effect was most brilliant in the Southern Hemisphere, where an eruption of Mount Hudson in Chile in August 1991 supplemented the Mount Pinatubo cloud.

In mid-1992, scientists were also investigating two less visible but potentially more significant effects of the Mount Pinatubo eruption. The first is the airborne debris's impact on Earth's climate. The cloud's dust and sulfuric acid droplets increase the amount of sunlight reflected back into space. This reduces the amount of energy reaching Earth's surface and lower atmosphere. From climate data collected after several large volcanic eruptions in the 1800's, scientists know that this effect can lead to noticeable reductions in surface temperatures. As a result of the 1815 eruption of Indonesia's Mount Tambora, for example, 1816 become known as the "year without summer."

Fortunately, the amount of volcanic material shot into the stratosphere from Mount Pinatubo was small compared to the gigantic eruption of Mount Tambora and that of Mount Krakatoa, also in Indonesia, in 1883. According to atmospheric scientists, the global cooling from Mount Pinatubo should be about 0.5 Celsius degree (0.9 Fahrenheit degree). This is far enough beyond the typical year-to-year global temperature variation of about 0.2 Celsius degree (0.4 Fahrenheit degree) that computers designed to measure

Mount Pinatubo in the Philippines erupts violently in June 1991. The series of volcanic eruptions sent between 15 million and 18 million metric tons (17 million to 20 million short tons) of ash and sulfurous gases into Earth's atmosphere.

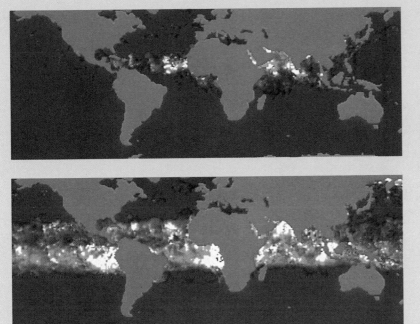

A globe-circling cloud
A satellite image taken three weeks before the eruptions of Mount Pinatubo, *top,* shows normal levels of *aerosols,* small particles suspended in the atmosphere (white and gold). A few weeks after the eruptions, winds had carried a huge cloud of aerosols from the volcano around the world, *bottom.* The cloud may temporarily cool Earth's climate and contribute to the destruction of the ozone layer.

global climate changes should notice it, according to atmospheric scientists. The cooling effects were expected to peak in autumn 1992 and return to normal two or three years later as the dust cloud and acid droplets gradually settle out of Earth's lower stratosphere.

Scientists were also greatly concerned that the contents of Mount Pinatubo's volcanic cloud might further deplete Earth's protective ozone layer. Ozone is a molecule made up of three oxygen atoms. In the stratosphere, ozone protects people and other organisms by absorbing most of the sun's damaging ultraviolet radiation before it reaches Earth's surface. Overexposure to ultraviolet radiation can weaken the immune system and increase the risk of developing skin cancer in human beings. The radiation can also damage crops.

Recent history provides an example of how volcanic debris may destroy ozone. In 1982, Mexico's El Chichón volcano erupted and sent a comparatively small amount of material into the lower stratosphere. Nevertheless, this appeared to have resulted in a 15 to 20 per cent reduction in ozone concentration in the regions where the volcanic dust was thickest.

The major threats to ozone from the volcano are ash particles, sulfuric acid droplets, and chlorine gas. In December 1991 and January 1992, aircraft observations above the Arctic suggested that these particles were causing chemical reactions that were further damaging the ozone layer.

According to Richard Turco, an atmospheric scientist at the University of California at Los Angeles, the gases shot aloft by Mount Pinatubo formed a band of sulfuric acid droplets that were causing the greatest disruption of the stratosphere observed during the 1900's. Sulfuric acid droplets provide surfaces on which chemical reactions occur. These reactions break down molecules of industrial chemicals called chlorinated fluorocarbons (CFC's) in the stratosphere. The CFC's then release chlorine, which reacts quickly with oxygen to form chlorine monoxide. In the presence of sunlight, this compound begins other reactions that destroy ozone.

In the stratosphere, the sulfuric acid droplets also react with nitrogen oxide, which normally protects ozone by combining with chlorine atoms to prevent them from forming chlorine monoxide. Data gathered by a NASA research plane showed that sulfuric acid droplets had combined with more than three-quarters of the nitrogen oxide in the cloud, preventing it from combining with chlorine.

By about 1994 or 1995, Mount Pinatubo's cloud of ash and acid droplets will gradually thin as the debris either mixes with the lower atmosphere, washes out in rain, or evaporates by the action of sunlight and stratospheric chemical reactions. As this occurs, first the enhanced sunsets, and then both the climate cooling and the increased ozone destruction, will fade.　　　　[John T. Snow]

equipped with scientific instruments in the Pacific near the equator. Scientists entered data from these instruments into computer climate models at the Lamont-Doherty Geological Observatory and at other locations to help predict whether El Niño would occur. With the help of these instruments and computers, meteorologists were able to say early in 1991 that El Niño would be likely to occur in autumn 1991.

Effects of oil fires. Some scientists had predicted that the smoke plumes from the 650 oil wells set on fire during the Persian Gulf War in early 1991 would cause a disastrous cooling of Earth's climate by rising into the atmosphere and blocking sunlight. But the threatening black plumes produced only regional cooling and other effects. Fire fighters capped the last burning well in mid-November 1991.

According to Lawrence Radke, an atmospheric scientist at the National Center for Atmospheric Research in Boulder, Colo., and a leader of the scientific effort to investigate the plumes, three factors limited the impact of the plumes. First, the fires burned hotter and more efficiently than expected, resulting in fewer airborne particles from incomplete combustion. Greater combustion efficiency resulted in the production of approximately 50 times less soot than scientists had predicted.

Soot particles from the fires were also much smaller than expected and contained compounds called sulfates. The particles were just the right size to be captured by clouds, and because most sulfates dissolve in water, water droplets in clouds easily absorbed the soot particles. Once incorporated into the clouds, the particles could not rise to higher levels of the atmosphere and tended to fall to Earth in rain before drifting too far from the area of the fires.

Perhaps most importantly, the burning oil also contained large quantities of naturally occurring salt, far more than scientists expected. As a result, the smoke plumes were much lighter in color than expected. Some burning wells even appeared to produce white smoke. The lighter-colored plumes stayed lower in the atmosphere than they would have had they been darker. Darker plumes tend to absorb more solar energy than lighter-colored ones. As they absorb en-

ergy, the darker plumes heat up, become lighter, and rise higher into the atmosphere.

The plume from Kuwait did not rise much above 5 kilometers (3 miles). As a result, the soot stayed out of the *stratosphere* (upper atmosphere), where high-speed winds would have taken it around the globe.

Ozone studies. Beginning in September 1991, the U.S. National Aeronautics and Space Administration (NASA) intensified studies on the problem of increasing ozone loss in Earth's stratosphere. In September, NASA launched its Upper Atmosphere Research Satellite (UARS), which began measuring stratospheric ozone levels. NASA also set up a special program to monitor ozone levels above the Arctic. Called the Airborne Arctic Stratospheric Expedition II, this program used instruments mounted in research aircraft to measure concentrations of ozone, ozone-destroying chemicals, and ozone-protecting chemicals from late October 1991 through April 1992.

Ozone is a gas molecule composed of three oxygen atoms. The ozone layer in the stratosphere protects people and other organisms by absorbing most of the sun's dangerous ultraviolet radiation. Chemicals called chlorofluorocarbons (CFC's) destroy ozone in the stratosphere. These chemicals are widely used in industry and in refrigeration equipment, and their concentration in the stratosphere is increasing.

When CFC's break down, they release chlorine atoms, which begin a series of chemical reactions that destroy ozone. The main ozone-destroying product of these chemical reactions is the molecule chlorine monoxide.

In December 1991, UARS recorded exceptionally high levels of chlorine monoxide—around 1 part per billion—over large areas north of 50 degrees latitude, a line just north of the United States-Canada border. (One part per billion equals one molecule in 0.3 cubic meter [10.6 cubic feet] of air.) These chlorine monoxide levels were comparable to those observed since the mid-1980's during the annual thinning in the ozone layer above Antarctica.

By February 1992, chlorine monoxide levels in the Arctic air had reached 1.5 parts per billion, the highest levels ever recorded over the Arctic or the Antarctic. This finding raised the possibility of serious ozone depletion over populated areas in the northern portions of Europe and Asia. Atmospheric chemist James Anderson of Harvard University in Cambridge, Mass., the project scientist for the Airborne Arctic Stratospheric Expedition II, suggested that if such high chlorine monoxide levels continued, total ozone losses of 30 to 40 per cent of normal could be expected.

Such losses did not occur in 1992, presumably because of the circulation pattern of winds in the stratosphere. High winter levels of chlorine monoxide must last into early spring for ozone damage to occur. Whether these levels last depends in turn upon how long a high-speed wind called the circumpolar vortex lasts above the Arctic each winter. During winter, the circumpolar vortex circles the polar regions. The vortex helps trap large concentrations of chlorine monoxide in the area.

Chemical reactions that break down CFC's are most efficient in the very cold stratospheric air of midwinter and late winter, so concentrations of chlorine monoxide increase rapidly then. Chlorine monoxide destroys ozone only in the presence of sunlight, however, so no ozone destruction takes place above the poles during the sunless winter. In late winter or early spring, when the sun begins to shine again on the polar regions, chemical destruction of ozone may begin.

In the Antarctic, the circumpolar vortex is very strong and lasts into spring—resulting in large concentrations of chlorine monoxide, which cause the Antarctic ozone hole. In the Arctic, however, the circling vortex is usually relatively weak, and air from lower latitudes mixes through it. This mixing has helped reduce concentrations of chlorine monoxide and helped break up the vortex before springtime sunlight appears. But scientists warn that if the Arctic circumpolar vortex lasts longer than usual, it may cause an Arctic ozone hole.   [John T. Snow]

In the Science Studies section, see GLOBAL CHANGE. In WORLD BOOK, see METEOROLOGY; OZONE.

Neuroscience

A study suggesting that there are physical differences between the brains of homosexual men and those of heterosexual men was reported in August 1991 by neuroscientist Simon LeVay of the Salk Institute for Biological Studies in La Jolla, Calif. LeVay concluded that these neurological differences might account at least in part for the different sexual orientations of male homosexuals and heterosexuals.

LeVay examined the brains of 41 adults who had died of various causes. They included 19 homosexual men, 16 heterosexual men, and 6 heterosexual women.

LeVay found that a tiny structure in the *hypothalamus* (a region of the brain believed to be involved in sexual behavior) was significantly smaller in the homosexual males' brains than in the brains of male heterosexuals. The size of the structure appeared to be the same in the homosexual men and the heterosexual women.

These findings suggest that heterosexual and homosexual orientations in males have some biological basis. Experts say that further studies are needed to determine the degree to which sexual behavior and preference may be biologically determined.

Regenerating brain cells. The possibility that adult brain tissue can be stimulated to grow new cells was reported in March 1992 by neuroscientists Samuel Weiss and Brent Reynolds of the University of Calgary in Canada. Neuroscientists have previously assumed that the brain tissue of mammals cannot repair itself or regrow cells lost to damage or disease. Experts thought that new brain cells in mammals grow only until shortly after birth, and that lost cells cannot be replaced. This new work suggests that even mature mammalian brains can be repaired.

Working with mouse brains, the researchers removed cells from a part of the brain called the corpus striatum and placed them in a shallow laboratory dish. They added a protein called epidermal growth factor to keep the cells alive. Most of the cells died quickly. But a small number of them survived and multiplied.

After two to three weeks, the cells began to develop and separate into the two types of cells that make up the brain—the *neurons*, which receive, store, and transmit information; and the *glia*, which make up the brain's connective and supportive tissue. The scientists reported that the epidermal growth factor had somehow prompted these cells not merely to grow and multiply, but also to differentiate into the two types of brain cells.

Neuroscientists say that if these preliminary findings are confirmed in further experiments, a fundamental part of our understanding of how the brain operates will be changed. Such findings may also provide a basis for repairing and replacing cells lost to brain injury and disease.

Seeing memory. A way to view the brain activity involved in recalling a memory was presented in November 1991 by neuroscientists Larry R. Squire of the University of California at San Diego and Marcus Raichle of the Washington University School of Medicine in St. Louis, Mo. In their study, Squire and

Raichle used positron emission tomography (PET). This imaging technique allows neuroscientists to observe blood flow, and hence chemical activity, in the brain.

First, scientists inject a harmless radioactive solution into the bloodstream. The concentration of the solution in the brain is visible on images called PET scans. Active regions of the brain take up more of the radioactive solution than do inactive regions and appear as lighter or more intensely colored areas on the image.

In one of several series of experiments, researchers used PET scanning to monitor the brain activity of 18 volunteers. The scientists first showed the volunteers 15 common words. Then, while activity in the brain was being monitored, the volunteers were shown the first three letters of what could be a variety of words.

The volunteers were asked to name words that began with the three-letter groups they were shown. Sometimes the researchers asked the volunteers to name words that they remembered from

Mature brain cells multiply
A brain cell from an adult mouse, *below left,* divides into a clump of cells over a period of several days, *below center* and *right,* in an experiment providing unexpected evidence that some brain cells in mature mammals have the capacity to multiply. In the experiment—which was conducted at the University of Calgary in Canada and reported in March 1992—researchers encouraged the cells to grow by treating them with a protein called epidermal growth factor.

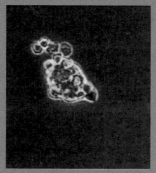 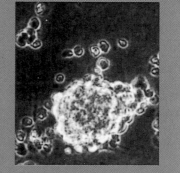

Image of a memory

A positron emission tomography (PET) scan of a human brain, *right,* reveals the brain activity of a person in the act of remembering a word. Neuroscientists in November 1991 reported using the imaging technique to monitor blood flow—and thus brain activity—in the brains of volunteers asked to perform recall tasks. The researchers found unusual levels of activity in three distinct regions of the brain, *below*, during these tasks.

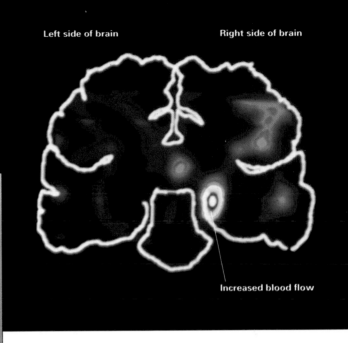

Left side of brain   Right side of brain

Increased blood flow

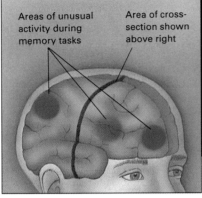

Areas of unusual activity during memory tasks

Area of cross-section shown above right

the list seen earlier. At other times, the volunteers were instructed to simply name the first words that came to mind.

The PET scans showed increased blood flow to different parts of the brain, depending on whether the volunteers were consciously trying to recall the list or just naming the first word that came to mind. The *hippocampus*, a seahorse-shaped structure in the middle of the brain, was active when a volunteer tried to remember the list of words. When the volunteers were not trying to remember the list, blood flow increased in another part of the brain called the visual cortex, which plays an important role in visual perception. This indicates that such recollections had more to do with the perception of the shapes of the letters than with conscious memory. Finally, the scientists reported that in some experiments, a part of the brain called the prefrontal cortex was active during the memory tasks.

Retinal implants. Transplants of retina cells might restore vision to the visually impaired or the blind, according to animal experiments by neuroscientist

Manuel del Cerro and his colleagues at the University of Rochester Medical School in New York. The researchers first reported their work in September 1991.

The retina is a light-sensitive layer of nervous-system cells at the back of the eyeball. It receives light signals and transmits them to the back of the brain to produce vision. In previous experiments, scientists had discovered that when cells from the retinas of *fetal* (unborn) rats were grafted onto the retinas of blind rats, the new cells developed and formed working contacts in the blind rats' visual system.

In the new experiments, del Cerro and his colleagues transplanted fetal retinal cells into the damaged retinas of blind rats. In one experiment, nine rats received the new cells, and nine others did not.

The vision of the animals in both groups was tested by measuring their responses to loud noises that followed flashes of light. By measuring how high the mice jumped after hearing the noise, the scientists were able to determine whether the mice had seen the light and thus had anticipated the noise.

The rats that had not received the new cells continued to be startled by the noise whenever it was repeated. The rats that had received the transplants appeared less startled by the noise.

Del Cerro and his colleagues concluded that the rats that received the transplants were able to detect the light flash. Some amount of the animals' vision, they decided, had been restored. Experts said that these first steps in exploring the usefulness of retina transplants might eventually lead to techniques to help people suffering from vision disorders and blindness.

Alzheimer's disease. New information on a substance produced in the brain and involved in Alzheimer's disease was reported in February 1992 by a team led by neurologist Steven Younkin of Case Western Reserve University in Cleveland. Hundreds of thousands of Americans suffer from Alzheimer's disease, which mainly strikes older people. It causes memory loss, dementia, and eventually death. There is no known cause or cure.

Younkin's research centered on *beta amyloid*, a protein that forms the center core of *plaques* (deposits) that are found in the brains of people with Alzheimer's disease. The researchers compared cells removed from the brains of people who had died of Alzheimer's disease with those of people who had died of other causes.

The scientists found *amyloid precursor protein*, a biochemical that breaks down into beta amyloid, in the normal brains as well as in those of the Alzheimer's patients. Equally surprising, the scientists found beta amyloid itself in the brains of people with and without Alzheimer's disease. However, far larger quantities of beta amyloid had accumulated in the brains of the people with Alzheimer's disease.

The researchers theorized that the large quantities of beta amyloid in the brains of Alzheimer's patients are linked to the presence of certain lysosomes in cells. Lysosomes are tiny structures that contain *enzymes*, proteins that break down biochemicals.

Younkin and his colleagues found that people with Alzheimer's disease have lysosomes containing enzymes that break down amyloid precursor protein into beta amyloid. The presence of these lysosomes—perhaps as a result of a genetic mutation—may be the source of the large quantities of beta amyloid that are found in Alzheimer's disease brain plaques.

According to the researchers, gaining a better understanding of the role of these lysosomes in Alzheimer's disease may lead to drugs that can block the creation of beta amyloid. Such drugs could conceivably prevent or slow the progression of the disease.

Dyslexia. New findings that relate the basis of dyslexia to a visual system defect and that may suggest new ways of treating dyslexia were reported in September 1991. Dyslexia is a broadly defined reading disorder that may cause severe learning disabilities. People with dyslexia have normal intelligence but are deficient in reading skills. Neuroscientists at Harvard Medical School and Beth Israel Hospital in Boston were the authors of the new study.

In one part of the study, the scientists tested five adults with dyslexia and seven nondyslexic adults for their responses to changes in the appearance of a computer-generated image of a checkerboard. The dark and light squares in the checkerboard were reversed at different speeds and with different levels of contrast.

The researchers found that when the squares were changed at low speeds and with high levels of contrast, the subjects who had dyslexia responded just as the nondyslexics did, recognizing each succeeding image distinctly. But when the images changed quickly and the contrast between the squares was low, the adults with dyslexia failed to notice the changes.

In another part of the study, the researchers examined the brains of 10 deceased people. Five had suffered dyslexia, and five had not. The researchers found a significant difference between the two groups in an area of the brain that processes visual information presented quickly. Both parts of the study thus suggested that the brains of people with dyslexia have some abnormality in the ability to rapidly process visual information.　　　　[George Adelman]

See also MEDICAL RESEARCH; PSYCHOLOGY. In WORLD BOOK, see BRAIN.

In 1991, for the first time since 1948, no Americans were among the Nobel Prize winners in the sciences. The Nobel Prize in chemistry in October 1991 was awarded to a Swiss scientist, the Nobel Prize in physics went to a French scientist, and the prize in physiology or medicine was shared by two German scientists. For the first time ever, the value of a Nobel Prize rose to $1 million.

The chemistry prize was awarded to physical chemist Richard R. Ernst of the Federal Institute of Technology in Zurich, Switzerland, for improving nuclear magnetic resonance (NMR) spectroscopy. The Royal Swedish Academy of Sciences in Stockholm, Sweden, cited Ernst for making several important contributions over the previous 25 years to NMR spectroscopy, which the academy described as "perhaps the most important instrumental measuring technique within chemistry."

The technique enables scientists to determine the identity and structure of chemical compounds. But when NMR was first developed in the mid-1940's, chemists were limited by the number of compounds they could study using this technique.

In the 1960's and 1970's, Ernst introduced several refinements that improved the accuracy of NMR. These refinements, the academy pointed out, made it possible to study complex molécules consisting of thousands of atoms, rather than molecules having only hundreds of atoms. Ernst's development of the technique also paved the way for *magnetic resonance imaging,* a diagnostic tool that is now used widely in medicine. This tool enables physicians to image soft tissues within the human body, which cannot be imaged using X rays.

The physics prize went to physicist Pierre-Gilles de Gennes of the Collège de France in Paris. The Royal Swedish Academy called de Gennes "the Isaac Newton of our time" because of his insight in applying generalized mathematical formulas to many different phenomena. "Some of the systems de Gennes has treated have been so complicated that few physicists had earlier thought it possible to incorporate them at all in a

Chemist Richard R. Ernst of the Federal Institute of Technology in Zurich, Switzerland, won the Nobel Prize in chemistry in October 1991 for his contributions to improving nuclear magnetic resonance spectroscopy, a technique for identifying chemical compounds.

French physicist Pierre-Gilles de Gennes of the Collège de France in Paris, named the winner of the Nobel Prize in physics in October 1991, works in the laboratory where he specialized in the study of liquid crystals.

Nobel Prizes Continued

general physical description," the academy noted.

De Gennes has specialized in the study of liquid crystals, complex substances in which molecules can be induced to undergo changes from ordered to disordered states. His findings have had practical applications in the use of liquid crystals to display information on laptop computer screens and to light up numbers on digital watches and calculators. But more importantly, de Gennes showed that the mathematical relationships that govern the changes from ordered to disordered states in liquid crystals could also be applied to similar changes in other substances. These included magnetic materials, *superconductors* (materials that conduct electricity with little or no resistance at extremely low temperatures), and *polymers* (long chainlike molecules).

The physiology or medicine prize was awarded to Erwin Neher of the Max Planck Institute for Biophysical Chemistry in Göttingen and Bert Sakmann of the Max Planck Institute for Medical Research in Heidelberg, both in Germany.

In announcing the award, the Nobel Assembly of the Karolinska Institute in Stockholm noted that "Neher and Sakmann's contributions have meant a revolution for the field of cell biology" and "for the understanding of different disease mechanisms."

Neher and Sakmann demonstrated in great detail the way in which charged atoms known as ions flow in and out of cells. The two scientists discovered protein molecules called ion channels in cell membranes. The ion channels control the passage of ions. When ions pass through these channels, they produce an electric current that scientists can measure using a technique developed by Neher and Sakmann known as patch clamping.

The patch clamp technique, in turn, enabled researchers to study how ion channels regulate a cell's internal levels of ions, such as sodium and potassium ions. It also made it possible to investigate defects in ion channels, which underlie such diseases as cystic fibrosis and diabetes. [Rod Such]

In WORLD BOOK, see NOBEL PRIZES.

The American Cancer Society in March 1992 signaled a change in its approach to fighting cancer when it announced that it will support more research studying the role of diet in cancer prevention. This shift reflected the findings of recent studies showing that some foods or nutrients seem to play a protective role against cancer, while others appear to promote the disease.

Diet and colon cancer. A high-fat, low-fiber diet may encourage the formation of precancerous growths in the colon. Epidemiologist Edward Giovannucci and his colleagues at the Harvard School of Public Health in Boston reported this finding in January 1992.

In the two-year study, the Harvard researchers studied the incidence of *adenomas,* small, harmless growths that can turn into *polyps* (tumorlike masses of tissue that can become cancerous) in 7,284 male health professionals. The men had completed a questionnaire in 1986 concerning their dietary habits. During the next two years, they received colon exams to check for possible adenomas or cancers.

The men who consumed diets high in fat and low in fiber were 3.7 times more likely to develop adenomas than those who ate a low-fat, high-fiber diet. Men who ate more red meat than chicken and fish also had greater risks of developing adenomas.

The Harvard researchers had found similar results in previous studies of fiber and fat intake among women. The findings also supported research by other scientists that related high fat intake and low fiber consumption with an increased risk for colon cancer, which claims the lives of 58,000 Americans each year.

Folate and cervical cancer. Inadequate amounts of the nutrient folate, or folic acid, in the body may increase a woman's risk of cervical cancer, according to a study published in January 1992. Researchers led by nutritionist Charles E. Butterworth at the University of Alabama in Birmingham discovered that folate deficiencies in the blood increased the incidence of a precancerous condition known as *cervical dysplasia* (abnormal cell growth in the *cervix,* the opening to the uterus) in women who were already at risk for the disease. Cervical cancer is the ninth leading cause

of cancer deaths in the United States.

Low folate levels seem to magnify the harmful effects of such risk factors as smoking, having multiple sexual partners, and infection with a sexually transmitted virus called human papilloma virus (HPV).

In the study, the researchers compared folate levels in 294 women who had cervical dysplasia with 170 women who did not. Among both groups, the level of folate in the blood did not by itself seem to increase the risk of cervical dysplasia. But women who had both low folate levels and other risk factors were up to five times more likely to have cervical dysplasia than were women with normal folate levels.

The researchers hypothesized that folate may protect cells from cancer-causing agents by making the cells' genetic material less vulnerable to HPV infection. Folate is a vitamin found in such foods as leafy, green vegetables and some meats.

Children's cholesterol levels. Total dietary fat intake for children over age 2 should not exceed 30 per cent of the total daily calories consumed, and saturated fats should make up no more than 10 per cent of those calories. Thus concluded the Expert Panel on Blood Cholesterol Levels in Children and Adolescents in its September 1991 report. The panel, which was sponsored by the United States National Institutes of Health, also recommended that children consume no more than 300 milligrams of dietary cholesterol per day. These guidelines paralleled those that a similar panel recommended for adults in 1990.

The group reached its conclusions after reviewing numerous studies indicating that high blood-cholesterol levels in children play a role in the development of coronary artery disease later in life. Coronary artery disease—the leading cause of death among Americans—occurs when cholesterol builds up on the inner walls of the arteries and restricts the flow of blood to the heart. Research has found that this build-up can start in childhood. Saturated fats, which are found mainly in animal products, seem to contribute to this process.

The panel called on schools and the food industry to provide children with appetizing alternatives to high-fat and high-cholesterol foods. It also suggested

Food Irradiation: Facts and Myths

The first commercial plant in the United States for preserving food through irradiation opened in January 1992. Its first product was 3,400 pints of strawberries. But not everyone hailed this as a breakthrough in food technology. As the fruit went to market, picketers lined up to protest irradiation as a process fraught with risk to human health. Most scientists rebutted the charges, declaring irradiation not only safe but also a major step toward preventing food-borne illnesses.

The irradiation process destroys bacteria, fungi, insects, larvae, and other organisms that can spoil food and cause illness in human beings. Irradiation may be used with fruits and vegetables, meat, poultry, and other foods. Scientists say that consumers' concerns about the safety of irradiation arise from misperceptions about the process.

The food irradiation process is a simple one. The new U.S. plant, Vindicator of Florida Incorporated in Mulberry, Fla., uses a material called cobalt 60 to irradiate food. Cobalt 60 is a radioactive *isotope* (form) of the metallic element cobalt. Cobalt 60, which gives off radiation in the form of gamma rays, is also used for radiation therapy for cancer patients and for sterilizing hospital equipment. The radioactive isotope is created by bombarding cobalt with subatomic particles in a nuclear reactor. However, irradiation plants do not themselves contain nuclear reactors.

In the irradiation plant, food is exposed to thin rods of cobalt 60. The rods give off gamma rays, which disrupt chemical processes in contaminating organisms. The disruption breaks down the cell walls of organisms or destroys their genetic material. The dose, set by the U.S. Food and Drug Administration (FDA), is enough to kill organisms on food, but not enough to produce significant changes in the food itself.

To prevent workers at the plant from being exposed to radiation, the cobalt 60 rods are kept in a processing chamber with concrete walls 1.8 to 2.4 meters (6 to 8 feet) thick. Workers outside the

The food irradiation process

A worker loads strawberries into aluminum carriers, which move along a rail and pass into a thickly walled chamber that contains racks of a radioactive metal called cobalt 60. As the food passes by the cobalt 60 racks, it is exposed to gamma rays, a form of electromagnetic radiation. The gamma rays kill bacteria, insects, fungi, and other organisms that make food spoil and may cause disease if eaten. After food leaves the irradiation chamber, it is ready for marketing. When not in use, the cobalt 60 racks are lowered into an underground storage tank containing water, which absorbs gamma rays.

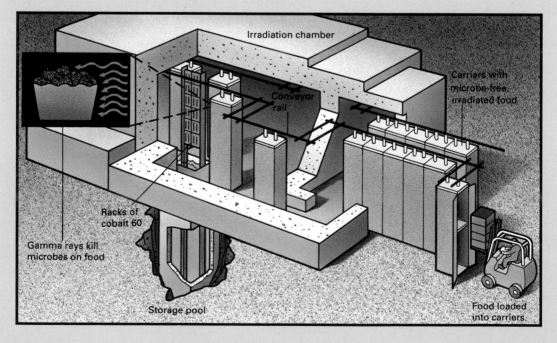

Irradiation chamber

Carriers with microbe-free, irradiated food

Conveyor rail

Racks of cobalt 60

Gamma rays kill microbes on food

Storage pool

Food loaded into carriers

chamber load food to be irradiated into carriers. The carriers move along a mechanical rail into the irradiation chamber and past the cobalt 60 rods. Different types of foods are exposed to the gamma rays for varying lengths of time. When the cobalt 60 is not in use, the rods are lowered into a pool of water, which absorbs the gamma rays.

Although irradiation slightly decreases the nutritive value of foods, the loss is less than that produced by some other methods of food preservation. Canning, for example, results in a much greater loss of nutrients.

Those who object to irradiation say that the process may create substances not found in nonirradiated food. Since the 1960's, researchers have studied irradiated food at microscopic levels to try to find such substances, called unique radiolytic products. After reviewing these studies, the FDA determined that compounds formed during irradiation are similar to substances found in nonirradiated foods and are not dangerous to consume.

In the early 1960's, the FDA first approved irradiation for bacon, wheat, wheat flour, and potatoes. The food industry, however, was not interested in irradiation because chemical pesticides killed insects in grain and prevented sprouting in potatoes. But as the industry became more aware of consumers' perceptions of hazards associated with chemical pesticides, food irradiation began to look more attractive.

In 1983, the FDA allowed irradiation for preserving spices. In 1985 and 1986, the FDA approved irradiation for pork and fresh fruits and vegetables. Pork irradiation can destroy the larvae of a parasite that causes the food poisoning known as trichinosis. In 1990, the FDA endorsed irradiation for poultry, a major cause of the bacterial illness salmonellosis.

Destruction of microorganisms that cause illness is an important goal of irradiation. About 250 million cases of food poisoning—or 1 per person—occur every year in the United States, according to FDA estimates. Food poisoning can cause vomiting, diarrhea, fever, headache—and, occasionally, death.

Because of the apparent safety of food irradiation, and the problems presented by contaminated food, scientific groups—including the American Medical Association, the World Health Organization, and the United Nations Food and Agriculture Association—have voiced nearly universal support for the process. Worldwide, 38 nations have approved irradiation for 355 products.

Like microwave ovens, food irradiation has aroused apprehension and misunderstanding. Yet it has been scrutinized more thoroughly than other methods of food treatment that we have come to regard as safe, and it appears to be a method whose time has come.   [F. J. Francis]

Nutrition Continued

that health professionals, government agencies, and the media take a more active role in educating the public on healthy dietary habits.

Diet and mental development. When young, undernourished, and developmentally stunted children are given extra nutrition and attention, their mental development significantly improves, according to a report published in July 1991. A British study of malnourished children in Jamaica found that developmentally stunted children's mental capacities could become equivalent to those of healthy children after they received proper nutrition and the stimulation of playing with their mothers.

For two years, the researchers studied 129 stunted infants and toddlers who ranged from 9 months to 24 months in age. Thirty-two healthy children served as a basis for comparison. The stunted children were examined to make sure that their poor growth was due to malnutrition rather than to illness or some other disorder. The researchers then assigned the children to one of four groups.

The first group received no intervention at all. The second group received food supplements only. The mothers of the third group received special instruction and encouragement for one hour each week in playing with their children. The fourth group received both nutritional supplements and the weekly play sessions.

At the beginning and the end of the study, the researchers administered tests to measure the children's development in such areas as hand-eye coordination and the ability to recognize shapes and use building blocks. Initially, the stunted children's test scores were lower than those of the well-nourished children. At the end of the two years, the scores of the children who had either received extra food or extra attention were higher than the scores of the children who received no intervention. The group that received both food and play showed the greatest increase in mental development, and they performed almost as well on their tests as did the healthy children.   [Johanna T. Dwyer]

In the Special Reports section, see GETTING THE FAT (AND SUGAR) OUT. In WORLD BOOK, see CANCER; CHOLESTEROL; HEART; NUTRITION.

Dolphins may form alliances to control other dolphins, according to a study reported in October 1991 by biologists Richard C. Connor and Andrew F. Richards, along with psychologist Rachel A. Smolker, all of the University of Michigan at Ann Arbor. The researchers, who observed the behavior of 21 male dolphins for 25 months in Shark Bay, Australia, found that groups of two or three dolphins cooperate to isolate and control the movements of females, a behavior the researchers described as "herding."

Herding begins when males pursue a female. Each member of a dolphin "team" appeared to cooperate in the chase. Instead of swimming directly behind the female, the males often slipped off to either side to limit the female's movements more completely. The pursuing dolphins often executed simultaneous underwater turns or leaps into the air, and engaged in biting or other aggressive behaviors. The researchers theorized that herding may be a strategy for monopolizing females that are not pregnant.

Data compiled between 1985 and 1989 confirm that the male pairs and triplets remained stable for years. Shifting alliances occurred when the males were not herding a female, however.

So far, scientists have observed long-term, stable alliances and alternating hostile and cooperative behavior only in human beings and dolphins. Although scientists have no generally acceptable explanation for this complex social behavior, some have speculated that it may be linked to these animals' large brain size.

Endangered turtles. A team of scientists reported in August 1991 that genetic tests confirm that the endangered Kemp's ridley sea turtle is a distinct species. Genetic tests are used to study genes, which all living things inherit from their parents and which determine physical characteristics. Geneticists Brian W. Bowen and John C. Avise of the University of Georgia in Athens and Anne B. Meylan, a marine biologist at the Florida Marine Research Institute in St. Petersburg, made the finding.

Their discovery is important because

Unusually warm water in the Pacific Ocean (red areas) is visible on an image of *infrared* (heat) radiation released in April 1992. Water temperatures in the area have been rising since about 1982 and are as much as 4 Celsius degrees (7.2 Fahrenheit degrees) higher than surrounding water. Complex climate and weather patterns appear responsible for the hotspot.

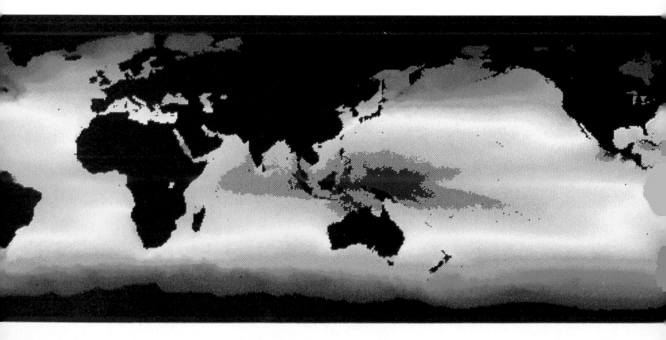

identification by physical appearance alone has often led scientists to confuse Kemp's with other sea turtles, including the loggerhead, the hawksbill, and the olive ridley. The finding will allow scientists to protect Kemp's ridley populations that may be mistaken for other turtle species.

Kemp's ridley turtles nest almost exclusively on a beach in Tamaulipas, Mexico, on the Gulf of Mexico. Since the late 1940's, the number of adult nesting females has plunged from more than 40,000 to about 200.

The scientists took samples of genetic material from six Kemp's ridleys, and compared these with samples drawn from two widely separated populations of olive ridleys—one from the Atlantic Ocean and the other from the Pacific Ocean. The genetic material showed that the Atlantic and Pacific olive ridleys were indistinguishable, but that the Kemp's ridleys were sharply different from both populations of olive ridleys.

Under the terms of the United States Endangered Species Act and similar international regulations, legal protection may only be extended to distinct species, subspecies, or populations. Biologists must thus rely on more precise data than geographical location or physical similarities in determining whether an animal population is in danger of extinction. Genetic testing provides an important tool for obtaining these data.

Deepest hole in the ocean. In November 1991, scientists aboard the ocean drillship *JOIDES Resolution* deepened a hole in the ocean floor to 2 kilometers (1.2 miles). The hole, 320 kilometers (200 miles) west of Ecuador, is the deepest hole ever drilled into the ocean's crust.

The hole is the only location in the world where scientists can observe a section of ocean crust evolve. Scientists bored the hole into the Nazca tectonic plate, which formed some 5.9 million years ago and moves southward at about 3 centimeters (1 inch) a year. The Earth's surface is composed of about 30 such plates, which shift on a layer of extremely hot rock.

Ocean crust usually contains three layers. The deepest level holds the solidified remains of ancient *magma* (molten rock) chambers beneath the mid-ocean ridges. Molten rock in these chambers cools slowly and forms coarse, crystalline rock called *gabbros*. The drilled hole enables scientists to examine the physical and chemical transition from the middle layer to the deepest layer. These studies may help explain how the ocean crust forms.

Although the scientists did not penetrate the deepest level of crust, much of the rock recovered from the hole contained fragments of gabbros. These rocks indicated to geologists that an ancient magma chamber lies beneath the bottom of the hole.

Ancient extinction. A sudden temperature increase in deep waters about 57 million years ago caused a widespread extinction of creatures that live in the ocean depths. Marine geologists James P. Kennett of the University of California at Santa Barbara and Lowell D. Stott of the University of Southern California in Los Angeles reported evidence of the warming in September 1991. Their studies indicated that 35 to 50 per cent of the ocean's deep-sea species disappeared at that time—one of the largest extinctions in the last 90 million years.

The scientists analyzed fossils of plankton and other one-celled organisms in sediment cores recovered from water 2,914 meters (9,560 feet) deep in the Weddell Sea in the Antarctic. To determine the extinction rate, the scientists studied changes in the types and numbers of these tiny fossils over time. To discover what caused the extinction, the researchers analyzed evidence of the deep water's temperature, salt content, and other factors.

The scientists measured the ratios of *isotopes* (forms) of oxygen and carbon in the sediment to determine the difference in deepwater temperature over time in the ancient seas. Colder water produced sediment with heavier isotopes.

The scientists estimated that global temperatures rose suddenly, causing seawater temperatures to climb as much as 6 degrees Celsius (11 degrees Fahrenheit) within 3,000 years. As the difference between the deepwater and surface water temperatures disappeared, warmer water killed the deep-sea organisms.   [Lauriston R. King]

See also GEOLOGY. In WORLD BOOK, see OCEAN.

Astrophysicists in April 1992 announced they had found new evidence for the big bang, the event believed to have given birth to the universe some 10 billion to 20 billion years ago. The evidence was revealed by measurements of microwave radiation throughout the universe taken by the Cosmic Background Explorer satellite. (See PHYSICS [CLOSE-UP].)

Toward controlled nuclear fusion. A major step was taken toward the controlled release of energy from nuclear fusion, the reaction that powers the sun and other stars, in November 1991 by researchers in Abingdon, England. Working on the Joint European Torus (JET) experiment, a team of more than 700 physicists, engineers, and technicians sustained a fusion reaction for two seconds at a peak power level of almost 2 million watts—enough to power a town with a population of 2,000.

It was the first time scientists had produced substantial energy from a controlled fusion reaction, something they have been working toward since the explosion of the first hydrogen bomb in 1952. The fusion reactions of hydrogen bombs are uncontrolled.

Fusion releases energy by joining the *nuclei* (cores) of two atoms. The JET reactor produced energy in a reaction called deuterium-tritium (DT) fusion, which combines nuclei of two *isotopes* (forms) of hydrogen. The nucleus of an ordinary hydrogen atom contains a single proton. A deuterium nucleus, however, contains one neutron and one proton, while a tritium nucleus has two neutrons and one proton.

When deuterium and tritium nuclei fuse, they form a helium nucleus containing two protons and two neutrons. The process releases a neutron and energy.

Water in lakes and oceans could provide an inexpensive and almost inexhaustible source of fuel for fusion. Each molecule of water contains two hydrogen atoms. And about 1 hydrogen atom in every 6,500 on Earth has a deuterium nucleus. Deuterium's abundance makes fusion exciting as a potential source of energy. Tritium can be produced in nuclear reactors.

But fusion reactions are difficult to initiate and control. They require very high temperatures—from tens of millions to hundreds of millions of degrees

Celsius—because only at such temperatures can nuclei get close enough to fuse. The higher the temperature, the faster the nuclei move. Their speed enables the nuclei—each of which carries a positive electrical charge—to overcome the electrical repulsion that keeps them apart.

Matter becomes difficult to handle at such high temperatures. At extremely high temperatures, matter *vaporizes* (turns into a gas), and its atoms are *ionized* (stripped of some or all of their electrons). This creates a state of matter called a plasma. Confining a plasma—which would melt the walls of any container—presents difficulties.

But because a plasma consists of electrically charged atoms and electrons, scientists can manipulate it with magnetic forces. Machines like the JET reactor create a kind of magnetic "bottle" that holds the hot plasma but prevents it from touching the reactor's walls.

This method, called *magnetic confinement*, poses its own problems. One problem arises because a plasma moving in response to magnetic forces generates magnetic fields of its own that can disrupt the ones that are holding it in the bottle. Scientists try to force the plasmas to generate magnetic fields that actually help keep the plasmas bottled up.

Another problem lies in keeping the hydrogen plasma pure. If atoms of heavier elements enter the plasma, they can quickly radiate away its heat, making it hard to sustain the high temperatures needed for fusion.

Since the early 1950's, plasma researchers around the world have built a succession of increasingly larger machines in the quest for magnetic confinement. Since the 1970's, the largest and most successful magnetic confinement machines have been based on the doughnut-shaped tokamak design pioneered by Russian physicists Andrei Sakharov and Igor Y. Tamm.

A 14-nation effort. The JET tokamak, built as a joint effort by 14 European nations, is currently the largest machine of its kind. At its heart is a hollow metal ring about 7.6 meters (25 feet) in diameter. The ring, or doughnut, has an oval cross section about 1.8 meters (6 feet) high and 1.2 meters (4 feet) wide. An electric coil wound around it generates part of the confining magnetic field.

A major step toward nuclear fusion

Researchers at the Joint European Torus (JET) project in England made a breakthough in November 1991, when they produced 1.7 million watts of power from nuclear fusion—the joining of atomic nuclei—inside a reactor. It was the first time scientists had produced substantial energy from controlled fusion, but the experiment required more energy than it yielded.

To produce nuclear fusion, the JET team heated two forms of hydrogen gas inside a doughnut-shaped nuclear reactor to create a type of matter called a *plasma*. Magnets surround the JET reactor chamber, and their magnetic fields push the superhot plasma away from the walls, *right*. A technician makes an adjustment inside the JET reactor, *below*, where plasmas reach temperatures higher than the sun's.

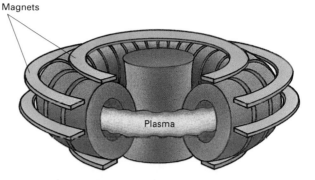

Magnets

Plasma

The rest comes from a current created by the plasma as it flows around the doughnut. The walls of the doughnut have many *ports* (openings) to allow technicians to insert instruments and inject beams of high-speed particles and radio waves that heat the plasma.

Plasma researchers rarely use tritium in their experiments, because this form of hydrogen is highly radioactive and creates health hazards, especially for the technicians who work on the machine. The neutrons released in the DT reaction add to the problem: By absorbing the neutrons, the doughnut's metal walls become radioactive.

For this reason, the JET team, like other plasma scientists, experimented for years with pure deuterium plasmas. These plasmas behave in a similar fashion to DT mixtures but achieve fusion at higher temperatures. Because the deuterium plasma produces little fusion at DT fusion temperatures, researchers could use it to study reactor conditions without having to deal with radiation.

The researchers' strategy has been to learn how to control three key factors that contribute to the fusion reaction: temperature, plasma density, and confinement time. By multiplying numbers representing each of these three factors, researchers obtain a so-called triple product. This number indicates how close they have come to their goal of confining a sufficient amount of plasma at a high enough temperature and for a long enough time for fusion to occur. The higher the triple product, the better the result. The JET researchers hold the current world record for the highest triple product.

The optimum fuel mixture for generating power from DT fusion would contain a bit more than 50 per cent tritium. But for their November run, the JET team used a mixture containing 11 per cent tritium. They did this partly to reduce radioactive contamination of the machine and partly because the walls of the doughnut could not handle the energy produced in such a *burn*, as test runs are called.

The results of the November test were impressive, even so. During the burn, the plasma reached a peak temperature of 200,000,000 °C (360,000,000 °F) and a peak power output of 1.7 million watts. The test did not produce an overall gain in energy, however, because it took 15 million watts of power to heat the plasma.

After two seconds, the JET reaction came to a halt, and scientists are not sure what quenched it. Carbon vapor produced by the heating of carbon tiles that line the doughnut walls might have cooled the plasma. Or instabilities in the confining magnetic field might have disrupted the reaction.

The next goal of the JET team is to reach *scientific break-even*—the magic value of the triple product at which the power generated by fusion equals the power used to heat the plasma. Computer analysis of data taken during the JET burn indicated that the burn would have reached break-even if the machine had confined the plasma for its record time of eight seconds, set during a previous run, and if the plasma had contained 50 per cent tritium. The JET team plans to modify the inside of the doughnut to handle a 50 per cent mixture and hopes to try the burn by 1996.

Scientists who work with the largest tokamak in the United States, the Tokamak Fusion Test Reactor (TFTR) at Princeton, N.J., plan to try a full-scale DT burn sometime in 1993. Since the best triple product values for TFTR fall somewhat below those for JET, it seems unlikely that this test will reach scientific break-even.

But scientific break-even will not end the long quest for fusion power. Scientists first must reach *ignition,* the state in which the plasma generates enough energy to keep itself hot without any additional heating from outside. Ignition requires a triple product nearly 10 times higher than the break-even value. Even then, engineers will still have to solve the vexing problem of designing a machine that can stand up to a flood of neutrons. Long exposure to such intense radiation makes metals brittle and liable to rupture.

Despite JET's moment of triumph, fusion power still remains a long way off. It is unlikely to provide a major share of our energy before the middle of the next century.

A heavy neutrino? An elementary particle that University of Chicago physicist Michael Turner called "the neutrino from hell" continued to haunt particle physics in 1991 and early 1992. Four of

The development of the world's tiniest laser—so small that 10,000 of the microscopic light-amplifying devices could fit on the head of a pin—was reported by physicists at AT&T Bell Laboratories in Murray Hill, N.J., in November 1991. Such devices may someday find a use in computers or telecommunications equipment that would use light rather than electrons to process data.

five new experiments completed during 1991 reported evidence that about 1 per cent of the electron neutrinos released in a common form of radioactivity called beta decay have a mass too great to be consistent with current theories.

Neutrinos play a crucial role in the nuclear reactions that power the sun and other stars. But they interact so feebly with matter that they can fly through Earth with only a small chance of being absorbed.

The electron neutrino resembles an electron but carries no electric charge. It is one of three varieties of neutrino, and none of them had been shown to have any mass prior to the recent experiments. These experiments indicated that some electron neutrinos had a mass of 17,000 electronvolts (17 keV), about 30 times less than that of an electron. (One electronvolt is the amount of energy that an electron gains when it moves across an electric potential of one volt.) Although physicists have no objection to a neutrino with a slight mass, 17 keV seems far too heavy.

The possible existence of this "un-

wanted" particle has been debated since 1985, when physicist John Simpson of the University of Guelph in Canada reported an experiment that indicated its presence. In the years since, several attempts to confirm his result failed. One of the 1991 experiments supporting Simpson's conclusion was the work of his own team. The others were performed at Britain's Oxford University, the University of California at Berkeley, and the Rudjer Boscovic Institute in Zagreb, Croatia. The fifth experiment, performed at the California Institute of Technology (Caltech) in Pasadena, failed to see the effect.

In beta decay, a neutron is transformed into a proton by emitting an electron and a neutrino. The electron and the neutrino share the energy released in beta decay. But only the electron can be easily observed and its energy measured. What Simpson observed was that about 1 per cent of the electrons emitted had an energy level about 17 keV below the expected level. It appeared as if this fraction of the electrons had to give up 17 keV of their energy to

A Glimmer of Creation

Astrophysicists have long sought a "missing piece" in their picture of the universe's violent birth, the explosion of matter and energy called the big bang that occurred an estimated 15 billion years ago. The missing piece was evidence of how stars and galaxies formed out of the seemingly uniform distribution of matter created by the big bang. In 1992, that piece seemed to have been found.

In April, a team of United States scientists analyzing data from the Cosmic Background Explorer (COBE) satellite reported finding a "lumpy" residue from the big bang. Astrophysicist George Smoot of the University of California at Berkeley, who headed the project, said the COBE data show that when the universe was still very young—about 300,000 years old—it already contained tiny irregularities in density that became the stars, galaxies, and other structures that we see today.

This finding, called one of the most significant discoveries in astronomy in this century, was the culmination of years of study of the *cosmic background radiation*. This radiation is a faint "glow" left over from the incredible energy of the big bang. Over billions of years, as the universe expanded, the wavelengths of the energy were stretched out, so that what began as visible light we see today as the longer wavelengths of radio signals. But despite this shift in wavelength and the passage of so much time, these waves can tell us what the early universe was like.

The existence of the cosmic background radiation was predicted in 1948 by U.S. physicist George Gamow. In 1965, physicists Arno Penzias and Robert Wilson at Bell Telephone Laboratories became the first investigators to detect the

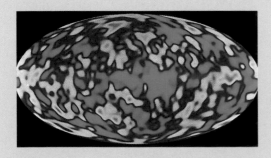

Regions in the early universe that may have become clumps of matter from which stars and galaxies evolved appear as blue areas in this image based on data from the COBE satellite.

weak signals. They did so by accident, having been unaware of Gamow's theoretical work.

The Bell researchers' discovery gave a major boost to the big bang theory, but it also raised a difficult question. The problem was that the background radiation seemed to be exactly equal throughout space. Stars and galaxies form as a result of gravity, which draws matter together by mutual attraction. But how could this process have gotten started in the early universe if the density of matter and energy created by the big bang was everywhere the same? In a completely uniform universe, gravity would have pulled equally in all directions, and no large clumps of matter could have formed.

In 1989, the National Aeronautics and Space Administration (NASA) launched COBE to enable astronomers to make extremely exact observations of the cosmic background radiation. In April 1992, Smoot reported that the COBE data showed that the background radiation was not uniform after all. The energy difference detected by the satellite between the areas of higher density and other parts of space was very small, registering as a temperature difference of just a few millionths of a degree. Without that tiny irregularity, however, our familiar universe of galaxies, stars, and planets could never have come to be.

The COBE discovery not only provided the very first evidence of the "lumpiness" that led to the formation of the objects we see today, but also began to cast light on two other mysteries—the nature of the matter in the universe and the origin of the variations in density.

The total amount of matter in the universe is not known. Scientists do know that in addition to the matter we can see—stars and clouds of dust or gas—the universe contains invisible *dark matter*. Many cosmologists believe that dark matter is a new form of matter left over from the earliest moments of the universe, and that there is enough of it for the force of gravity to eventually reverse the expansion of the universe and bring everything together again in a final "big crunch."

Both the amount and the composition of the dark matter are important to understanding how the objects in the universe formed from the lumpiness that COBE detected. The nature and origin of the lumpiness itself is equally important. Some cosmologists believe that it arose in the earliest moments of the universe, during an exceedingly rapid period of expansion called *inflation*. The ideas that a new form of matter makes up the bulk of the universe and that lumpiness arose during inflation are together known as the *cold dark matter theory*. The COBE measurements were consistent with the predictions of this theory and thus give astrophysicists a sharper understanding of the universe.   [Robert H. March]

form the mass of the heavy neutrino.

Like other experiments that have failed to see the effect, the Caltech experiment measured the electron energy with a device called a magnetic spectrometer. All the confirming experiments used electronic detection devices. Thus, the possibility remains that the disagreement results from the instruments: Either the electronic devices occasionally miss some of the electron energy or the spectrometers are insufficiently precise to observe the effect.

The discovery of a neutrino with some mass—though far less than 17 keV—would solve some outstanding questions in physics. A neutrino several thousand times lighter, for example, would be an ideal candidate for *dark matter*—the halo of invisible mass that seems to surround galaxies. Scientists expect that, for every atom of visible matter, the universe contains billions of neutrinos left over from the big bang. And so, even if each neutrino had a small mass, neutrinos would be the dominant form of mass in the universe. A small percentage of 17-keV neutrinos, however, would yield far more mass than expected. If this heavy neutrino exists, it must be unstable and break down into something else.

A neutrino a million times lighter than 17 keV might help explain another mystery: why detectors on Earth see fewer electron neutrinos than expected coming from the sun. The most likely explanation is that the "missing" solar neutrinos change into other types of neutrinos on their way out of the sun— neutrinos that today's detectors cannot pick up. If neutrinos had a tiny mass, then interactions inside the sun could convert electron neutrinos to other neutrino types.

A rare decay. Studies of the rarest form of radioactivity, double beta decay, revealed possible indirect evidence for the existence of neutrino mass in December 1991. In double beta decay, two neutrons in a nucleus are simultaneously transformed into protons by emitting two electrons and two neutrinos.

For example, the uranium isotope known as U-238 usually decays into thorium by emitting an alpha particle—two protons and two neutrons. But, rarely, U-238 transforms into the plutonium isotope Pu-238 through a double beta decay.

Physicists Anthony Turkevich and Thanasis Economou of the University of Chicago, working with George Cowan of the Los Alamos National Laboratory in New Mexico, found that double beta decay occurs about once each year in one gram (0.04 ounce) of U-238. As rarely as the double beta decay of uranium occurs, it happens about 100 times more frequently than had been predicted by theory—if the neutrinos emitted in the reaction are assumed to have zero mass. But if the neutrinos have a mass of 14 electronvolts, more than a thousand times less than a 17-keV neutrino, the theory would predict the rate that the physicists observed.

A decay rate this slow makes direct observation of double beta decay nearly impossible. The 1991 measurement rested instead on a lucky find. The experimenters came across 8,470 grams (299 ounces) of a pure uranium salt, uranyl nitrate, that had been sealed in a container in 1956 and put away. They computed the decay rate by detecting the radioactivity of the plutonium in the salt.

The age of the sample was crucial. After 1956, small quantities of Pu-238 entered the atmosphere in fallout from nuclear tests. Any sample of uranium after 1956 would contain minuscule amounts of Pu-238 from nuclear fallout.

The experimenters insisted, however, that their work should not be taken as a measurement of neutrino mass. Theoretical estimates of the rates for double beta decays are notoriously unreliable, because the rates are sensitive to fine details of the motions of the neutrons inside the nucleus. Studies of double beta decays of other isotopes have set upper limits of a few electronvolts on the neutrino mass.

A more accurate measurement of neutrino mass may come from an older and much larger sample of uranium in Vienna, Austria. This sample was seized at the end of World War II (1939-1945) from an unsuccessful German project to develop an atomic bomb. The experimenters could be certain that all Pu-238 in the sample came from double beta decay, because it was sealed before the very first nuclear test took place in July 1945.   [Robert H. March]

In the Special Reports section, see SEEKING THE ULTIMATE COLD. In WORLD BOOK, see PHYSICS.

Genes can influence whether a man becomes heterosexual or homosexual, according to a December 1991 report. The study by psychologist J. Michael Bailey of Northwestern University in Evanston, Ill., and psychiatrist Richard C. Pillard of Boston University School of Medicine raised controversy while not identifying specific genes involved in homosexuality.

Bailey and Pillard recruited and interviewed 161 gay or bisexual men. Each man had an identical twin brother, a fraternal twin brother, or an adopted brother. Identical twins have the same genetic material, while fraternal twins have some but not all genes in common. Unrelated adoptive siblings would have no more genetic similarities than any other unrelated pair.

The researchers questioned the men's brothers to determine their sexual orientation. The interviewers found that in 50 per cent of the identical twins, both brothers were homosexual, compared with 24 per cent of the fraternal twins and 19 per cent of unrelated brothers.

The researchers concluded that genes may equal or outweigh environmental influences on the development of male homosexuality and heterosexuality. Critics of the study charged that a larger sample of twins or different interview questions about sexuality might have produced different results.

Dyslexia reinterpreted. A January 1992 report on the reading disorder known as dyslexia challenged two widespread assumptions: that a clear distinction exists between normal reading abilities and dyslexia, and that dyslexic children cannot shed their reading problems. Pediatrician Sally E. Shaywitz of Yale University School of Medicine in New Haven, Conn., and her colleagues found that dyslexia covers a range of reading problems from mild to severe and often disappears as children progress through elementary school.

While the definition of dyslexia remains controversial, a common description holds that dyslexic children exhibit normal intelligence but have difficulty translating strings of letters into words. For example, a dyslexic person might read the word *saw* as the word *was*.

The researchers studied data compiled from the Connecticut Longitudinal Study, whose subjects consisted of 414 randomly selected Connecticut children who had entered kindergarten in 1983. Intelligence and achievement tests had been administered to the children at various intervals. The researchers compared the scores from these tests to determine if the children had achieved reading scores that had been predicted on the basis of their intelligence scores. The scientists diagnosed as dyslexic only those children who showed reading scores far below the level predicted by their intelligence.

These children displayed a range of reading problems that gradually approached normal reading skills, Shaywitz said. This showed that dyslexia was not an "all-or-nothing" characteristic, but a phenomenon that could be measured in degrees and was part of a normal continuum of reading skills. Moreover, the childrens' reading ability could change markedly over time. For example, of first-graders diagnosed with dyslexia, only 1 in 6 retained that label in the sixth grade.

Children of divorce. Parental conflict prior to divorce—rather than divorce itself—accounts for many of the emotional and academic problems that children of divorced parents typically experience, according to a June 1991 report. A research team led by sociologist Andrew Cherlin at Johns Hopkins University in Baltimore took a new look at data from surveys of families conducted in Great Britain in the 1960's and in the United States in the 1970's.

The British study had compiled academic achievement scores and parent and teacher ratings of behavior for 11,837 unrelated children at age 7 and then at age 11. During the intervening four years, the parents of 239 of the youngsters had divorced or separated. The U.S. survey charted parent's ratings for 822 children. These ratings were also done at four-year intervals. During those four years, 65 divorces or separations occurred.

In analyzing the data, the researchers found that for boys in both surveys, academic and behavior problems existed prior to divorce and did not significantly increase after divorce. Girls in the British study also showed problems prior to parental divorce, but compared with boys, they had a slightly higher rate of problems after divorce.

Alcoholism in families. Environmental influences, rather than genes, play a major role in alcoholism among women of all ages and among men whose drinking problems begin during adulthood, psychologists reported in February 1992. In contrast, genes play a predominant role among men whose alcoholism develops during their teens, said the study's director, psychologist Matt McGue of the University of Minnesota in Minneapolis. The study lends support to the theory that there is more than one type of alcoholism, one of which primarily affects males and begins in adolescence.

The group studied consisted of 356 pairs of twins. One twin in each pair had received hospital treatment for alcohol problems.

McGue's team found that both brothers in some pairs of male identical twins suffered from alcoholism more often than did both brothers in pairs of male fraternal twins. This was the case only when the treated twin had developed alcohol problems during his teens.

By contrast, alcoholism occurred at about the same rate among female identical and fraternal twins, who rarely became alcoholic during adolescence. This finding indicated that environmental factors, which are shared by both identical and fraternal twins, played a more important role than genetic factors in these cases.

Drug for autism. Scientists reported in March 1992 that a drug known to help *obsessive-compulsive disorder* (a mental disorder characterized by obsessive thoughts or compulsive habits such as constant hand washing or hair pulling) helps autistic children more than does the drug normally used to treat autism. Psychiatrist Charles T. Gordon and his associates at the National Institute of Mental Health in Bethesda, Md., studied seven autistic children who took two types of antidepressants for five weeks each. The researchers noted that the drug clomipramine worked better than the drug desipramine to reduce the compulsive behaviors, anxiety, social withdrawal, and self-injury that characterize autism.   [Bruce Bower]

In WORLD BOOK, see PSYCHOLOGY.

Public Health

The largest annual increase since 1953 in the number of new tuberculosis (TB) cases in the United States occurred in 1990, according to a 1992 report from the U.S. Centers for Disease Control (CDC) in Atlanta, Ga. With the resurgence came new strains of the bacterium that causes TB and a threat to the goal of the U.S. Public Health Service to eradicate the disease by the year 2010.

TB cases had declined from 84,304 in 1953 to 22,201 in 1985. But starting in 1986, the numbers began to rise steadily. The number of cases reported to the CDC in 1990 was 9.4 per cent higher than the number reported in 1989, and 15.5 per cent greater than what had been reported in 1984.

The increase in TB has occurred primarily among racial and ethnic minorities. The incidence of cases is greatest among people with AIDS and among immigrants from countries that have high rates of TB.

Cholera makes a comeback. Thirty-one passengers on a commercial airline flight from Buenos Aires, Argentina, to Los Angeles in February 1992 developed cholera, becoming victims of an epidemic first identified in Peru in January 1991. The cholera epidemic—the first in the Americas in 50 years—had spread through South America and into Mexico, Panama, and other Central American nations. By April 1992, the Pan American Health Organization reported 533,646 cases of cholera and 4,762 deaths from the disease throughout the Americas.

A microorganism in food or water causes cholera, which results in severe diarrhea and dehydration. International health officials believed Peru's failure to chlorinate its entire water supply contributed to the start of the epidemic.

Problems in Russia. A team of U.S. health experts in February 1992 recommended that public health assistance to the new Russian republic should focus on water purification systems, medical supplies, essential medications, and immunizations for children. The team, from the U.S. Food and Humanitarian Assistance Bureau, had traveled to Russia in January 1992, after the region had suffered months of economic upheaval prior to declaring its independence.

The team reported that hospitals had shortages of medicine and supplies. Russia also was unable to maintain vaccine production plants, and during 1991 there was a dramatic rise in some childhood diseases. In Siberia, water-purification systems were not adequately maintained, causing increases in cases of bacterial dysentery and other diseases. Because of the high cost and scarcity of food, the team also voiced concern over potential cases of malnutrition—especially among infants, young children, and the elderly.

Targeting tobacco ads. U.S. Surgeon General Antonia Novello in March 1992 asked the R. J. Reynolds Tobacco Company to withdraw its popular "Old Joe" camel cartoon used to advertise Camel cigarettes. She also called on retailers and the media to stop displaying the cigarette ads.

Novello's appeal followed the December 1991 publication of a study showing that almost 30 per cent of 3-year-old children and 91 per cent of 6-year-old children could match the Old Joe logo

with a picture of a cigarette. Researchers at the Medical College of Georgia in Augusta and the University of North Carolina in Chapel Hill reported these findings after asking 229 children, ranging from 3 to 6 years in age, to match logos with 12 products.

Unhealthy habits of adolescents. Many high school students practice unhealthy behaviors in such areas as exercise, sexual activity, and smoking, according to results of the national Youth Risk Behavior Survey. The CDC published in 1991 and 1992 a series of reports detailing the conclusions of this 1990 survey of 11,631 U.S. students in grades 9 through 12.

The reports showed that the students were less physically active than those polled in previous years. Only 36 per cent of students in grades 10 through 12 exercised vigorously for at least 20 minutes three times per week. In contrast, 62 per cent of students in 1984 exercised at these levels.

Boys reported engaging in vigorous exercise more regularly than did girls. Half of the boys exercised vigorously at

Tuberculosis on the rise
After several decades of decline, the number of tuberculosis (TB) cases reported each year in the United States is on the upswing. According to public health reports in 1991 and 1992, the increase is mainly due to TB among AIDS patients and among immigrants from nations with high rates of TB.

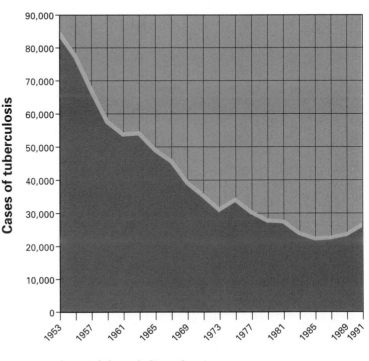

Source: U.S. Centers for Disease Control.

least three days per week, compared with only 25 per cent of the girls. The survey also showed that older girls were less physically active than younger ones.

A high percentage—36 per cent—of the students also reported using tobacco during the month prior to the survey. Forty per cent of white youths reported ever having smoked cigarettes, compared with 32 per cent of black students and 17 per cent of Hispanics.

Of all students surveyed, 54 per cent said that they had engaged in sexual intercourse. Forty per cent of 9th graders and 72 per cent of 12th graders had experienced intercourse.

The majority—78 per cent—of sexually active students said that they relied on some method of contraception. However, fewer than half of all sexually active students used condoms—putting themselves at risk for sexually transmitted diseases and AIDS.

Nearly one in five students reported carrying a weapon during the month prior to the survey. Boys were more likely than girls to carry a weapon. Twenty-nine per cent of white males had carried a weapon at least once during the preceding month, compared with 39 per cent of black males, and 41 per cent of Hispanic males. Of the students who had reported carrying a weapon, 55 per cent carried a knife or razor, 24 per cent carried a club, and 21 per cent carried a firearm, usually a handgun.

Finally, more than one-third of the high school females and more than one-fifth of the high school males surveyed in 1990 said that they had thought about attempting suicide at some time during the preceding 12 months. Eight per cent had attempted suicide, and 2 per cent required medical attention for their action.

The statistics represent a disheartening long-term trend. From 1950 to 1990, the suicide rate among youths aged 15 to 19 increased fourfold. In 1950, there were 2.7 suicide deaths for each 100,000 persons in this age group. In 1988, the suicide rate had increased to 11.3 per 100,000 youths.   [Richard A. Goodman and Deborah Kowal]

In WORLD BOOK, see CHOLERA; PUBLIC HEALTH; TUBERCULOSIS.

Science Student Awards

Winners in the 51st annual Westinghouse Science Talent Search were announced on March 9, 1992, and winners of the 43rd annual International Science and Engineering Fair were named on May 15. Science Service, a nonprofit organization in Washington, D.C., conducts both competitions.

Other science student competitions include international olympiads in mathematics and physics. Both events were held in July 1991.

Science Talent Search. Forty finalists in the Westinghouse competition were chosen from 1,705 entrants from high schools throughout the United States. The top 10 finalists received scholarships totaling $175,000 from the Westinghouse Electric Corporation of Pittsburgh, Pa.

First place and a $40,000 scholarship went to Kurt S. Thorn of Shoreham-Wading River High School in Shoreham, N.Y., for detecting trace elements, such as strontium, in clamshells. Thorn showed that the levels of the trace elements in the shells correlated with the levels of those elements in the seawater in which the clams grew. Thorn used X rays produced by a *synchrotron* (particle accelerator) at the Brookhaven National Laboratory in Upton, N.Y., to obtain his measurements.

Second place and a $30,000 scholarship went to Claudine D. Madras of The Winsor School in Boston. Madras observed the way sunlight was reflected from the asteroid Gaspra and compared those light-reflection patterns with a laboratory model to predict the asteroid's egglike shape and rotation rate. The National Aeronautics and Space Administration used Madras' findings to program cameras on board the Galileo spacecraft when it flew past and photographed Gaspra in 1991.

Third place and a $20,000 scholarship were awarded to Michael S. Agney of Melbourne High School in Melbourne, Fla., for using his personal computer to simulate a neural network that directed a simulated robot arm to grab a simulated ball.

Fourth place and a $15,000 scholarship went to Leonid Reyzin of Sinai Academic Center in New York City.

Fifth place and a $15,000 scholarship were awarded to Patricia Bachiller of Scotch Plains-Fanwood High School in Scotch Plains, N.J.

Sixth place and a $15,000 scholarship were awarded to Christopher Bouton of St. Ann's School in New York City.

Seventh place and a $10,000 scholarship went to Erica Goldman of Hunter College High School in New York City.

Eighth place and a $10,000 scholarship went to Peter Khalifah of Shawnee Mission South High School in Overland Park, Kans.

Ninth place and a $10,000 scholarship were awarded to Benjamin Jun of Montgomery Blair High School in Silver Spring, Md.

Tenth place and a $10,000 scholarship went to Robin Niles of Commack High School in Commack, N.Y.

Science fair. The 43rd annual International Science and Engineering Fair took place in Nashville from May 10 to 16, 1992. The 752 participants were selected from finalists at high school science fairs in 47 states in the United States, and at fairs in American Samoa, Puerto Rico, Guam, Canada, Germany, Ireland, Japan, Taiwan, Sweden, and Great Britain.

Four main awards recognized the most outstanding scientific accomplishments from among the fair's First Award winners. The two top awards were all-expense-paid trips to the Nobel Prize ceremonies in Stockholm, Sweden, in December 1992. Two other awards were all-expense-paid trips to the European Community Contest for Young Scientists in Seville, Spain, in September 1992.

Selected for the Glenn T. Seaborg Nobel Prize Visit Award were Laura E. Becvar, 16, of Coronado High School in El Paso, and Adam R. Healey, 17, of Paul D. Schreiber High School in Port Washington, N.Y. Selected to represent the United States as guest observers at the European Community Contest were Jonobie D. Baker, 15, of Theodore Roosevelt High School in Kent, Ohio, and Barnas G. Monteith, 16, of Randolph High School in Randolph, Mass.

Becvar won for creating a new technique for detecting toxic chemicals. The technique involves using bacteria that emit blue light. When the bacteria are exposed to toxic chemicals, their light is extinguished. The technique has been used to identify a number of pollutants.

Healey was selected for developing a biological sensor that detects antibodies to Lyme disease, indicating the presence of the bacterium that causes the disease. Healey combined a gold-plated quartz crystal with a homemade electronic device and coated the crystal with a protein from the bacterium. Healey found that antibodies in a drop of blood bind to the protein and increase the crystal's mass, which can be measured.

The First Award winners of $500 each in the 13 disciplinary categories were:

Behavioral and social sciences. Tippony E. Scott, 17, of Carlisle Area High School in Carlisle, Pa.

Biochemistry. Lisa M. Castaneda, 18, of Lincoln Park High School in Chicago, and Jose R. Barreto, 17, of University Gardens High School in Rio Piedras, Puerto Rico.

Botany. Nathaniel S. E. L. Shortridge, 16, of Winona Senior High School in Winona, Minn.; Dianella G. Howarth, 16, of Moanalua High School in Honolulu, Hawaii; and Isaac S. Bruck, 15, of Cary Senior High School in Cary, N.C.

Chemistry. David S. Fieno, 18, of Walnut Hills High School in Cincinnati, Ohio, and Laura E. Becvar.

Computer science. Jonobie D. Baker.

Earth and space sciences. Robin C. Bond, Jr., 17, of Mid-Pacific Institute in Honolulu, Hawaii, and Barnas G. Monteith of Randolph (Mass.) High School.

Engineering. Brian D. Gerardot, 16, of R. Nelson Snider High School in Fort Wayne, Ind.; Syndi L. Nettles, 18, of Roy High School in Roy, Utah; Michael M. Serbinis, 18, of Scherwood Secondary School in Hamilton, Canada; and Simon P. Mehalek, 17, of Mehalek Home School in Santa Fe, N. Mex.

Environmental sciences. Joseph P. Salyards II, 17, of Valley Baptist High School in New Market, Va.; Erik J. Edoff, 17, of Athens High School in Troy, Mich.; Kenna R. Mills, 15, of Thomas A. Edison High School in Alexandria, Va.; Julie C. Clay, 18, of Capital High School in Helena, Mont.; and Aaron S. Reames, 18, of Bellefontaine High School in Bellefontaine, Ohio.

Mathematics. Mahesh K. Mahanthappa, 16, of Fairview High School in Boulder, Colo.

Medicine and health. Christopher P.

The top three winners of the Westinghouse Science Talent Search—from left, Claudine D. Madras, Kurt S. Thorn, and Michael S. Agney—celebrate their scholarship awards in March 1992.

Stone, 18, of Bloomington High School South in Bloomington, Ind.; Aaron M. Laing, 17, of Sandia High School in Albuquerque, N. Mex.; and Andrea V. Page, 16, of Waterdown District High School in Waterdown, Canada.

Microbiology. Rory H. Todd, 17, of Bay High School in Panama City, Fla.; Jennifer J. Casaletto, 18, of Thomas Jefferson High School for Science and Technology in Alexandria, Va.; and Adam R. Healey.

Physics. Melissa C. Mazumder, 16, of Little Rock Central High School in Little Rock, Ark.; and Brian R. D'Urso, 15, of Portsmouth Abbey in Portsmouth, R.I.

Zoology. Robin N. Nazaretian, 17, of Long Beach High School in Long Beach, Miss.; Paul J. Plummer, 16, of Central Bucks West High School in Doylestown, Pa.; and Freddy A. Medina, 16, of Carvin High School in Carolina, Puerto Rico.

Math Olympiad. The 32nd annual International Mathematical Olympiad was held in Sigtuna, Sweden. Teams from 55 nations competed by working on six challenging math problems. The top

three places went to the former Soviet Union, China, and Romania.

Every member of the six-member team from the United States won a medal. Joel E. Rosenberg of Hall High School in West Hartford, Conn., won a gold medal. Silver medals were awarded to Kiran S. Kedlaya of Georgetown Day High School in Washington, D.C.; Robert D. Kleinberg of Iroquois High School in Elma, N.Y.; Lenhard L. Ng of Chapel Hill Senior High School in Chapel Hill, N.C.; and Michail G. Sunitsky of Stuyvesant High School in New York City. Ruvim Y. Breydo of Stuyvesant won a bronze medal.

Physics Olympiad. The 22nd annual International Physics Olympiad was held in Havana, Cuba, and drew participants from 31 nations. Five-member teams competed by testing their experimental skills and understanding of theoretical physics. Derrick Bass of North Miami Beach Senior High School in North Miami Beach, Fla., won a gold medal, and R. Michael Jarvis of Fox Lane High School in Bedford, N.Y., won a silver medal.   [Rod Such]

329

A new space shuttle, Endeavour, joined the United States shuttle fleet in 1992 to replace Challenger, the spacecraft that exploded on launch in January 1986. Endeavour went aloft for the first time on May 7, 1992. The mission was the 47th U.S. shuttle flight and the 22nd since the Challenger disaster.

The Endeavour crew was made up of six men and one woman. The National Aeronautics and Space Administration (NASA) selected its chief astronaut, Navy Captain Daniel C. Brandenstein, to lead the crew.

During the nine-day flight, the astronauts walked in space four times. On one spacewalk, for the first time ever, three astronauts worked together outside their spacecraft. They captured an errant communications satellite and attached a rocket booster to it.

The stranded satellite, an Intelsat VI telephone relay satellite owned by an international telecommunications group, occupied most of the crew's time. A mistake in the wiring of the Intelsat's booster rocket had left the satellite in a useless low orbit when it was launched in March 1990.

The Endeavour astronauts, using a specially designed tool, failed in two attempts to grab the satellite, which is shaped like a drum 5.3 meters (17.4 feet) long and 3.6 meters (11.8 feet) in diameter. On May 13, three of the crew members went into the shuttle's cargo bay and, using just their gloved hands, grabbed the satellite. They then attached the special tool, which allowed the shuttle's manipulator arm to hold the satellite while they then attached a new rocket motor to it. The rocket propelled the satellite to its correct orbit 35,900 kilometers (22,300 miles) above Earth.

During the fourth spacewalk, on May 14, two astronauts practiced assembling and moving large structures. The construction and handling techniques could be useful in building the space station that NASA hopes to have in orbit by the end of the 1990's.

Experiments aboard Columbia. Seven astronauts—four men and three women—flew aboard the space shuttle Columbia in June 1991 to conduct life sciences research. The shuttle carried the Spacelab module in its cargo bay. The long module, designed for conduct-ing experiments in space, connects to the cabin of the space shuttle.

During the nine-day flight, the crew carried out a variety of medical experiments to test the effects of space flight on the human body. Scientists, who had been planning the mission for 13 years, said the flight exceeded their expectations. Results of the tests should help in planning for extended space voyages, such as a flight to Mars sometime in the next century.

Atlantis missions. The shuttle Atlantis went aloft three times in late 1991 and early 1992. The crews launched two satellites and conducted atmospheric experiments.

On the first mission, in August 1991, Atlantis carried a large communications satellite aloft. The satellite, called TDRS-5, is used to track other spacecraft and relay data to Earth. The crew also conducted physiological experiments inside the orbiter.

In November 1991, Atlantis flew a seven-day mission for the U.S. Department of Defense. The astronauts, working in concert with controllers on the ground, deployed a large Defense Support Program (DSP) satellite. DSP satellites have telescopes that use infrared light to watch for missiles and rockets fired from anywhere on Earth.

Atlantis flew again in March 1992. The shuttle orbiter carried 13 instruments in its cargo bay to study the atmosphere and the sun. Called Atlas-1, the flight was the first of several such missions NASA hopes to fly over the course of an entire 11-year solar cycle. During that cycle, the number of sunspots rises and falls as the sun goes through periods of turbulence separated by times of relative calm.

Studying planet Earth. The first satellite in a program NASA calls Mission to Planet Earth was placed in orbit by the space shuttle Discovery in September 1991. The 6.8-metric-ton (7.5-short-ton) Upper Atmosphere Research Satellite (UARS) will provide information about the chemistry and motion of the atmosphere above an altitude of about 16 kilometers (10 miles).

Mission to Planet Earth is conceived as a multiyear program in which NASA will use a number of satellites and other data-gathering systems to monitor the environmental health of the planet. Sci-

Clouds swirl around Antarctica in the first photographic image made of the Earth as viewed from above the South Pole. The image—in which parts of Australia, South America, and Africa appear as reddish areas—was released in November 1991 by astronomer W. Reid Thompson of Cornell University in Ithaca, N.Y. Reid created the picture by combining 21 photographs taken by the Galileo space probe as it swung past the Earth in December 1990.

entists hope that the project will enable them to determine how various human activities, such as logging, industry, and agriculture, might be altering the global climate.

Discovery flew again in January 1992, carrying the Spacelab. The mission was called the First International Microgravity Laboratory. The crew carried out 54 experiments, designed by more than 200 scientists from 16 countries, to test the effects of low gravity on various processes in the life sciences and materials research.

Space probes and telescopes. The space probe Galileo produced the first close-up pictures of an asteroid in late 1991. But because Galileo's main antenna was stuck, the images of the asteroid, named Gaspra, were relayed to Earth very slowly by a smaller antenna. Galileo, launched from a shuttle in 1989, is bound for Jupiter, where, in 1995, it is scheduled to begin making observations of the large planet's chemical composition and magnetic field. (See ASTRONOMY, SOLAR SYSTEM.)

Two orbiting spacecraft began pro-

ducing important astronomical data in 1992. The Hubble Space Telescope—despite the optical flaw in its 2.4-meter (94.5-inch) primary mirror discovered soon after the telescope was put into orbit in April 1990—started yielding good images of stars, galaxies, and other celestial objects. Computer techniques were used to clarify the images that the Space Telescope relayed to Earth, thereby enabling astronomers to compensate somewhat for the deficiency in the telescope's mirror.

The Compton Gamma-Ray Observatory also produced a wealth of new data. The spacecraft, launched in April 1991, carries the most sensitive gamma-ray detectors ever orbited. (In the Special Reports section, see OBSERVING THE GAMMA RAY SKY.)

Space station. In October 1991, the U.S. Congress approved $2.03 billion in funding to continue NASA's efforts to build an international space station. The European Space Agency, Canada, and Japan are participating in the effort. The aim is to have a permanent base in low Earth orbit by the year 2000. Astro-

Using only their gloved hands, astronauts capture a communications satellite while standing in the cargo bay of the U.S. space shuttle Endeavour. The maneuver took place during the shuttle's maiden flight in May 1992—and during the first-ever three-person spacewalk. The Intelsat VI satellite had been stranded in a useless low orbit. After bringing the satellite into the cargo bay, the astronauts fitted it with a rocket booster that propelled it to its correct orbit 35,900 kilometers (22,300 miles) above Earth.

nauts would live and work there the year around.

The project began in 1984 and has progressed much more slowly than had been anticipated. The station has been redesigned several times to simplify its assembly and maintenance in space and to save money. By NASA's own estimate, the space station will cost $30 billion through 1999.

Critics of the project have expressed concerns that the cost would grow, causing other space programs to suffer for lack of funds. In 1991, in an effort to halt the space station, those opponents provoked the broadest congressional debate on U.S. space policy since the 1970's. Although the space station program survived, few people on either side of the issue believed in mid-1991 that the fight was over.

New NASA director. The first astronaut to serve as administrator of NASA, Navy Rear Admiral Richard H. Truly, resigned in February 1992. He was succeeded by an industry executive, Daniel S. Goldin, the former vice president and general manager of TRW Incorporated's Space & Technology Group. Goldin, who was installed in his new position on April 1, said many of NASA's programs had become too expensive and took too long to produce scientific results.

Soviet space program: What now? The disintegration of the Soviet Union in December 1991 raised many questions about the fate of the Soviet space program. Although that program continued to be the world's most active, the breakup of the union caused disruptions in the Soviet space establishment, and one man was forced to stay on board the space station Mir months longer than planned before he could be returned to Earth.

The division of the former Soviet Union into the Commonwealth of Independent States (CIS) has resulted in different parts of the space program being located in different nations. Cosmonauts, as the Soviets called their space travelers, will now be launched from a facility in Kazakhstan, while their flights will be directed from a control center in Russia.

The struggle of the CIS to convert from a centrally planned economy to one based on free-market forces also af-

A global view of the planet Venus, based on radar data from the Magellan spacecraft, was released in October 1991 by the National Aeronautics and Space Administration (NASA). The most prominent feature in the image is a bright band of volcanoes and lava flows stretching for some 10,000 kilometers (6,200 miles) along the planet's equator. Magellan's mapping of Venus continued in 1992.

fected the space program. To raise much-needed cash, the CIS in 1991 ordered many organizations, including those that build space equipment and conduct missions in space, to begin trying to sell their products and services to the world.

Ironically, the United States, which had been the Soviet Union's main adversary, became a customer. The United States in 1992 bought several kilograms of plutonium, a radioactive element that is used to power space probes that travel too far away from the sun to run on solar power. Other U.S. purchases were a small nuclear reactor called Topaz 2, which is also used to power spacecraft, and some small electrically powered thrustors that are used to maneuver space vehicles.

Adding to the irony, the U.S. customer for the reactor and the space thrustors was the Strategic Defense Initiative (SDI), the proposed antimissile defense system that is known popularly as "Star Wars." The Soviets had consistently criticized SDI as a dangerous and foolhardy United States program that would have

the effect of extending the arms race into space.

The fall of Communism also lifted the veil of secrecy that had concealed many Soviet space activities. For decades, the Soviets had denied that they were ever in a race with the United States to land people on the moon. In September 1991, however, the Russians revealed plans and photographs of a colossal four-stage rocket called the N1, upon which the Soviets had pinned their hopes of reaching the moon. But the rocket failed to work properly in four unmanned flights, and it never carried a crew into space.

Other space programs. Japan and Europe also conducted noteworthy space missions in 1991 and 1992. The European company Arianespace continued to be the largest provider of commercial launch services. Both the European Space Agency and Japan placed Earth-observing satellites into orbit. The satellites use radar, which enables them to make images of the Earth at night and through clouds.   [James R. Asker]

In WORLD BOOK, see SPACE TRAVEL.

Zoology

Researchers may have found out why the pronghorn is the fastest animal in the Western Hemisphere and the second fastest animal in the world, the first being the cheetah. A pronghorn, which resembles an antelope, can run 11 kilometers (6.8 miles) in 10 minutes because of the way it breathes, reported physiologists from the University of Wyoming in Laramie and from the University of Bern in Switzerland in October 1991.

Before conducting laboratory tests, the scientists calculated how much oxygen a pronghorn would need to attain speeds of 65 and 100 kilometers (40 and 62 miles) per hour. Then, they measured the actual amount of oxygen that two pronghorns inhaled as they galloped on a tilted treadmill at speeds of 10 meters (33 feet) per second—faster than most race horses run. The scientists found that the pronghorn used oxygen three times faster than the scientists had thought.

The researchers also compared the oxygen use of pronghorns to that of goats that were similar in size. He found

that the pronghorns used five times the amount of oxygen that goats used while running at top speed. Lindstedt attributed the difference to the pronghorn's larger lungs, greater ability to move oxygen from the lungs to the muscles, greater amount of *hemoglobin* (the pigment in blood that transports oxygen), stronger heart, and greater number of *mitochondria* (structures that produce most of a cell's energy) in its muscles.

Dolphins ride wakes behind boats to make swimming long distances easier, according to physiologist Terrie M. Williams and her colleagues at the Naval Oceans Systems Center Hawaii Laboratory in Kailua on the island of Oahu.

For the experiments, reported in February 1992, Williams trained two bottlenose dolphins to swim alongside a moving boat. Each dolphin wore a special harness that measured its heartbeat. The researchers also measured lactic acid in the animal's blood. The blood levels of lactic acid indicate how hard the muscles are working.

At medium and slow speeds, the dolphins swam alongside the boat. But at high speeds, about 4 meters (13 feet) per second, they swam in the boat's wake. Williams reported that the animals swam twice as fast in the wake behind the boat as they did alongside the boat, and they used only 13 per cent more energy doing so.

Jumping maggots. The Mediterranean fruitfly maggot is the first example of a legless, soft-bodied larva that can jump. Physiologist David Maitland at the University of Witwatersrand in Johannesburg, South Africa, reported this finding in January 1992. Other animals without backbones can jump, but they have legs and hard bodies.

To jump, the maggot first tucks its body into a loop by contracting muscles that run the length of its body. Then, it grasps its tail with its mouth hooks and contracts its round body into a tighter loop. Finally, as the maggot contracts its body one more time, it releases the mouth hooks. This sudden release of tension causes the tail to push hard against the ground, which quickly propels the maggot into the air in an unpredictable direction.

The fruitfly maggot usually takes five seconds to crawl 8.5 millimeters (0.3 inch), a distance equal to the length of its body. By jumping, it can travel 300 times as far in the same amount of time. The fruitfly maggot may have developed this type of locomotion to escape predators, such as ants, according to Maitland. He observed that ants failed to locate their maggot prey after the maggots had jumped.

Fathers recruit sons. Some birds pester their sons into helping raise the father's younger offspring, two biologists from Cornell University in Ithaca, N.Y., reported in March 1992. For five years, Stephen T. Emlen and Peter H. Wrege studied the social behavior of white-fronted bee-eaters. These birds live on the African plains and nest in groups of up to 200 members.

The biologists marked a number of these birds for identification, then observed 47 encounters of older birds interfering with the mating efforts of younger males. In 16 of the encounters, the young birds gave up mating to help raise the older bird's chicks.

Dad prefers daughters
A bluebird father, *right*, feeds daughters up to twice as often as he feeds sons, perhaps because daughters do not compete with fathers for mates, reported Clemson University biologists in January 1992. The scientists studied bluebirds because the bright blue feathers of male nestlings, *above* right, make it easy to identify young birds' sex.

California Condor: Wild Again

As the early morning sun warmed the rugged mountains of California's Los Padres National Forest, four large black birds emerged from a boxy structure onto a platform. Two of the birds were California condors, North America's largest land-based bird species. Their companions were Andean condors, a South American species. Wearing a featherweight radio transmitter on each wing, the condors flapped and hopped about, recognizing that something was different—there was no net around the platform. The birds, who were all 8 to 9 months old, had been conceived and raised in zoos. But on this day, Jan. 14, 1992, they were finally free to fly into the wilderness.

About 2.4 kilometers (1.5 miles) away, biologists from federal and state wildlife agencies and two zoos, representatives from conservation organizations, and a crowd of journalists cheered the birds' every move. Chumash Indians, who believe that California condors carry the souls of the dead to heaven, chanted and beat drums. All celebrated the California condor's return to the wild after nearly becoming extinct in the 1980's.

On the day of the release, the condors were cautious. Robert Mesta, condor program coordinator for the United States Fish and Wildlife Service (FWS), described the scene. "It was not very dramatic," he said. "The birds made only a few short flights away from their home base." By early April, however, the young condors had become better fliers and were beginning to soar a bit, traveling a few kilometers on each voyage.

Although the event was cause for celebration, it was not the end of the struggle to save the California condor. Reintroducing captive-bred animals into the wild is a difficult process that requires careful monitoring.

About 100,000 years ago, birds of this species flew as far east as Florida and New York. By the time Europeans began settling the Pacific Coast in the 1700's and early 1800's, condors were still fairly numerous in a territory that extended from British Columbia in Canada to the Baja Peninsula in Mexico. As the human population grew, however, the condor's habitat shrank, and the number of birds declined dramatically. Hunters, including museum collectors, also killed many of the birds. Scientists estimate that by the early 1900's, only a few hundred condors remained, all in California. By 1985, only six remained in the wild.

With extinction virtually certain, the FWS removed some condor nestlings and eggs and put them in the San Diego and Los Angeles zoos. The first of these eggs hatched in 1983. In 1987, the agency captured the last remaining condor in the wild. The first chick bred in captivity hatched in 1988, and four more arrived the following year.

Meanwhile, biologists had begun preparing for the species' return to the wild. As a trial run, they equipped with radio transmitters 13 zoo-bred Andean condors, which are not endangered, and released them into the California countryside between 1989 and 1991. Tracking the birds not only provided valuable information about condor behavior but also helped train the scientists assigned to the California condor recovery project.

For example, condors flap their wings to become airborne and then catch air currents that allow them to soar and glide. Therefore, the biolo-

Four California and Andean condors await their release into the wild on a netted platform in California's Los Padres National Forest. The birds lived on the platform and in an adjoining shelter for several months, exercising their wings and getting used to their surroundings.

A scientist equipped with a radio antenna and receiver, *above,* tracks one of the condors reintroduced into the California mountains. All the released birds wore a featherweight radio transmitter on each wing (inset), so that scientists could determine the birds' whereabouts and monitor their activities.

gists realized, the cliffs that condors need as launch sites must face into prevailing winds. "The Andean experiment is why we're so confident of success," Mesta said. "Most reintroduction programs don't have the luxury of a substitute species."

In mid-1991, the condor recovery team selected 2 of the 52 condors then in captivity for release—one from the Los Angeles Zoo and another from San Diego. Two Andean condors joined them because condors seem to function better in groups.

The recovery team moved the four condors to the Sespe Condor Sanctuary, a 21,700-hectare (53,500-acre) area in the Los Padres National Forest, about 80 kilometers (50 miles) northwest of Los Angeles. The birds were housed in a box designed to look like a cave—a standard condor refuge and nest site. The box was attached to a platform covered with netting. This allowed the birds to safely exercise their wings and become familiar with their surroundings. Because condors, like all vultures, eat *carrion* (the flesh of dead animals), the scientists fed them stillborn calves, dropped into the "cave" at night. The night before the condors were to be released, the biologists quietly removed the net.

If the birds' attempt at flying the next morning seemed tentative, it was because condor flight is a two-step process. Young eagles and hawks just take off, but condors must master basic flapping and then learn to soar on rising air currents. While young, they also learn regular routes—"air highways"—which they use throughout their lives.

To keep the released birds from eating contaminated food, scientists planned to provide carrion indefinitely. During the 1970's and 1980's, many condors died after eating deer and other prey killed with lead bullets or eating poisoned animal remains that ranchers had set out for coyotes.

The food was also being used to extend the condors' range. Biologists moved the feeding stations regularly in order to lure the birds farther north, deeper into the mountain wilderness and as far as possible from human activity.

The biologists planned to release other condors each year, as long as the captive flock keeps reproducing. The biologists also hope to free condors outside southern California, probably in Arizona, just north of the Grand Canyon. This area was once a part of the species' range.

The project's long-term goal is to create three self-sustaining populations of 100 birds each. Two of these groups would live in the wild, the other would remain in captivity. But that goal is many years in the future. First, the reintroduced birds must survive to maturity and begin reproducing. So far, they are off to a flying start.

[Eugene J. Walter, Jr.]

The biologists found that the more closely the older bird was related to the younger, the more successful the older bird was. Fathers who interfered with their sons were the most successful at getting them to help. A typical father visited a son's nest dozens of times a day, blocking the young bird's return and begging for food intended for a young female in preparation for egg-laying. About 40 per cent of the time, the son returned to the nest of his father, at times leaving his own mate with eggs that had little chance to survive as chicks without his help.

When the son helped the father, the survival rate of the father's new chicks was almost double the survival rate of chicks brought up without helpers. The biologists suggested that the sons cooperate in order to pass on their fathers' genes, in which they too have a share.

Dangers of cannibalism. There is a good reason why very few organisms like to eat their own kind, biologists at Arizona State University in Tempe reported in October 1991. Cannibalism can cause death.

David Pfennig and his colleagues studied cannibalism in tiger salamanders because these animals come in two types: those that eat other tiger salamanders and those that do not. Cannibal tiger salamanders in the laboratory ate their weaker—often sick—neighbors. When they did so, they also consumed the disease-causing viruses or bacteria common to the species and potentially harmful to all members. Many of the cannibals became sick and died from the same diseases as their prey.

The biologists also surveyed the two types of tiger salamanders in 10 lakes. The lakes with high levels of bacteria had fewer cannibal salamanders than noncannibals. The scientists concluded that the cannibal salamanders had eaten infected members of the species and subsequently died. Thus, they said, cannibalism is rare in nature because of the high risk for spreading disease.

Strange mammals. Although the naked mole rat is a mammal, biologists are discovering that it defies certain aspects of the definition of mammal. For example, all mammals have hair, but

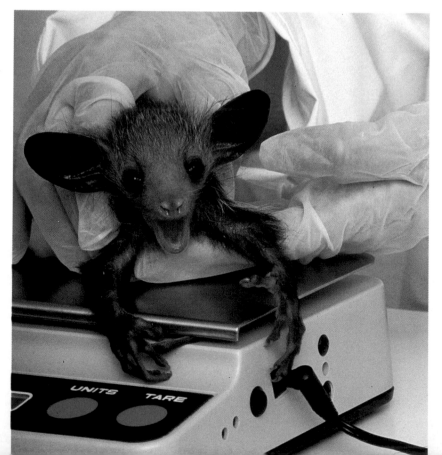

The first aye-aye born in the Western Hemisphere is weighed at the Duke University Primate Center in Durham, N.C., a few days after its birth in April 1992. The tiny male weighed in at 142 grams (5 ounces). Aye-ayes are an endangered primate species native to Madagascar, an island off the east coast of Africa. Large ears help the aye-aye hear tree-boring insects—its food—and the animal's long fingers enable it to dig the bugs out of their tunnels.

Black-footed ferrets make their official comeback

Federal and state wildlife officials released 49 black-footed ferrets into the Shirley Basin in southeast Wyoming during September and October 1991. The animals were the offspring of the last surviving community of wild ferrets, which were rounded up in 1986 in order to establish a captive-breeding program.

Wyoming wildlife employees, *left,* check a black-footed ferret in a cage placed on the range to help the animal adapt to its new home.

Before being released, each ferret was fitted with a special collar, *right,* to help officials track the animal's movements in the wild.

Once freed, *below,* the ferrets faced harsh winters and natural predators such as coyotes for the first time. Although several died in 1991 and 1992, 50 more ferrets were scheduled for release in South Dakota or Montana in 1993.

the mole rat is hairless except for a few snout whiskers. And mammals are able to maintain their body temperatures even though the temperature of the air surrounding them changes. But biologists at the University of Witwatersrand reported in October 1991 that naked mole rats lack this ability.

Naked mole rats are blind, hot-dog-sized mammals that live in colonies in underground burrows in the semiarid, tropical parts of northeast Africa. Their burrows tend to be humid and warm with little temperature variation—always between 28 °C and 32 °C (82.4 °F and 89.6 °F). Because of their stable, warm environment, naked mole rats have no need for the fur or the fat under the skin that most mammals have.

In a laboratory, the biologists tested the mole rat's temperature-regulating ability in a temperature range greater than that found in the animal's natural habitat. The researchers found that the body temperature of these animals was never more than a fraction above the surrounding temperature in the range of 12 °C to 37 °C (53.6 °F to 98.6 °F).

The scientists also tested the mole rat's response to sudden temperature drops—again, a condition generally not found in their natural environment. Typically, mammals respond to cold by breathing faster to generate more body heat. The mole rats responded by breathing more slowly. The scientists suggested that breathing slowly and failing to generate more body heat suits the animal's life in tunnels, which have low levels of oxygen. It also might serve to reduce the chance of overheating the enclosed tunnels.

Monkey medicine. Female muriqui monkeys may change their diets to control when they can have babies, primatologist Karen Strier at the University of Wisconsin in Madison reported in February 1992. For the past 10 years, Strier and her co-workers have been studying the muriqui monkeys, an endangered species that lives in 12 small areas of rain forest along the coast of Brazil.

The researchers observed that female muriqui monkeys wait until the start of Brazil's rainy season—about six months after they stop nursing their young—to mate again. Then, they seek out the fruit of a rare tree that grows on the border of the protected forest where they

live. This fruit contains stigmasterol, a substance chemists have long used to synthesize progesterone. Progesterone is a female sex hormone that prepares the lining of the *uterus* (womb) to receive a fertilized egg. If the muriqui females absorb stigmasterol from the fruit, then eating the fruit may be their way of promoting fertility, Strier reported.

Biologist Richard Wrangham of Harvard University in Cambridge, Mass., also reported in February 1992 his observations of chimpanzees in Uganda eating leaves of plants that contain a toxic compound. Each morning, the chimpanzees ate the young leaves of a plant called *Aspila,* barely chewing them before swallowing, so that the leaves passed through the animals' intestinal tract nearly whole. In contrast, chimpanzees thoroughly chew leaves that make up the balance of their diet.

Eloy Rodriguez at the University of California in Irvine, also reporting in February, found that these leaves contain a compound that kills nematode worms, which are common parasites in the chimp's gut. The compound is released from structures on the leaf's surface as the leaf passes through the animal's intestinal tract. The researchers reasoned that if the chimpanzees chewed the leaves too much, the structures that produce the toxic substance would be destroyed.

A zebra without stripes. A foal that looks like the quagga, a zebra without stripes, was born in October 1991 at the Vrolijkheid Breeding Center in Cape Province in South Africa. The quagga, however, became extinct more than 100 years ago.

Using DNA testing techniques, geneticist Russell Higuchi at the University of California in Berkeley showed in the 1980's that the brown quagga was really a zebra with a different coat pattern. Since Higuchi's discovery, biologists have carried out selective breeding of zebras to try to bring back the quagga color. The new foal, one of eight born in the project since 1988, looks the most like the quagga, with a dark brown coat and just a hint of stripes visible on its rear end. [Elizabeth J. Pennisi and Thomas R. Tobin]

In the Special Reports section, see SCIENCE STALKS THE DOMESTIC CAT. In WORLD BOOK, see ZOOLOGY.

Science You Can Use

In areas selected for their current interest, *Science Year* presents information that the reader as a consumer can use in understanding everyday technology or in making decisions—from buying products to caring for personal health and well-being.

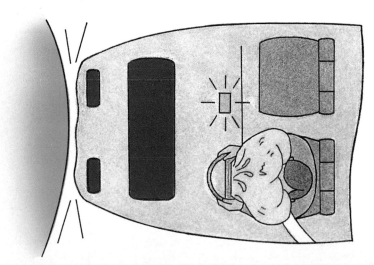

Airbags: Split-Second Protection

As a safety device for automobiles, the seat belt is hard to beat. Drivers and passengers who buckle up with shoulder and lap restraints are about 40 per cent less likely to be killed in an automobile accident than are unrestrained riders, according to estimates by some safety experts. But there's another safety device that, used with a seat belt, can reduce passenger fatalities in head-on collisions by an additional 5 to 10 per cent. That device is the airbag.

Automobile airbags are pillowlike cushions that protect passengers during head-on crashes. Safety experts consider airbags the best mass-produced safety feature since the seat belt for minimizing injuries in such crashes, which account for an estimated 59 per cent of all accidents.

Most serious injuries in automobile accidents occur when passengers strike the interior surfaces of a vehicle after the vehicle comes to a sudden stop as the result of a crash. Padding on the steering wheels, dashboards, and door panels of many modern cars may make it seem that a collision with these soft surfaces couldn't result in serious injury. Perhaps for this reason, some people believe they can brace or otherwise restrain themselves—without the aid of a seat belt—during a crash. But, in fact, self-restraint is nearly impossible.

When a car traveling at, for example, 48 kilometers per hour (kph) (30 miles per hour [mph]) crashes head-on into a stationary object, the car itself may slow from 48 to 0 kph in 0.1 second. However, the passengers will continue moving inside the car at 48 kph. That's about the speed at which you would hit the ground if you jumped from the top of a three-story building. And in such a collision, a layer of padding the same thickness as that on steering wheels and dashboards would provide little protection from injury.

The United States government's first attempts to make cars safer, beginning in the mid-1960's, focused on requiring such items as shatterproof windshields, padded dashboards, and collapsible steering columns. In 1968, the government ordered automakers to equip the front seat of all passenger cars with lap and shoulder seat belts, often called *three-point belts* because they restrain the rider at three points: one near the shoulder and two on either side of the hips.

Although standard three-point seat belts are effective in reducing both injuries and deaths from auto accidents, they have two limitations. First, they are *active restraints*—that is, drivers and passengers have to buckle them on if the belts are to provide any protection. And many people dislike wearing or forget to wear their seat belt.

Second, three-point belts act almost like rubber bands, allowing passengers to move some distance forward in their seat before their movement is halted. This is particularly true in head-on collisions. It's not that the seat belts are defective. In fact, they are designed to stretch in order to reduce the force of the belts on the body. This means, however, that in accidents occurring at high speeds, the force exerted by the moving belted rider stretches the belt so far that the rider could still be thrown against the steering wheel, dashboard, or windshield.

Because of these two limitations and government safety concerns, automotive engineers developed the first driver's-side airbag in the early 1970's. The uninflated airbag is like a pillowcase tightly packed inside the *hub* (center) of a steering wheel. On impact, the bag inflates and pops out of the steering wheel. The cushion first slows and then stops the driver's forward movement. This action prevents the driver's face and chest from hitting the steering wheel, dashboard, or windshield.

The major components of an airbag system are tiny devices called *sensors* that detect sudden *deceleration* (slowing down), a computerized control unit, and the bag itself. The sensors are connected to the car's battery. The control

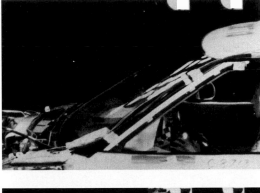 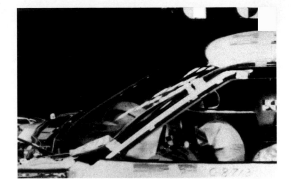

 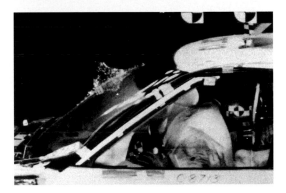

Instant protection
A driver's-side airbag deploys instantly during the head-on crash of a car with two test dummies in the front seats, *top, left*. The entire process from impact to airbag inflation takes less than 0.003 second, about the time it takes to blink the eyes. The dummy behind the wheel is unharmed, but the other crashes into the windshield, *bottom, right*.

unit monitors the system for malfunctions and also serves as a power reserve in case the battery is damaged in the crash.

Airbag systems often employ at least three sensors—an arming sensor in the control unit (usually in the passenger compartment) and two impact sensors located in the front corners of the engine compartment. The arming sensor is usually a tube-shaped device that contains liquid mercury, a good electrical conductor. The impact sensor might consist of a small metal ball held by a magnet.

During a sudden, large deceleration—such as that which occurs when a car collides with another object—the mercury in the arming sensor slides forward and touches two electrical contacts at the front of the device. At the same time, the metal ball in one or both of the impact sensors breaks away from the magnet and rolls forward, touching two electrical contacts.

At this point, the electrical circuit for the airbag has been completed. Electric current then flows to a wire, called a *squib*, in the steering wheel. The squib, a

charge of explosive powder, pellets that generate gas, and the uninflated airbag itself are inside the hub of the steering wheel.

The electric current from the control unit rapidly heats the squib. The squib's heat ignites the charge, which ignites the pellets. In most cases, the pellets are made of sodium azide and produce nitrogen gas. The gas expands quickly, inflating the airbag, which then breaks through the plastic cover of the steering wheel hub.

The whole operation from impact to inflation usually takes less than 0.003 second. That interval is short enough to assure that the bag is fully inflated by the time the driver hits it, even in high-speed collisions. Once the bag is inflated, the gas quickly escapes through two large vents on either side of the bag, deflating the bag, so that the driver can leave the vehicle.

In general, airbags are designed to deploy only in impacts in which the car is moving at more than about 18 kph (11 mph). The bag will not inflate if the car receives a hard bump. And, since the arming sensor and one impact sen-

How an airbag works

A typical airbag system includes the bag itself, a computerized control unit that monitors the system for malfunctions, and sensors that detect the *deceleration* (sudden slowing) that occurs during an impact. Airbag systems often employ at least three sensors: an arming sensor in the control unit and two impact sensors in the front corners of the engine compartment.

When the front of the car strikes another object at a speed of at least 18 kilometers (11 miles) per hour, the sudden deceleration triggers the arming sensor and at least one impact sensor, thus completing an electrical circuit for the airbag.

The activation of at least two sensors tells the computerized control unit that a malfunction has not occurred. The electric current is sent to a wire called a squib in the steering wheel. The current heats the squib, which ignites a charge of explosive powder. The powder, in turn, ignites pellets that produce nitrogen gas.

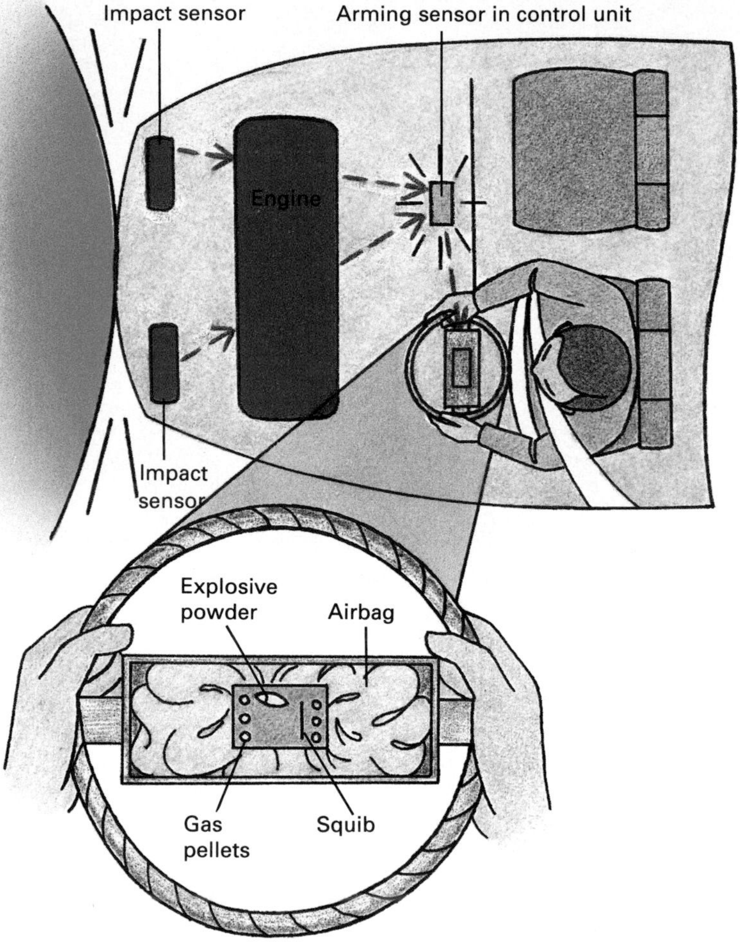

Impact sensor

Arming sensor in control unit

Engine

Impact sensor

Explosive powder

Airbag

Gas pellets

Squib

sor must both be activated before the squib will heat, the bag will not inflate if an auto mechanic accidentally strikes an impact sensor while repairing the car.

In addition, airbags will inflate only if the force of impact is within 30 degrees to either side of the centerline of the car. This range covers only the front of the car. Airbags don't provide protection in side- or rear-impact accidents or in rollovers, where the occupants can be ejected from the car.

Airbags deployed in head-on collisions can reduce or prevent head and chest injuries. Drivers protected by air-

bags have walked away from head-on crashes that would otherwise have sent them to the hospital.

Airbags are most effective when used with lap and shoulder restraints. Unfortunately, the presence of an airbag may provide a false sense of security for those who don't buckle up. Riders who rely on airbags alone are only 18 per cent less likely to be killed in a front-end crash than they would be if they used no restraints at all, and they offer no protection for other types of accidents. In comparison, people who use both airbags and seat belts are about 50

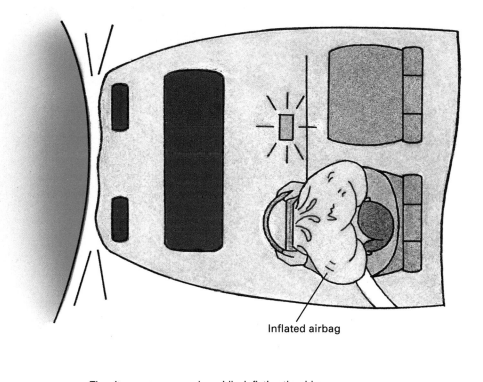

Inflated airbag

The nitrogen gas expands rapidly, inflating the airbag, which breaks through the plastic covering on the hub of the steering wheel. After the bag is inflated, the gas quickly escapes through two large vents on either side of the bag, which deflates within several seconds.

per cent less likely to be killed in a head-on collision.

In 1987, the federal government began requiring automakers to phase in *passive restraints* of some type in their cars. (Passive restraints, such as automatic seat belts, are those that work without any action by the rider.) In 1988, 25 per cent of cars had to have front-seat passive restraints. But that year, only 2 per cent of the new passenger cars sold in the United States were equipped with airbags. The remaining cars with mandatory passive restraints were equipped with some type of automatic seat belt. By 1991, the percentage of cars with airbags sold in the United States had increased to 34 per cent.

Although consumer demand for airbags has surged in recent years, carmakers have responded slowly, in part because of the cost of the devices. The typical driver's-side airbag system costs about $300. An airbag that protects the front-seat passenger costs about the same. Soon, however, automakers will not have a choice. Beginning in 1994, federal law will require them to equip all new cars with at least a driver's-side airbag.   [Don Schroeder]

Making Sense of Opinion Polls

Public opinion polls figured prominently in the 1992 political season. Polls sponsored by newspapers, magazines, and broadcast news organizations focused on the public's views and preferences regarding issues and candidates. Polls conducted privately helped the political candidates map their campaign strategies.

Public opinion polls, whether public or private, are basically tools for estimating the division of opinion among an entire population by interviewing just a part, or *sample,* of the total population. *Pollsters,* the people who conduct opinion polls, begin by selecting the sample to be interviewed and designing the questions to be asked. Interviewers then contact the people in the sample by telephone or in person. Finally, computers tabulate the answers to the questions, and then the pollsters release the results.

The basic idea of a public opinion poll is that each person in the population has at least some chance of being interviewed. Pollsters can tell how representative their samples will be if, as they draw their samples, they keep track of the probability each individual selected had of falling into the sample.

A *random sample,* in which everyone in the population has an equal chance of being interviewed, is the ideal. But purely random samples are seldom possible because of the difficulties in conducting a poll. For example, some people are not at home when the interviewers call. Not all people will agree to be interviewed, and some will refuse to answer certain questions or will not complete the interview.

Most polls in the United States are done by telephone, which has many advantages over interviewing in person. Phone polls are less expensive to conduct than than are polls based on in-person interviews, because the interviewing, or field work, can be done from a central, closely supervised location rather than having interviewers sent to *sampling points* (specific locations, such as selected blocks in a city, at which a certain number of interviews are to be completed).

Telephone samples are usually drawn by first selecting telephone area codes and exchanges from master lists kept by the phone company. The pollster then adds to them random numbers for the last digits, in this way making up the list of numbers to call. Using this procedure ensures that unlisted phone numbers will also have a chance of being called.

Only one-fourth of all possible combinations of phone numbers belong to phones at private residences, however. The rest ring at offices and institutions, such as schools or hospitals, or they are not working numbers.

Once a residence has been contacted, good sampling practice gives each individual in the household an equal chance of being interviewed. For example, the interviewer may question the adult with the most recent birthday. If the person selected to be interviewed is not at home at the first call, interviewers are instructed to call back to reach him or her. Failure to contact hard-to-reach individuals because they are not at home can produce a sample that does not include enough men, younger people, less-educated people, and racial minorities.

One drawback to telephone polls is that, by definition, they exclude households without telephones. About 1 household in 14 in the United States has no telephone and the proportion is higher in the South, among racial minorities, and among the less educated and less well-to-do.

Pollsters often adjust, or *weight,* their samples to make up for biases that may result from not making callbacks to reach hard-to-find people or from missing people who live in households without phones. Weighting brings the proportion of each subgroup in the sample into line with its actual proportion in the population as a whole.

Because an infinite number of possible samples could be drawn from a population, there is always the chance that a poll's sample is not representative. *Sampling error* is the term pollsters use to assess the chance that the sample they have drawn is unrepresentative of the entire population. Sampling error is expressed as a specific number of percentage points above and below a reported per cent. This is a margin pollsters allow within which they can calculate the amount of confidence they have in their sample.

For example, suppose a public opinion poll finds that 64 per cent of those polled approve of the President's performance. If the poll's sampling error is 3 percentage points, the pollster is reasonably confident that, if everyone in the population had been interviewed, the approval rating would be between 61 and 67 per cent (64 plus or minus 3 percentage points), with 64 per cent being the most likely rating.

Sampling error is based on the size of the sample, not the size of the population from which the sample is drawn. The larger a poll's sample, the smaller the sampling error will be. This is because the larger the sample, the more precise its estimate of a given characteristic in the total population is likely to be. Pollsters have calculated that a sample of 1,000 cases will have a sampling error of 4 percentage points regardless of whether it is a sample of a community, a state, or the entire country. Other sampling errors associated with the sample sizes of most polls reported in the news are 5 percentage points for 600 cases and 3 percentage points for 1,500 cases.

Equally as important as sampling error when interpreting a poll's findings are the nonsampling considerations that affect the poll's results. These considerations include the questions that interviewers ask, how those questions are worded, the order in which they are asked, and how well the interviewers do their job.

The importance of nonsampling issues can be illustrated by two polls conducted in December 1990. These polls produced conflicting results about what the public thought the United States should do about Iraq's invasion of Kuwait. A poll by *The Wall Street Journal* and NBC News found that more than half of the public (54 per cent) favored going to war if Iraq did not withdraw its troops from Kuwait, and 34 per cent were opposed. A poll conducted at exactly the same time by *The New York Times* and CBS News found that less than half of the public (45 per cent) favored military action against Iraq, while 48 per cent wanted to see if economic sanctions would force Iraq to withdraw from Kuwait.

Because both polls were based on representative samples, their different findings can be explained only by the questions that were asked. The *New York Times*/CBS question mentioned giving sanctions more time to work, but the *Wall Street Journal*/NBC question did not.

Research shows that poll questions that spell out alternative positions on an issue will get different results from questions that state one position and merely ask people whether they favor or oppose it. Careful pollsters try to present balanced alternatives when asking questions about issues.

Public opinion researchers have also found that as much as one-fifth of the public will answer a question on an issue even though they have no opinion. Careful pollsters deal with this by first asking people whether they have heard or read enough about an issue to have an opinion on it. Only if the answer is "yes" do the interviewers then ask questions about the issue.

It is possible to judge the quality of a poll only when the purposes for which it has been conducted are known. In an election year, polls are used in many ways. Consider three types of election polls: preelection polls, tracking polls, and exit polls:

• **Preelection polls.** Although the object of preelection polls is to estimate as closely as possible the outcome of an election, they should not be thought of as predictions. Rather they are measurements of the thinking of voters in the last days before the election. To increase the chances of accurately measuring last-minute public preferences among the candidates, pollsters usually increase the size of their samples. They may interview as many as 4,000 people just before a presidential election in November.

Because not all people of voting age

The art of polling

Pollsters concentrate on several important considerations in their efforts to assemble accurate polls. They try to write fair, balanced questions that will draw out each respondent's views, *below.* Pollsters also try to interview large numbers of people, *opposite page,* so that their poll results have the best possible chance of reflecting the views of the population as a whole.

▼ **Do you agree or disagree with this statement: Any able-bodied person can find a job and make ends meet.**

▼ **Some people feel that any able-bodied person can find a job and make ends meet. Others feel there are times when it is hard to get along, and some able-bodied people are not able to find work. Whom do you agree with most?**

How a question is phrased can affect the results of a poll. The first question, *above,* calls for a simple yes or no response. The second question offers the respondent alternative positions. Most pollsters would say that the second question would reflect the views of the population more accurately than the first question.

cast a ballot on election day, pollsters also need to determine which respondents in preelection polls are most likely to vote. This is a difficult task.

In 1992, for example, less than 40 per cent of the voting-age population in New Hampshire cast ballots in the state's presidential primary. This meant that more than 6 out of every 10 people approached by interviewers were not going to vote. The pollsters' challenge was to identify correctly the 40 per cent of the potential respondents most likely to vote. To determine whether a person is a likely voter, interviewers may ask if he or she is registered, has voted in previous elections, is interested in the current election, and knows where to vote.

• **Tracking polls** are polls conducted daily just before primaries or the general election. In conducting these polls, news organizations and political campaigns monitor the effect of events and political ads on voter preferences. Speed is important, so the interviews are short, usually about five minutes, and the samples small, ranging from 150 to 200 interviews. Because of the small samples, most tracking polls report the average results of three nights' interviewing.

• **Exit polls** are conducted by news organizations and involve interviews with a sample of people just after they have voted. These polls explore what issues influenced the way people voted and what support the candidates had among subgroups of voters, such as women, young people, or members of labor unions.

Regardless of the type of poll, elections provide a real test for their results. If polls were not reasonably accurate before elections, who would believe the

A *sample* is the part of the total population that the pollsters contact and question. *Sampling error* is a term pollsters use to assess the chance that the particular sample they have interviewed is not representative of the population as a whole. A poll's sampling error is expressed as a number of percentage points above and below the reported per cent, *below.* Larger samples have smaller sampling errors.

Results of a preelection poll with a sampling error of 3 percentage points		
	Level of support reported in poll	Actual level of support when sampling error is taken into account
Candidate A	49%	46% to 52% (with 49% being the most likely)
Candidate B	46%	43% to 49% (with 46% being the most likely)
Undecided	5%	

Sample size	Sampling error
200	± 9 percentage points
400	± 6 percentage points
600	± 5 percentage points
1,000	± 4 percentage points
1,500	± 3 percentage points

If the sampling error for a preelection poll is plus or minus 3 percentage points, *above,* the level of support for a candidate may be 3 percentage points larger or smaller than indicated. Thus, in this example, there is a small chance that support for Candidate A could be equal to or less than that for Candidate B, though it is most likely that Candidate A leads Candidate B by 3 percentage points.

polls between elections? But even if the polls are seen as believable, how well do they serve our political process?

The oldest worry about the role of the polls is that public opinion itself may be influenced by what the polls say. Will some people be inclined to vote for candidates who appear to be ahead while other people are drawn to candidates who are behind? Pollsters have long said there was no evidence of such "bandwagon" or "underdog" effects. Studies have revealed that voter preferences can be influenced by the polls early in a campaign. But once the campaign gets underway, poll reports hold less sway because voters have other reasons to make up their minds.

A newer concern about the role of polls has to do with their effect on the way news organizations cover election campaigns. Some observers wonder whether political reporters may be influenced by the apparent precision and objectivity of polls, and whether this might keep them from writing stories that suggest conclusions that are different from what the latest polls show. This can lead to a kind of "pack journalism," in which reporters come to see and report an election campaign in the same way.

All in all, carefully conducted and reported polls can help our democratic process work. They help hold elected officials accountable by providing measures of the public's approval. They serve as a check on claims special interests make about the public's thinking on important issues. Most importantly, the polls can strengthen democracy by bringing the public's concerns and priorities into the competition among political interests.   [Albert H. Cantril]

The Chemistry of Cleaning Clothes

Have you ever wondered how a cup of detergent cleans soiled jeans, towels, socks, and other articles in your wash, or how cleaning fluid at the dry cleaner whisks away that grease stain from your suit? And why are hair spray, vinegar, club soda, and baking soda surprisingly effective dirt and stain removers in an emergency? The answers lie both in the chemical properties of various types of dirt and stains and in the ways that the cleaning agents chemically interact with them.

Dirt and stains typically consist of particles, such as minerals from soil, protein and other organic matter from living things, or bits of black carbon. The particles are trapped on cloth fibers by grease and oil, which cannot be dissolved in water. Anything that can loosen the grease and oil from the fibers and *disperse* (scatter) these substances in the wash water or dry-cleaning solution will remove the dirt and stains.

Soaps, detergents, cleaning fluids, and many emergency stain removers are effective cleaners because they can dissolve and *emulsify* (break up and suspend) the oil and grease that holds dirt in place. The grease and trapped soil particles then can be carried away in the water or dry-cleaning solution. But these agents differ widely in their dirt-fighting activities and the conditions under which they work. To understand why, we must understand the chemical nature of soaps and detergents.

The words *soap* and *detergent* are often used interchangeably, but the two cleaners differ considerably. Soaps are generally made from natural fats and oils. Soaps are excellent for cleaning our hands, face, and body, because the loosened dirt is rinsed away immediately. But soaps have definite drawbacks for cleaning laundry. For example, soaps often allow dirt lifted from clothes to redeposit on the clothes before the wash cycle is finished. And in *hard water* (water containing high levels of minerals), soaps react with minerals to form scum, called soap curd. Soap curd does not dissolve. It is difficult to remove from fabrics, and it makes the fabric feel stiff.

Because of these drawbacks, laundry soaps have largely been replaced by detergents. Detergents are *synthetic* (artificial) mixtures of ingredients that not only clean clothes but also prevent redeposition of dirt, discourage scum formation, and possess other useful properties. The most important advantage of detergents is the ability to clean effectively in hard water.

Both soaps and detergents contain cleaning ingredients known as *surfactants*. Surfactant compounds are *molecules* (linked groups of atoms) attracted to the boundary between two liquids that normally do not dissolve in each other, such as oil and water. One end of the surfactant molecule is attracted to water but not oil, and the other end is attracted to oil but not to water.

This dual nature of surfactant molecules boosts the "wetting" ability of water. This means that water containing surfactants can more easily penetrate and disperse dirt and stains. One end of the surfactant molecule dissolves and emulsifies the grease that traps soil particles on fabrics. The other end dissolves in the surrounding water. As a result of this action, one portion of the molecule pulls away from the other, and this force pulls the grease from the clothes and suspends it in the form of tiny droplets. Washing machine agitation also helps loosen the greasy soil. After the soil droplets are suspended in the water, the thin layer of surfactant molecules around them keeps them separated from the fabric and prevents them from resettling on the clothes. The suspended droplets and the soil clinging to them are then easily rinsed away by the water.

The same principle enables hair spray to remove ink and certain other stains from clothes. Some hair sprays contain alcohol, which behaves chemically in a way similar to surfactants in detergents. One portion of the alcohol molecule penetrates and emulsifies the oils that hold the ink pigments in place. Another portion of the alcohol molecule dissolves in the alcohol solvents also found in hair spray. In this way, hair spray loosens the ink pigments, which can then be removed by conventional laundering with water and detergents.

Compounds called *enzymes* enhance the cleaning action of surfactants. Enzymes are complex molecules made by living organisms. Often called "biological catalysts," enzymes promote certain chemical reactions without themselves being changed. Enzymatic action is similar to digestive juices in the stomach, which break down food in preparation for digestion in the intestines. Detergent enzymes, made by bacteria in factory production vats, react with and break up stains that are made of proteins. Such stains include blood, meat gravy, milk, eggs, and grass. Enzymes break down these substances into simpler forms that can be removed by other components in the detergent.

If you're out of enzyme detergents and the stores are closed, try using a meat tenderizer on a protein stain. The tenderizer contains enzymes intended to partially digest proteins in meat before it is cooked. But when poured onto clothing or carpets, the enzymes can also break up protein molecules in stains. (But make sure to rinse the stain with water to wash away the salt, spices, and coloring that are included with the enzymes in the tenderizer.)

Another group of chemical compounds used in detergents are called *builders*. Builders typically make up more than half the weight of a box of detergent. Their principal function is to soften hard water. These chemicals react with and remove from wash water certain minerals, particularly those containing calcium and magnesium. Such minerals can react with surfactants to form scums that deposit on clothes and interfere with cleaning action. Minerals can also promote redeposition of removed soil particles.

Another function of builders is to make the wash water alkaline. *Alkali builders* are chemicals that neutralize acids in the water and aid the breakup of oil and fat molecules by rupturing their chemical bonds. Some builders act as buffering agents to maintain the proper alkaline level in the wash water.

Removing dirt and stains by making water "wetter"

Chemical compounds in soap and detergents called surfactants account for much of the cleaning power of these products. Surfactants are molecules that boost the "wetting" ability of water so that the water can more easily penetrate dirt and stains on fabrics.

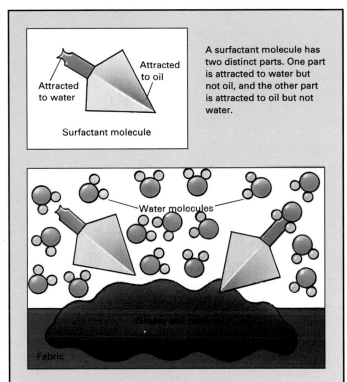

A surfactant molecule has two distinct parts. One part is attracted to water but not oil, and the other part is attracted to oil but not water.

When one part of the surfactant molecule attaches to water and the other part attaches to the oil in greasy dirt, the surfactant is pulled in opposite directions. The force of one part of the surfactant molecule pulling away from the other also pulls the greasy soil particle away from the fabric.

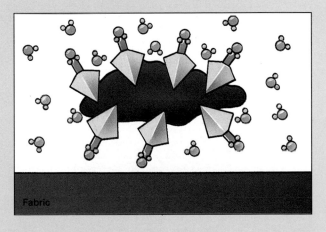

Surfactant molecules surround the dirt, keeping it suspended in the wash water.

Removing stains in an emergency

Some products commonly found at home are surprisingly effective in removing certain stains because of the way these products chemically interact with stains.

Emergency stain remover	Stains removed	Why it works	How to use
Baking soda	Toilet-bowl cleaner and other acid stains	Alkali in baking soda neutralizes the acid	Sprinkle on stain
Carbonated water	Hard-water residues and other alkaline stains	Weak acid in carbonated water dissolves alkaline stains	Pour on stain
Denture cleaner	Coffee, tea	Acts like oxygen bleach to decolorize stains	Rub on stain
Hair spray	Ink	Alcohol in hair spray emulsifies oils that hold ink pigments in place	Spray on stain, launder as usual
Hydrogen peroxide	Blood	Liberates oxygen atoms, which turn red blood pigments into less brightly colored stains	Pour on stain
Lemon juice	Tomato juice	Citric acid in lemon juice lightens red pigments	Rub on stain
Meat tenderizer	Blood, grass, gravy, and other protein stains	Enzymes in meat tenderizer break up protein molecules	Sprinkle on stain, rinse
Vegetable shortening	Oils and ink on nonwashable fabrics, such as silk	Dissolves oils	Rub on stain, follow with hair spray
Vinegar	Hard-water residues and other alkaline stains	Weak acid in vinegar dissolves alkaline stains	Pour on stain

Because ordinary baking soda contains an alkali—sodium bicarbonate—baking soda is handy for neutralizing and removing acid stains such as those made by toilet-bowl cleaners. Because vinegar contains acetic acid, which is mildly acidic, it is useful for breaking up and dissolving such alkaline stains as hard-water residues. You also could use club soda on these residues, because it contains weakly acidic carbonic acid, a compound not found in plain water.

Some builders also boost the action of surfactants. For example, certain builders help surfactants suspend loosened dirt and keep it from settling back on clothes. Other builders help surfactants emulsify greasy soil by breaking the oily particles into tiny globules.

In the 1960's, chemicals called phosphates were the most common builders in detergents. Phosphates remove minerals from hard water by combining with them. The compound thus formed is then rinsed away with the water after the clothes are washed.

But phosphates in waste water were found to harm the environment. Detergent phosphates ultimately ended up in streams and lakes, and because phosphates are nutrients for algae, the chemicals overfertilized the streams and lakes. The result was excessive growth of algae. Eventually, the abundance of algae clogged streams and lakes, setting in motion a process that could kill most of the life in the water. Because of this, detergent manufacturers drastically reduced the phosphate content of their products and began using builders that were less harmful to the environment.

Interestingly, there is no relationship between a detergent's sudsing action and its cleaning ability. Nevertheless, manufacturers may recommend the use of low sudsing detergents for front-loading tumbler-type washing machines because high levels of suds would cushion clothes as they drop back into the water after being lifted out in the tumbling action. Such a cushioning effect would interfere with the machine's washing action. To appeal to consumers who prefer various amounts of suds, detergent manufacturers include in their formulas special sudsing modifiers. These compounds are long-chain molecules, made from natural fats, that can either boost or depress levels of suds made by dissolved detergents.

Bleaches do not remove dirt particles but make them colorless or nearly colorless. Liquid chlorine bleach is the most powerful of the chemical bleaches used as laundry aids. Chlorine bleach not only whitens clothes, but also disinfects and deodorizes them. It can, however, remove color from clothes.

A less powerful chemical bleach is oxygen bleach. Because it is safe to use on most fabrics, oxygen bleach is the one most frequently added to detergents. It is also used in presoak products to aid in cleaning heavily soiled clothes or in helping to remove stubborn stains before clothes are put through a normal washing machine cycle.

Some presoak products use enzymes, but these require more time to work than do products using only oxygen bleach. Also, enzyme presoak products should not be used at the same time as chlorine bleach, because chlorine bleach destroys enzymes. By using the products separately, you will get the maximum benefit of each.

Other laundry aids also do not remove dirt or stains, yet they can make clothes appear cleaner. *Whiteners,* also known as optical bleaches, consist of *organic* (carbon-containing) molecules that can absorb invisible forms of light and, through a complex process at the atomic level, reemit it as visible blue light. Clothes treated with these compounds come out of a wash looking both brighter and whiter than they did before being washed.

The hydrogen peroxide found in many medicine cabinets for the treatment of wounds behaves comparably to the bleach we add to washes. When applied to blood stains, for example, peroxide liberates oxygen atoms, which turns red blood pigments into less brightly colored stains. Denture cleaning tablets, which contain oxygen in the same form found in oxygen bleaches, can similarly decolorize stains made by tea and coffee.

Unfortunately, laundry cleaning agents function only in water, a medium that can damage some natural fabrics, such as silk and wool, which are water-sensitive. When they are wet, water-sensitive fibers swell in diameter and shorten, causing the garment to shrink.

The most effective way of removing dirt and stains from water-sensitive articles is dry cleaning. Dry cleaning is a process in which a liquid other than water is used to dissolve and flush away oil and grease along with underlying soils. The most useful solvents in dry cleaning are water-insoluble liquids derived from petroleum, particularly a carbon- and chlorine-containing compound called perchloroethylene. Dry-cleaning solvents, unlike water-based detergents, do not repel oil and grease molecules. Instead, the solvents surround and dissolve these molecules. Many commercial dry cleaners also add special detergents to their solvents to further loosen soil particles.

A primitive form of dry cleaning is possible using vegetable shortening as a "solvent." The shortening dissolves oils—for example, those in deep-fried snacks or those that hold ink pigments in place. Then a follow-up treatment with hair spray will remove the dissolved oils and pigments.

So, the next time you're studying late on a Sunday night, and your pen slips from the paper onto your white pants, where a greasy snack fell without your knowing it, remember your chemistry. A little shortening and hair spray could prevent an ugly stain.   [Gordon Graff]

Weather Terms— Cloudy or Clear?

We are all interested in what the weather forecast has to tell us: Will it rain when we want to go to the beach, to the park, or to a ball game? Will there be a heavy snow tomorrow, so that commuter trains and school buses may run on a delayed schedule (or maybe not at all)?

The forecast itself becomes more interesting and more understandable if we look into the meanings of the terms that forecasters use. Some parts of the weather forecast seem easy enough to understand—for example, the predicted high and low temperatures. But weather terms such as "high-pressure system," "occluded front," or "temperature-humidity index" sound more complicated. The meanings of these terms become clear, however, once you know something about the major factors that produce the weather and how these factors influence one another.

Precipitation refers to rain, snow, sleet, and hail—types of moisture that fall from the atmosphere. Moisture enters the atmosphere through the evaporation of water from lakes, rivers, soil, and even green plants on Earth's surface. This evaporated water is called *water vapor*.

At a given temperature and pressure, the air can hold only a certain amount of moisture, and colder air can hold less than can warmer air. The *dew point* is the temperature of the air at which water vapor begins to *condense* (turn to liquid). The vapor may condense on Earth's surface as dew or frost or in the air around tiny particles of dust or pollution.

High in the air, the tiny water droplets form the clouds; near ground, they create fog. If the temperature of the air is below freezing, the water vapor that forms clouds turns into microscopic ice crystals.

Rain falls when the microscopic water droplets in clouds collide, merge, and finally become too heavy for the air to support them. If the air temperature is above about 4 °C (39 °F), ice crystals in clouds melt as they fall to Earth, also creating rain. At slightly lower temperatures, the result is sleet. Below about 3 °C (37 °F), the moisture falls as snow.

Hailstones are frozen raindrops or ice pellets that are swept up by powerful *updrafts* (upward movements of air) in storm clouds and coated with a layer of icy water that freezes. The pellets drop and then get carried back up again to freezing heights by the updraft. As this process repeats, the hailstones grow until they find their way into a downdraft that carries them to the ground. If the hailstones are large enough, they will not completely melt as they fall to Earth, even on a warm summer day.

In weather forecasts, forecasters often refer to the chance of precipitation as a percentage. A 30 per cent chance of rain, for example, means that it rained in the past on 30 days out of every 100 with similar weather conditions.

Humidity is a measure of the water vapor in the air. *Absolute humidity* is the actual amount of water vapor in a given volume of air. Weather forecasts more often refer to *relative humidity*—a ratio between the actual moisture and the maximum amount of moisture that air at that temperature could hold. If the temperature outside drops to the dew point, relative humidity becomes 100 per cent and fog is likely to form.

Relative humidity affects our comfort. In hot weather, high relative humidity slows the evaporation of water from the skin and makes us feel uncomfortably hot and sticky. In cold weather, high relative humidity conducts heat away from the body and makes the air feel cold and raw.

The *temperature-humidity index* (THI) sometimes mentioned in forecasts was once called the discomfort index. This scale estimates the degree of discomfort caused by hot, moist weather. The higher the reading, the more discomfort people feel. Most people feel comfortable with a THI below 75.

Air pressure is the weight of the atmosphere pressing down on the surface of Earth. Meteorologists call it *barometric pressure* because the instrument used

Reading a weather map

Weather maps that appear in newspapers predict daily weather conditions, including areas of rain and snow and the high and low temperatures in selected cities. They also show factors that influence those conditions, such as zones of high and low pressure and zones called fronts, where masses of cool and warm air meet.

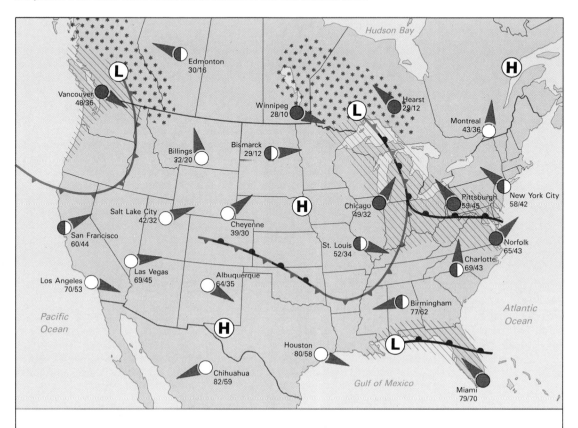

H

A high-pressure zone forms where the force exerted by the atmosphere on Earth is fairly great. It usually brings clear skies.

L

A low-pressure zone forms where the force exerted by the atmosphere on Earth is fairly low. It usually brings cloudy skies.

Wind direction shows the direction in which the wind is blowing.

A warm front occurs where a warm air mass overtakes a colder air mass. It brings gradual changes in the weather, often accompanied by high humidity and light, steady precipitation. As the front passes, the temperature rises.

A cold front forms where a cool air mass overtakes a warmer air mass. It brings sudden changes in the weather, often accompanied by heavy precipitation. As the front passes, the temperature drops.

A stationary front, where two air masses meet but do not move, usually brings stagnant, unsettled weather that lasts several days.

An occluded front occurs where two cold air masses meet beneath a warmer air mass. The front can resemble a cold front or a warm front, but it usually brings less severe weather.

52/34
High and low daily temperatures (°F)

▨ **Area of rain**

✳ **Area of snow**

○ **Clear skies**

◑ **Partly cloudy skies**

● **Cloudy skies**

to measure air pressure is called a *barometer*. The barometer was invented in 1643 by Evangelista Torricelli, an Italian physicist, who demonstrated that the pressure of the atmosphere at sea level could push a column of mercury 76 centimeters (30 inches) up a glass tube. Hence, standard barometric pressure is about 30 inches of mercury at sea level.

In the United States, weather forecasts give barometric pressure in inches. Meteorologists who use the metric system express barometric pressure in units called *bars* and *millibars*. A millibar is $\frac{1}{1000}$ of a bar, and standard barometric pressure averages 1,013 millibars at sea level.

Zones of high atmospheric pressure, also called *highs,* contain dense air. In the Northern Hemisphere, many highs form in polar regions because the colder a mass of air gets, the denser it becomes, and this increases its pressure. A high also occurs where an air mass cools in relation to the surrounding air. As the cooling air becomes denser, it sinks. This further compresses the air, warming it somewhat and increasing its ability to hold moisture. As a result, the water drops that make up clouds evaporate, and the sky over a high-pressure zone is usually clear.

Low-pressure zones, or *lows,* contain air that is less dense. Lows form where the air is warm and rises. The warm air cools as it rises, and the water vapor it holds begins to condense. As a result, the sky over a low is generally cloudy.

Changes in barometric pressure help forecast weather conditions. A high with rising barometric pressure typically signals fine, clear weather ahead, whereas a low with falling barometric pressure often indicates bad weather ahead— usually heavy, prolonged rain.

Fronts, where most abrupt changes in the weather occur, are the boundaries between huge masses of air, each with its own temperature and moisture content. The movements of these air masses influence local weather. For example, an air mass from the equator can produce balmy weather, while an air mass from northern Canada can bring a cold spell. Air masses of different temperatures meet and do battle along fronts. Fronts were discovered toward the end of World War I (1914-1918) and are so named because the clashing of air masses reminded meteorologists of the clashing of armies along a battlefront.

Strong fronts, which occur where there is a large difference in temperature or moisture between air masses, bring high winds and stormy weather. Weak fronts, where the two air masses are close in temperature, often pass unnoticed, except by meteorologists. In North America, highs, lows, and fronts generally move from west to east and follow curving paths. A front may be warm or cold, depending upon which air mass—the warmer or the colder—is pushing the air ahead of it.

A *warm front* occurs where a relatively warm air mass advances on a colder air mass. The warm air, which is lighter, pushes up and over the edge of the cold air. As the warm air rises, it cools and thereby loses some of its ability to hold moisture. If the air is fairly humid, some of this moisture may turn into rain or snow. If the air is dry, clouds may form but precipitation will be slight. The gentle rain or drizzle that warm fronts often bring usually lasts several days. After the front passes, the temperature rises and the sky clears.

A *cold front* forms where a relatively cool air mass overtakes a warmer air mass. The cold air, being denser, slides under the edge of the warmer air, lifting it rapidly. Tall clouds form as the warm air quickly cools on its steep ascent. The more moisture in the air, the larger the clouds are.

Cold fronts bring bad weather, but they move faster than warm fronts, and the bad weather usually ends soon. If a cold front moves very fast, it may slide under a warm air mass, lift it off the ground, and collide with another cold air mass on the far side of the warm air. In this case, an *occluded front* forms. The word *occlude* comes from a Latin word meaning *to close off,* and the two cold air masses essentially "close off" the warm air mass. Occluded fronts usually bring less severe weather than warm or cold fronts and tend to stay in one place for a longer time.

Sometimes air masses meet and do not move, forming a *stationary front.* This kind of front usually brings unsettled weather that lasts a while.

A *thermal inversion* is a weather condition that occurs when a mass of warm air forms over cooler air near the ground. The lighter warm air sits like a lid atop the cooler air, blocking the normal air circulation. In large cities such as Los Angeles, a thick haze of automobile exhaust, industrial chemicals, and other pollutants may build up during the thermal inversion. The warm air above is very stable and prevents the pollutants from rising and scattering and results in a type of air pollution often called *smog.*

Winds and wind speed. Wind is simply air in motion over Earth's surface. The sun's uneven heating of Earth's surface sets air in motion. As warm air rises, cool air rushes in to replace it.

The uneven heating of land and water surfaces along coastlines creates local winds. During the day, the land warms faster than the water and heats the air above it. As this warm air rises, cooler air over the water rushes in to replace it. At night, the land cools faster than the water, and cooler air blows from land to replace warm air rising over the water.

But the strongest winds occur along fronts. The greater the differences in temperature and pressure along the front, the stronger the winds are.

Winds also spiral into low-pressure zones, like water into a whirlpool. For this reason, meteorologists call low-pressure zones *cyclones,* a term that comes from the Greek word for *circle.* A high-pressure zone is called an *anticyclone* because wind flows out of it in the direction opposite that of a cyclone. North of the equator, the winds move counterclockwise around a cyclone and clockwise around an anticyclone due to Earth's rotation. South of the equator, cyclone winds move clockwise; anticyclone winds, counterclockwise.

A *jet stream* is a band of strong winds at a high altitude. Jet streams follow meandering paths from west to east at speeds up to 400 kilometers per hour (kph) (250 miles per hour [mph]), changing their course frequently. Over the Northern Hemisphere, cold air masses predominate to the north of a jet stream and warm air masses to its south.

Wind chill provides an estimate of the effect of wind speed on air temperature. Wind accelerates the loss of heat from the body, even on a hot day. The faster the wind blows, the more heat the body loses and the colder the temperature feels. On a day with a temperature of 1.7 °C (35 °F), for example, a wind of 8 kph (5 mph) has the effect of lowering the temperature to 0 °C (32 °F). A wind that is blowing twice as fast appears to lower the wind-chill temperature to -5.6 °C (22 °F).

Wind shear is a rapid change in the speed or direction of wind. Wind shear can be dangerous for airplane travel, especially if the change is a *downburst,* a gust of wind that blows straight to the ground. Downbursts may develop when precipitation falls through dry air, suddenly cooling the air and making it more dense. The air may then plummet to the ground.

Storms. A *hurricane* or *typhoon* is a violent, swirling storm that develops in a low-pressure area over tropical ocean regions. Hurricanes grow in size and strength as they travel, feeding on heat from the warm water. They peter out when they pass over land or cold water, which robs them of their source of energy. As hurricanes move onto land, their heavy rains often cause floods.

A *tornado* is a small, intense funnel of wind that extends downward from the dark clouds that form during thunderstorms. Wind speeds in a tornado can exceed 320 kph (200 mph). Strong updrafts of wind inside the funnel are powerful enough to lift automobiles and mobile homes into the air. In the United States, tornadoes occur most frequently in the Midwest in spring.

Winter storms and thunderstorms often form when air that is moist and relatively warm is set in motion, perhaps by an advancing cold front. Water vapor in the air quickly condenses as the warm air rises, forming massive, towering clouds that produce heavy rains, blizzards, or ice storms.

In thunderstorms, the motion of the air also causes electric charges to build up inside the cloud, producing lightning. Flashes of lightning heat the surrounding air, causing the air to expand violently and create the sound waves known as thunder.

Even when such severe weather is not threatening, it's still a good idea to understand the meaning of common weather terms. And knowing about the actions of fronts, highs, and lows can help you understand why the forecaster predicts that the weather will be fair or foul. 　　　　[Peter R. Limburg]

EnergyGuide Labels: Help for the Appliance Shopper

Operating home appliances costs consumers in the United States about $100-billion a year in gas, fuel oil, and electricity bills—more than $1,000 for the average household. The U.S. government has lent a helping hand to consumers trying to lower their energy costs by requiring a yellow EnergyGuide label to be affixed to most large appliances being offered for sale.

Large appliances consume most of the energy used in homes. Thus, small appliances are not required to carry EnergyGuide labels. The requirement has also been waived for some major appliances, such as clothes dryers and kitchen ranges, because all brands and models are similar in their efficiency.

The cost of operating a major appliance can be quite high. In fact, over the lifetime of the appliance, which may be 15 to 20 years, energy costs may amount to several times the purchase price.

Consider, for example, the purchase of a new refrigerator that costs $660 and consumes $72 worth of electricity a year. If the refrigerator lasts 20 years, the cumulative electricity costs for it would be $1,440. Of course, that total is based on the assumption that the price of electricity won't go up during the 20-year period—a highly unlikely possibility. So the eventual energy cost is apt to be much more than $1,440.

The combination of purchase price and operating costs over the useful lifetime of an appliance is known as the machine's *life cycle cost*. The life cycle cost of the $660 refrigerator would be $2,100—the purchase price plus the total cost of energy at current rates, $1,440. Because the energy costs involved with operating an appliance can be so high, it may be useful to consider the purchase price as just a down payment. Additional "installments" on the appliance will be paid in monthly electricity, gas, or oil bills.

The latest home appliances are generally much more energy efficient than older models. The most striking improvements have been made in the design of refrigerators. Most refrigerators made in 1992 use only about half as much electricity as ones sold in 1972.

Appliance manufacturers were prodded into making their products less energy hungry because of U.S. government efficiency standards and rising energy costs in the 1970's and 1980's. Technological innovations enabled the appliance industry to meet and exceed those new standards. The greater efficiency of the newer refrigerators, for instance, was made possible by advanced insulation materials, better motors and compressors, and improved systems for getting rid of heat.

Although such changes have greatly improved the efficiency of most appliances, there are still wide differences between various brands and models. EnergyGuide labels can help you distinguish highly efficient models from those of only average efficiency. There are three types of labels: energy cost labels, energy efficiency rating labels, and general information labels.

Energy cost labels give estimates of the yearly cost of operating an appliance, based on national average energy prices. These labels appear on refrigerators, freezers, water heaters, dishwashers, and clothes washers.

Energy efficiency rating labels appear on central and room air conditioners and on central heat pumps. These labels show the efficiency of an appliance in terms of an energy efficiency rating (EER) for room air conditioners, a seasonal energy efficiency rating (SEER) for central air conditioners, and both an SEER and a heating season performance factor (HSPF) for heat pumps. The higher the rating, the more efficient the equipment.

To enable consumers to compare the efficiencies of different appliance models, EnergyGuide labels include a horizontal bar scale. The scale shows the extremes of the most- and least-efficient models available for a particular type of appliance of a specific size or work capacity. An arrow indicates the point on the scale representing the relative efficiency of the model the shopper is looking at.

The energy cost labels for refrigerators, freezers, and electric water heaters are based on an estimate of the amount of electricity the model would consume in a year. Electricity consumption is measured in *kilowatt-hours* (kwh). One kwh represents a kilowatt (1,000 watts) of power consumed for one hour.

A typical new refrigerator today uses about 850 kwh per year. The national average price of electricity for residential customers is about 8.5 cents per kwh. Multiplying the price per kwh by the number of kilowatt-hours the appliance uses each year gives the annual energy cost, in this case $72.25. That is, $850 \times \$0.085 = \$72.25$.

The costs listed on EnergyGuide labels for gas water heaters are based on the model's estimated annual consumption of natural gas. Natural gas consumption is commonly measured in *therms,* a unit equal to 2.8 cubic meters (100 cubic feet) of gas. A typical new gas water heater uses about 300 therms a year. The national average price of gas is 60 cents per therm, so a gas water heater using 300 therms a year would have an annual operating cost of $180 ($0.60 × 300 = $180).

The expense of heating household water is even higher with electricity than with gas. The considerable cost of operating a water heater can be an important factor when purchasing a dishwasher or clothes washer, since both those appliances use large amounts of hot water. Energy cost labels for dishwashers and clothes washers therefore include two sets of information, one giving the annual cost of operating the appliance in connection with an electric water heater, the other figuring the cost with a gas heater.

In calculating the long-term savings that one appliance model offers over another, consumers may sometimes discover that the model with the highest purchase price is ultimately the cheapest. The average water heater, for example, lasts about 13 years. Over that period, a high-efficiency model might yield

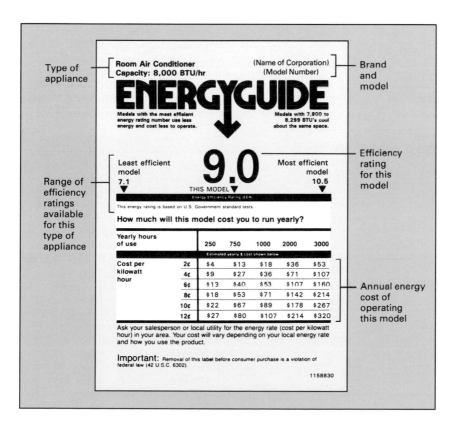

An EnergyGuide label for a room air conditioner shows that this model has an energy efficiency rating of 9.0, considerably better than the least efficient model on the market, rated 7.1. The best available model has a rating of 10.5. A chart at the bottom of the label tells how much it will cost to run the air conditioner each year, based on local electricity costs and estimates of how many hours the appliance will be used during the year.

Using EnergyGuide labels

How to calculate savings

By following three steps, a buyer can determine the long-term savings from purchasing a more efficient appliance—in this case, a $630 refrigerator with an annual operating cost of $60, compared with a $600 refrigerator costing $70 a year to operate. The operating cost of an appliance is determined by consulting the per-kilowatt-hour chart at the bottom of the EnergyGuide label. Some labels also give annual operating costs based on national-average electricity rates.

Step 1. Subtract the purchase price of the less expensive refrigerator from that of the more expensive model ($630–$600=$30).

Step 2. Subtract the lower yearly operating cost from the higher yearly operating cost ($70–$60=$10).

Step 3. Divide the difference in purchase price by the difference in yearly operating cost ($30÷$10=3). Thus, the price difference would be made up in three years. Because the average lifetime for refrigerators is 19 years, the owner could expect to look forward to 16 years of "profits" from energy savings.

Average life expectancies of appliances

Appliance	Life expectancy
Central air conditioner	12 years
Clothes washer	13 years
Dishwasher	12 years
Freezer	21 years
Furnace	23 years
Heat pump	12 years
Refrigerator	19 years
Room air conditioner	15 years
Water heater	13 years

savings of nearly $300 in energy costs over a less efficient water heater—more than the initial cost difference between the two models.

Estimating the operating costs of new air conditioners can be more difficult than for other kinds of appliances. That is because the energy efficiency of air conditioners is commonly expressed in efficiency ratings—SEER's—rather than dollars.

Many older central air conditioners have SEER's below or near 8. New federal efficiency standards have set the minimum allowable SEER for new units at 10, and very-high-efficiency models are now available with SEER's of about 15. The numbers indicate relative efficiency: A unit rated 12 is twice as efficient as one rated 6 and would cost half as much to operate.

When shopping for an air conditioner or any other major appliance, the consumer should be aware that while EnergyGuide labels are useful, they are not perfect. For one thing, the horizontal bar showing the range of efficiencies for available models is often outdated.

Because manufacturers introduce new models constantly, it is difficult for the government to keep up with every improvement, so the high-efficiency end of the horizontal bar may show a figure that has long since been surpassed by some manufacturers. Therefore, a model whose efficiency rating is near the posted high-end figure may seem to be more efficient, relative to other models, than it really is.

Another problem is that different manufacturers may use different energy prices when they are calculating the estimated cost of operating their products. Consumers would thus be wise to check the information table beneath the bar to compare different models at consistent energy prices. These EnergyGuide tables give yearly operating costs at varying kilowatt-hour prices.

Because of these shortcomings in the EnergyGuide labeling system, the Federal Trade Commission, which administers the program, was expected to propose new labels in late 1992. Any suggested changes, however, would be subject to review by appliance manufacturers and the public and would probably not take effect until late 1993 or early 1994.   [John H. Morrill]

World Book Supplement

Four new or revised articles reprinted from the 1992 edition of *The World Book Encyclopedia.*

© Eslami Rad, Gamma/Liaison   Park Snavely, U.S. Geological Survey

Earthquakes are among the most destructive and powerful forces in nature. An Iranian, *left,* mourns the damage caused by a 1990 quake. The course of a stream, *right,* was changed by shifting rock along the San Andreas Fault. Such rock shifts can cause devastating quakes.

Earthquake

Earthquake is a shaking of the ground caused by the sudden breaking and shifting of large sections of the earth's rocky outer shell. Earthquakes are among the most powerful events on earth, and their results can be terrifying. A severe earthquake may release energy 10,000 times as great as that of the first atomic bomb. Rock movements during an earthquake can make rivers change their course. Earthquakes can trigger landslides that cause great damage and loss of life. Large earthquakes beneath the ocean can create a series of huge, destructive waves called *tsunamis* (pronounced *tsoo NAH meez*) that flood coasts for many miles.

Earthquakes almost never kill people directly. Instead, many deaths and injuries in earthquakes result from falling objects and the collapse of buildings, bridges, and other structures. Fire resulting from broken gas or power lines is another major danger during a quake. Spills of hazardous chemicals are also a concern during an earthquake.

The force of an earthquake depends on how much rock breaks and how far it shifts. Powerful earthquakes can shake firm ground violently for great distances. During minor earthquakes, the vibration may be no greater than the vibration caused by a passing truck.

On average, a powerful earthquake occurs less than once every two years. At least 40 moderate earthquakes

Karen C. McNally, the contributor of this article, is Professor of Geophysics and Director of the Charles F. Richter Seismological Laboratory at the University of California at Santa Cruz.

cause damage somewhere in the world each year. About 40,000 to 50,000 small earthquakes—large enough to be felt but not damaging—occur annually.

How an earthquake begins

Most earthquakes occur along a *fault*—a fracture in the earth's rocky outer shell where sections of rock repeatedly slide past each other. Faults occur in weak areas of the earth's rock. Most faults lie beneath the surface of the earth, but some, like the San Andreas Fault in California, are visible on the surface. Stresses in the earth cause large blocks of rock along a fault to *strain,* or bend. When the stress on the rock becomes great enough, the rock breaks and snaps into a new position, causing the shaking of an earthquake.

Earthquakes usually begin deep in the ground. The point in the earth where the rocks first break is called the *focus,* also known as the *hypocenter,* of the quake. The focus of most earthquakes lies less than 45 miles (72 kilometers) beneath the surface, though the deepest known focuses have been nearly 450 miles (700 kilometers) below the surface. The point on the surface of the earth directly above the focus is known as the *epicenter* of the quake. The strongest shaking is usually felt near the epicenter.

From the focus, the break travels like a spreading crack along the fault. The speed at which the fracture spreads depends on the type of rock. It may average about 2 miles (3.2 kilometers) per second in granite or other strong rock. At that rate, a fracture may spread more than 350 miles (560 kilometers) in one direction in less than three minutes. As the fracture extends along the fault, blocks of rock on one side of the fault may drop down below the rock on the other side, move up and over the other side, or slide forward past the other.

How an earthquake spreads

When an earthquake occurs, the violent breaking of rock releases energy that travels through the earth in the form of vibrations called *seismic waves*. Seismic waves move out from the focus of an earthquake in all directions. As the waves travel away from the focus, they grow gradually weaker. For this reason, the ground generally shakes less farther away from the focus.

There are two chief kinds of seismic waves: (1) body waves and (2) surface waves. Body waves, the fastest seismic waves, move through the earth. Slower surface waves travel along the surface of the earth.

Body waves tend to cause the most earthquake damage. There are two kinds of body waves: (1) compressional waves and (2) shear waves. As the waves pass through the earth, they cause particles of rock to move in different ways. Compressional waves push and pull the rock. They cause buildings and other structures to contract and expand. Shear waves make rocks move from side to side, and buildings shake. Compressional waves can travel through solids, liquids, or gases, but shear waves can pass only through solids.

Compressional waves are the fastest seismic waves, and they arrive first at a distant point. For this reason, compressional waves are also called *primary (P) waves*. Shear waves, which travel slower and arrive later, are called *secondary (S) waves*.

Body waves travel faster deep within the earth than near the surface. For example, at depths of less than 16 miles (25 kilometers), compressional waves travel at about 4.2 miles (6.8 kilometers) per second, and shear waves travel at 2.4 miles (3.8 kilometers) per second. At a depth of 620 miles (1,000 kilometers), the waves travel more than 1½ times that speed.

Surface waves are long, slow waves. They produce what people feel as slow rocking sensations and cause little or no damage to buildings.

There are two kinds of surface waves: (1) Love waves and (2) Rayleigh waves. Love waves travel through the earth's surface horizontally and move the ground from

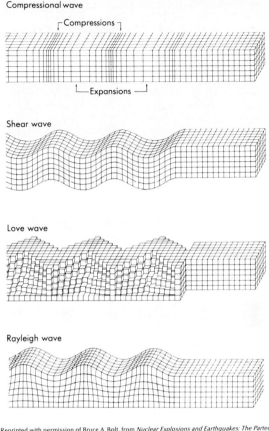

Reprinted with permission of Bruce A. Bolt, from *Nuclear Explosions and Earthquakes: The Parted Veil* (San Francisco: W. H. Freeman and Company. Copyright © 1976).

Different seismic waves travel through rock in different ways. A *compressional wave* travels through the earth, compressing and expanding the rock. When a compressional wave hits the surface, it can cause houses and other structures to contract and expand. A *shear wave* also travels through the earth, moving rock back and forth. At the earth's surface, it can shake structures violently. A *Love wave* travels along the earth's surface and moves the ground from side to side. A *Rayleigh wave* also travels through the rock at the earth's surface, making the surface roll like waves on the ocean.

side to side. Rayleigh waves make the surface of the earth roll like waves on the ocean. Typical Love waves travel at about 2¾ miles (4.4 kilometers) per second, and Rayleigh waves, the slowest of the seismic waves, move at about 2¼ miles (3.7 kilometers) per second. The two types of waves were named for two British physicists, Augustus E. H. Love and Lord Rayleigh, who mathematically predicted the existence of the waves in 1911 and 1885, respectively.

Damage by earthquakes

How earthquakes cause damage. Earthquakes can damage buildings, bridges, dams, and other structures, as well as many natural features. Near a fault, both the shifting of large blocks of the earth's crust, called *fault slippage,* and the shaking of the ground due to seismic waves cause destruction. Away from the fault, shaking produces most of the damage. Undersea earthquakes

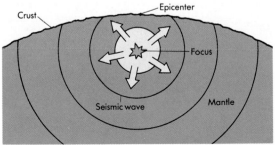

WORLD BOOK illustration by Doug DeWitt

An earthquake occurs when the earth's rock suddenly breaks and shifts, releasing energy in vibrations called *seismic waves*. The point in the earth where the rock first breaks is called the *focus*. The point on the surface above is known as the *epicenter*.

may cause huge tsunamis that swamp coastal areas. Other hazards during earthquakes include rockfalls, ground settling, and falling trees or tree branches.

Fault slippage. The rock on either side of a fault may shift only slightly during an earthquake or may move several feet or meters. In some cases, only the rock deep in the ground shifts, and no movement occurs at the earth's surface. In an extremely large earthquake, the ground may suddenly heave 20 feet (6 meters) or more. Any structure that spans a fault may be wrenched apart. The shifting blocks of earth may also loosen the soil and rocks along a slope and trigger a landslide. In addition, fault slippage may break down the banks of rivers, lakes, and other bodies of water, causing flooding.

Ground shaking causes structures to sway from side to side, bounce up and down, and move in other violent ways. Buildings may slide off their foundations, collapse, or be shaken apart.

In areas with soft, wet soils, a process called *liquefaction* may intensify earthquake damage. Liquefaction occurs when strong ground shaking causes wet soils to behave temporarily like liquids rather than solids. Anything on top of liquefied soil may sink into the soft ground. The liquefied soil may also flow toward lower ground, burying anything in its path.

Tsunamis. An earthquake on the ocean floor can give a tremendous push to surrounding seawater and create one or more large, destructive waves called tsunamis, also known as *seismic sea waves.* Some people call tsunamis *tidal waves,* but scientists think the term is misleading because the waves are not caused by the tide. Tsunamis may build to heights of more than 100 feet (30 meters) when they reach shallow water near shore. In the open ocean, tsunamis typically move at speeds of 500 to 600 miles (800 to 970 kilometers) per hour. They can travel great distances while diminishing little in size and can flood coastal areas thousands of miles or kilometers from their source.

Structural hazards. Structures collapse during a quake when they are too weak or rigid to resist strong, rocking forces. In addition, tall buildings may vibrate wildly during an earthquake and knock into each other.

A major cause of death and property damage in earthquakes is fire. Fires may start if a quake ruptures gas or power lines. The 1906 San Francisco earthquake ranks as one of the worst disasters in United States history because of a fire that raged for three days after the earthquake.

Other hazards during an earthquake include spills of toxic chemicals and falling objects, such as tree limbs, bricks, and glass. Sewage lines may break, and sewage may seep into water supplies. Drinking of such impure water may cause cholera, typhoid, dysentery, and other serious diseases.

Loss of power, communication, and transportation after an earthquake may hamper rescue teams and ambulances, increasing deaths and injuries. In addition, businesses and government offices may lose records and supplies, slowing recovery from the disaster.

Reducing earthquake damage. In areas where earthquakes are likely, knowing where to build and how to build can help reduce injury, loss of life, and property damage during a quake. Knowing what to do when a quake strikes can also help prevent injuries and deaths.

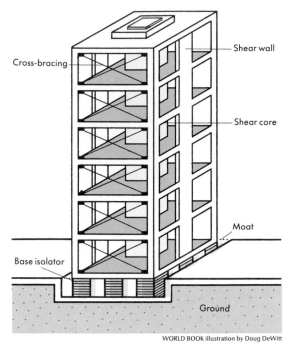

WORLD BOOK illustration by Doug DeWitt

An earthquake-resistant building includes such structures as *shear walls,* a *shear core,* and *cross-bracing. Base isolators* act as shock absorbers. A moat allows the building to sway.

Where to build. Earth scientists try to identify areas that would likely suffer great damage during an earthquake. They develop maps that show fault zones, *flood plains* (areas that get flooded), areas subject to landslides or to soil liquefaction, and the sites of past earthquakes. From these maps, land-use planners develop zoning restrictions that can help prevent construction of unsafe structures in earthquake-prone areas.

How to build. Engineers have developed a number of ways to build earthquake-resistant structures. Their techniques range from extremely simple to fairly complex. For small- to medium-sized buildings, the simpler reinforcement techniques include bolting buildings to their foundations and providing support walls called *shear walls.* Shear walls, made of *reinforced concrete* (concrete with steel rods or bars embedded in it), help strengthen the structure and help resist rocking forces. Shear walls in the center of a building, often around an elevator shaft or stairwell, form what is called a *shear core.* Walls may also be reinforced with diagonal steel beams in a technique called *cross-bracing.*

Builders also protect medium-sized buildings with devices that act like shock absorbers between the building and its foundation. These devices, called *base isolators,* are usually bearings made of alternate layers of steel and an elastic material, such as synthetic rubber. Base isolators absorb some of the sideways motion that would otherwise damage a building.

Skyscrapers need special construction to make them earthquake-resistant. They must be anchored deeply and securely into the ground. They need a reinforced framework with stronger joints than an ordinary skyscraper has. Such a framework makes the skyscraper strong enough and yet flexible enough to withstand an earthquake.

Earthquake-resistant homes, schools, and workplaces have heavy appliances, furniture, and other structures fastened down to prevent them from toppling when the building shakes. Gas and water lines must be specially reinforced with flexible joints to prevent breaking.

Safety precautions are vital during an earthquake. People can protect themselves by standing under a doorframe or crouching under a table or chair until the shaking stops. They should not go outdoors until the shaking has stopped completely. Even then, people should use extreme caution. A large earthquake may be followed by many smaller quakes, called *aftershocks.* People should stay clear of walls, windows, and damaged structures, which could crash in an aftershock.

People who are outdoors when an earthquake hits should quickly move away from tall trees, steep slopes, buildings, and power lines. If they are near a large body of water, they should move to higher ground.

Where and why earthquakes occur

Scientists have developed a theory, called *plate tectonics,* that explains why most earthquakes occur. According to this theory, the earth's outer shell consists of about 10 large, rigid plates and about 20 smaller ones. Each plate consists of a section of the earth's crust and a portion of the *mantle,* the thick layer of hot rock below the crust. Scientists call this layer of crust and upper mantle the *lithosphere.* The plates move slowly and continuously on the *asthenosphere,* a layer of hot, soft rock in the mantle. As the plates move, they collide, move apart, or slide past one another.

The movement of the plates strains the rock at and near plate boundaries and produces zones of faults around these boundaries. Along segments of some faults, the rock becomes locked in place and cannot slide as the plates move. Stress builds up in the rock on both sides of the fault and causes the rock to break and shift in an earthquake. See **Plate tectonics.**

There are three types of faults: (1) normal faults, (2) reverse faults, and (3) strike-slip faults. In normal and reverse faults, the fracture in the rock slopes downward, and the rock moves up or down along the fracture. In a normal fault, the block of rock on the upper side of the sloping fracture slides down. In a reverse fault, the rock on both sides of the fault is greatly compressed. The compression forces the upper block to slide upward and the lower block to thrust downward. In a strike-slip fault, the fracture extends straight down into the rock, and the blocks of rock along the fault slide past each other horizontally.

Most earthquakes occur in the fault zones at plate boundaries. Such earthquakes are known as *interplate earthquakes.* Some earthquakes take place within the interior of a plate and are called *intraplate earthquakes.*

Interplate earthquakes occur along the three types of plate boundaries: (1) mid-ocean spreading ridges, (2) subduction zones, and (3) transform faults.

Mid-ocean spreading ridges are places in the deep ocean basins where the plates move apart. As the plates separate, hot lava from the earth's mantle rises between them. The lava gradually cools, contracts, and cracks, creating faults. Most of these faults are normal faults. Along the faults, blocks of rock break and slide down away from the ridge, producing earthquakes.

Near the spreading ridges, the plates are thin and weak. The rock has not cooled completely, so it is still somewhat flexible. For these reasons, large strains cannot build, and most earthquakes near spreading ridges are shallow and mild or moderate in severity.

Where earthquakes occur

Most earthquakes occur near and along the boundaries of the rocky plates that cover the earth's surface. Each dot on the map represents a major earthquake that occurred during the past 30 years.

WORLD BOOK map

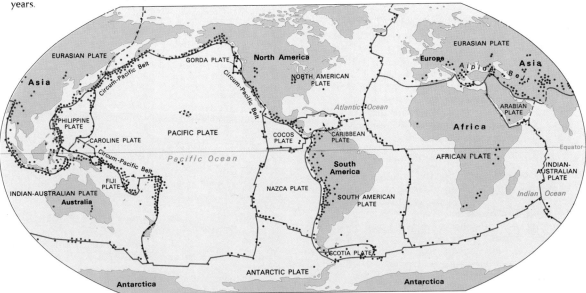

Types of faulting

Movement of the earth called *faulting* causes most earthquakes. In *normal faulting, left,* two blocks of earth move apart and one drops down. In *reverse faulting, center,* two blocks collide and one is pushed under the other. In *strike-slip faulting, right,* the blocks slide past each other.

WORLD BOOK illustration by Sarah Woodward

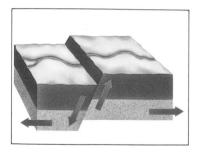 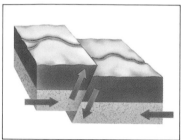 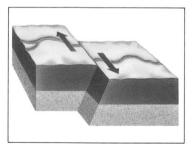

Subduction zones are places where two plates collide, and the edge of one plate pushes beneath the edge of the other in a process called *subduction.* Because of the compression in these zones, many of the faults there are reverse faults. About 80 per cent of major earthquakes occur in subduction zones encircling the Pacific Ocean. In these areas, the plates under the Pacific Ocean are plunging beneath the plates carrying the continents. The grinding of the colder, brittle ocean plates beneath the continental plates creates huge strains that are released in the world's largest earthquakes.

The world's deepest earthquakes occur in subduction zones down to a depth of about 450 miles (700 kilometers). Below that depth, the rock is too warm and soft to break suddenly and cause earthquakes.

Transform faults are places where plates slide past each other horizontally. Strike-slip faults occur there. Earthquakes along transform faults may be large, but not as large or deep as those in subduction zones.

One of the most famous transform faults is the San Andreas Fault. The slippage there is caused by the Pacific Plate moving past the North American Plate. The San Andreas Fault and its associated faults account for most of California's earthquakes.

Intraplate earthquakes are not as frequent or as large as those along plate boundaries. The largest intraplate earthquakes are about 100 times smaller than the largest interplate earthquakes.

Intraplate earthquakes tend to occur in soft, weak areas of plate interiors. Scientists believe intraplate quakes may be caused by strains put on plate interiors by changes of temperature or pressure in the rock. Or the source of the strain may be a long distance away, at a plate boundary. These strains may produce quakes along normal, reverse, or strike-slip faults.

Studying earthquakes

Recording, measuring, and locating earthquakes. To determine the strength and location of earthquakes, scientists use a recording instrument known as a *seismograph.* A seismograph is equipped with sensors called *seismometers* that can detect ground motions caused by seismic waves from both near and distant earthquakes. Some seismometers are capable of detecting ground motion as small as 1 billionth of a meter, or about 40 billionth of an inch.

Scientists called *seismologists* measure seismic

ground movements in three directions: (1) up-down, (2) north-south, and (3) east-west. The scientists use a separate sensor to record each direction of movement.

A seismograph produces wavy lines that reflect the size of seismic waves passing beneath it. The record of the wave, called a *seismogram,* is imprinted on paper, film, or recording tape or is stored and displayed by computers.

Probably the best-known gauge of earthquake intensity is the *local Richter magnitude scale,* developed in 1935 by United States seismologist Charles F. Richter. This scale, commonly known as the *Richter scale,* measures the ground motion caused by an earthquake. Every increase of one number in magnitude means the energy release of the quake is 32 times greater. For example, an earthquake of magnitude 7.0 releases 32 times as much energy as an earthquake measuring 6.0. An earthquake

© Doug Wechsler, Earth Scenes

A seismologist examines the record of vibrations from a quake as registered by an instrument called a *seismograph.*

Largest earthquakes

This table includes the largest earthquakes since 1922 for which moment magnitude is known. Moment magnitude measures the world's largest earthquakes more accurately than the conventional Richter magnitude.

Year	Location	Magnitude	Year	Location	Magnitude
1922	Central Chile	8.5	1952	Tokachi-Oki, Hokkaido Island, Japan	8.1
1923	Kamchatka, Soviet Union	8.5		Kamchatka, Soviet Union	9.0
	Kanto Plain, Japan	7.9	1957	Aleutian Islands	9.1
1932	Jalisco, Mexico	8.1		Southwestern Mongolia	8.1
1933	Pacific Ocean floor, near Japan	8.4	1958	Kuril Islands	8.3
1938	Banda Sea floor, near Indonesia	8.5	1960	Southern Chile	9.5
	Pacific Ocean floor, near Alaska Peninsula	8.2	1963	Kuril Islands	8.5
1944	Southern Honshu, Japan	8.1	1964	Southern Alaska	9.2
1946	Pacific Ocean floor, near Japan	8.1	1965	Aleutian Islands	8.7
1949	Queen Charlotte Islands,		1968	Pacific Ocean floor, near Japan	8.2
	British Columbia	8.1	1977	Sumbawa Island, Indonesia	8.3
1950	Arunachal Pradesh, India	8.6	1989	South Pacific Ocean floor, near	
1951	Southeastern Tibet	7.5		Macquarie Island, Australia	8.2

Sources: K. C. McNally in *The Encyclopedia of Solid Earth Geophysics*, Van Nostrand Reinhold, New York, 1989; Program GEOSCOPE, Centre National de la Recherche Scientifique, Paris, France.

with a magnitude of less than 2.0 is so slight that usually only a seismometer can detect it. A quake greater than 7.0 may destroy many buildings. There are about 10 times as many quakes for every decrease in Richter magnitude by one unit. For example, there are 10 times as many earthquakes with magnitude 6.0 as there are with magnitude 7.0.

Although large earthquakes are customarily reported on the Richter scale, scientists prefer to describe earthquakes greater than 7.0 on the *moment magnitude scale*. The moment magnitude scale measures the total energy released in an earthquake, and it describes large earthquakes more accurately than does the Richter scale.

The largest earthquake ever recorded on the moment magnitude scale measured 9.5. It was an interplate earthquake that occurred along the Pacific coast of Chile in South America in 1960. The largest intraplate earthquakes known struck in central Asia and in the Indian Ocean in 1905, 1920, and 1957. These earthquakes had moment magnitudes between about 8.0 and 8.3. The

largest intraplate earthquakes in the history of the United States were three quakes that occurred in New Madrid, Mo., in 1811 and 1812. The earthquakes were so powerful that they changed the course of the Mississippi River. During the largest of them, the ground shook from southern Canada to the Gulf of Mexico and from the Atlantic Coast to the Rocky Mountains. Scientists estimate the earthquakes had moment magnitudes of about 7.5.

Scientists locate earthquakes by measuring the time it takes body waves to arrive at seismographs in a minimum of three locations. From these wave arrival times, seismologists can calculate the distance of an earthquake from each seismograph. Once they know an earthquake's distance from three locations, they can find the quake's focus at the center of those three locations.

Predicting earthquakes. Scientists can make fairly accurate long-term predictions of where earthquakes will occur. They know, for example, that about 80 per cent of the world's major earthquakes happen along a belt encircling the Pacific Ocean. This belt is sometimes called the Ring of Fire because it has many volcanoes, earthquakes, and other geologic activity.

Scientists are working to make accurate forecasts on when earthquakes will strike. Geologists closely monitor certain fault zones where quakes are expected. Along these fault zones, they can sometimes detect small quakes, the tilting of rock, and other events that might signal a large earthquake is about to occur.

Exploring the earth's interior. Most of what is known about the internal structure of the earth has come from studies of seismic waves. Such studies have shown that rock density increases from the surface of the earth to its center. Knowledge of rock densities within the earth has helped scientists determine the probable composition of the earth's interior.

Scientists have found that seismic wave speeds and directions change abruptly at certain depths. From such studies, geologists have concluded that the earth is composed of layers of various densities and substances. These layers consist of the crust, mantle, outer core, and inner core. Shear waves do not travel through the outer core. Because shear waves cannot travel through liquids, scientists believe the outer core is liquid. Scientists believe the inner core is solid because of the movement

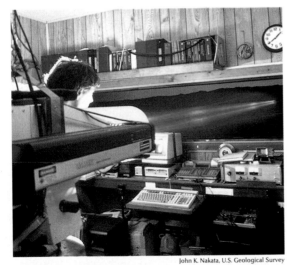

John K. Nakata, U.S. Geological Survey

A geologist monitors a fault for ground movement to look for signs of a potential quake. He fires a laser beam across the fault to a reflector. Measurements of the time it takes the beam to return enable the geologist to detect ground movement.

of compressional waves when they reach the inner core.

Karen C. McNally

Plate tectonics is a theory that explains the origin of most of the major features of the earth's surface. For example, the theory tells us why most volcanoes occur where they do, why there are high ridges and deep trenches in the oceans, and how mountains form.

According to this theory, the earth has an outer shell made up of about 30 rigid pieces called *tectonic plates.* Some of these plates are gigantic. For instance, most of the Pacific Ocean covers a single plate.

The plates move about on a layer of rock that is so hot it flows, even though it remains solid. The plates are moving very slowly relative to one another. They move at speeds up to about 4 inches (10 centimeters) per year.

Plates have been moving about for hundreds of millions of years. So, in spite of their very low speeds, some of them have moved vast distances. In fact, over the past several hundred million years, plate movement has changed the map of the earth drastically. Earth scientists have determined that before about 200 million years ago, all the continents were part of a supercontinent called *Pangaea* (pronounced *pan JEE uh*).

Structure of tectonic plates

Tectonic plates are made up of the earth's *crust* and the outermost part of its *mantle.* The crust is the outermost layer of the earth. It is thin and rocky. All the dry land, all the ocean floors, and the beds of all the other bodies of water on earth are part of the crust. The mantle is a thick layer of hot rock under the crust and above the *core,* a dense sphere at the earth's center.

The continents are embedded in the tops of plates, so as these plates move, they carry the continents along with them. The plates that carry continents do not have the same boundaries as their continents; they include both continents and ocean floor.

Plates are typically about 60 miles (100 kilometers) thick. However, they may be less than 5 miles (8 kilometers) thick at certain places in the oceans and as much as 120 miles (200 kilometers) thick under parts of continents. The plates as a whole make up the earth's *lithosphere.* The layer of mantle rock under the plates is the *asthenosphere* (pronounced *uhs THEEN uh sfihr*). This rock reaches temperatures between about 2400 °F and 3600 °F (1300 °C and 2000 °C).

Plate interactions

As the tectonic plates move about on the asthenosphere, they interact with one another at their boundaries. There are three types of boundaries: (1) *divergent,* where plates move apart from each other, (2) *convergent,* where plates move toward each other, and (3) *transform,* where plates slide alongside each other.

Divergent plate boundaries are mostly on ocean floors. There, the separation of plates, or *rifting,* creates lithosphere. Rifting on continents creates gaps into which water flows to form major river systems, lakes, and even oceans.

The rifting of the ocean floor enlarges the floor. *Magma* (liquefied rock) rises from the asthenosphere, filling the gap between the separating plates. The magma hardens, creating equal amounts of new crust on the edges of the two plates. The process of separa-

tion of plates and formation of new crust is called *sea-floor spreading.* This process creates about 1 square mile (2.4 square kilometers) of ocean crust a year.

The build-up of ocean crust on plate boundaries generates long underwater mountain ranges called *ocean ridges.* Some of these mountain ranges occur along the center of ocean basins and are called *mid-ocean ridges.* One such mid-ocean ridge, called the *Mid-Atlantic Ridge,* extends from waters east of Newfoundland in Canada to an area off the southern tip of South America.

Earthquakes occur at ocean ridges when one plate edge drops down and grinds against the edge of a neighboring plate. These earthquakes occur a short distance beneath the surface of the plates, indicating that newly formed plate edges are very thin. See **Earthquake** (Mid-ocean spreading ridges).

The rifting of continents creates new seas as ocean waters fill a gap in continental crust. The Red Sea region, for example, is in an advanced stage of rifting. The rift is already flooded by ocean waters—the Red Sea, an extension of the Indian Ocean.

The East African Rift, a unit of the Great Rift Valley that extends from Ethiopia to Mozambique and connects to the Red Sea, is in an early stage of rifting. There, the gap is not yet deep enough to become filled with ocean water from the Indian Ocean. However, scientists believe that in 50 million years an extension of that ocean may cut into southeastern Africa.

Convergent plate boundaries are places where lithosphere created at divergent boundaries is destroyed by recycling into the mantle. At a convergent boundary, the edge of a plate sinks, thrusting under the margin of its neighboring plate. This process is called *subduction.* The sinking plate can create deep ocean trenches where it plunges into the asthenosphere. Because the earth is not changing in size, scientists believe that *subduction zones* consume the same amount of ocean crust as ocean ridges create.

The subducting plates generate powerful earthquakes and usually create a line of volcanoes along the overriding plate boundary. A volcano forms when magma, hot gases, and fragments of rock burst through the surface. Subduction zones generate magma at a depth of about 75 miles (120 kilometers) by melting three kinds of material: oceanic crust at the top of the descending plate, ocean sediment dragged to great depths, and asthenosphere caught in the corner between the converging plates.

At some convergent plate margins, the overriding plate scrapes a thick mass of sediment off the descending plate. This process of *subduction accretion* (pronounced *uh KREE shuhn*), adds material to the edge of the overriding plate. In California, for example, subduction accretion formed a large part of the coastal mountain ranges.

At other convergent plate boundaries, the edge of the descending plate, all its cover of sediment, and even pieces from the edge of the overriding plate disappear beneath the overriding plate. This process, *subduction erosion,* causes continents to shrink. Such erosion is occurring in the Pacific Ocean along the coasts of Peru and Chile and east of the Mariana Islands.

At boundaries where plates carrying continents collide, layers of rock in the overriding plate crumple and

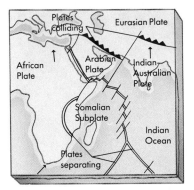

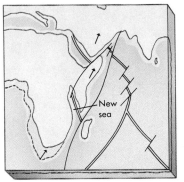

A rift has already formed in eastern Africa, where molten rock of the asthenosphere is rising, pushing apart tectonic plates of the lithosphere. In time, a sea will form along Africa's eastern coast.

WORLD BOOK illustration by Charles Wellek

WORLD BOOK illustration by Charles Wellek

Plate movements are reshaping Africa. The African Plate, in which most of the continent is embedded, is moving north and northeast, *above left,* while the small Somalian Subplate is separating from the African Plate. If these movements continue for 50 million years, *above right,* a new sea will open up along the eastern coast of Africa.

fold like a tablecloth that is pushed across a table. About 40 million years ago, a plate that includes what is now the country of India collided with the southern edge of the Eurasian Plate, which includes Europe and most of Asia. The Indian-Australian Plate began to push beneath the Eurasian Plate, causing rock in the Eurasian Plate to crumple and fold. Over millions of years, the Himalaya, the world's highest mountain system, was formed.

Transform plate boundaries, where plates slide horizontally against each other, neither create nor destroy lithosphere. However, at these boundaries, or *transform faults,* powerful earthquakes can occur. For example, devastating earthquakes have occurred in California along parts of a transform plate boundary known as the San Andreas Fault.

The San Andreas Fault forms part of the boundary between two large plates—the North American Plate and the Pacific Plate. The fault connects a spreading ridge in the Gulf of California to a trench off the coast of northern California. The parts west of the fault are attached to the Pacific Plate and are moving northwest.

Plate movement

Rate. Earth scientists measure the speed of plate movement by monitoring how rapidly a plate moves relative to the plate next to it. Today, plates move about 4 inches (10 centimeters) a year—about as rapidly as human hair grows. In the past, plates may have moved as fast as $6\frac{1}{4}$ inches (16 centimeters) per year.

The overall pattern of movement of the tectonic plates is a widening of the Atlantic Ocean and a shrinkage of the Pacific Ocean. The Atlantic is widening because sea-floor spreading at the Mid-Atlantic Ridge continues to create lithosphere. The Pacific is shrinking because much of it is ringed by convergent plate boundaries that are consuming its lithosphere.

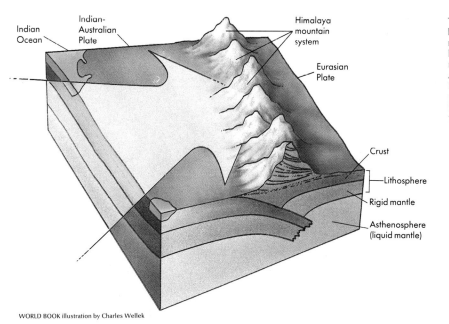

The Himalaya, the world's highest mountain system, is a result of the collision of two huge tectonic plates about 40 million years ago. The Indian-Australian Plate struck the Eurasian Plate and began to plunge beneath it. Layers of rock in the Eurasian Plate folded like a tablecloth that is pushed across a table, forming the Himalaya. Today, the Indian-Australian Plate continues to push against the Eurasian Plate.

WORLD BOOK illustration by Charles Wellek

Scientists have traced the movements of tectonic plates millions of years into the past. According to the commonly accepted description of plate movement, all the continents once formed part of an enormous single land mass called Pangaea. This mass was surrounded by a giant ocean known as *Panthalassa.*

About 200 million years ago, Pangaea began to break up into two large masses called *Gondwanaland* and *Laurasia.* These masses, in turn, broke up into the continents, which drifted to their present locations.

Evidence of plate movement. Earth scientists find much evidence of plate movement at the boundaries of plates. They study surface features, such as mountains and ocean trenches, and investigate the frequencies and locations of earthquakes and volcanic eruptions.

Volcanoes that rise within plates are also evidence of plate movement. Scientists believe that these volcanoes are caused by *mantle plumes,* columns of very hot mantle that rise from deep inside the earth to the base of the lithosphere. These plumes generate magma that rises through the lithosphere and erupts in places called *hot spots.* As a plate moves over a hot spot, the spot can generate a chain of volcanoes. For example, a hot spot under the Pacific Plate generated volcanoes that became the Hawaiian islands.

Paleomagnetism (the study of magnetism in ancient rocks) also provides evidence of plate movement. The evidence is in rocks that contain magnetic particles.

When such a rock was hot and liquid, the magnetic particles were free to align themselves with the earth's magnetic field, like tiny compass needles. Once the rock has cooled and solidified, however, the earth's magnetic field can no longer influence the direction in which the magnetized particles point. Thus, the particles continue to point in the direction of the magnetic field that was present when the rock cooled.

So when the plate containing the rock either drifts to a different latitude or rotates, the particles no longer align with the earth's magnetic field. A comparison of the direction in which the particles now point in the rock with the direction of the earth's present magnetic field provides information about where the plate was when the rock solidified.

Causes of plate movement. Tectonic plates slide mostly because of temperature changes and gravity. As an edge that has formed on the ocean floor cools, it shrinks, becoming denser. After about 25 million years of cooling and shrinking, the edge becomes so dense that gravity can pull it down into the asthenosphere. There, the intense heat and increased pressure due to the great depth change the crust of the sunken plate edge into even denser rock. Because of the additional density, gravity pulls the plate edge into the asthenosphere even more strongly.

This sinking action is known as *slab-pull* because the sinking edge pulls the remainder of the slablike plate behind it. Many scientists believe that slab-pull is the main action driving the motion of plates with sinking edges.

Gravity also causes plates to slide downhill away from ocean ridges. This sliding force is called *ridge-push.*

Another cause of plate movement is the simple pushing of plates against one another. Scientists believe that large plates shove some small plates about.

The drifting continents

The maps below illustrate the theory of continental drift. The top map shows a single land mass—*Pangaea*—about 200 million years ago. The middle map shows Pangaea broken into the land masses *Laurasia* and *Gondwanaland,* and the present continents forming. The arrows show the direction in which the continents moved. The bottom map shows the continents today and where they may drift during the next 50 million years, *black outlines.*

Pangaea: The supercontinent 200 million years ago

The land masses after 65 million years of drift

The continents today and 50 million years from now

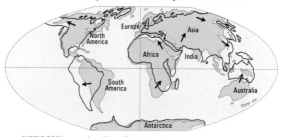

The rise of mantle plumes and other movements of mantle rock may also affect the motion of tectonic plates slightly. The circulation of mantle rock as it rises to the top of the asthenosphere, cools, and then sinks is known as a *convection current.*

Earth scientists once thought that convection currents caused continental drift. Today, however, most earth scientists believe that such currents are primarily a result of the sinking of plates, rather than the cause of plate motion.

Maintaining tectonic activity. The interior of the earth has generated enough heat energy to keep the planet tectonically active since it formed at least 4.5 billion years ago. This energy has maintained tectonic activity by keeping the asthenosphere so soft that the lithosphere can sink into it.

The interior of the earth generates heat energy mainly through the radioactive decay of atoms in the crust and mantle. In radioactive decay, radioactive atoms release energetic particles and rays. Material near these atoms absorbs energy from the particles and rays, becoming hotter.

The production of heat within the earth is declining, mainly because decay is decreasing the number of radioactive atoms. As the earth's heat production is slowing, its interior is cooling. During perhaps the next 5 billion or 10 billion years, this cooling will harden the asthenosphere so much that plate motion will cease. After that occurs, volcanic eruptions will stop and earthquakes will become infrequent. The earth will be tectonically inactive.

History of tectonic theory

The theory of plate tectonics developed from a theory of *continental drift,* presented in 1912 by German meteorologist Alfred Wegener. Wegener's theory proposed that the continents move about the surface of the earth. It explained why the shape of the eastern coast of the Americas and that of the western coast of Africa seem to fit together like pieces of a jigsaw puzzle. Evidence for the drift came from the presence of certain rock deposits that indicate the continents have changed position over time. For example, rock deposits from glaciers that existed hundreds of millions of years ago are found in India, Australia, Africa, and South America, indicating that these continents were once in a very cold climate, probably near the South Pole. Fossils of tree ferns and other tropical features in North America indicate that it was once at the equator.

Wegener was not sure what caused continents to drift, however. His theory of continental drift became a subject of much debate among scientists. Then, in the 1920's, British physicist Harold Jeffreys proposed that the deep interior of the earth was very strong and therefore could not flow. As a result, most scientists rejected Wegener's theory.

However, evidence supporting the theory gradually accumulated. In the late 1930's, American geologist David Griggs demonstrated that apparently solid rock can flow slowly when subjected to high temperatures and pressures. In the 1940's and 1950's, other researchers showed that the ocean floor contains much less sediment than would be expected if the floor were a permanent depression. A permanent sea floor would have accumulated more sediment due to the erosion of soil from the continents. In addition, the oldest sea-floor rocks that could be found were less than 150 million years old.

In the 1950's, scientists developed techniques for studying rock magnetism that enabled them to determine the positions of the continents millions of years ago. By the late 1950's, scientists completed mapping a system of ocean ridges extending for about 37,000 miles (60,000 kilometers) and reaching nearly around the world.

In 1960, Harry H. Hess, an American geologist, proposed a theory of what came to be called sea-floor spreading. Shortly after that, scientists discovered that most earthquakes occur along lines parallel to ocean ridges and trenches. In 1967, American geophysicist Jason Morgan and British geophysicist D. P. McKenzie independently proposed the idea that the earth's surface consists of a number of movable plates. The following year, American earth scientists Bryan L. Isacks, Jack E. Oliver, and Lynn R. Sykes combined the idea of sea-floor spreading with new results from earthquake detection and proposed that rigid plates of lithosphere move about on a soft, flowing asthenosphere.

In 1969, the drillship *Glomar Challenger* completed its first scientific cruise. Material drilled from various locations on both sides of the Mid-Atlantic Ridge indicated that the age of the ocean crust was exactly as predicted by the analysis of paleomagnetism and sea-floor spreading. This discovery and the continuing accumulation of other evidence convinced most earth scientists that the theory of plate tectonics is valid.   Mark Cloos

Nutrition is the science that deals with food and how the body uses it. People, like all living things, need food to live. Food supplies the energy for every action we perform, from reading a book to running a race. Food also provides substances that the body needs to build and repair its tissues and to regulate its organs and systems.

What we eat directly affects our health. A proper diet helps prevent certain illnesses and aids in recovery from others. An improper or inadequate diet increases the risk of various diseases. Eating a balanced diet is the best way to ensure that the body receives all the food substances it needs. Nutrition experts recommend that the daily diet include a certain number of servings from each of five food groups: (1) vegetables, (2) fruits, (3) breads, cereals, rice, and pasta, (4) milk, yogurt, and cheese, and (5) meat, poultry, fish, dried beans and peas, eggs, and nuts.

Workers in the field of nutrition coordinate school food services, plan menus for hospitalized patients, and provide nutrition counseling for individuals. They administer international food programs and investigate the relationship between diet and health. They seek improved ways of processing, packaging, and distributing foods, and they create new foods.

How the body uses food

Food provides certain chemical substances needed for good health. The substances, called *nutrients,* perform one or more of three functions. (1) They provide materials for building, repairing, or maintaining body tissues. (2) They help regulate body processes. (3) They serve as fuel to provide energy. The body needs energy to maintain all its functions.

The body breaks food down into its nutrients through the process of digestion. Digestion begins in the mouth. As food is being chewed, saliva moistens the particles. The saliva begins to break down such starchy foods as bread and cereals. After the food is swallowed, it passes through the *esophagus,* a tube that leads into the stomach. In the stomach, the food is thoroughly mixed with a digestive juice. The juice, called *gastric juice,* speeds up the digestion of such foods as meat, eggs, and milk.

Johanna T. Dwyer, the contributor of this article, is Professor of Medicine and Community Health at Tufts University Medical School and Director of the Frances Stern Nutrition Center, New England Medical Center Hospital.

© Lawrence Migdale

A balanced diet is the key to good nutrition. It supplies all the food substances the body needs. The family shown above enjoys a breakfast that includes fruit, cereal, bread, and milk. The daily diet should include several servings of these foods.

The partly digested food, called *chyme,* passes from the stomach into the small intestine. In the small intestine, other juices complete the process of digestion. They break down the food into molecules that pass through the walls of the intestine and into the bloodstream.

The blood distributes the nutrients to cells and tissues throughout the body. There the nutrients are broken down to produce energy or are used to rebuild tissues or to regulate chemical processes. Some of the nutrients are stored in the body, and others are used over and over again. But most of the nutrients undergo chemical changes as they are used in the cells and tissues. These chemical changes produce waste products, which go into the bloodstream.

Some of the wastes are carried to the kidneys, which filter the wastes out of the blood. The body expels these wastes in the urine. The liver also filters out some wastes and concentrates them into a liquid called *bile.* Bile is stored in the gall bladder until it is needed to aid in the process of digestion. Then the gall bladder empties bile into the small intestine. From there, any remaining bile passes into the large intestine, along with those parts of the food that could not be digested in the small intestine. The large intestine absorbs water and small amounts of minerals from this waste material. This material, along with bacteria present in the large intestine,

becomes the final waste product, the *feces,* and it is eliminated from the body.

Kinds of nutrients

The foods we eat contain thousands of different chemicals. However, only a few dozen of these chemicals are absolutely essential to keep us healthy. These few dozen are the nutrients—the substances we must obtain from the foods we consume.

Nutritionists classify nutrients into six main groups: (1) water, (2) carbohydrates, (3) fats, (4) proteins, (5) minerals, and (6) vitamins. The first four groups are called *macronutrients,* because the body needs them in large (or macro) amounts. The last two groups are required in only small quantities and so are known as *micronutrients.*

Water is needed in great amounts because the body consists largely of this substance. Usually, between 50 and 75 per cent of a person's body weight is made up of water.

The body requires large quantities of carbohydrates, fats, and proteins because these nutrients provide energy. The energy in food is measured in units called *calories.* A calorie is the amount of energy required to raise the temperature of one gram of water one degree Celsius. A calorie is equal to 1,000 kilocalories.

Although minerals and vitamins are needed in only

small amounts, they are as vital to health as any of the other classes of nutrients. Minerals and vitamins are needed for growth and to maintain tissues and regulate body functions.

Water is, perhaps, the most critical nutrient. We can live without other nutrients for several weeks, but we can go without water for only about one week. The body needs water to carry out all of its life processes. Watery solutions help dissolve other nutrients and carry them to all the tissues. The chemical reactions that turn food into energy or tissue-building materials can take place only in a watery solution. The body also needs water to carry away waste products and to cool itself.

Adults should consume about $2\frac{1}{2}$ quarts (2.4 liters) of water a day. This intake can be in the form of beverages we drink or water in food.

Carbohydrates include all sugars and starches. They serve as the main source of energy for living things. Each gram of carbohydrate provides about 4 calories. (A gram is about 0.035 ounce.)

There are two kinds of carbohydrates—*simple* and *complex.* Simple carbohydrates, all of which are sugars, have a simple molecular structure. Complex carbohydrates, which include starches, have a larger and more complicated molecular structure that consists of many simple carbohydrates linked together.

Most foods contain carbohydrates. The main sugar in food is *sucrose,* ordinary white or brown sugar. Another important sugar, *lactose,* is found in milk. *Fructose,* an extremely sweet sugar, comes from most fruits and many vegetables. Foods containing starches include beans, breads, cereals, corn, *pasta* (macaroni, spaghetti, and similar foods made of flour), peas, and potatoes.

Fats are a highly concentrated source of energy. Each gram of fat provides about 9 calories.

All fats are composed of an alcohol called *glycerol* and substances called *fatty acids.* A fatty acid consists of a long chain of carbon atoms, to which hydrogen atoms are attached. There are three types of fatty acids: *saturated, monounsaturated,* and *polyunsaturated.* A saturated fatty acid contains as many hydrogen atoms as its carbon chain can hold. A monounsaturated fatty acid is lacking a pair of hydrogen atoms. In a polyunsaturated fatty acid, the carbon chain contains at least four fewer hydrogen atoms than it could hold.

Certain polyunsaturated fatty acids must be included in the diet because the body cannot manufacture them. These essential fatty acids serve as building blocks for the membranes that make up the outer border of every cell in the body.

Polyunsaturated fatty acids are found in the oils of such plants as sunflowers and sesame seeds and in such fish as salmon and mackerel. Common sources of monounsaturated fatty acids include olives and peanuts. Most saturated fatty acids are contained in foods derived from animals, such as butter, lard, dairy products, and fatty red meats.

Proteins provide energy—like carbohydrates, 4 calories per gram—but more importantly, proteins serve as one of the main building materials of the body. Muscle, skin, cartilage, and hair, for example, are made up largely of proteins. In addition, every cell contains proteins called *enzymes,* which speed up chemical reactions. Cells could not function without these protein en-

zymes. Proteins also serve as *hormones* (chemical messengers) and as *antibodies* (disease-fighting chemicals).

Proteins are large, complex molecules made up of smaller units called *amino acids.* The body must have a sufficient supply of 20 amino acids. It can manufacture 11 of them in sufficient amounts. Nine others, called *essential amino acids,* either cannot be made by the body or cannot be manufactured in sufficient amounts. They must come from the diet.

The best sources of proteins are cheese, eggs, fish, lean meat, and milk. The proteins in these foods are called *complete proteins* because they contain adequate amounts of all the essential amino acids. Cereal grains, *legumes* (plants of the pea family), nuts, and vegetables also supply proteins. These proteins are called *incomplete proteins* because they lack adequate amounts of one or more of the essential amino acids. However, a combination of two incomplete proteins can provide a complete amino acid mixture. For example, beans and rice are both incomplete proteins, but when they are eaten together they provide the correct balance of amino acids.

Minerals are needed for the growth and maintenance of body structures. They are also needed to maintain the composition of the digestive juices and the fluids that are found in and around the cells. As mentioned earlier, we need only small amounts of minerals in our daily diet.

Unlike vitamins, carbohydrates, fats, and proteins, minerals are *inorganic compounds.* This means that they are not created by living things. Plants obtain minerals from the water or soil, and animals get minerals by eating plants or plant-eating animals. In addition, unlike other nutrients, minerals are not broken down within the body.

The required minerals include calcium, chlorine, magnesium, phosphorus, potassium, sodium, and sulfur. Calcium, magnesium, and phosphorus are essential parts of the bones and teeth. In addition, calcium is necessary for blood clotting. Milk and milk products are the richest sources of calcium. Cereals and meats provide phosphorus. Whole-grain cereals, nuts, legumes, and green, leafy vegetables are good sources of magnesium in the diet.

Still other minerals are needed only in extremely tiny amounts. These minerals, called *trace elements,* include chromium, copper, fluorine, iodine, iron, manganese, molybdenum, selenium, and zinc. Iron is an important part of hemoglobin, the oxygen-carrying molecule in red blood cells. Copper helps the body to make use of iron to build hemoglobin. Manganese and zinc are required for the normal action of various protein enzymes. Green leafy vegetables, whole-grain breads and cereals, seafood, liver, and kidney are good sources of most of the trace elements.

Vitamins are essential for good health. Small amounts of these compounds should be supplied daily in the diet. Vitamins regulate chemical reactions by which the body converts food into energy and living tissues. There are 13 vitamins: vitamin A; the vitamin B complex, which is a group of 8 vitamins; and vitamins C, D, E, and K.

Scientists divide vitamins into two general groups, *fat-soluble vitamins* and *water-soluble vitamins.* The fat-soluble vitamins—vitamins A, D, E, and K—dissolve in fats. The vitamins of the B complex and vitamin C dissolve in water.

Vitamin A is necessary for healthy skin and development of the bones. Sources of this vitamin include liver, green and yellow vegetables, and milk.

Vitamin B₁, also called *thiamine,* is necessary for changing starches and sugars into energy. It is found in meat and whole-grain cereals.

Vitamin B₂, or *riboflavin,* is essential for complicated chemical reactions that take place during the body's use of food. Milk, cheese, fish, liver, and green vegetables supply vitamin B₂.

Vitamin B₆ (also called *pyridoxine*), *pantothenic acid,* and *biotin* all play a role in chemical reactions in the body. Many foods contain small amounts of these vitamins.

Vitamin B₁₂ and folate (also called *folic acid* or *folacin*) are both needed for forming red blood cells and for a healthy nervous system. Vitamin B₁₂ is found in animal products, especially liver. Folate is present in green leafy vegetables.

Niacin is also part of the B complex. Cells need niacin in order to release energy from carbohydrates. Liver, yeast, lean meat, fish, nuts, and legumes contain niacin.

Vitamin C, or *ascorbic acid,* is needed for the maintenance of the ligaments, tendons, and other supportive tissue. It is found in fruits—especially oranges and lemons—and in potatoes.

Vitamin D is necessary for the body's use of calcium. It is present in fish-liver oil and vitamin D-fortified milk. It is also formed when the skin is exposed to sunlight.

Vitamin E, or *tocopherol,* helps maintain cell membranes. Vegetable oils and whole-grain cereals are especially rich in this vitamin. It is also found in small amounts in most meats, fruits, and vegetables.

Vitamin K is necessary for proper clotting of the blood. Green leafy vegetables contain vitamin K. It is also manufactured by bacteria in the intestine.

Nutrition guidelines

Eat a balanced diet. The key to good nutrition is a varied diet that includes every kind of nutrient. To simplify the planning of a varied diet, nutritionists have devised systems that group foods according to nutrient content. One such system divides foods into five groups: (1) vegetables, (2) fruits, (3) breads, cereals, rice, and pasta, (4) milk, yogurt, and cheese, and (5) meat, poultry, fish, dried beans and peas, eggs, and nuts. The illustration in this article of the basic food groups shows the nutritional value and recommended daily number of servings for each group.

Additional guidelines, called *Recommended Dietary Allowances (RDA's),* are provided in the United States by the Food and Nutrition Board of the National Academy of Sciences. In other countries, similar groups provide national nutrition guidelines. The RDA's give health experts' estimates of the amounts of essential nutrients needed daily to maintain good nutrition in healthy people. This article includes a table of RDA's.

The RDA for a particular nutrient may vary depending on a person's sex and age. The RDA for iron, for example, is 12 milligrams for males age 11 to 18 and 15 milligrams for females age 11 to 50. The RDA for calcium

ranges from 400 milligrams for infants under the age of 6 months to 1,200 milligrams for males and females age 11 to 24 and for pregnant women.

People also vary in their needs for energy. A person who plays sports daily, for example, needs more calories than someone who does little physical work. Children need more calories than their size would indicate because they are growing. Pregnant women also need extra calories to provide enough nutrients for a healthy baby.

Include fiber. Dietary fiber consists of cellulose and other complex carbohydrates that cannot be absorbed by the body. It passes out of the body as waste. Fiber moves food along through the stomach and intestines, thus helping to prevent *constipation* (difficulty in emptying the bowels). Many experts believe that it also helps reduce the risk of such rectal and intestinal disorders as hemorrhoids, diverticulitis, and, possibly, cancers of the colon and rectum. Good sources of fiber include whole-grain breads and cereals, beans and peas, vegetables, and fruit.

Limit your intake of saturated fats and cholesterol. Health experts recommend a diet that is low in saturated fats and *cholesterol,* a waxy substance found in many animal foods. Consumption of saturated fats and cholesterol raises the level of cholesterol in a person's blood. A high level of blood cholesterol increases the risk of heart disease. Animal products are the source of most saturated fats and all dietary cholesterol. To reduce the intake of saturated fats and cholesterol, health experts suggest choosing lean meats, fish, poultry without skin, and low-fat dairy products. They also advise using fats and oils sparingly.

Limit your intake of sodium and sugar. A diet that includes a great deal of sodium may increase the risk of high blood pressure. Sodium is found in many foods, including canned vegetables, frozen dinners, pickles, processed cheeses, table salt, and such snack foods as pretzels, potato chips, and nuts. One way to reduce sodium intake is to use herbs and other seasonings instead of salt in cooking and at the table. Another way is to select fresh foods rather than canned or frozen foods.

Foods that contain a lot of sugar are often high in calories and fat but low in minerals, proteins, and vitamins. Nutritionists sometimes call them "empty calorie" foods, because they may make a person feel full but provide few nutrients. In addition, sugar that remains in and around the teeth contributes to tooth decay. Foods that have a large amount of sugar include candies, pastries, many breakfast cereals, and sweetened canned fruits. In place of sugary foods, nutritionists advise people to snack on such foods as fresh fruits and vegetables. They also recommend that people drink unsweetened fruit and vegetable juices instead of soft drinks.

Beware of alcohol. Alcoholic beverages supply calories, but they provide almost no nutrients. In addition, alcohol is a powerful drug, and habitual drinking can lead to many health problems. Health experts recommend that if people choose to drink alcoholic beverages, they consume only small amounts. They suggest that certain people avoid alcohol altogether: children and adolescents, pregnant women, people who are about to drive, anyone who is taking medicine, and those who are unable to limit their drinking.

Basic food groups   Nutritionists group foods in order to make it easier to plan a balanced diet. They recommend eating a certain number of daily servings of each food group. These servings will provide the proteins, vitamins, and other substances the body needs to function.

WORLD BOOK photo by Ralph J. Brunke

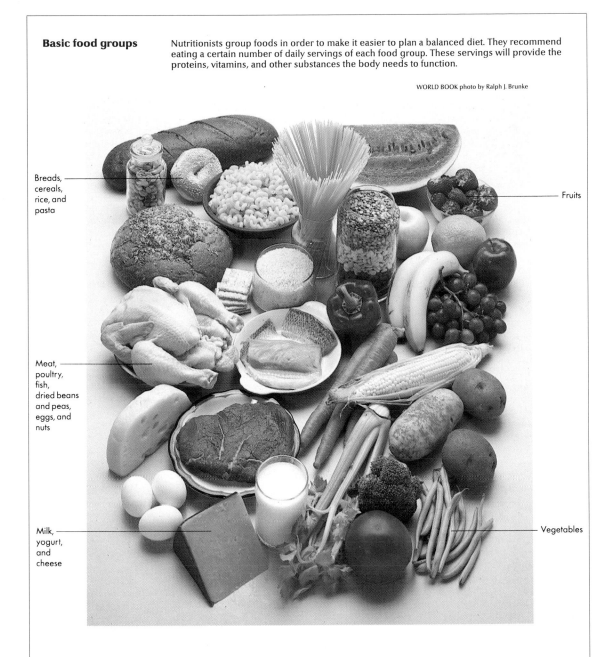

Breads, cereals, rice, and pasta

Fruits

Meat, poultry, fish, dried beans and peas, eggs, and nuts

Milk, yogurt, and cheese

Vegetables

Breads, cereals, rice, and pasta. This group consists largely of carbohydrates, the main source of energy. Nutritionists recommend 6 to 11 servings a day.

Meat, poultry, fish, dried beans and peas, eggs, and nuts. This group is a chief source of proteins. Nutritionists recommend 2 to 3 servings a day.

Milk, yogurt, and cheese. This group provides vitamin A, vitamin B$_2$, calcium, and proteins. The recommended daily number of servings is 2 to 3.

Fruits are excellent sources of vitamin C. They also provide dietary fiber. Nutritionists recommend 2 to 4 servings of fruits a day.

Vegetables are excellent sources of vitamin A, the B vitamins, vitamin C, and calcium and iron, as well as fiber. Nutritionists recommend 3 to 5 servings a day.

Don't overeat. When a person consumes more calories than are needed, the body stores most of the excess calories as fat. This can result in *obesity*. An obese person has too much body fat for good health. Obesity increases the risk of such diseases as adult-type diabetes, stroke, high blood pressure, gall bladder disease, heart disease, and certain cancers. Health problems such as osteoarthritis and lower back pain are often worsened by the pressure of excess weight.

A number of techniques can help a person avoid obesity. For one thing, be careful not to use food as a reward or as a way to overcome loneliness or boredom. It is also a good idea to avoid snacking on foods that are high in fat or sugar. Instead, try substituting fruits, fruit juice diluted with water, skim milk and unsalted crackers, nonfat yogurt, and sparkling water. Another way to combat obesity is to be as physically active as possible. Most health experts recommend that a person engage in physical exercise to help reduce weight.

Store and cook foods properly to retain their nutritional value. Many fresh foods should be kept in the refrigerator. They should be washed thoroughly and eaten as soon as possible. Frozen foods must be stored in a freezer. Foods in cans or jars do not need to be refrigerated until after they have been opened.

Vegetables should be cooked quickly and in as little water as possible so that vitamins are not lost in the water. Cooking meats and other animal foods by such methods as broiling, stir-frying, braising, or poaching results in food that is tasty but free of added fat and extra calories. Microwave cooking enables one to cook or reheat food quickly and keep nutrient values high.

Be cautious about food myths and misinformation. Often, ideas about foods become popular, but they are not necessarily correct. For example, some people believe that if they take a vitamin pill every day they can eat whatever they choose. But, in fact, people who rely on vitamin pills may not get the amount of calories, minerals, or proteins that they need. Another common, but incorrect, idea is that such starchy foods as potatoes are fattening. In fact, starches provide fewer calories than do such fats as butter or margarine. However, when starches are combined with fats, the combination is high in calories. There is no evidence that gelatin strengthens fingernails, that fish is a brain food, or that celery is a nerve tonic. Eggs with brown shells are not more nutritious than white-shelled eggs. The color depends on the breed of hen. It is best to use caution and common sense when faced with claims about food products.

Nutrition and disease

An improper or inadequate diet can lead to a number of diseases. On the other hand, good nutritional habits can help prevent certain diseases.

Heart disease in its most common form is called *coronary artery disease* (CAD). CAD narrows the coronary arteries and so reduces the blood supply to the heart. It can lead to crippling attacks of chest pain and, eventually, to life-threatening heart attacks. High blood pressure and high levels of blood cholesterol are two of the major risk factors for CAD. Each of these risk factors can often be lessened by following good nutritional practices.

Many people with mild high blood pressure can reduce it by limiting their intake of salt and calories. Similarly, many people can lower their blood cholesterol level by reducing the amount of cholesterol, fat—particularly saturated fat—and calories in their diet. They can do so by avoiding such foods as butter, cakes, cookies, egg yolks, fatty meats, tropical oils, and whole-fat dairy products.

Cancer. Scientists do not know exactly why cancer develops. But they have found that heredity, environment, and life style all play a role in causing the disease. They have also learned that good nutrition can help prevent certain kinds of cancer in laboratory animals. Large doses of vitamins A and C have been proven to prevent some cancers in animals. Many scientists believe that certain foods contain substances that may help prevent some cancers in people. Such foods include broccoli, cabbage, carrots, cauliflower, fruits, spinach, whole-grain breads and cereals, and some seafoods. Lessening intake of fats and increasing the intake of fiber may also help prevent some cancers from forming.

Deficiency diseases. Many diseases result from the *deficiency* (lack) of certain nutrients in the diet. When the missing nutrient is provided, the disease usually can be eliminated. Deficiency diseases are most widespread in developing countries, where people often lack access to adequate food supplies. The availability of a variety of foods the year around, along with vitamin and mineral fortification of many foods, have made deficiency diseases less common in most developed countries.

Protein-calorie malnutrition occurs when the diet is low in both proteins and calories. If the diet is especially low in proteins, the condition is called *kwashiorkor*. Signs of kwashiorkor include changes in the color and texture of the hair and skin, swelling of the body, and damage to the intestines, liver, and pancreas. The disease, which is common in some developing nations, usually attacks children who are suffering from an infectious disease. Kwashiorkor is fatal unless the patient is given protein along with food providing calories. If the diet is especially low in calories, the condition is called *marasmus*. Marasmus usually attacks infants and young children, and it causes extreme underweight and weakness.

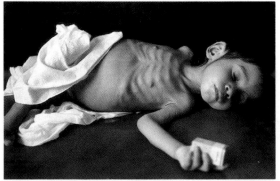

Fred Griffing, UNICEF

A diet especially low in proteins may cause *kwashiorkor,* a disease that generally strikes children. In severe cases, the muscles waste away and the skin swells with body fluids.

Recommended daily dietary allowances of some nutrients

	Age	Weight In lbs.	In kg	Calories	Protein (g)	Calcium (mg)	Iron (mg)	Vitamins A (mcg R.E.)	C (mg)	D (mcg)	Thia-mine (mg)	Ribo-flavin (mg)	Niacin (mg N.E.)
Children	1-3	29	13	1,300	16	800	10	400	40	10	0.7	0.8	9
	4-6	44	20	1,800	24	800	10	500	45	10	0.9	1.1	12
	7-10	62	28	2,000	28	800	10	700	45	10	1.0	1.2	13
Males	11-14	99	45	2,500	45	1,200	12	1,000	50	10	1.3	1.5	17
	15-18	145	66	3,000	59	1,200	12	1,000	60	10	1.5	1.8	20
	19-24	160	72	2,900	58	1,200	10	1,000	60	10	1.5	1.7	19
	25-50	174	79	2,900	63	800	10	1,000	60	5	1.5	1.7	19
	51+	170	77	2,300	63	800	10	1,000	60	5	1.2	1.4	15
Females	11-14	101	46	2,200	46	1,200	15	800	50	10	1.1	1.3	15
	15-18	120	55	2,200	44	1,200	15	800	60	10	1.1	1.3	15
	19-24	128	58	2,200	46	1,200	15	800	60	10	1.1	1.3	15
	25-50	138	63	2,200	50	800	15	800	60	5	1.1	1.3	15
	51+	143	65	1,900	50	800	10	800	60	5	1.0	1.2	13

lbs=pounds; kg=kilograms; g=grams; mg=milligrams; mcg=micrograms; R.E.=retinol equivalents; N.E.=niacin equivalents
Above recommendations designed for the maintenance of good nutrition of practically all healthy people in the United States.
Source: *Recommended Dietary Allowances*, Tenth Ed., 1989. Food and Nutrition Board, National Academy of Sciences.

Vitamin deficiencies. The signs and symptoms of vitamin deficiencies vary according to the missing vitamin. Vitamin C deficiency, also called *scurvy,* causes sore and bleeding gums, slow repair of wounds, and painful joints. Vitamin D deficiency, also called *rickets,* causes an abnormal development of the bones. A deficiency of niacin and the amino acid tryptophan, found in protein, causes *pellagra.* The early symptoms of pellagra include weakness, lack of appetite, diarrhea, and indigestion.

Mineral deficiencies. The most common mineral deficiency disease is *iron-deficiency anemia,* which results from a lack of iron. In a person with this disease, the blood does not have enough healthy red blood cells and cannot supply the tissues with sufficient oxygen. Thus, the person feels weak or tired. Other symptoms include dizziness, headaches, rapid heartbeat, and shortness of breath. A lack of iodine can cause *goiter,* a disease in which the thyroid gland becomes enlarged.

Other diseases may result from poor nutritional habits. For example, the excessive intake of alcohol causes some forms of liver disease. Obesity increases the risk of gall bladder disease and of diabetes in adults. The risk of *osteoporosis* (loss of bone tissue) is higher for women whose intake of calcium and level of physical activity are low. To prevent osteoporosis, physicians recommend a lifelong combination of regular exercise and a diet with adequate calcium.

Careers in nutrition

Nutrition offers a variety of careers in work settings that range from restaurants to research laboratories. Jobs in this field require at least a high school education. Some positions require a two-year associate degree or a bachelor's degree. High school students interested in a career in the field of nutrition should take such science courses as biology and chemistry. College students preparing for a career in nutrition study physiology—the science that deals with how the body works—as well as biochemistry—the science of the various chemical reactions that take place in the body. They also take courses in bacteriology and general chemistry. Those interested in careers in medical nutrition learn how diseases affect the body. Students pursuing careers in food service take such courses as food preparation, food purchasing, accounting, and personnel management.

Work as a *dietetic technician* requires an associate degree. Dietetic technicians work as members of a food service staff or a health care team, under the supervision of or in consultation with a *registered dietitian.* They supervise support staff, develop nutrition care plans, and provide nutrition counseling for individuals or small groups.

A bachelor's degree and a period of supervised practice are necessary to become a registered dietitian. Candidates must also pass a registration examination. Many registered dietitians manage food services in schools, nursing homes, and restaurants. Others work in hospitals or clinics, planning special diets for people who are ill. Some registered dietitians coordinate disease prevention programs for public health organizations or work with community food programs. Others work for corporations, helping to develop food products. A num-

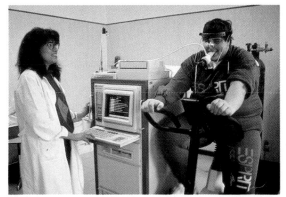

© R. Benzi, Custom Medical

Obesity may result from poor nutrition. Medical personnel should be consulted to develop and monitor a weight-loss program involving both diet and physical exercise.

Food services in schools, nursing homes, and restaurants offer career opportunities in the field of nutrition. The nutritionist pictured above, *left*, directs the preparation of meals.

© Joseph Sterling, Tony Stone Worldwide from Click/Chicago

ber of registered dietitians offer personal nutrition counseling directly to the public.

People with advanced degrees in nutrition and food science may teach; conduct research projects for government, business, industry, and health care institutions; or hold administrative positions in international food or agricultural programs. These experts may investigate the effect of diet on health or develop improved methods for processing and packaging food. Some create new foods, such as artificial sweeteners and the foods used in space exploration.   Johanna T. Dwyer

Related articles in *World Book* include:

Dietary diseases

<table>
<tr><td>Allergy</td><td>Goiter</td><td>Pellagra</td></tr>
<tr><td>Anemia</td><td>Kwashiorkor</td><td>Rickets</td></tr>
<tr><td>Beriberi</td><td>Malnutrition</td><td>Scurvy</td></tr>
</table>

Nutrients

<table>
<tr><td>Albumin</td><td>Gluten</td><td>Protein</td></tr>
<tr><td>Amino acid</td><td>Iron</td><td>Starch</td></tr>
<tr><td>Carbohydrate</td><td>Lipid</td><td>Sugar</td></tr>
<tr><td>Fat</td><td>Potassium</td><td>Vitamin</td></tr>
</table>

Other related articles

<table>
<tr><td>Baby (Feeding procedures)</td><td>Home economics</td></tr>
<tr><td>Biochemistry</td><td>Meat</td></tr>
<tr><td>Calorie</td><td>Metabolism</td></tr>
<tr><td>Cholesterol</td><td>Rice (Food)</td></tr>
<tr><td>Diet</td><td>Starvation</td></tr>
<tr><td>Digestive system</td><td>Trace elements</td></tr>
<tr><td>Food</td><td>Vegetarianism</td></tr>
<tr><td>Food preservation</td><td>Weight control</td></tr>
<tr><td>Food Stamp Program</td><td>Wheat (Food for people)</td></tr>
</table>

Outline

I. How the body uses food
II. Kinds of nutrients
    A. Water
    B. Carbohydrates
    C. Fats
    D. Proteins
    E. Minerals
    F. Vitamins

III. Nutrition guidelines
    A. Eat a balanced diet
    B. Include fiber
    C. Limit your intake of saturated fats and cholesterol
    D. Limit your intake of sodium and sugar
    E. Beware of alcohol
    F. Don't overeat
    G. Store and cook foods properly
    H. Be cautious about food myths and misinformation
IV. Nutrition and disease
    A. Heart disease
    B. Cancer
    C. Deficiency diseases
    D. Other diseases
V. Careers in nutrition

Questions

Why is water an essential nutrient?
How do complete proteins differ from incomplete proteins?
What are some symptoms of iron-deficiency anemia?
Why must essential fatty acids be included in the diet?
What is *kwashiorkor*? *Marasmus*?
What are the dangers of obesity?
What are some ways to reduce sodium intake?
What three main functions do nutrients perform?
What are some roles of a registered dietitian?
Why is it important to include fiber in the diet?

Additional resources

Level I
Encyclopedia of Good Health: Nutrition. Ed. by Mario Orlandi and Donald Prue. Facts on File, 1988.
Lee, Sally. *New Theories on Diet and Nutrition.* Watts, 1990.
Peavy, Linda, and Smith, Ursula. *Food, Nutrition, & You.* Scribner, 1982.

Level II
Brody, Jane E. *Jane Brody's Nutrition Book: A Lifetime Guide to Good Eating for Better Health and Weight Control.* Norton, 1981.
The Columbia Encyclopedia of Nutrition. Ed. by Myron Winick and others. Putnam, 1987.
Garrison, Robert H., Jr., and Somer, Elizabeth. *The Nutrition Desk Reference.* Rev. ed. Keats Pub., 1990.
Mayer, Jean, and Goldberg, J. P. *Dr. Jean Mayer's Diet and Nutrition Guide.* Pharos Bks., 1990.

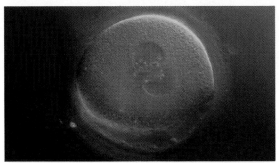

Copyright © Lennart Nilsson, 1990. From *A Child is Born,* Dell Publishing Company

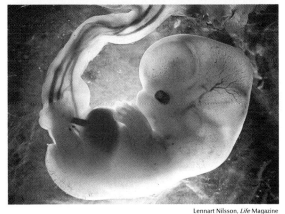

Lennart Nilsson, *Life* Magazine

© Dan McCoy, Rainbow

Human reproduction begins when a sperm from the father unites with and fertilizes an egg from the mother. The egg divides rapidly, *top left,* and soon becomes an embryo, *above left,* that develops and grows within the mother's body. After about nine months, a baby is born, *right.*

Human reproduction

Reproduction, Human, is the process by which human beings create more of their own kind. Human beings reproduce sexually. That is, a new individual develops from the joining together of two sex cells, one from a female parent and one from a male parent. The union of these cells is called *fertilization.*

Biologists refer to sex cells as *gametes.* Females produce gametes called *eggs* or *ova.* Male gametes are called *sperm.* Fertilization may occur after a male delivers sperm to the female's egg by means of sexual intercourse. Fertilization begins a remarkable period of development in which the egg develops into a fully formed baby within the body of the female. This period of development, called *pregnancy,* takes about nine months.

At the beginning of pregnancy, the fertilized egg is smaller than the period at the end of this sentence. The egg develops into a growing mass of cells called an *embryo.* Gradually, the cells rearrange themselves to form tissues. By the end of the second month of pregnancy,

Lynn J. Romrell, the contributor of this article, is Associate Dean for Education and Professor of Anatomy and Cell Biology at the University of Florida College of Medicine.

all the major body organs and organ systems have formed and the embryo looks distinctly human. During the rest of pregnancy, the embryo is called a *fetus.* The fetus grows while its systems prepare for the day when they must function outside the mother's body. Pregnancy ends when the new baby passes out of the mother's body at birth.

Human beings are born with the body organs needed for reproduction. But reproduction cannot actually occur until these organs mature. This maturation process takes place during *puberty,* a period of several years in which a boy or girl goes through dramatic physical changes. These changes are regulated by certain *hormones* (chemicals produced by the body). Puberty begins during or just before the early teen-age years.

The reproductive systems of females and males differ greatly in shape and structure. But both systems are specifically designed to produce, nourish, and transport the eggs or sperm.

In females, the reproductive system consists primarily of a group of organs located within the pelvis. A woman or girl has external organs called the *vulva* between her legs. The outer parts of the vulva cover the opening to a narrow canal called the *vagina.* The vagina leads to the *uterus,* a hollow, pear-shaped, muscular organ in which a baby develops. Two small, oval organs called *ovaries* lie to the right and left of the uterus. The ovaries produce, store, and release eggs. These organs also produce two types of hormones—*progesterone* and *estrogens*. Eggs from the ovaries reach the uterus through tubes called *fallopian tubes* or *oviducts*.

Females produce eggs as part of a monthly process called the *menstrual cycle,* which begins during puberty. Each menstrual cycle, the female reproductive system undergoes a series of changes that prepares it for fertilization and pregnancy. If the egg is not fertilized, a shedding or loss of tissue in the uterus called *menstruation* occurs. Bleeding is associated with this process and lasts three to seven days. Menstruation marks the beginning of each menstrual cycle. Each cycle lasts about 28 days.

Other changes during a menstrual cycle involve cells in the ovaries called *oocytes.* Eggs develop from these cells. At birth, each ovary has about 400,000 oocytes. These cells remain inactive until the first menstrual cycle. Thereafter, many oocytes grow and begin to mature each month. Normally, only one oocyte in either of the ovaries reaches full maturity. This fully developed cell—the mature egg—is released from the ovary in a process called *ovulation.* This process occurs at about the midpoint of the menstrual cycle. After ovulation, the egg travels toward the uterus through one of the fallopian tubes by means of wavelike contractions of muscles and the beating of *cilia* (hairlike structures) located on cells in the walls of the oviduct. Fertilization may occur in one of the tubes. An unfertilized egg lives for about 24 hours after it leaves the ovary.

Important changes also occur in the *endometrium* (lining of the uterus). During the first half of the menstrual cycle, the ovaries release relatively large amounts of estrogens, which cause the endometrium to thicken. The endometrium reaches its maximum thickness at about the time of ovulation. After ovulation, the ovaries release relatively large amounts of progesterone. This

hormone maintains the thickness of the endometrium, so that a fertilized egg can attach to the uterus.

If fertilization occurs, the endometrium continues to develop. If fertilization does not occur, the egg breaks down and the production of progesterone decreases. The thickened endometrium also breaks down and passes out of the body during menstruation.

Most women produce eggs until the ages of about 45 to 55, when the menstrual cycles become increasingly infrequent and then stop. This period of a woman's life is called *menopause.* The completion of menopause marks the end of a woman's natural childbearing years.

In males, the reproductive system includes the *testicles,* a *duct system, accessory glands,* and the *penis.* The testicles, also called *testes,* are the organs that produce sperm. The duct system, which includes the *epididymis* and the *vas deferens,* transports the sperm. The accessory glands, mainly the *seminal vesicles* and the *prostate gland,* provide fluids that lubricate the duct system and nourish the sperm. The sperm leave the body through the penis, a cylindrical organ that is located between the legs.

The testicles are contained in the *scrotum,* a pouch behind the penis. The location of the scrotum keeps the testicles about 4 to 5 Fahrenheit degrees (2.2 to 2.8 Celsius degrees) cooler than the normal body temperature of 98.6 °F (37.0 °C). Unlike other cells of the body, sperm cells cannot develop properly at normal body temperature. In addition to producing sperm, the testicles also produce hormones, particularly *testosterone.*

Sperm develop in the testicles within a complex system of tubes called *seminiferous tubules.* At birth, a male baby's tubules contain only simple round cells. But during puberty, the testicles begin to produce testosterone and other hormones that make the round cells divide, and undergo changes to become slender cells

The human reproductive system

The reproductive systems of males and females are specifically designed to produce, nourish, and transport the sperm or egg. After sperm are deposited in the vagina, they pass through the uterus and into the fallopian tubes, where fertilization usually occurs.

WORLD BOOK diagrams by George Suyeoka

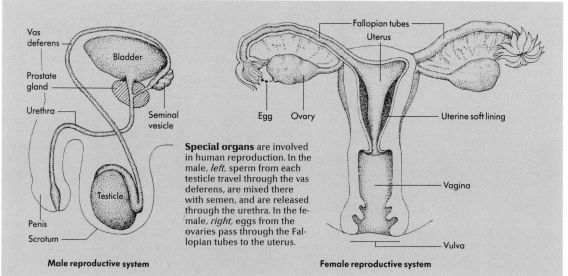

Special organs are involved in human reproduction. In the male, *left,* sperm from each testicle travel through the vas deferens, are mixed there with semen, and are released through the urethra. In the female, *right,* eggs from the ovaries pass through the Fallopian tubes to the uterus.

Male reproductive system

Female reproductive system

with a tail. A sperm cell uses its tail, called a *flagellum,* to propel itself forward. Sperm pass from the testicles into the epididymis and complete their development there in about 12 days.

A healthy adult male normally produces about 200 million sperm per day. Although sperm production begins to decline gradually at about 45 years of age, it normally continues throughout life.

From the epididymis, sperm move to the vas deferens, a long tube that stores the sperm. The seminal vesicles and prostate gland produce a whitish fluid called *seminal fluid.* This fluid mixes with sperm from the vas deferens to form *semen.* The vas deferens leads to the *urethra,* a tube that runs through the penis.

Semen, which contains the sperm, is expelled from the body through the urethra. This process is called *ejaculation.* The penis usually hangs limp. But when a male becomes sexually excited, special tissues in the penis fill with blood, and the organ becomes stiff and erect. When the erect penis is stimulated, muscles around the reproductive organs contract. This contraction forces fluid from the glands and propels the semen through the duct system and the urethra. The amount of semen ejaculated varies from 2 to 6 milliliters (0.07 to 0.2 fluid ounce). Each milliliter of semen contains about 100 million sperm.

Fertilization

A pregnancy begins when a sperm fertilizes an egg. Fertilization, also called *conception,* normally occurs by means of sexual intercourse. Sexual intercourse takes place when the man's erect penis is inserted in the woman's vagina. When a man ejaculates, semen containing the millions of sperm is deposited in the vagina.

Scientists have developed techniques of achieving fertilization without sexual intercourse. In a process called *artificial insemination,* sperm are collected from a man and later injected into a woman's uterus. In another technique, called *in vitro fertilization,* collected sperm are used to fertilize eggs in a laboratory dish. The fertilized eggs are then inserted into the woman's uterus.

After ejaculation, the sperm pass from the vagina into the uterus and then into the fallopian tubes. Most sperm die along the way. Only a few thousand reach the *ampulla,* an area near the end of each fallopian tube. If a sperm fertilizes an egg, it usually does so in this part of the fallopian tube.

Some sperm may reach the fallopian tubes in as little as five minutes. Others take hours to reach the tubes. Sperm can survive in the fallopian tubes for up to 48 hours. It takes an egg about 24 hours to pass through a fallopian tube. The egg can be fertilized only during this period. Therefore, intercourse must take place at about the time of ovulation for fertilization to occur.

The surface of a newly released egg is covered with a jellylike layer of cells called the *zona pellucida.* A second layer of cells, called the *cumulus oophorus,* surrounds the zona pellucida. A sperm must pass through both layers to fertilize the egg. The *acrosome* (tip) of the sperm releases special enzymes that scatter the cells of both layers. Although several sperm may begin to penetrate the zona pellucida, usually only one can fertilize the egg. After the first sperm enters, the egg releases substances that prevent other sperm from entering.

How sex is determined. Fertilization is complete when the *chromosomes* of the sperm unite with the chromosomes of the egg. Chromosomes are threadlike structures that contain *genes,* the units of heredity that determine each person's unique traits. Most body cells have 46 chromosomes that occur in 23 pairs. However, as each egg or sperm develops, it undergoes a special series of cell divisions called *meiosis.* As a result, each sperm or egg cell contains only one member of each chromosome pair, or 23 unpaired chromosomes. During fertilization, the chromosomes pair up so that the fertilized egg has the normal number of 46 chromosomes. The fertilized egg is called a *zygote.*

Special *sex chromosomes* determine whether the zygote will develop into a boy or a girl. Each body cell contains a pair of sex chromosomes. In females, the two sex chromosomes are identical. Each of the chromosomes is called an *X chromosome.* The cells of males have one X chromosome and a smaller chromosome called the *Y chromosome.*

After meiosis, each sperm or egg cell has only one sex chromosome. All egg cells carry one X chromosome. Half the sperm cells carry an X chromosome, and the other half have a Y chromosome. At fertilization, a sperm with an X chromosome uniting with an egg will develop into a girl baby because the fertilized egg will have two X chromosomes. A sperm with a Y chromosome uniting with an egg will form a boy baby because the fertilized egg will have the X and Y combination.

Multiple birth. In most cases, a single egg is fertilized and develops into one baby. Occasionally, however, two or more infants develop and are born at the same time. The birth of more than one baby from the same pregnancy is called *multiple birth.*

Multiple births can result from separate zygotes or from a single zygote. For example, if two eggs are released during ovulation, each may be fertilized by a separate sperm, producing separate zygotes. The two zygotes develop into *dizygotic twins,* also called *fraternal twins.* Monozygotic twins develop from a single zygote that divides into separate cells, with each cell developing independently. The infants born have the same genetic makeup and usually resemble each other. Such twins are also called *identical twins.* See **Multiple birth.**

Development of the embryo

The zygote goes through a series of changes before it reaches the uterus. In the uterus, the zygote develops into a form called the embryo. The embryo develops rapidly. Within two months, all the tissues and organs of the body have begun to form.

The first days of pregnancy. After fertilization, the zygote travels through the fallopian tube toward the uterus. Along the way, the zygote begins to divide rapidly into many cells with no increase in overall size. The resulting cell mass is called a *morula.* By the third or fourth day after fertilization, the morula enters the uterus. At that time, the morula is still surrounded by the zona pellucida and consists of about 12 to 16 cells.

The embryo develops from the central cells of the morula. These cells are called the *inner cell mass.* The outer cells of the morula are called the *outer cell mass.* They develop into the *placenta,* an organ that connects the embryo to the blood supply of the mother.

The development of a human embryo

During the first two months of pregnancy, an embryo develops from a single cell to a recognizably human shape about $1\frac{1}{4}$ inches (3 centimeters) long. After this period, the embryo is called a *fetus*.

WORLD BOOK illustrations by Barbara Cousins

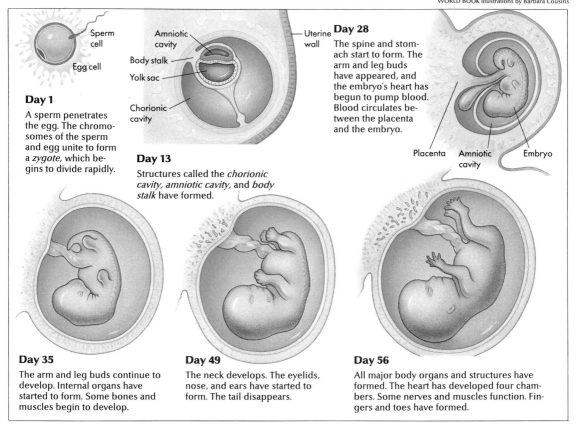

Day 1

A sperm penetrates the egg. The chromosomes of the sperm and egg unite to form a *zygote,* which begins to divide rapidly.

Sperm cell

Egg cell

Amniotic cavity

Body stalk

Yolk sac

Chorionic cavity

Day 13

Structures called the *chorionic cavity, amniotic cavity,* and *body stalk* have formed.

Uterine wall

Day 28

The spine and stomach start to form. The arm and leg buds have appeared, and the embryo's heart has begun to pump blood. Blood circulates between the placenta and the embryo.

Placenta

Amniotic cavity

Embryo

Day 35

The arm and leg buds continue to develop. Internal organs have started to form. Some bones and muscles begin to develop.

Day 49

The neck develops. The eyelids, nose, and ears have started to form. The tail disappears.

Day 56

All major body organs and structures have formed. The heart has developed four chambers. Some nerves and muscles function. Fingers and toes have formed.

After the morula enters the uterus, it continues to divide. A fluid-filled cavity forms between one side of the inner cell mass and the outer cell mass, and the zona pellucida begins to disintegrate. At this stage, the ball of cells is called a *blastocyst* or *blastula.* The cells of the blastocyst divide as it floats free in the uterus for one or two days.

About the fifth or sixth day of pregnancy, the blastocyst becomes attached to the internal surface of the uterus. The outer cells of the blastocyst, called the *trophoblast,* secrete an enzyme that breaks down the lining of the uterus. The trophoblast begins to divide rapidly, invading the uterine tissue. The process of attachment to the uterine wall is called *implantation.* By the 11th day of the pregnancy, the blastocyst is firmly implanted in the uterus.

Nourishing the embryo. Various structures develop in the uterus to help the embryo grow. These structures include the placenta and certain membranes.

By the 13th day of pregnancy, a space called the *chorionic cavity* has formed around the embryo. Two membranes surround the chorionic cavity. The outer membrane is called the *chorion,* and the inner membrane is called the *amnion.* The chorion interacts with tissues of the uterus to form the placenta. The chorion pushes into the wall of the uterus with fingerlike projections called

chorionic villi. The chorionic villi are the embryo's first blood vessels. The chorion is attached to the embryo by a structure called the *body stalk.* The body stalk develops into the *umbilical cord,* which joins the embryo to the placenta.

The amnion forms a sac around the embryo and is filled with fluid. The embryo floats in this fluid, called *amniotic fluid.* The amniotic fluid protects the embryo by absorbing jolts to the uterus. It also allows the embryo to move without damaging the amnion and other tissues.

About the 21st day of pregnancy, blood begins to circulate between the placenta and the embryo. The blood vessels of the mother and those of the embryo exchange substances through a thin layer of cells called the *placental barrier.* Waste products from the embryo are carried away through the barrier. Likewise, nutrients and oxygen from the mother's blood pass through the thin walls of the barrier and enter the embryo's blood. However, such organisms as viruses and bacteria, as well as chemical substances, including drugs, also may cross the placental barrier and harm the embryo.

Origin of tissues and organs. At about the same time that the placenta begins to form, the inner cell mass flattens and develops into three layers of cells in what is called the *embryonic disc.* The three types of cell layers are the *ectoderm,* the *mesoderm,* and the *endoderm.* In a process called *differentiation,* cells from each layer move to certain areas of the embryonic disc and then fold over to form tubes or clusters. These tubes and clusters develop into various tissues and organs of the body.

Cells from the ectoderm form the brain, nerves, skin, hair, nails, and parts of the eyes and ears. Cells from the mesoderm form the heart, muscles, bones, tendons, kidneys, glands, blood vessels, and reproductive organs. The linings of the digestive and respiratory systems develop from cells of the endoderm.

Development of organs and organ systems. The body's organs and organ systems grow rapidly from the third through eighth weeks of pregnancy. The major structures include the central nervous system and the circulatory system, as well as such organs as the eyes, ears, and limbs. Defects in the development of these structures often occur during these weeks. Such defects sometimes are caused by substances introduced from the mother's body through the placental barrier. These substances are called *teratogens.* They include medications taken by the mother, as well as viruses, bacteria, and other infectious organisms. Other teratogens include nonmedicinal drugs, alcoholic beverages, and cigarette smoke.

The central nervous system, which consists of the brain and spinal cord, starts to develop in the middle of the third week of pregnancy. It begins as a flattened strip of cells within a long cylinder of cells called the *neural tube.*

At about the 25th day of pregnancy, one end of the neural tube closes. The brain develops from three sacs formed in this end of the tube. The other end of the tube closes two days later. Failure of the tube to close can result in birth defects, especially *spina bifida,* a disorder of the spine.

The circulatory system also begins to develop in the third week of pregnancy. Two tubes of cells combine to form a single tube that becomes the heart. By the fourth week, a simple circulatory system is functioning and the heart has begun to pump blood. During the fourth to seventh weeks of pregnancy, the heart tube divides into four chambers. Any irregularity in the normal pattern of development during this period can produce a defect in the heart.

The eyes and ears begin to develop in the fourth week of pregnancy. Both these organs form rapidly. The external parts of the ears appear by the sixth week. Defects in the eyes or ears often stem from abnormalities that occur during the fourth to sixth weeks of pregnancy.

The arms and legs appear as buds of tissue during the fifth week of pregnancy. The arms develop a few days ahead of the legs. The fingers and toes become recognizable in the sixth week. They form when certain cells die and leave spaces in the remaining tissue.

The structures of the mouth, such as the lips and palate, begin to form during the fourth and fifth weeks of pregnancy. The lips and palate form during the sixth to ninth weeks. Each forms from paired structures that gradually move from the sides toward the middle of the face and *fuse* (join). If anything interferes with normal development during this period, a split in the upper lip

or palate may develop. Such a defect is called *cleft lip* or *cleft palate.*

Growth of the fetus

From the ninth week of pregnancy until birth, the developing baby is called a fetus. In the first three months of this period, the fetus increases rapidly in length. It grows about 2 inches (5 centimeters) in each of these months. In the later months of pregnancy, the most striking change in the fetus is in its weight. Most fetuses gain about 25 ounces (700 grams) in both the eighth and ninth months of pregnancy.

Stages of growth. Physicians commonly divide pregnancy into three, three-month parts called *trimesters.* At the end of the first trimester, the fetus weighs about 1 ounce (28 grams) and is about 3 inches (7.6 centimeters) long. At the end of the second trimester, the fetus weighs about 30 ounces (850 grams) and measures about 14 inches (36 centimeters) long. At the end of the third trimester, the fetus measures about 20 inches (50 centimeters) and weighs about 7 pounds (3.2 kilograms).

The mother can feel movements of the fetus by the fifth month of pregnancy. By this time, fine hair called *lanugo* covers the body of the fetus. Hair also appears on the head. Lanugo disappears late in pregnancy or shortly after birth. The eyelids open by the 26th week of pregnancy. By the 28th week, the fingernails and toenails are well developed.

Until the 30th week of pregnancy, the fetus appears reddish and transparent because of the thinness of its skin and a lack of fat beneath the skin. In the last six to eight weeks before birth, fat develops rapidly and the fetus becomes smooth and plump.

The mother also experiences many physical changes during pregnancy. For example, a pregnant woman gains weight and her breasts increase in size. For more information on such changes, see **Pregnancy.**

Checking the fetus. Physicians can use several procedures to monitor the development of the fetus in the mother's uterus. Two of the most commonly used techniques are *ultrasonography* and *amniocentesis.*

Ultrasonography, also called *ultrasound,* involves the use of high-frequency sound waves to produce an image of the fetus on a screen. By viewing the shape and body features of the fetus, a physician can measure its growth and detect malformations. Fetal abnormalities also can be detected through amniocentesis. This technique involves the removal of a sample of the amniotic fluid, which contains cells of the fetus. The fluid and cells are then analyzed and examined.

Birth

The process of giving birth is called *parturition* or *labor.* By this process, the fetus and the placenta are pushed out of the uterus. Scientists believe that labor is triggered by the release of certain hormones from the adrenal glands of the fetus.

A fetus that undergoes the normal period of development before labor begins is considered to have reached *term.* Labor occurs at term if it begins during the 37th to 43rd week of pregnancy. Labor that starts before the 37th week is called *preterm labor.* Labor that begins after the 43rd week is *postterm labor.* Babies born at term or postterm have the best chance for survival. Most

The birth of a baby   Before birth (1), the head of the baby lies near the opening of the uterus. As muscle action forces the baby out of the uterus (2), the head turns and (3) the baby passes through the vagina.

WORLD BOOK illustrations by Joann Harling

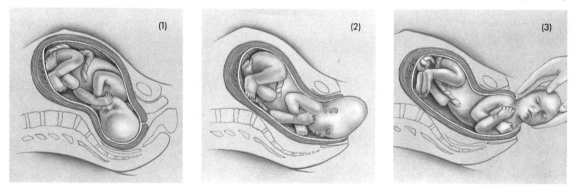

babies born from the 26th to 36th weeks of pregnancy also will live, but some of these babies may experience serious health problems because their respiratory and central nervous systems are not fully developed at birth. Babies born before the 26th week have a poor chance of surviving.

The stages of labor. Labor has three stages. The first stage begins with an alternating tensing and relaxing of muscles in the uterus. These muscle contractions are called *labor pains.* When labor begins, the fetus lies within its protective membranes and is held in place by the *cervix* (neck of the uterus). During the first stage of labor, the cervix begins to *dilate* (open). This stage ends when the cervix has fully dilated to a diameter of about 4 inches (10 centimeters). The first stage of labor is the longest, averaging about 14 hours in women giving birth for the first time. In women who have had children before, this stage normally takes 8 hours or less.

The second stage of labor begins at full dilation of the cervix and ends with the delivery of the baby. This stage may last from one to five hours. The muscle contractions of the uterus and abdomen help push the baby through the cervix and out the vagina. Most babies are born headfirst, but some are born with their shoulders or buttocks first. After the head comes out, the rest of the baby follows easily.

The third stage of labor starts after the baby's delivery and ends when the placenta, now called the *afterbirth,* is expelled from the uterus. This stage lasts about 30 minutes. A few minutes after the baby is born, the umbilical cord is clamped and cut. The placenta then detaches from the uterus and passes out the vagina.

Sometimes, the smallness of a woman's pelvis or some other condition makes it difficult to deliver a child through the vagina. In these situations, doctors may perform surgery to remove the baby through the mother's abdomen. This procedure is called a *Caesarean section.*

The newborn infant. At birth, most babies weigh about 7 pounds (3.2 kilograms) and measure about 20 inches (50 centimeters) long. The newborn infant is fed with the mother's breast milk or with a formula of milk and other nutrients. The baby can now survive outside its mother's body but needs constant care.

Lynn J. Romrell

Related articles in *World Book* include:

Abortion	Hormone (Other	Pregnancy
Baby	hormones)	Prostate gland
Birth control	Infertility	Reproduction
Birth defect	Menstruation	Sex
Childbirth	Miscarriage	Sterility
Embryo	Multiple birth	Testicle
Fertilization	Ovary	Uterus
Genetics	Penis	Vagina
Heredity	Placenta	Venereal disease

Outline

I. The human reproductive system
  A. In females
  B. In males
II. Fertilization
  A. How sex is determined
  B. Multiple birth
III. Development of the embryo
  A. The first days of pregnancy
  B. Nourishing the embryo
  C. Origin of tissues and organs
  D. Development of organs and organ systems
IV. Growth of the fetus
  A. Stages of growth
  B. Checking the fetus
V. Birth
  A. The stages of labor   B. The newborn infant

Questions

What are the three stages of labor?
How many chromosomes does a fertilized egg have?
What is *lanugo?*
How long does an egg survive after being released by an ovary?
Where in a woman's body does fertilization usually occur?
What is *menopause?* When does it occur?
How long does pregnancy last?
What are *dizygotic twins? Monozygotic twins?*
How does a sperm propel itself?
What are *teratogens?*

Additional resources

Grabowski, Casimer T. *Human Reproduction and Development.* Saunders Coll. Pub., 1983.
Jones, Richard E. *Human Reproduction and Sexual Behavior.* Prentice-Hall, 1984.
Stein, Sara B. *Making Babies: An Open Family Book for Parents and Children Together.* Walker, 1984. First published in 1974. For younger readers.
Ward, Brian R. *Birth and Growth.* Watts, 1983. For younger readers.

Index

How to use the index
This index covers the contents of the 1991, 1992, and 1993 editions of *Science Year,* The World Book Science Annual.

Each index entry gives the last two digits of the edition year, followed by a colon and the page number or numbers. For example, this entry means that information on marshes may be found on pages 15 through 22 of the 1993 *Science Year* and on page 45 of the 1991 edition.

When there are many references to a topic, they are grouped alphabetically by clue words under the main topic. The clue words under **Mathematics** group the references to that topic under five subtopics, from "books" to "science student awards."

A main entry in all capital letters indicates that there is a Science News Update article with that name in at least one of the three volumes covered in this index.

An entry that only begins with a capital letter indicates that there are no Science News Update articles with that title but that information on this topic may be found in the editions and on the pages listed.

The indication (il.) after a page number means that the reference is to an illustration only.

The "see" and "see also" cross references indicate that references to the topic are listed under another entry in the index.

Index

A

Index

Index

Index

N

Index

Index

Acknowledgments

The publishers of *Science Year* gratefully acknowledge the courtesy of the following artists, photographers, publishers, institutions, agencies, and corporations for the illustrations in this volume. Credits should read from top to bottom, left to right on their respective pages. All entries marked with an asterisk (*) denote illustrations created exclusively for *Science Year*. All maps, charts, and diagrams were prepared by the *Science Year* staff unless otherwise noted.

2	NASA; Gustavo Gilabert, JB Pictures; George Ross, Gamma/Liaison
3	U.S. Department of Fish and Wildlife; Sygma; NASA; Joint European Torus; Massimo Sestinita, Gamma/Liaison
4	David Muench; Yoshi Onuki, University of Tokyo
5	U.S. Department of Agriculture; Jet Propulsion Laboratory; LuRay Parker, Wyoming Game and Fish Department
10	C. C. Lockwood; Jan Wills*
11	Thomas Hoepker, Magnum; Frank L. Warren, TRW after NASA illustration
12	Ian J. Adams
15	Greg Guirard
16	C. C. Lockwood; Volo Bog Natural Area, Illinois Department of Conservation
17	David Muench; Jim Brandenburg, Minden Pictures
20	Ian J. Adams; Nancy Lee Walter*; Larry C. Cameron
21	Scott Nielsen, Ducks Unlimited, Inc.; Nancy Lee Walter*; C. C. Lockwood
22	C. C. Lockwood
23	Greg Guirard; Jim Brandenburg, Minden Pictures
24	Volo Bog Natural Area, Howard W. Phillips, Illinois Department of Conservation
25	Diane Mitchell; Diane Mitchell; Bob Frenkel
28	Tom Herzberg*; Jet Propulsion Laboratory; Francois Gohier, Photo Researchers
32	Tom Herzberg*; Tom Herzberg*; NASA
33	John Sanford, SPL from Photo Researchers; Tom Herzberg*
34	Francois Gohier, Photo Researchers; Alan Hildebrand, Geological Survey of Canada; Richard Grieve, Geological Survey of Canada
36-39	Tom Herzberg*
40	D. H. Hill, University of Arizona; Harry Przekop, *Discover* Magazine; Tom Herzberg*
41	Tom Herzberg*
44	Richard Burger; Yoshio Onuki, University of Tokyo
45	Shelia and Thomas Pozorski
48	Bob Hersey*
52	Robert A. Feldman; Richard Burger
53	Bob Hersey*
55	Shelia and Thomas Pozorski
56	Bob Hersey*
59	John Bigelow Taylor, American Museum of Natural History; Richard Burger
62	David R. Frazier Photolibrary; Andy Miller from Graham Studios
65-66	Andy Miller from Graham Studios
69	General Motors Corporation
72	Andy Miller from Graham Studios
74	General Motors Corporation
76	Nancy Lee Walter*; Howard Sochurek, The Stock Market; *World Book* photo; Roy Morsch, The Stock Market; *World Book* photo; Stephen Green-Armytage, The Stock Market
79	Fritz Prenzel, Bruce Coleman Ltd.
80	Nancy Lee Walter*; Stephen C. Kaufman, Bruce Coleman Ltd.
82	Nancy Lee Walter*; Kim Taylor, Bruce Coleman Ltd.; Nancy Lee Walter*
83	Gerard Lacz, Natural History Photographic Agency
85	Stephen Dalton, Natural History Photographic Agency, Nancy Lee Walter*; Stephen J. Kraseman, DRK Photo
86	Nancy Lee Walter*; *World Book* photo; Ken Cole, Animals Animals
87	Gunter Ziesler, Bruce Coleman Ltd.; Hans Reinhard, Bruce Coleman Ltd.; Nancy Lee Walter*
88	Nancy Lee Walter*; Hans Reinhard, Bruce Coleman Ltd.; Belinda Wright, DRK Photo
92	AP/Wide World; Steve Spicer*
94	Steve Spicer*
95	AP/Wide World
97	Rick Maiman, Sygma
100	Bill Nation, Sygma
102	Steve Spicer*
104	UPI/Bettmann
106	Jan Wills*
110	Musee de l'Homme, Paris (© David L. Brill); Musee de l'Homme, Paris (© David L. Brill); Jan Wills*
111	© Ira Block
112	Jan Wills*; Denise de Sonneville-Bordes, Centre Francois Bordes, Université de Bordeaux (© David L. Brill)
115	© Ralph S. Solecki, Texas A&M University; Jan Wills*
120	Steve McCurry, Magnum
124	Thomas Hoepker, Magnum; Abbas, Magnum
126-127	Steve McCurry, Magnum
128	Mark Rattin*
129	Compton J. Tucker, NASA/GSFC
131	Steve McCurry, Magnum
134-138	Jan Jones*
140	A. E. Staley Company
142	NutraSweet Company
145	Jan Jones*
148	National Science Teachers Association; Fred J. Maroon*
149	National Science Teachers Association
151	Michele Noiset*
152-153	Fred J. Maroon*
154	Fred J. Maroon*; Michele Noiset*
156	Fred J. Maroon*; Michele Noiset*
157	Fred J. Maroon*
158	Fred J. Maroon*; Michele Noiset*
159	Michele Noiset*
160	TSW/Chicago Ltd.; Gabe Palmer, The Stock Market
163-165	JAK Graphics*
166	Art: JAK Graphics*—photo: Cornell University
167	Art: JAK Graphics*—photo: AT&T Bell Laboratories
169	J. F. Allen, University of St. Andrews
171	Kaku Kurita, Gamma/Liaison; Biomagnetic Technologies, Inc.
174	NASA
177	Ernest Norcia*
178	Roberta Polfus*
180	NASA; Roberta Polfus*
182	Frank L. Warren, TRW after NASA illustration; Roberta Polfus*
184	C. P. O'Dea and F. N. Owen, NRAO/AUI; Roberta Polfus*; NASA; Roberta Polfus*
186	National Optical Astronomy Observatory (NOAO); Roberta Polfus*; Roberta Polfus*; NASA
188	NASA/GSFC
191	Roberta Polfus*; Brown Bros.
194	Roberta Polfus*; © Bar-Brown, Camera Press Ltd.
195	Roberta Polfus*
196	Peter Menzel, Stock, Boston
197-198	Roberta Polfus*
201	Roberta Polfus*; AP/Wide World
204	NASA; Gustavo Gilabert, JB Pictures; P. Durand, Sygma
205	Jim Brandenburg, Minden Pictures
207	John Roberts, The Stock Market; JAK Graphics*
208	JAK Graphics*
210	Larry Hamill; Will McIntyre, Photo Researchers; JAK Graphics*
211	Rob Crandall, Picture Group; Jim Brandenburg, Minden Pictures
212	P. Durand, Sygma; Jon Lamar, The Stock Market
214	Roberta Polfus*; NASA
216	Skin Cancer Foundation
217-219	JAK Graphics*
220	Oxford Illustrators*
222	Luis C. Marigo from Peter Arnold; Gustavo Gilabert, JB Pictures
223	John Maier, Picture Group
226	© Sygma; Oluf Nielsen and Barney Magrath
227	Lawrence Livermore Laboratory; Martha Weiss; Jim Wallace, Duke University
229-230	U.S. Department of Agriculture

World Book Encyclopedia, Inc., provides high-quality educational and reference products for the family and school. They include THE WORLD BOOK MEDICAL ENCYCLOPEDIA, a 1,040-page fully illustrated family health reference; THE WORLD BOOK OF MATH POWER, a two-volume set that helps students and adults build math skills; THE WORLD BOOK OF WORD POWER, a two-volume set that is designed to help your entire family write and speak more successfully; and HOW TO STUDY video, a video presentation of key study skills with information students need to succeed in school. For further information, write WORLD BOOK ENCYCLOPEDIA, INC., P.O. Box 3073, Evanston, IL 60204-9974.